D0492997

CHURCHILL

HIS LIFE AND TIMES

Photo by Walter Stor

MALCOLM THOMSON

CHURCHILL

HIS LIFE AND TIMES

ODHAMS PRESS LIMITED

LONG ACRE, LONDON

Revised New Edition 1954

MADE AND PRINTED IN
GREAT BRITAIN BY ODHAMS (WATFORD) LTD.
WATFORD, HERTS

CONTENTS

WINSTON SPENCER CHURCHILL IN HIS LIBRARY

Winston Churchill is among the most versatile of our contemporaries. Though he is a great statesman his abilities in other directions are also astounding. As an author, his historical sense is highly developed, and though picturesque, his style is characteristically incisive. His many publications include history, biography and autobiography.

CHAPTER I

CHURCHILL THE MAN

WINSTON CHURCHILL will in the years to come be remembered most of all as the man who was Prime Minister of Britain during the Second World War. But he had made good his foothold in history long before that conflict. For forty years he had been a well-known public figure, a statesman who had held a record number of different Cabinet offices, an author of several massive historical works which were acknowledged as masterpieces, and beyond all this, a vivid and picturesque personality about whom violent controversy raged. He had many admirers, if few followers; and even his bitterest opponents admitted his brilliance, however little they trusted his judgment.

Throughout his political career Churchill has been an outstanding figure, with a magnetic attraction for the limelight. Failures could never abash, nor setbacks dishearten him. Whether his contemporaries were with him or against him, they could never thrust him aside and leave him out of account. And they were often against him, for during a large part of his public life Churchill inspired more interest than confidence. His very cleverness, allied as it was with an element of dare-devilry and schoolboy recklessness, counted against him, for in quiet, peaceful days those qualities in a statesman are not regarded with much favour by a democracy, certainly not by the British democracy, which is rather suspicious of cleverness in its rulers. Dash and daring are equally unwelcome, for they may land the nation all unawares in some rash adventure or entanglement. Solid ability, sure-footed caution, and matter-of-fact common sense are the political virtues that normally win the nation's confidence. And on Winston's luggage these are hardly the labels which have chiefly caught the eye of his fellow-passengers.

But with the outbreak of the Second World War, Churchill found the proper field for the exercise of his special talents. He came into his own, and through the war years he captured and held the confidence and affectionate loyalty of the mass of the nation to a degree rivalled

7

WINSTON CHURCHILL PLAYING POLO

When he went out to India in 1896 as a young officer, Churchill discovered that the most serious business of life in the army there was polo. This was an expensive hobby as it required a whole stud of ponies. His regiment won the All-India Cavalry Cup and Churchill himself was in the team in spite of the handicap of an injured shoulder.

by few other statesmen in the country's history. In the tense hours of that grim and deadly struggle, when the need was for brilliance of vision and imagination to outplan the enemy, when risk and peril were on every side, and unstinted daring was the only path to victory, the people recognized that Churchill's gifts, however dubious their value for peacetime politics, were admirably suited to the national emergency. His clever and fertile intellect, ever-youthful courage and power of firm, self-confident decision were just the qualities the nation longed to find in its wartime leader. Daring, cleverness and originality were the needs of the hour.

AN INCARNATION OF JOHN BULL

His bulldog face, twinkling eyes, confident, dominating smile; cigar thrust out jauntily between firm lips; a hat looking too small for the broad head it tried to cover; hand uplifted, brandishing a stick or waving two fingers in a "V" for victory sign, came to be a familiar and cheering picture during those years to the whole of Britain, and indeed to the free peoples of two hemispheres. With the addition of side-whiskers and the appropriate costume, he might have stood as an incarnation of the traditional John Bull. Indeed, his stubborn independence of judgment, his warm-heartedness, generosity and deep-rooted patriotism were quite in keeping with the character of that burly symbol in the union-jack waistcoat. He was, perhaps, less true to type in his quickness of wit and speech, but his wartime oratory truly voiced the mind of the British people. The world outside was not mistaken when it saw in him the embodiment of the temper and determination of the nation whose leader and spokesman he was.

Future historians writing the account of the great struggle against the Nazi-Fascist dictators will be compelled to record that Britain was the mainstay of the forces of liberty, and that Churchill was the dominating figure among the democratic leaders in the conflict. America and Russia both threw immense efforts into the fight, but Britain will take the centre of the stage because, but for her original defiance and her lonely stand, there might have been no organized and ultimately successful resistance to Hitler, only a collapse of one country after another in face of external attack and internal treachery. Had Britain fallen, and had her industrial potential thereby been added to the Nazi resources, the assault on Russia would have ended differently, and with Europe, Asia and Africa subject to Germany

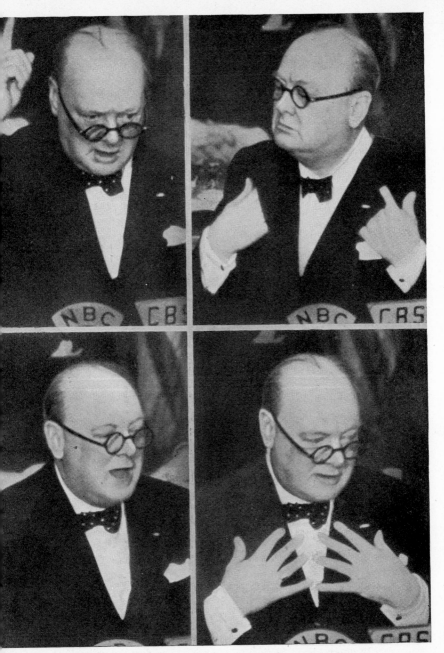

BROADCASTING TO THE EMPIRE AND AMERICA

The voice of Winston Churchill is better known than that of any one else in Britain. He combines great force and vivid phraseology with a simplicity which can be understood by the man-in-the-street. Some of his speeches have become classics of the spoken word.

and Italy, America herself would have faced disaster. Civilization owes Winston Churchill a great debt because he not only led and inspired the resistance of Britain, but succeeded in drawing the United Nations together into a strongly woven partnership, and maintained their unity and co-operation throughout the war by his tireless efforts.

DETESTED, CRITICIZED, ATTACKED AND APPLAUDED

At one time or another in his long and varied career Churchill has been detested by every political party. He has been savagely attacked, criticized, derided by men of responsible judgment. He has been approved, admired and applauded on other occasions as wholeheartedly by those very same men.

It may be taken for granted that there was reason behind both verdicts. For all mortal men are faulty and fallible, and the bigger the scale of the man, the more visible are his defects. Gulliver was repelled by the coarse skins of the giants of Brobdingnag, while he marvelled at the smooth complexions of the Lilliput dwarfs. However golden the head of the idol, its feet will be common clay. Winston is no exception to that rule.

In recent times it has been the fashion for biographers to concentrate on the clay, to exhaust themselves in "debunking" their heroes, stressing their faults and frailties and trying to belittle their greatness. No doubt they get a great satisfaction from this game—for game it is, not honest biography. None but a fool can seriously contend that a man whose capacities and achievements have raised him head and shoulders above his contemporaries is really nothing but a mean little fellow in the bottom class. If great men are not always without blemish as their admirers pretend, if they have the defects of their virtues, they may still be great.

Winston is a great man. Bonar Law, his bitter critic, was yet compelled to admit: "In mental power and vital force, he is one of the foremost men in the country." He is not by any means always wise or infallible. There are lights and shadows in his character, and we can look frankly at them both, not expecting perfection, but knowing, nevertheless, that when the account is cast, the lights will show a big credit balance over the shadows.

In any review of Winston's qualities one fact thrust itself at once to the fore: he is at heart a soldier.

12

LEISURE MOMENT

Holding political office from 1906 to 1915, from 1917 to 1922, from 1924 to 1929, and from 1939 through the Second World War till after "V-E." Day, 1945, Winston Churchill's moments of leisure have been few. Yet in that period he has still found the time to publish at least twenty books, including his great "Life of Marlborough."

BRICKLAYER AND ARTISAN

Churchill has himself done a considerable amount of building on his own grounds and is an accomplished bricklayer. He is essentially an open-air man with strong and capable hands. The photograph, taken in 1928, shows him assisted by his daughter, Sarah, hard at work building the wall of a house on his estate at Westerham in Kent.

The career of arms was his own first choice; and although the years he actually spent in military service were few, they were crowded with battle experience eagerly sought and whole-heartedly enjoyed. "Don't you like war?" he blithely asked one of his officers as they stood in a trench under heavy bombardment. He has a very full measure of that physical courage which revels in the thrill of danger. In his writings about his experiences, he may confess to moments of fear, but that feeling never seems to have deterred him from taking the wildest risks.

The fact is that Winston delights in action; and battle, where action is at its keenest intensity and the stakes are life and death, is of all human occupations the one which gives the richest satisfaction to such a craving. Action is one of the keys to his character. He is not in the accepted sense of the term a thinker. He thinks, of course; thinks with quite remarkable vigour and clarity. But the aim and object of his thinking is not abstract knowledge but concrete performance. He thinks in order to act. Quiet meditation upon the truth behind the face of things does not lure him. His natural bent is not towards matters of mind, and when in his writings he occasionally wanders into some such problem there is an air of childish simplicity about his remarks. As a young man, he found himself once involved in a discussion with some learned friends fresh from Oxford, and was soon swept far out of his depth by their clever reasoning. "I must go to Oxford," he resolved. But he never went. It was not his spiritual home.

ARTIST, ORATOR AND AUTHOR

Winston is not a philosopher; he is an artist. Mere activity is not enough. It must be a finished performance. Whatever he does—and he is eager always to do anything to which his active hands can be set—is done with technical efficiency and that infinite capacity for taking pains which is proverbially the mark of genius.

He is an artist with his pen. As a man of letters he ranks very high indeed. Though a master of classic elegance, he is never too polished and dignified to be arresting, exciting and hugely entertaining in his books. He has produced tales of travel, biography, autobiography, history, and even, in his early days, a novel. The novel is not perhaps in the front rank of its kind; but the high place of his other work is assured.

About his performance as an orator there can be no two opinions. Here his desire to excel came up against the crippling handicap of a speaking defect—a kind of lisp that thickens his S's—which might have kept a less determined man off the platform. So well has he overcome that vocal difficulty that his hearers are hardly aware of it, and are swiftly caught up and carried forward on the tide of an eloquence that grips, delights and inspires them. His language is direct, vivid, magnificent. He puts immense pains into the preparation of these speeches, even of the apparently impromptu jests. He is unequalled as a phrase-maker. He can clothe ideas in words that men remember; quaint and unexpected at times, as in the description of an inaccurate statement as a "terminological inexactitude"; splendid at others, as in his tribute to the airmen heroes of the Battle of

DINING OUT AT BURLINGTON HOUSE

Winston Churchill entertains lavishly and is fond of all the good things of life. He is an accomplished after dinner speaker, epigrammatic and witty, and he has the power to appreciate these qualities in others. In this photograph, taken in 1932, he is seen listening to a speech at the Royal Academy banquet at Burlington House.

Britain: "Never in the field of human conflict was so much owed by so many to so few."

His delight in craftsmanship finds many outlets; for he must ever be making something. His skill as a painter is well known, and landscapes from his brush have found an honoured place in the homes of eminent art collectors. For years past his easel and canvases have gone with him on all his holiday travels. He has in earlier days frequently piloted his own aeroplane. He has turned his hand to bricklaying, and acquired the art of building a wall well and truly at the correct trade union rate of progress. Some giant intellects are housed

16

in very helpless and unhandy bodies, devoid of practical skill. Their fingers, as the saying runs, are all thumbs. Churchill is not of their number. He has a craftsman's hands and a craftsman's temperament.

PERTINACITY AND PREMONITION

To his tireless industry he adds another gift—that of quite extraordinary pertinacity. If Winston wants something, he goes for it till he gets it, and nothing will deter him. When he wanted to join Kitchener's Sudan campaign, he hammered at every door, up to that of the Prime Minister himself, and when none opened, still persisted till he found a back entrance. He treads the earth with the confident step of one who feels himself an owner, not a trespasser, wherever he goes.

One gift he has, which from time to time has shown itself uncannily—the power of premonition. It is not always active, and normally he can look ahead only as well as any other knowledgeable and clear-thinking man. But now and again he utters a prophecy edged with more than ordinary foresight. Shrewd deduction? Lucky guesswork? Maybe. Maybe not. Is there in the complex web of his ancestry some Celtic strain that momentarily and unpredictably sharpens his subconscious mind with the penetration of second sight, as it often tinges his speech with an Irish quality of wit?

Some of these forecasts find mention in the following pages. Another, perhaps less precise but no less heavy with premonition, occurred in February, 1938, at the end of his speech deploring Eden's departure from the Foreign Office:

> "I predict that the day will come at some point or other, on some issue or other, when you will have to make a stand, and I pray to God that when that day comes we may not find, through an unwise foreign policy, we may have to make that stand alone!"

Two and a quarter years later that warning was fulfilled to the letter.

The widespread distrust which has pursued Churchill throughout the greater part of his political career has sought its justification in his successive changes of party, his open disagreement with his party leaders, his advocacy at different times of conflicting policies. He labours under the charge of unreliability.

On the face of it, there is good warrant for this charge. Winston

17

started in politics as a Tory—a Tory Democrat of the school founded by his father, Lord Randolph Churchill. He criticized his leaders, quarrelled with them, attacked them and crossed the floor of the House to join their opponents, the Liberals. There for some years he associated with the Radical wing, and supported them in urging a reduction of naval expenditure. Then, at the Admiralty, he became a zealous spender on the Navy and a problem to his former allies. He served as a Coalition Liberal under Lloyd George, but when the Coalition fell, he drifted away from the party and called himself a Constitutionalist, under which title he rejoined the Tories. Later on, however, he challenged his leader, Baldwin, on the Indian question, and slid into the position of an independent Tory critic of the substantially Tory government.

WHEN CHURCHILL CHANGED SIDES

These changes of side are facts of his history. When they were thrown up at him once in the House, he blandly retorted: "To improve is to change. To be perfect is to have changed often." But the answer was hardly a true explanation of his changes. They were the result, not of some effort of self-improvement, but of fidelity to what he already was. He was most true to himself when most indefinite in his party loyalties. For the fact is that Winston is not, in the accepted sense, a good party man. He will not swallow and digest the policies thrust on him by any party. Always he must choose and decide for himself. His party has but one member—Winston Churchill.

If he must wear a label, then that of Tory Democracy suits him best. Born in a ducal palace, with the blue blood of a long aristocratic lineage in his veins, he instinctively inclines towards a benevolently feudal outlook. He has warm human interests, the kindliest goodwill to his fellow-citizens, and a healthy confidence in their essential worth. He is ready to be a big brother to them all, so long as they give the rôle of leadership to him. He can call himself a Tory. He can call himself a Liberal. He can never call himself a Socialist, for any suggestion of dictatorship by the proletariat is abhorrent to him.

Leadership, however, means service, and to Churchill the notion that those in authority should use their power to pursue personal ends, to feather private nests, while leaving those they govern in

SIGNING AUTOGRAPHS IN THE NORTH COUNTRY

Winston Churchill has become a very popular character in recent years and his familiar features and cigar (missing above) make him recognized wherever he goes. He is a tireless traveller and during the Second World War he made himself known personally over the whole country through frequent visits to areas devastated by enemy action.

poverty, wretchedness or suffering, is no less abhorrent. He broke with the Tories over Tariff Reform, when he saw their big business interests plotting a protectionist racket to exploit the public for the benefit of their own pockets. He left the Liberals when he deemed them to be betraying the country to the Socialists in the hope of saving thereby the remnants of their shattered party. He quarrelled with Baldwin when he thought the Tory leader was letting go the Empire; weakly shirking his responsibilities to the masses of India for the sake of his own tranquillity and failing to maintain Britain's

EXPERIENCE JOINS HANDS WITH YOUTH

Winston Churchill is as well known to the public in his less formal
moments as in his public appearances. This photograph was taken
in the grounds of the British Embassy at Cairo, in 1942, and the child
to whom General Smuts and Mr. Churchill are talking is the son of
Sir Miles Lampson (Lord Killearn), then British Ambassador to Egypt.

tradition of care for her dependent peoples. To himself, Churchill
seemed always consistent, however inconsistent his course might
appear to others, and however faulty might be the judgment upon
which he based his attitude.

His consistency is, however, the practice of uniformly acting
according to his nature and his immediate judgment with regard to
each particular situation. His reactions to current events are swift
and vigorous. He is no crafty plotter or schemer, pursuing long-
distance plans and subtle intrigues. His nature is frank, open and
ingenuous, and within the limits of honour, kindliness and fair play
his course tends to be opportunist. It is natural, therefore, that those

who judge him by the standard of their own fixed party loyalties and undeviating plans and purposes should deem him erratic, elusive and unreliable.

DEVOTION TO HIS OWN OPINIONS

It must be admitted that Winston's rather exaggerated devotion to his own personal view of affairs often proves embarrassing and exasperating to those with whom he teams up. They find him lacking in the team spirit; and it is not, to speak the truth, highly developed in him. Morley once said of him and Lloyd George: "Whereas Winston knows his own mind, Lloyd George is always more concerned to know the minds of other people." It was a shrewd analysis of the contrast between the two men, and drew attention to that feature in Winston's character which strongly colours the whole of it. Winston is intensely subjective. What he himself is thinking, feeling, planning, experiencing, is all-important. What other people think or experience is of very little consequence to him, except in so far as it affects his own affairs. No doubt we all tend to look out on life rather in this fashion, but in Churchill the personal view is very pronounced. His natural instinct is always to take the lead. Others are at liberty to follow if they will.

"The proper study of mankind," said Alexander Pope, "is man." Winston pursues this study upon the man nearest to him—himself—with eager interest and ceaseless curiosity. The curiosity becomes at times almost detached and impersonal, as for instance when he was knocked down by a motor in New York in 1932, and proceeded to record from his sick-bed a detailed account of his exact sensations at the time of the accident, and picturesque calculations of the stresses his body had undergone. This exaggerated interest in his own mental and physical processes and experiences is shown again and again in his writings. It comes out in his speeches. It dominates his thought.

Such a quality is of course far more excusable in him than it would be in a lesser man. For after all, Winston is quite the most lively and gifted and exciting personality that Winston has ever met or is likely to meet, with a wider range of experience and a more varied assortment of talents than any of his contemporaries. He knows that this is so, and as he is by temperament incapable of false modesty, as he is of any other form of duplicity, he makes no pretence

21

of thinking that other people's ideas are as important or well-founded as his own.

Although he has a generous and kindly nature, with plenty of goodwill to his neighbours, this self-absorption interferes with the growth of a steady fellowship with them. Pursuing his own ideas and trains of thought, he is suddenly surprised to find that he is out of step with his companions—or they, as he judges, with him—and is rather hurt that they blame him for the discord. Obviously, it must be their fault, and he is puzzled by their antagonism. "I have never joined in any intrigue," he protested in 1912. "Everything I have got, I have worked for; and I've been more hated than anybody."

AMBITIOUS, WILFUL AND MISCHIEVOUS

No doubt there was warrant for his complaint, and yet the fault did not altogether lie with his critics. They were excusably annoyed at the young man's undisguised ambition and his air of infallibility. Besides it must be embarrassing for a group of politicians when their colleague takes the bit between his teeth and goes boring along on his own course, heedless of the generally accepted policy. Especially must this be so when that course has been chosen on the spur of the moment, on grounds which are not clear to them or seem inadequate. And Winston has a natural preference for an original way of his own. When he was going up Vesuvius in 1910, he ignored the beaten track, and insisted on choosing his own more direct route. He nearly broke his neck.

He has yet another characteristic which helps to explain the hostility that has pursued him during so much of his career. As a small boy, he was very wilful and mischievous, and he has never entirely grown up. Still, from time to time, that streak of mischief comes to the surface.

H. G. Wells once wrote: "There are times when the evil spirit comes upon him, and then I can only think of him as an intractable little boy, a mischievous, dangerous little boy, a knee-worthy little boy. Only by thinking of him in that way can I go on liking him." Age has not quenched the imp in him. In party controversy he will sometimes startle the public and disconcert his allies by his reckless utterances, or by explosions of childish petulance. And while he enjoys opposition he cannot bear criticism.

We have still to reach that quality in Churchill which warrants us

IMPERIAL CONFERENCE OF 1944

On 1 May, 1944, the Imperial Conference to discuss the conduct of the war against Germany opened at 10 Downing Street and lasted until 16 May. In the photograph, reading from left to right, are:—General Smuts (South Africa), Mr. Mackenzie King (Canada), Mr. Churchill, Mr. John Curtin (Australia), Mr. Peter Fraser (New Zealand).

calling him great. For a man may be gifted far above the ordinary, a remarkable figure in his generation, without earning a title to real greatness. For that, he must devote himself to a great cause, use his abilities in a mighty enterprise. Only the man who can lose his life in the service of some noble purpose will save it unto life eternal.

Churchill has brilliant gifts. He is, in addition, driven by a limitless ambition. Without such ambition, men rarely rise to greatness.

> *"Fame is the spur that the clear spirit doth raise*
> *(That last infirmity of noble mind)*
> *To scorn delights, and live laborious days."*

But had Churchill been no more than a clever egoist, concerned merely to outshine his fellows, and grasp all the prizes, he would not be truly great. He might only be a disturbing nuisance. A man must have something bigger and finer than himself as the object of his ambition if he is to win enduring fame.

Men are made great by the causes they serve. George Washington was ennobled by his service to the freedom of the American colonies; Lincoln by his fight to free the slaves and establish a united American democracy. Gladstone had a passion for liberty—the liberty of small nations everywhere. Lloyd George was dominated by an instinctive

23

"CHARLES MORIN," LANDSCAPE PAINTER

Churchill is a very able landscape painter, and under the pseudonym of "Charles Morin" exhibited and sold pictures at public exhibitions in France and Britain. He had three pictures in the Royal Academy in 1947, signed "Charles Winter," and three under his own name in 1948, when he was made an "Honorary Academician Extraordinary."

craving to help the under-dog. All had great gifts. But it was the purpose to which they used those gifts which stamped their fame on history.

What is Winston's deepest passion? What in him is stronger than his personal ambition?

He has at one time or another used his great abilities on behalf of various causes. Free Trade evoked his first major political efforts, even to the sacrifice of his party loyalties. Later, he devoted himself wholeheartedly to the problem of alleviating the lot of the unemployed. "I would give my life," he once declared, "to see them placed on a right footing in regard to their lives and means of living." But in fact neither of these issues quite gripped the central core of the man. His Free Trade convictions were largely accepted from the economic doctrines of the day. He is not himself an economist. His activities in social reform owed much of their inspiration and most of their content to his close association with Lloyd George, who planned the measures which Churchill carried out for Unemployment Insurance. Later on in his career, Winston acquiesced in a policy of protective tariffs, and showed a much diminished zeal about current unemployment problems.

THE SERVICE OF HIS COUNTRY

It was left for the Second World War to demonstrate and to bring into full prominence that central passion which is bigger in Winston than any self-seeking ambition, and makes him the giant figure which the world admiringly recognizes today. Fighter, reformer, artist, Winston is above all a patriot, with a flaming and overmastering loyalty to Britain, to her honour, her greatness, her Empire, her destiny. He may hold lightly by party ties. He may abandon and oppose former colleagues. He may forget the old time-honoured doctrines and ignore or disavow the policies he once acclaimed. But round one pivot he always swings truly. Bigger than his thirst for fame, his hopes of success and dreams of greatness, is his limitless devotion to the service of his country.

His interest has always centred chiefly on Imperial and international affairs. Britain's defence by sea, land and air; her dealings with her Colonial possessions, and with the great Dominions joined with her in the British Commonwealth; her friendship with that other mighty English-speaking democracy, the United States; and her relations with allied or rival Powers; these have been throughout his career the matters of first concern to Winston.

Happy is the man who has found his right place and task. Winston Churchill has always felt himself to be destined and fore-ordained to some mission of supreme importance for his country. The many almost miraculous escapes from death which have studded his career gave support to that faith. Like General Gordon, he might assert the conviction: "I am immortal till my work is done!" In the fullness of time his hour arrived, and the task for which he had been born.

Britain may well be grateful to the Providence which, at the moment when her need was most desperate, brought forth the man ideally equipped by ability, experience and warlike temper to lead her through her darkest night of peril.

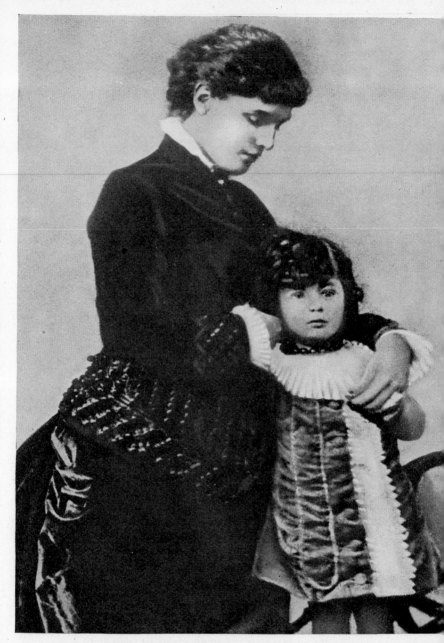

WINSTON CHURCHILL AND HIS MOTHER

*Winston Churchill was born on 30 November, 1874, and this photo-
graph was taken when he was about four years old. With him, is his
brilliant American mother, whom he loved dearly but of whom he
was, at the same time, a little afraid. His real companion in those
early days was Mrs. Everest, his nurse, to whom he was devoted.*

CHAPTER II

MAKINGS OF A SOLDIER

O N the last day of November, 1874, a cry shattered the stately silences of Blenheim Palace, ancestral seat of the Dukes of Marlborough. It was the yell of a new-born baby; an aggressive yell, one fancies, for even in birth this was an impetuous youngster. The notice that appeared in *The Times* three days later announced:

"On the 30th November at Blenheim Palace, the Lady Randolph Churchill, prematurely, of a son."

He was, in fact, a seven-months child, and in his eagerness to be out and about there was something prophetic to hint that tireless energy and activity, that restless thirst for living and doing, which would characterize his whole career.

He was christened Winston Leonard Spencer Churchill. The name was a cameo of his ancestry. The first "Winston" Churchill, ten generations back, was the father of the great Duke of Marlborough. He was a Cavalier squire of Dorsetshire, who married a relative of Francis Drake, and fought gallantly on the Royalist side in the Civil War. Subsequently he sold out his estate, but regained it at the Restoration, and wrote a book on the Divine Right of Kings which had some vogue in the days of the Merry Monarch, Charles II. "Leonard" was the name of his maternal grandfather, Leonard Jerome, an American who made and lost fortunes in New York. He owned and edited the *New York Times,* and had once armed his staff with rifles and artillery, to defend his newspaper office against the mob when it disagreed with his views and tried to break into the premises. A lover of the turf, he founded the first great racecourses in America, the Jerome Park course and the Coney Island Jockey Club.

Winston's father, Lord Randolph Churchill, was the third son of the seventh Duke of Marlborough, and in his heyday the liveliest and most popular member of the nobility. This year, 1874, was one to be marked in red in his calendar. It began with a General Election, at which he stood for Woodstock, in Oxfordshire, and was returned

WINSTON CHURCHILL'S PARENTS

Winston's father (inset), Lord Randolph Churchill, entered Parliament as member for Woodstock in 1874. He was leader of the "Fourth Party," Secretary of State for India (1885) and Chancellor of the Exchequer (1886). Winston's mother, Lady Randolph Churchill, was the daughter of Mr. Leonard Jerome of New York. A prominent figure in both Victorian and Edwardian society, she died in 1921.

triumphantly to Parliament. Lord Randolph was barely twenty-five.

In April he dashed across to Paris to marry Miss Jeannette Jerome. He had met her at a ball at Cowes in the previous August, fallen in love at first sight, proposed next day and been accepted. But his ducal father had frowned upon the idea of bringing an American bride into the family, and Leonard Jerome, not to be outdone in pride, had carried off his daughter and imposed a delay on the young couple. That was over now, however, and both families beamed on the match. To crown the year, November brought Lord Randolph a son and heir, destined, though he did not then suspect it, to become one of the most brilliant and distinguished of the sons of Britain, and to write his name in world history.

A SETTING OF FEUDAL MAGNIFICENCE

Lord Randolph had brought his bride back to Blenheim Palace, and so young Winston first saw the light in a setting of feudal magnificence. The vast estates of great landowners were still maintained in their traditional splendour. Sir William Harcourt's death duties, which were ultimately to cripple and break them up, would not be invented for another twenty years.

In the early seventies Dukes were Dukes. When a local court had the impertinence to fine the Duke of Portland for driving a primitive motor-car along the road at more than four miles an hour, and without two men walking ahead carrying red flags, His Grace's steward attended the court and paid the fine but with the protest: "I must warn you that the Duke will be much displeased."

The countryside was emptier than of yore. Enclosures had wiped out its small peasantry. Their children had mostly been drawn off into the great new industrial towns that were growing fast in the Midlands and the North. The mail coaches had long since ceased to run, and post horses were no longer ready in relays for travellers at the country inns. The railway system had come into full flower, and Britain's roads were now deserted, except for local farm traffic, carriers' carts and the doctor's gig. As yet there were no motor-cars, and the bicycles were penny-farthing boneshakers. People all lived very near their work, and most of them travelled little. They had no telephones, no radio and no cinemas.

Life for most people at that time was simple and inexpensive. Food was cheap. Rents were low. The country was more prosperous than it had ever been, and large families were the custom. Income tax in 1874 was threepence in the pound, and Gladstone promised that he would abolish it if he was returned to power at the General Election. But he was defeated, and income tax is still with us. Farm wages averaged ten shillings a week. Wages of domestic servants were about five pounds a year. Many a professional or business man lived in dignified comfort and brought up a large family on an income that never exceeded £300 a year.

Class distinctions were clearly marked and calmly accepted. *"The rich man in his castle, the poor man at his gate,"* were regarded as the divinely appointed social order, to quarrel with which was blasphemy. When Lady Ashburton took Thomas Carlyle, the world-famous writer, and his sick wife, to Scotland, she packed them with her maid and doctor into a second-class carriage, while she herself travelled first-class. Everyone, including the cantankerous Carlyle himself, thought this entirely right and proper. There was a formula for daily conduct, nearly as stiff and stifling as the high-boned, tightly laced corsets which imprisoned the unnatural wasp-waists of ladies of fashion.

THE WORLD AT PEACE

The world was then at peace, and looked forward to years of peace. The Franco-Prussian war of 1870 had been fought and the French, the traditional enemies of England, had been defeated. The strength of the British Navy was unchallenged, for Germany, now the most powerful nation on the Continent, had no fleet. It seemed inconceivable that any enemy could threaten our shores.

There were, however, two portents of change ahead, though few realized their significance. The 1870 Education Act had ordained schooling for every child and School Boards were empowered to frame bye-laws enforcing attendance where it seemed desirable; and, in the 1874 parliament, fifty-eight Irish Home Rule members made their appearance.

Winston was just over a year old when the Duke of Marlborough, his grandfather, was appointed Lord Lieutenant of Ireland and took Lord Randolph with him as his private secretary. So Winston's earliest memories are of Dublin, where he spent the next four years. The Little Lodge, in the grounds of the Vice-Regal Lodge, was his home, and its shrubberies were his playground. Vast jungles to him then, they appeared very small when he revisited them twenty years later. There were not many stirring events to make those years memorable. The bogey of those Irish days was the Fenians. On one occasion the little boy fell from a donkey when racing away from a column of men whom his nurse averred to be Fenians—though they were probably troops making a route-march.

It would be untrue to suggest that Winston was ever a notably "good" boy. All accounts seem to agree that he was lively, mischievous and often tiresome. He was red-haired and snub-nosed. Deeply as he admired and revered his parents, there was throughout his boyhood no bond of sympathetic understanding between him and them. His mother was being whirled along in the midstream of society life, and young Winston was no ornament to be produced with pride in the drawing-room. His father was wrapped up in his political work, and viewed his barbarian offspring with somewhat distant affection. In fact, Winston was a rather lonely urchin. His one real friend was his nurse, Mrs. Everest. More than anyone else, perhaps, she gave him love and understanding, and shaped his character to a sturdy and uncompromising honesty.

A RESTLESS WINSTON SENT TO SCHOOL

By the time that Winston was seven he had become too restless an inmate of the home for his parents, so they packed him off to school. It was a private school, and its head was a clergyman who indulged in periodic orgies of brutal thrashing. Winston naturally got his full share of those canings. They did not break his spirit, and in revenge for one of them he kicked the headmaster's hat to pieces. But they impaired his health, and after a year he became seriously ill, and was taken away. His next school was at Brighton, a gentler establishment, run by maiden ladies, where he remained for three years. Miss Eva Moore, the actress, was the dancing mistress. It is recorded by her that he was "the naughtiest boy in the class. I used to think him the naughtiest small boy in the world!"

Despite the bracing air of Brighton, Winston's chest was still weak. In fact, he nearly died of pneumonia there. So when at thirteen and a half he went on to his public school, it was not to the family's traditional school of Eton, lying among the damp meadows of the Thames Valley, but to Harrow-on-the-Hill.

How he got in must remain a mystery. Latin was reckoned there

31

as the supreme essential, and Winston knew no Latin. He hated it from the first lesson at his first school, and at the Harrow entrance examination he confesses that his Latin paper consisted of the figure 1, in brackets, a blot and some smudges. No doubt something of his erratic ability was shown in other papers. Anyhow, Dr. Welldon, the headmaster, admitted him in faith and hope, not unmixed with charity, to the tail of the bottom form. There he was content to stay. Indeed, he never climbed out of the Junior School during his days at Harrow.

A DUNCE WHO OFTEN WAS BRILLIANT

He was that curious mixture, a dunce who often was brilliant. He had plenty of brains when he chose to use them. He had a magnificent memory, and could learn anything he liked. In his first term he won a prize by repeating twelve hundred lines of Macaulay's "Lays." That retentive memory was to serve him well later on in the delivery of his carefully prepared speeches. But what he didn't like he made no attempt to learn. He liked history and English—especially English, and as he was too low in the school to be herded to Latin, he spent his time under a master who knew how to teach English, exploring the secrets of its syntax and the rich texture of its literature. We owe a debt to that master.

He was still an undisciplined boy. He had no patience with organized games. At the swimming bath he enjoyed the joke of pushing other small boys into the water unawares. One day he made the mistake of pushing in Leo Amery, who, though diminutive, was a senior, in the sixth form and gymnastic champion. Amery's retribution was swift and drastic. Afterward Winston essayed an apology for his mistake. "You are so small," he explained; then, with an effort at tact, "My father, who is a great man, is also small!"

At home his favourite amusement was playing with toy soldiers, of which he had an immense army, powerfully equipped. His younger brother, John, was allowed to manoeuvre the native troops, without artillery, and accept defeat from the masses of Winston's white forces. That toy army was of historical importance for Winston's career. His father, Lord Randolph, came up one day to inspect the troops, and spent twenty minutes studying their competent disposition. He had been wondering what to do with this disappointing boy, whose scholastic backwardness made it hopeless to think of

CHURCHILL'S BOYHOOD

*Top, left: a photograph of
Winston taken after 1876 while
Lord Randolph Churchill was
secretary to his father, the Duke
of Marlborough, in Ireland.
Below, left: at the time of this
picture "the naughtiest small boy
in the world" was at a private
school in Brighton. Top, right:
a picture taken during Winston's
early years at Harrow School.*

entering him for the bar. But the toy soldiers gave him an idea. Here was evidence of real interest and even ability. "Would you like to go into the Army?" he asked. Would he? From his earliest boyhood, Winston had longed to be a soldier! His future was settled there and then.

At Harrow he duly sat and passed the preliminary Army examination. This success was due to one of those amazing strokes of luck which have spangled his life-story. The examination would include drawing a map. He put the names of all the countries on the atlas into a hat and drew one out: New Zealand. He studied its outline thoroughly and next day picked up his examination paper to find the instruction: draw a map of New Zealand.

THE ARMY CLASS AT HARROW

He passed into the Army class at Harrow, but did not distinguish himself in it. Twice he failed in the entrance examination for Sandhurst, and at last was sent to an army coach who managed to pump enough mathematics into him to squeeze him through—too low in the list to gain admittance as anything better than a cavalry candidate. Cavalry commissions were less sought after than those in the infantry, as they involved heavier expenses. Lord Randolph was keenly disappointed, for he had designed to get Winston into the 60th Rifles. Winston himself was jubilant. He liked the prospect of riding about on a horse, fighting sword in hand. His one outstanding success at Harrow had been the winning of the Public Schools Fencing Championship just before he left.

Between leaving Harrow at the end of 1892 and entering Sandhurst in the summer of 1893, Winston grew up. Some will perhaps deny that. They will say that he never grew up. And indeed, the German philosopher's dictum is truer of him than of most:

"Im echten Manne ist ein Kind versteckt; das will spielen!"
(In the true man there lurks a child, who wants to play.)

But though Winston had not entirely lost his small-boy quality, the year 1893 marked a new maturity and compactness of his character. The ungainly, erratic, undisciplined vagaries of his incalculable urchin days fell away, and a young man emerged with definite aims and quite remarkable abilities.

Several circumstances may have contributed to this. The most dramatic was no doubt an accident. At Christmastime, larking with

34

SCHOOL HOUSE, HARROW, 1892

This photograph was taken in Winston's second year at Harrow School. He is the boy at the top of the fire-escape. Dr. Welldon (sixth from the right, second row), a distinguished cleric and writer, was the Headmaster. He showed his foresight by taking a keen interest in young Churchill, who did not at that time show much promise.

his younger brother and cousin in the pinewoods on his aunt's estate at Bournemouth, he was cornered on a rustic bridge. He tried to escape by jumping into a pine tree, but fell thirty feet and lay unconscious for three days. A ruptured kidney was diagnosed, and he was convalescing for many weeks.

That enforced rest gave him time to think; to pull himself together mentally. It did more. Living at home, he had leisure to see something of his father's political activities and friends—and Lord Randolph was on intimate terms with the leading figures of the day.

The Liberals had ousted the Tories in 1892, and Gladstone was again in power for a last brief spell. Lord Randolph, the most popular personality on the Tory side, had wrecked his standing with his party in 1886 through trying to hustle them into social reform. Now, in their time of defeat, he hoped for a comeback. His son, listening to the conversation of great men at the dinner-table, caught

LORD RANDOLPH AT WORK

After an early career of great promise, ill-health curtailed the political activities of Lord Randolph Churchill, Winston's father. His last term of office as Chancellor of the Exchequer ended in 1886. Although in Parliament until his death in 1895 at the age of 46, he was in the end a chronic invalid. He is shown above, preparing a speech.

visions of causes and purposes and policies to be fought for. Life took on a deeper meaning for Winston Churchill.

Winston was passionately on his father's side. He would have loved to help him. Perhaps it was the young man's bitterest tragedy that he could win no intimacy with Lord Randolph, who still held aloof from this perplexing boy and rejected his offers of assistance. Well, perhaps in the years to come. . . . But there were to be no years to come. Lord Randolph never regained his lost position. A shadow was beginning to fall across him—that creeping, malignant disease which was to eat away body and mind and within two years bring him to an untimely grave.

RELATIONS WITH HIS FATHER

In all his life, Winston could count up only three or four really frank and intimate talks with his father. The failure to gain his confidence and friendship was the sadder because Lord Randolph was a brilliant and lovable figure. The crowds adored him. Even to the end when he rose in the Commons to attempt a speech, his fellow-members, friends and opponents alike, sat listening to the stricken man with no feeling but of sympathy and affection. Huge multitudes lined the streets to watch his funeral pass.

Although his accident may have played a valuable part in Winston's sudden maturity, it did not help him to a high place in the Sandhurst entrance examination. Once there, however, he embarked on a new life. Gone were the schoolboy studies of bewildering mathematics and loathsome Latin. He was now learning real practical things such as fortification and tactics and military administration, riding and drill—though he wasn't very fond of the drill!

Winston was never a scholar, who loved learning for its own sake. Yet his brilliant mind could readily master any subject for which he could see a real use, and his Sandhurst days were as successful as his schoolboy days had been aimless. It was as if the early morning mists had suddenly cleared and the sun was now shining radiantly in a cloudless sky. He was no longer a dunce, but an able and successful embryo officer. He made friends—many friends. Today their graves stud the South African veldt and the fields of France and Flanders.

At Christmas, 1894, Winston finished his Sandhurst course, and in contrast with his lowly place in the entrance examination passed out eighth out of a hundred and fifty. In the spring of 1895 he was gazetted to the 4th Hussars.

To an onlooker it might seem that he had chosen a blind alley. The world was at peace, and seemed likely to remain at peace. Few officers in the British Army below field rank had ever seen active service on any battlefield.

England in the middle of the "Naughty Nineties" was passing through spiritual doldrums. The great tide of Victorian effort and achievement had passed its flood. Most of the giants had fallen. Palmerston and Disraeli, Dickens and Thackeray, Tennyson and Browning—all were dead. Gladstone and Ruskin had finished their work and were near the end. The harvest of Victorian industry and commerce was being reaped in an ever-widening prosperity. The nation was confident, self-satisfied, and tending to mental inertia.

Conventional propriety had fastened on the nation, and the smallest tradesman or clerk had his frock coat and silk hat for Sundays. This was the best of all possible worlds, and everything wrong in it was a necessary evil. The British Empire was a divinely ordained institution, and the British felt a smug self-righteousness at being called on to shoulder "the White Man's Burden," and to rule for their own good the "lesser breeds without the law."

It was a stuffy and relaxing atmosphere. Restless spirits among the young generation found no fertile inspiration in it. The old emphasis on duty and respectability began to be invaded by a rather inartistic craving for enjoyment, of which the music-hall became the crude and rowdy temple.

POLITICS AT A LOW EBB

Politics, too, were at a low ebb when Winston got his commission in 1895. His father had just died. Gladstone had retired, and that summer Lord Rosebery, his successor and a close friend of Lord Randolph, was displaced by the elderly Marquess of Salisbury. Irish Home Rule, on which the Liberal party had foundered, was regarded with amused impatience by the nation as a whole, who were entertained by the antics of the Irish members in Parliament, but did not take them or their cause seriously. To take things seriously was almost bad form.

Happily for himself—and for his country—Winston did not succumb to this atmosphere. He had no mind to be an aimless play-

CAVALRY CADET AT SANDHURST

After passing his entrance examinations with difficulty, Churchill entered Sandhurst in 1893 as a cavalry cadet. What he was to be had greatly worried his father, but his interest in toy soldiers had decided Lord Randolph that he was cut out for a military life. Winston certainly found his army training more enjoyable than his schooldays.

FAMILY GROUP AT COWES

This photograph, from the collection of the late Lady Leonie Leslie, aunt of Winston Churchill, was taken at Cowes in the early nineties. Churchill is sitting on the right with the dog on his knees. Lady Randolph Churchill, his mother, is seated on the arm of his chair. Next to her is Major John Churchill, Winston's younger brother.

boy. He had become a soldier. A soldier's job was not just parades and steeplechases, mess dinners and society functions. It was fighting. So he looked round the peace-blanketed world for somewhere to fight. There seemed to be peace everywhere.

The only war to be found was in Cuba, where the Spanish Government was at last trying to stamp out the endemic rebellion which had dragged on for years past. Winston had a spell of leave coming—two and a half months of it. The other subalterns would spend it hunting. He would spend it in visiting a real battlefield and studying war at first hand.

Pulling wires with the British Embassy at Madrid was easy

enough for a Churchill. He persuaded another young subaltern, Reginald Barnes, to join him, and with a sheaf of letters of introduction to the Spanish authorities in Cuba they sailed for the Caribbean.

Before leaving, Winston did one thing that was perhaps of crucial influence for his future. He contracted with the *Daily Graphic* to write them descriptive letters about his experiences at £5 a letter. His idea was that it would help to pay his expenses. But it did far more; it initiated him in a practice of journalism which was ultimately to open to him a royal road, not only out of the limitations of a subaltern's life, but into national fame and public service.

THE WRONG WAY TO MAKE WAR

In Cuba, Winston got a rather confused glimpse of the wrong way to make war. The force to which he attached himself set out from the fever-ridden town of Sancti Spiritus and wandered through tropical forests and thickets, having occasional brushes with the elusive guerillas. It stood as much chance of crushing the rebels by such an expedition as a man would have of exterminating a swarm of mosquitoes, attacking him on a river bank, by slashing them with his fishing-rod.

Winston came under fire. A bullet whistled past his head as he sat eating his lunch, and killed a horse picketed just behind him. Trying to sleep in a hammock slung inside a hut, he listened to bullets crunching through the thatch, and wondered if the Spanish officer slung beside him was fat enough to stop anything coming his way. He even saw some sort of a battle when a rebel force made a stand, and the Spanish troops deployed and advanced against their position, while the officers and himself sat on horseback close behind the line and watched the fray.

He investigated rum cocktails, discovered the merits of the siesta —a knowledge which was to be invaluable to him in later days of strain and feverish activity—and as his leave of absence from the regiment neared its end he returned from Cuba, bearing the Spanish Military Medal (1st Class) and a scepticism which later years were to deepen about the infallibility of army commanders.

Back in England Winston found his regiment getting ready to sail for India. A few weeks were spent at Hounslow Barracks before their departure, and during this time he was able to attend a number

41

of society functions, and widen his already wide circle of acquaintance. At Lord William Beresford's house, Deepdene, near Dorking, he met Sir Bindon Blood, and made him promise that if there were any more trouble in the Malakand Pass on the Indian frontier— where the general had just carried out a successful minor campaign —he might come along and join in.

TO INDIA WITH THE 4TH HUSSARS

Presently the 4th Hussars went off to India. When they reached Bombay Winston was so eager to get on shore that he put off from the ship in a small boat, reached the quay and grabbed at a ring with such reckless impatience that he dislocated his shoulder. It was never reliable again, and he, the public schools champion fencer, had thereafter to fall back on a revolver when real fighting came his way. Perhaps it was all for the best: his injury may have saved his life. For a revolver disposes of your assailant quickly and thoroughly and at a distance. It has a longer reach than a sword.

In India he found that apparently the be-all and end-all of a cavalry subaltern's life was polo. He revelled in polo, and came to the front as a crack player, despite his game shoulder. But his mind, too, was awake and eager for exercise. He began to read, widely and indiscriminately, the writings of historians, philosophers, scientists. It is worth mention that he started this banquet with Gibbon and Macaulay. The rolling, eloquent music of their works captivated him: and one may catch in his own writings and speeches familiar echoes of the magniloquence of Gibbon's prose, and the vivid, dramatic quality of Macaulay's "History."

In the summer of 1897, Sir Bindon Blood led a punitive expedition against the rising Pathans in the Malakand Pass. Winston was just back in England on three months' leave when he heard of it, and he dashed off to India to claim his promised share of the fun. There was no room for him on Sir Bindon's staff, but he collected commissions to cover the campaign for the *Allahabad Pioneer* and the *Daily Telegraph,* and in the role of a war correspondent he was presently accompanying a mixed force of British and Indian troops up the Mahmund Valley.

The tribesmen sniped at them. They spread out, rather recklessly, into a number of small parties to deal with their assailants, and narrowly escaped being all cut to pieces. Winston at one moment

IN THE 4TH HUSSARS

In 1895, Winston Churchill obtained his commission in the army. He found his time as a recruit-officer which lasted for six months most arduous but at the same time much to his liking. In the same year he went out to Cuba to gain experience of war at first hand.

found himself isolated and fighting with a hairy Pathan across the corpse of the company adjutant. He abolished the foe with his revolver and managed to get back to the remains of his detachment.

THE FIRST OF MANY BOOKS

The losses were heavy, and Winston ceased to be supernumerary. He was posted to the 31st Punjab Infantry, of whose language he knew three words, and served with them for the rest of the campaign till his leave from the Hussars had long expired and his colonel insisted on his return. But he did not abandon his war correspondent job, and when he got back to Bangalore he devoted his spare time to writing a full account of the expedition. This, *The Malakand Field Force,* was the first of many books from his pen.

It was a great success. Financially, it brought him in the equivalent of two years' pay. In reputation it pushed him into notice as an able and original young author. It even won him a warm letter of appreciation from the Prince of Wales. But it was not so successful with the higher dignitaries of the Army, who were annoyed that a junior officer should criticize, as freely and confidently as Winston did, the blunders of his superiors.

The misfortunes of the Malakand campaign stirred the Indian Government to launch a bigger thrust against the Afridi tribesmen—the Tirah expedition. Winston moved heaven and earth to get in on this show, but only achieved a belated success when most of the fighting was over.

While the Tirah expedition was petering out into a peaceful political settlement, news began to come through of another pending war—Kitchener's expedition to clean up the Sudan, revenge the death of Gordon and make a final settlement with the Khalifa and his rebel Dervishes.

The previous history of this affair can be sketched briefly. The Suez Canal was opened in 1869, and six years later Disraeli bought for Britain the canal shares of the bankrupt Egyptian Khedive. In 1882 Arabi Pasha started a revolt in Egypt against the increasing foreign influence, and massacres broke out. Both the French and British sent fleets, but the French backed out and left the British to settle the affair. After the victory of Tel-el-Kebir the country was pacified. But meanwhile the Sudan had revolted from the Khedive, under the leadership of the Mahdi, a Moslem fanatic. The British

IN THE INDIAN ARMY

In 1897, Lieutenant Churchill went to India. Later he was attached to the 31st Punjab Infantry and was with the Malakand Field Force where he was mentioned in despatches and obtained a medal with clasp. He was later on the staff of Sir William Lockhart.

and Egyptian forces sent against him were defeated. Khartum was threatened, and General Gordon was sent to carry out its evacuation.

Gordon had no mind to evacuate Khartum. He resolved to force the British Government's hand and make it dispatch an army to recover the Sudan. Gladstone, then in power, was no less stubbornly against fresh Imperialist adventures and would send Gordon no help. When at last British public opinion compelled the dispatch of a relief expedition, it arrived two days too late. Khartum had fallen and Gordon was dead.

MILITARY EXPEDITION AGAINST THE DERVISHES

The British and Egyptian forces were withdrawn from the Sudan, which after the Mahdi's death continued in Dervish hands under his successor, the Khalifa. In 1890 Kitchener was appointed Sirdar (Commander of the Egyptian Army). He maintained with growing success the struggle against the Dervishes, and in the spring of 1898, with the backing of Lord Salisbury's Government, launched a final drive to retake Khartum and crush the Khalifa.

Winston was determined to get into this expedition. But he found the door barred against him. Kitchener did not approve of young men in a hurry who wrote for the papers and criticized their superiors. He returned a firm rebuff to every approach on Winston's behalf—even when the Prime Minister himself cabled the Sirdar to request a place for him. But Winston never was—either then or later—the man to accept defeat. On the strength of Lord Salisbury's backing, he persuaded Sir Evelyn Wood, the Adjutant-General, to give him a commission in the 21st Lancers, which were being sent to join the expeditionary force. The offer was subject to the chilling condition that Winston must pay his own expenses and get no compensation if killed or wounded.

The expenses problem was easily met, for he persuaded the *Morning Post* to commission him as its war correspondent. In this role he had now established his reputation. He rushed out to Egypt, and joined the Lancers just as they set off for the Sudan. Indeed, he had cut it so fine that he missed the command of the troop originally reserved for him in one of the leading squadrons—a circumstance which probably saved his life. At Assouan he was left to bring up the rear. This involved him in a lonely night ride through the unfamiliar desert, steering by the stars. In the morning he sought direction from friendly peasants. He could not talk to them, but he could draw with his sword-point, and the Egyptians, familiar through many ages with picture writing, grasped his signs and put him on his way.

The army moved cautiously across the desert, and it was nearly the end of August—four weeks from his arrival in Egypt—before Winston caught his first sight of a Dervish. On 1 September, at the head of a reconnoitring patrol, he was the first man to sight the Khalifa's army, drawn up in front of Omdurman. He was sent off post-haste to make his report to Kitchener in person. It was something of an ordeal for the young subaltern who was there in the teeth of the Sirdar's direct prohibition. But the interview passed off peacefully. Kitchener was either unaware of his identity, or too preoccupied to heed it. Yet the encounter held its concealed drama. The two men were to meet again, in the direction of a greater war; and the clash of their discordant temperaments was to cause embarrassment for the country they both aspired to serve.

BATTLE OF OMDURMAN

Next morning, in the early light of a tropic sun, twenty thousand British troops met an army three times their number on the field of Omdurman. The Dervishes swept forward with fanatical frenzy, buoyed up by the Khalifa's eloquent assurance that victory was foreordained, and that the joys of Paradise awaited any who fell. But Kitchener's artillery smashed and cut to pieces the advancing hordes, ploughing great furrows through their close-packed masses. Then, as they drew nearer, the British infantry met them with disciplined volleys of rifle fire that raised an impenetrable wall of lead against which they wavered and broke.

As the Dervishes began to fall away and scatter, the 21st Lancers were ordered to charge them and complete their rout. This was the last classic cavalry charge in the history of British warfare. Four squadrons of lancers—four hundred men and horses—swung into line abreast and swept with levelled lances across the desert plain upon what were thought to be the remnants of the Dervish army.

They found more than they expected. Behind a line of crouching snipers they came suddenly upon a wide nullah or desert ravine, thronged with about three thousand of the enemy. Into this ambush crashed the four hundred: into a wild mêlée of whirling swords and flying bullets. Winston himself, mindful of his game shoulder, had

FINAL CHARGE OF THE 21st LANCERS

In 1898, Churchill was attached to the 21st Lancers and served on the Nile Expeditionary Force. In the subsequent battle of Omdurman on the upper reaches of the Nile, Sir Herbert Kitchener broke the power of the Dervishes and revenged Gordon. Lieutenant Churchill was in the

sheathed his sword and drawn a Mauser pistol, which served him well. He shot his way through the nullah, scrambled out unhurt, plugged a prostrate Dervish who tried to hamstring his pony, and another who barred his way, and galloped on to rejoin his troop, most of whom won through safely.

"Did you enjoy yourself?" he asked one of his sergeants. The men laughed, and their tension was eased. But it had been a costly charge. Nearly a quarter of the regiment, and more than a quarter of their horses had been killed or wounded. They did not repeat the charge. They enfiladed the nullah with their carbines, and the surviv-

AT THE BATTLE OF OMDURMAN

final cavalry charge which routed the enemy. This contemporary drawing of the action, reproduced by courtesy of the "Illustrated London News," is by Caton Woodville, who lived from 1856 to 1927 and was acknowledged to be one of the most famous military artists of his time.

ing Dervishes made off. Robert Grenfell, who commanded the troop which had been at first reserved for Winston, struck the densest part of the nullah, where he was cut to pieces with most of his men.

With the victory of Omdurman the war to liberate the Sudan from the pitiless tyranny of the Dervishes came to an end. Winston returned down the Nile to England, where he set to work to write the history of the campaign. It was published in two volumes in the following year under the title of *The River War*. He also reached a momentous decision, which will be dealt with in a later chapter. He resolved to throw up his commission and enter Parliament.

IN THE "COCKYOLI BIRDS"

Churchill's two books, "The Malakand Field Force" (1898) and "The River War" (1899) made him famous in journalistic circles and when the South African War broke out in 1899, the "Morning Post" sent him out as war correspondent to South Africa. Later on in the War, he joined the South African Light Horse, the "Cockyoli Birds."

CHAPTER III

ADVENTURES IN SOUTH AFRICA

WHEN Winston got back from the Egyptian campaign he spent only a few weeks in London before starting off again on his travels. He had one last engagement to fulfil before resigning his commission. His regiment, the 4th Hussars, had set its heart on winning the All-India Cavalry Cup—the premier polo trophy—and Winston was No. 1 in its team. So at the end of November, 1898, he went out East, to make what he expected to be his farewell appearance as an officer.

The games were as fast and furious as desperate zeal could make them. Winston was under a heavy handicap because he managed to dislocate his groggy right shoulder again, just before the tournament, and had to play with his arm strapped to his side. Yet he scored the winning goal for his regiment in the final match. It was just the sort of success, in defiance of all the odds and all the rules, which has chequered his career. Then he resigned his commission and came back to London to get on with his book, *The River War*.

There was a second interlude in his labours of authorship when, during the summer of 1899, he dashed off to fight—this time without success—his first political contest, the Oldham by-election. But by October his task was finished, and he was eagerly looking forward to the publication of his two fat volumes, which he hoped might bring him distinction and some measure of fortune. In the event, they did both; but before they appeared he himself had embarked upon a fresh adventure that was to do far more for his reputation.

The storm-clouds which had long been gathering in South Africa suddenly broke, and Britain was at war with the Dutch republics of the Transvaal and Orange Free State. No sooner was the news out, than the *Morning Post* offered Winston the post of chief war correspondent; and it is testimony to the quality of his work as correspondent in the Sudan campaign that he was offered the highest rate of pay ever given, up to that time, to a British war correspondent. Needless to say, he jumped at the chance, packed his bags, and departed for the Cape in the same boat which was taking out General Sir Redvers Buller, the Commander-in-Chief. The one fear of all on board was that the war might be over before they arrived.

This is not the place to enter into a close examination of the causes of the South African War. At the time, the majority of people in this country approved, though a considerable minority denounced the war. Today nearly everyone applauds its outcome in the unification of South Africa, though there are few who can review without shame the actions of Britain in the events which led up to this great and bitter conflict between Boer and Briton.

The Cape had been settled by the Dutch in 1652, and for a century and a half the Dutch "boers" (farmers) gradually extended their colony into the fertile land. In the Napoleonic wars, the British took it under their protection to keep it out of French hands, and in 1814 they annexed it. British settlers came along, and in 1836-7 a large number of the Boers, irked by British rule and its interference with their treatment of the Kaffirs, set out on the "Great Trek," which carried them north to occupy the Orange Free State and the Transvaal.

TREATIES AND TROUBLES IN SOUTH AFRICA

Britain signed treaties acknowledging the independence of the Transvaal Republic in 1852, and of the Orange Free State in 1854. But two causes led to continued British interference with them. One was the recurring wars of the Boers with the natives. The British came to the aid of the Boers, and in 1877 annexed the Transvaal; but the Boers rose in rebellion, and in 1881 defeated the British at Majuba Hill. Queen Victoria refused to continue the war and acknowledged their independence. But a far more serious threat to peace developed five years later, when gold was discovered at Johannesburg and extensive diamond mines farther north. This brought a cosmopolitan rush of exploiters and adventurers, "Uitlanders," who were detested by the stolid Dutch farmers and their President, Paul Kruger—popularly known as "Oom Paul."

Wealth flowed into the Transvaal exchequer from the taxes levied on the gold and diamond mines. But the powerful interests to which those mines gave birth were not content to be at the orders of a nation of farmers and their archaic President. They intrigued, pulled wires, secured a backing in influential circles in London, and laid

52

plans to oust the Boer Government and gain control of the Transvaal.

The first attempt, the Jameson Raid of 1895, ended in failure. Dr. Jameson and his band of adventurers were laid by the heels. But the prime movers behind the affair regarded this as only a temporary set-back. When Sir William Butler was sent out to South Africa as High Commissioner and Acting Governor in 1895 he found that Cecil Rhodes and his party were straining every effort to precipitate a fresh conflict; and from some of the orders and proposals which the War Office sent out to him he realized to his dismay that in that Department forces were at work whose object was to provoke war with the Transvaal.

OUTBREAK OF THE BOER WAR

Munitions and stores were being sent out, together with horses and other supplies, and when Sir William refused on military grounds to move his scanty troops provocatively up into unsupported positions on the frontier of the Republic, he was recalled. His successor carried out these dangerous manoeuvres. Kruger sent the British Government an ultimatum demanding the withdrawal of these troops; and the long-planned war was launched.

The motives behind the whole affair were mixed, and some of them were very sordid. The idea of bringing all the closely related South African provinces and communities into a single Union had very much to commend it. It was indeed their obvious destiny. But it could have been sought by the better if slower process of developing co-operation between Boer and Briton.

When Winston arrived at the Cape he found that the war was very far from being over. The Boers had swept down into Natal, routed and killed General Symonds, bottled up Sir George White in Ladysmith and won a big victory at Nicholson's Nek. To the west of the Transvaal Baden Powell was besieged in Mafeking and, farther south, Kimberley was invested by the enemy.

It seems traditional with the British to start a war badly. But surely, never did the War Office and the military commanders make such a witless muddle of miscalculations and strategic blunders as at the outset of the South African War! They had utterly misjudged the nature of the conflict they would have to sustain, and the strength of the enemy they were so lightly engaging. Indeed, Chamberlain thought that Sir George White and his sixteen thousand men might

BRITISH TROOPS UNDER GENERAL SI[...]

*In 1899, a British force under Sir George White was so harassed by Boe[...]
Commandos that it was forced to fall back towards Ladysmith. Whit[...]
unwisely attempted to free his forces by an action at Lombard's Ko[...]
which only just escaped being a rout and cost 1,500 British dead. He wa[...]
able to retire into Ladysmith, where he was surrounded by the Boer.[...]*

GEORGE WHITE RETREAT TO LADYSMITH

Fortunately he had previously managed to evacuate his wounded. As a war correspondent, Churchill was almost in sight of the besieged garrison when the armoured train on which he was a passenger was derailed. He was later amongst the first to enter the town at its relief. In this photograph, General White's troops are seen as they marched into Ladysmith.

finish the affair in a month. It took three years, and drew the full strength of the Empire.

Winston was eager to get to the front. As all the heart of South Africa was in enemy hands, this meant a risky roundabout train journey, getting through just before the railway line was cut by the Boers. On the voyage through stormy weather along the coast he was very sick. From Durban he reached Estcourt, on the line to Ladysmith; beyond Estcourt the country was in enemy hands.

THE ADVENTURE OF THE ARMOURED TRAIN

An armoured train made a daily reconnaissance for a few miles up the line towards Ladysmith. One day the officer in charge, Captain Haldane, invited Winston to come along. They got as far as Chieveley, some fourteen or fifteen miles distant, but when they turned for home they ran into a Boer ambush and came under fire from two field guns and a Maxim. The engine-driver tried to run the gauntlet of the fire and, charging full tilt downhill round a curve, ran—as might have been guessed—into a big rock which the Boers had thoughtfully placed on the line. The engine was in the middle of the train, with three trucks in front and two more behind. The three front trucks of the train were derailed, and the last of them entirely blocked the line. Winston forgot that he was, as a war correspondent, merely an onlooker, and became very active indeed. He dashed forward to inspect the damage. Finding the engine-driver, who had been wounded by a shell fragment, about to run away, he hauled him back with the assurance that no man was hit twice the same day. The engine, fortunately, was still on the rails. Leaving Captain Haldane and the troops in the rear trucks to keep the enemy engaged, Winston took charge of the break-down operations, and for over an hour was running about under constant fire, making the engine pull and push at the truck that was blocking the line, till at last it got past.

It could not run back again to bring along the two trucks with Captain Haldane and his men; so Winston crowded more than forty wounded into the cab, told the rest of the men from the three wrecked trucks to walk along in the shelter of the engine, and started down the line. But the engine, pelted with shells and bullets, soon outstripped the walkers, and Winston, unaware that they had already been rounded up and forced to surrender, got out and went back.

As he hurried along a cutting some figures advanced down it to

ARMOURED TRAIN AMBUSHED AT ESTCOURT

On 15 November, 1899, Winston Churchill was with a body of troops at Estcourt who were in hourly expectation of attack and an armoured train was sent out on reconnaissance. Captain Haldane who was in charge, invited Churchill to accompany the expedition. The train was ambushed and Winston Churchill was among the prisoners.

meet him. They were not in uniform. Boers! He turned and started to scramble up the embankment, while their bullets whistled past and plunked unpleasantly into the earth beside him. But he reached the crest safely and ducked into cover, looking round for the best line of escape. Instead, he saw a Boer riding towards him with rifle poised. He grabbed for his revolver but found it was gone. There was nothing for it. Up went his hands; and presently he was travelling with Captain Haldane and the rest of the day's captures to a prisoner-of-war camp in Pretoria. Years after he discovered that the mounted Boer to whom he had surrendered was none other than Louis Botha, destined to become the first Prime Minister of the Union of South Africa and a loyal friend of Britain.

When Winston arrived at Pretoria he promptly demanded, with that impudent self-assurance which years since have mellowed but never quenched, to be set free as a non-combatant—a newspaper reporter. The Boers smiled grimly at the jest. "But for you, we should have got the whole train!" If they had been wiser, they would have

ESCAPE FROM CAPTIVITY

Winston Churchill was not a prisoner in the hands of the Boers for very long. On 12 December, he planned to escape with two comrades. He was the first to climb the enclosure and managed to elude the sentries. The other two, not so lucky, were unable to get clear.

chained him up; for his whole mind was given to planning an escape. Instead, they allowed him to "scrounge" a civilian suit, and the hat of a Dutch parson. Ever since, Churchill has shown a liking for unusual headgear.

With Haldane and a young lieutenant he planned and prepared a getaway. One evening, when the sentry's back was turned, he scrambled out over a ten-foot fence, and waited on the far side for his companions. They were unable to join him, for the sentry had no further lapses of vigilance that night. But Winston was not going back. Pulling down his clerical slouch hat, he strolled out of the garden into which he had jumped, passing an outside sentry without challenge. Making his way through the streets of Pretoria, he set off with the stars for guide to strike the railway to Delagoa Bay.

He found the line, started walking along it, and then decided that, as Delagoa Bay was three hundred miles away, it would be quicker to ride. He managed to board a goods train, slept among coal sacks till dawn was near, then jumped off and went into hiding under some trees. His food supply consisted of four slabs of chocolate and no water. A gigantic vulture settled uncomfortably near and watched him with greedy anticipation. With that simplicity of spirit which is a part of his contradictory make-up, he betook himself to prayer.

Meanwhile his escape had been discovered and the hunt was up all over the countryside. A notice was published offering the reward of twenty-five pounds for his capture, dead or alive. Unaware of the hornets' nest he had stirred up, Winston thirsted in his spinney through the hot African day. At dusk he drank from a stream, waited vainly for hours by the railway line in the hope of boarding another train, and finally started to trudge grimly on down the track, dodging the sentry posts at bridges and in occasional guard huts.

THE ONLY ENGLISH HOUSE

Across the veldt he saw distant lights, and stumbled toward them. They were the light from furnace engines in a mining village. Once before, as a schoolboy, he had drawn out of a hat the right name of a country from among a score of others. Now, a dazed fugitive, he chose a door, hammered on it, and was pulled quickly inside by an Englishman. It was the only English house for twenty miles around.

It held Mr. Howard, his impromptu host, and Mr. Dewsnap, an engineer from Oldham, of all places, and a couple of Scottish miners. They knew at once who he was, for the searchers had been there already looking for him. Howard gave him food and drink, and hid him down the mine, which had been brought to a standstill by the war. There he stayed for some days in darkness; swarms of enormous white rats, originally loosed there by Howard to act as scavengers, ate his candles and generally disturbed the rest that he needed so much. Meanwhile the hue and cry swept on and eventually died down.

His friends had been planning his further escape, and presently packed him under some bales of wool in a train going to Delagoa Bay. The train was searched at the frontier, but they did not find Winston. At Lourenço Marques a coal-smudged, dishevelled, unshaven loafer slid out of the train unnoticed and headed for the British Consulate.

CHURCHILL IN CAPTIVITY

Upon being taken to the prison camp at Pretoria, after the incident of the armoured train, Winston Churchill was somewhat anxious, as he had rendered himself liable to be shot as a civilian taking part in military operations. The Boers, however, were lenient and decided to treat him as an ordinary military prisoner-of-war. In the meantime, he was planning to escape and release the 200 British prisoners in captivity nearby, and, if possible, capture Pretoria itself. His companions refused to consider this rash scheme. Churchill had therefore to decide on a less ambitious but still enterprising method of escape. The photograph above shows him on parade with a group of British prisoners. Winston is the figure on the right in the cap, standing apart.

Luckier even than he had realized, Winston grasped the popular imagination by his escape. Even if his capture had prevented him from being first with the news for the *Morning Post* about the armoured-train adventure, other correspondents had told in their papers the full story of his gallant exploits. The wounded men who had got away on the engine had been eloquent in his praise. News of his break from the prison camp at Pretoria had delighted the public; and now the crown of the story, his triumphant return, came like a ray of sunshine through the dense gloom of war reports which were just then a succession of defeats. Winston was now a national hero.

60

British residents at Lourenço Marques formed an armed escort to take him to the boat for Durban. At Durban, amid flags and bands, he was given a royal reception by the mayor and naval and military commanders. He hurried back to the Army, where General Buller added his congratulations, and wanted to enrol him in the forces. Winston refused to give up his contract with the *Morning Post*, and it was now forbidden for serving officers of the British Army to act as newspaper correspondents. As a compromise he was given a commission in the South African Light Horse, an irregular force with gaily plumed hats, nicknamed the "Cockyoli Birds." They were raised and commanded by Col. Byng, known to a later generation as Lord Byng of Vimy, the most popular with the troops of all the Army Commanders in the First World War.

VARIOUS STORIES OF THE ESCAPE

Winston's escape from Pretoria was perhaps the most fantastically dramatic episode in a life holding many vivid moments and thrilling experiences. He has retold it often, in print and in lecture; and others, too, have recounted it—not without reason, for it is one of those true stories which are stranger than fiction. Small wonder if the British public, crestfallen at the reverses their arms were suffering at the moment, went wild with delight over this gay young champion whose courage, resource and good luck restored their national self-confidence and seemed a pledge of their victory.

But it seems to have been written in Winston's stars that, whenever he captivated popular imagination by some brilliant stroke, he should at the same time stir up a storm of detraction from envious or hostile critics. That section of the nation which opposed the Boer War found the enthusiasm for his feat quite intolerable, and made desperate efforts to fling mud at him. They went to fantastic lengths to decry his record.

Among the stories they put in circulation was one that he had broken his parole by escaping, and involved thereby his comrades in great unpleasantness and strict confinement. In fact, no parole had been asked or given, either by him or by the officers who shared his confinement and tried, but failed to share his escape. This story, put out by men in bitter mood who abhorred the war and abominated all who seemed to be gaining glory out of it, obtained a new and different circulation later on, when Churchill came to be a storm-

£25.—

(vijf en twintig pond stg.) belooning uitgeloofd door de Sub-Commissie van Wijk V voor den Specialen Constabel dezer wijk, die den ontvluchte Krijgsgevangene

Churchill

levend of dood te dezen kantore aflevert. —

Namens de Sub- Comm.
Wijk V
D. de Haas
Sec

Translation.

£25

(Twenty-five Pounds stg.) REWARD is offered by the Sub-Commission of the fifth division, on behalf of the Special Constable of the said division, to anyone who brings the escaped prisoner of war

CHURCHILL,

dead or alive to this office.

For the Sub-Commission of the fifth division,

(Signed) LODK. de HAAS, Sec.

NOTE.—The Original Reward for the arrest of Winston Churchill on his escape from Pretoria, posted on the Government House at Pretoria, brought to England by the Hon. Henry Mashew, and is now the property of W. R. Burton.

"£25 DEAD OR ALIVE"

No sooner was Churchill's escape discovered than a reward of £25 was offered for his recapture dead or alive. Above, is a facsimile of the notice offering this reward, while, right, is the photograph (from the collection of the late Lady Leonie Leslie) which the Boers published of the escaped prisoner and exhibited in all public places.

ARRIVAL AT DURBAN

Helped by an Englishman, Mr. Howard, who hid him, fed him and treated him with the greatest kindness, Churchill evaded recapture. He crossed the frontier into Portuguese territory hidden in a goods train bound for Lourenço-Marques. Here he went to see the British Consul, and established his identity. He was enabled to sail for Durban that same night, and on his arrival found himself to be a popular hero.

centre of politics. Then spiteful gossip gave a fresh lease of life to this shameful untruth, and on four occasions Winston had to take his slanderers into court and force them to retract and apologize for their false charges. There have always been some people whose temperament is so opposed to that of Churchill that their instincts have led them to detest him and believe ill of him. But this particular lie has long since been firmly nailed to the counter.

Winston was back in the Army again, but for the next few weeks his quick-working mind and restless spirit must have been irked intensely by the spectacle of the slow-moving, profoundly incompetent generalship of Buller. The British commander had no doubt been in his youth a gallant officer. But at this time he was a ponderous "Blimp," and under him were other elderly commanders, some of whom had risen by peacetime seniority and were incapable of seeing shrewdly, thinking clearly or acting quickly. Blunder after blunder was committed by these men. Winston was present at the battle of Spion Kop, where a British force, having seized that exposed hill, sat on it through a long day, being shelled to bits, while their commander had neither the energy to order an advance nor the discretion to withdraw. At nightfall they abandoned their position, leaving it covered with dead and wounded, for whom the Boers humanely allowed a removal truce.

ENTER "BOBS"

Fortunately for Britain, the higher ranks of her Army were not exclusively staffed with "Blimps." Lord Roberts—"Bobs," as he was affectionately known by the troops—was now in his sixty-eighth year, but was still younger in spirit and mind than many of his juniors. Kitchener, having completed the Egyptian campaign successfully, was also available. In December, 1899, the British Government decided to play these trump cards, and sent them out, Roberts as Commander-in-Chief, and Kitchener as his Chief of Staff.

They got to Cape Town on 10 January, 1900, and it took all Kitchener's great efficiency and ruthless drive to sort out the chaos of supplies and communications which existed there. But after a month's explosive work Roberts was able to start his drive north, along the western border of the Orange Free State. His movements were as swift and competent as those of Buller in Natal were vague, lumbering and fumbled. On 26 February, the anniversary of the defeat of Majuba, twenty-nine years before, he rounded up Cronje's army at Paardeburg and compelled its unconditional surrender. In March he raised the siege of Bloemfontein and started to thrust ahead for the Transvaal. His menace drew off much of the Boer strength from the east, so that even Buller could hardly help wobbling forward across the dozen miles which separated him from the starving defenders of Ladysmith.

Slow as was the progress of Buller's force during January and February, Winston himself was like quicksilver. With an unquenchable zest for adventure which left no room for personal fear, he was scampering round all the time to any part of the front that held out a promise of excitement, excusing his recklessness with the plea that he was looking for copy for the *Morning Post*. He bore a charmed life. Constantly he found himself near to groups of Boer marksmen and a

CHURCHILL ADDRESSES THE CROWD DURING HIS RECEPTION A

Upon landing at Durban, Winston was nearly torn to pieces in t
rapturous welcome he received from the crowd. He was seized and carrie
shoulder-high to the Town Hall where the multitude insisted on h
making a speech. Numberless telegrams poured in upon him. As
popular figure, he had his detractors also. There were some who spre

DURBAN AFTER HIS REMARKABLE ESCAPE FROM THE BOERS
*he rumour, quite unfounded, that when he escaped he broke parole.
*Ie had, in fact, never been asked to give it. That same night, he left
*nce more to rejoin the Army and was given a commission in the South
*African Light Horse, the "Cockyoli Birds". The photograph shows
Vinston Churchill making his speech before the Town Hall at Durban.

target for their purposeful bullets. But none of the bullets went home. Fate, or rather perhaps Providence, had other purposes in view for him.

When at last the British forces drew near to Ladysmith, Churchill got himself into the advance guard of cavalry which brushed through the retreating Boers and entered the beleaguered town. There he shared with White and his staff their last joint of beef. Then, eager for life with a more mobile force, he obtained permission to go over and join Lord Roberts in his advance on Johannesburg and Pretoria. The transfer was not easily come by, for Winston had annoyed "Bobs" mightily by a frank criticism, in one of his articles, of a stupid and inappropriate sermon by an army chaplain. But Winston was a very persistent young man, who was determined to get his own way in the end.

FURTHER ADVENTURE IN A SKIRMISH

He was to find still more adventure. One day the cavalry rode out on reconnaissance, and he attached himself to the Scouts, a troop of irregulars. They ran into a strong Boer force, and the Scouts dashed ahead into a wild skirmish, landing up against a Boer ambush. Winston's saddle-girth gave way, and his horse made off, leaving him on foot, running through a hail of bullets. He shouted to a trooper passing in front of him, and scrambled up on the horse's crupper. Their mount, though badly wounded, managed to bear the two of them to safety. The trooper did not share Winston's jubilation at their escape. He shook his head sadly. "Ah, but it's the horse I'm thinking about!" he grunted.

Among the first into Ladysmith, Winston was again the first into Johannesburg, for on the day before it fell he rode through it on a bicycle! He was with a force that had pushed up to the west of the town while Roberts was approaching from the south-east. He wanted to get off his dispatches to the *Morning Post*, for which purpose he had to reach Roberts' headquarters. Borrowing a bicycle, and with a French miner for guide, he audaciously trundled through Johannesburg, past crowds of armed Boers in its streets, and safely reached Lord Roberts' camp. The exploit won the old Field-Marshal's heart, and Winston's crime of criticizing a padre was forgiven and forgotten.

By the first week of June, "Bobs" and his army had made good their advance to Pretoria. As the cavalry vanguard reached the city, two horsemen darted ahead—Winston and his cousin, the Duke of Marlborough. Directed by a Boer, they headed for the prison camp, and the officers whose confinement Churchill had shared six months before saw a rider approaching, waving his slouch hat about a familiar red head. They yelled with delight, disarmed their guards, and streamed out to greet him with his message of deliverance.

For Winston this return to free his comrades from the Pretoria prison was the crowning moment of the campaign. Ten days later he resigned his commission in the "Cockyoli Birds," and started back for England.

With the hoisting of the Union Jack over Pretoria the first and most spectacular phase of the South African war came to an end. Most people thought it was now all over bar the shouting. In fact, it went on for another two years, thanks largely to De Wet and his adroit guerila tactics. The conflict had many of the characteristics of a civil war, for Boer and Briton dwelt side by side all over South Africa, and the perverse and deplorable course of events which had thrust them into two hostile camps created open or latent enemies for the British, not only in the Transvaal and the Orange River Colony, but also farther south down in Natal and even in Cape Province itself—a very wide area.

HIGH RESPECT FOR THE BOERS

From his contacts with the Boers Churchill came to conceive a high respect for them. In his articles he urged that as soon as victory was assured a policy of generosity should dictate the terms of settlement. He saw that Briton and Boer would have to go on living together when the fight was over, and that any display of vindictiveness in the hour of triumph would leave wounds in the social body of South Africa which might take long to heal. But this sanity of outlook was not shared by the populace at home, which had waxed delirious with war fever and wished to hear no good of the Boers. The *Morning Post* had to apologize for his articles, even while it printed them.

It was a generation and a half since Britain had been involved in any war against a white enemy; far longer still since she had been locked in conflict which imposed any real strain upon her manpower. Though South Africa was thousands of miles away, the spectacle of the City Imperial Volunteers marching through the streets of London to embark for the front, and the dispatch of the Yeomanry from the

69

countryside, made the war startlingly real. The shameful tale of disasters with which the campaign opened, and the long casualty lists that filtered through, were a bitter blow to the nation's pride, so that passions ran high. When Lloyd George went to Birmingham to speak against the Government's war policy, a savage crowd gathered with every intention of tearing him limb from limb. In that angry mood they had no patience with Winston's counsel that generous treatment should be meted out to the Boers.

The turn of the tide brought an almost intolerable relaxation to strained nerves and sore spirits. When news came through of the relief of Mafeking, London went wild with delight, and the decorous calm of Victorian respectability received that night a blow from which it never fully recovered. Yelling mobs swept the Strand, brandishing rattles and flags and ladies' ticklers, and playing football with the silk hats of the well-dressed, in an unbuttoned frenzy which took themselves by surprise. "Maffiking" passed into the language as a term for this new sport of reckless self-abandon, this shattering of tightly established inhibitions. Albert Chevalier came out with a song: "On Mafekin' Night!" that echoed round the country from every barrel-organ.

> *Wot oh! we cried*
> *On Mafekin' night!*
> *. . . . . We raved*
> *An' the old flag waved,*
> *The moke on 'is back wore a Union Jack,*
> *An' Par 'ad 'is whiskers shaved!*

It was to a nation in this uproarious mood that Winston returned after the fall of Pretoria. He came back to an extraordinary personal triumph. His gallantry in the armoured-train episode, his daring escape from the Boer prison, his adventurous ride through Johannesburg and his joyous rescue of the prisoners of Pretoria, had captivated the public imagination. He seemed a living symbol of the victorious irrepressible spirit of Britain, a means of renewing the nation's faith in herself. He was welcomed and fêted everywhere he went. It would be forty years before he again stood on so high a pinnacle of universal public favour.

CHAPTER IV

CHURCHILL TURNS POLITICIAN

OFF with the plumed hat of the "Cockyoli Birds"! On with the silk topper of civilian dignity! Winston now pursued his interrupted ambition of getting into Parliament.

Why did he decide to abandon the Army for politics? According to his own account, it was for the simple reason that he found Army life too expensive. In those days a subaltern's pay was meagre, and expenses in a crack cavalry regiment were heavy. Winston's mother, the widowed Lady Randolph Churchill, had been allowing him five hundred pounds a year. While comfortably off, she was not wealthy, and he was too fond of her to like being a continual burden on her limited income. Eager, capable, restless, he wanted to stand on his own feet. He had found a potential gold-mine in his pen. His books and newspaper articles were bringing in far more than he could hope to get in the Army for many years ahead. So he decided to write for a living, and to take up politics as a career.

This reasoning sounds very practical and long-headed. In fact, however, it played only a subordinate part in shaping his decision. There were two other reasons which were far more important.

The first was that Winston had outgrown the Army. In late Victorian times the British Army was small—in size, in function, in outlook. It was used partly to furnish an element of pageantry on state occasions, partly to police the outposts of the Empire. The fighting men themselves were sound enough at heart; but the army administration was hopelessly inefficient. Its red tape and bungling ineptitude were dismally exposed in the South African War. In atmosphere and outlook it was reactionary and out of date, hidebound by obsolete traditions. Initiative was suspect by the authorities. To ensure promotion, it was best to be of a solid, conventional type, to stick to the rules, cause no trouble, and display no embarrassing originality.

Winston was a cuckoo in this nest. True, he played polo superbly; but he read many strange books, wrote for the Press, was critical of

71

his superiors, and would not keep still. During his four years in the Army he had managed to wriggle into four campaigns—the Spanish-Cuban War; the Malakand Pass affair; the Tirah expedition; and the Sudan War, with its climax at Omdurman. In every one of them he was serving away from his own regiment, the 4th Hussars, which was out of them all. He saw more fighting in those four years than many officers had seen in forty.

Some of them looked at him askance, and muttered: "Medal-snatcher!" He was not that; he was just a young man of bursting energy, eager to savour to the full the adventure of life. He was temperamentally incapable of becoming a War Office pet. He snatched and sucked the orange of military danger and excitement. Then he tossed aside the skin, and looked round for fresh fruits to sample.

The second reason why Winston turned to politics was that politics was his pre-ordained destiny, to which he turned as naturally as a cat to cream. He had breathed politics from his earliest childhood. His father had been a leading statesman in his day, and even as a boy Winston had declared that he would be a soldier first, but later on would go into Parliament.

A SENSE OF MISSION

There was also a deeper urge, one of which he may not at first have been fully conscious. Lord Randolph had cherished a warm regard for the working man, and had tried to swing the Conservative party over to a programme of "Tory Democracy." In his day, he had founded and led the "Fourth Party," in opposition to the Tory reactionaries. He had lost his fight, and with it his office as Chancellor of the Exchequer. As a result his hopes of party leadership were destroyed. The "old gang" had stamped on him, and his days ended in shadow. His son had a feeling of a mission: to pick up the torch, to complete his father's unfinished work, lead the Tory party into the path of social reform, and, incidentally, pay off his father's score against the reactionaries.

It has been said that most thoughtful and warm-hearted young men pass through a phase of socialism, even if they do not remain Socialists. Churchill could never be regarded as a political Socialist, but he felt the human stir of a warm social sympathy with the humblest of his fellows, and that feeling he was never to outgrow. He sought a career in politics; but in return, he brought to politics great

CANDIDATE FOR OLDHAM

Before going out to Africa in 1899, Winston Churchill had resigned his commission on the grounds that he found life in the army too expensive. This had coincided with the serious illness of one of the members of the "two-member constituency" of Oldham.

gifts, such as few men in his own or any other time have had to offer. High among them ranked that hearty, honest fellowship with all classes of society, and that urge to make a positive contribution to national progress, which were to make him an outstanding leader in the coming great epoch of reform.

Winston played his qualifying rounds in politics during the interval between the Sudan and the South African campaigns. In November, 1898, on his return to Britain after the battle of Omdurhan, he visited the Conservative Central Office to find out what constituencies were available. The party officers were very affable to Lord Randolph's son, already becoming famous for his books and his brilliant journalism, until they found that he had little money and could not subsidize his electorate. At that time the best Tory seats went to the long purses, and cost their members anything up to five thousand pounds a year. So the only immediate result was a speaking engagement at a Primrose League fête in Bath.

SPEAKING IN PUBLIC

Churchill has the artist's capacity to take pains. With his command of language, he could write a fine speech. He did so, and learned it off by heart. For years afterward he was regularly to practise the same method. The speech went well; the audience cheered; the *Morning Post* gave it a column and a leaderette, and Winston decided that this game of political speech-making was great fun.

He spoke, too, in Rotherhithe Town Hall, waxing defiant towards France over the Fashoda incident—in which a French officer had tried to plant the French flag in the Sudan, and had been ordered off by Kitchener. The party agents who came to listen were as pleased as his audience, and marked him down as good material for a parliamentary candidate.

On his way home from the Nile Winston had travelled with G. W. Steevens, the *Daily Mail* correspondent, who was greatly impressed with him and proceeded to write him up in that paper, under the title of "The Youngest Man in Europe." "He may or may not possess the qualities that make a great general," wrote Steevens of the young subaltern, "but the question is of no sort of importance. . . . If they exist, they are overshadowed by qualities which might make him, almost at will, a great popular leader, a great journalist, or the founder of a great advertising business. . . . At the

LECTURER AND JOURNALIST

At the time he entered politics, Winston Churchill supplemented his earnings by a series of highly successful and very dramatic lectures both in this country and America on his experiences in South Africa. This caricature, reproduced by permission of the proprietors of "Punch," is by E. T. Reed (1860-1933), political cartoonist of "Punch."

rate he goes, there will hardly be room for him in Parliament at thirty, or in England at forty."

Despite his lack of wealth Winston did not have to wait very long for a chance to make a bid for parliament. His first electioneering battle ended in defeat; the first of many set-backs in his political career. But it furnished some significant revelations of his qualities, both the admirable and the disconcerting. Even at the outset he at once delighted and exasperated the party whose label he bore. In the years to come he was often to repeat that process.

In the early summer of 1899 Mr. Robert Ascroft, the senior Conservative member for Oldham—a two-member constituency—asked Winston Churchill to partner him at the next election, as the other Conservative member was retiring through ill-health. Winston jumped at the chance. An introductory meeting at Oldham had already been arranged, when Churchill's sponsor suddenly died. The other member thereupon resigned, and Winston found himself flung, not into a political meeting, but into an election campaign. It was rather significant that his fellow candidate in the Conservative interest was that unusual combination, a Tory Socialist—James Mawdesley, secretary of the Operative Spinners' Association.

They were foredoomed to defeat. The Tory Government was unpopular, while the constituency was almost wholly working-class and Radical in colour. Winston's Socialist partner was no asset in the eyes of the true blues, while their opponents were very able men —Emmott, a wealthy native of Oldham, and Walter Runciman, also wealthy, and destined to reach high rank in politics.

Winston fought fiercely, though in his inexperience he blundered tactically by taking sides against an unpopular Tithes Bill which the Government was then promoting. Already he was showing that inability to let his party do his thinking for him which always was to be characteristic of him. The Liberals won, and he returned to town, rather deflated, to face a good deal of criticism from the orthodox on his own side.

Arthur Balfour, who was then Leader of the House of Commons under the Premier, Lord Salisbury, wrote him a sympathetic letter, assuring him that the set-back would not be permanent. In fact, only a year later, Winston was to sweep into Parliament as junior member

76

MEMBER FOR OLDHAM

In 1900, there was a General Election (the Khaki Election) and Mr. Churchill again contested the seat at Oldham—this time successfully and held it until 1906. He was a member of King Edward VII's first Parliament. When the problem of Tariff Reform arose, Churchill proclaimed himself a Free-trader and joined the ranks of the Liberals.

for Oldham, defeating Walter Runciman by a narrow margin. Meantime, he went out to South Africa. His adventures there have already been narrated.

The general election of 1900 has become known in history as the "Khaki Election." The Tory Government, elected in 1895 for seven years, had still the best part of two years to go, but had become increasingly unpopular, and was looking to almost certain defeat. The South African War, however, had for the moment changed the picture. The British tend to close ranks round their government in time of national emergency. A series of successes in South Africa, after initial set-backs, led up to the capture of Johannesburg and

Pretoria. This looked like victory, though in fact the war was to drag on for another year and a half.

The Tory party managers decided that this was the ideal moment for an appeal to the country. Parliament was accordingly dissolved, and a General Election held, while the war fever was at its height. The Conservatives brandished the Union Jack, and denounced their opponents as pro-Boers and traitors to the country. The Liberals, taken at an immense disadvantage, declared the election to be a mean trick. Nevertheless, the trick worked. The Tory Government was returned for a fresh term.

Winston Churchill got back from his adventures in South Africa shortly before the decision to hold the election, and went to visit Oldham. There he had a wildly enthusiastic reception and related his war experiences to an appreciative audience. In the election contest which soon followed, he was riding the crest of a wave of personal popularity, which counterbalanced the fact that he carried the wrong party ticket for most of the Oldham electors. Oldham was one of the very first constituencies to poll (in those days elections were spread over several weeks) and so he was one of the first elected on the Government side. During the next weeks he toured the country, speaking for his side in other election fights, including that of his leader, Arthur Balfour. Everywhere he had a successful time. When Parliament opened he had already established a reputation in politics to add to those he had won in authorship, journalism and military adventure.

The political world at the beginning of the century was in many ways strangely different from the one we know today. An epoch, the great Victorian Age, was ending. Indeed, Queen Victoria herself passed away between the election of December, 1900, and Winston's first appearance in Parliament in February, 1901. A time of chaos and transition was about to set in, marked by very swift and far-reaching changes in the political and social life of the country.

At this time the Gilbertian assertion still held true that:

> "Ev'ry boy and gal
>   That's born into this world alive
> Is either a little Liberal
>   Or else a little Conservative!"

These two big groups divided the political field between them,

78

and alternated in and out of office. From time to time they stole one another's policies. But in the main their dividing lines were inherited from the past. The Tories, party of Church and Crown, were firmly entrenched in the Services, the parsonages, the squirearchy. The Liberals still bore signs of their origin as a coalition of Whigs and Radicals. They retained a number of great Whig families, which, in their past fights to preserve their aristocratic privileges against encroachments by the Crown, had established the principle of the liberty of the subject. Their Radical wing drew its strength from the new industrial and mercantile classes which had sprung up in the nineteenth century, and were bent on sweeping away the elements of feudalism which still survived in the social structure of the nation.

THE "LITTLE ENGLANDERS"

Latterly the Liberals had fallen on evil days. Their leader, Gladstone, had split his party in 1885 when he had tried to carry its principle of liberty into effect by offering Home Rule to Ireland. A large section, headed by the Whig Duke of Devonshire and the Radical Joseph Chamberlain, broke away and joined the Conservative party as "Liberal Unionists." The rest were split into two factions—the right wing of Liberal Imperialists, and the left wing of Radical Home Rulers. These latter wanted to give the widest liberty and self-government to all parts of the Empire, and concentrate on domestic reform—an attitude which won them the nickname of "Little Englanders."

It should be added that, whatever party was nominally in power, affairs of State were still largely settled behind the doors of Mayfair mansions, in the drawing-rooms and dinner parties of a few great families whose influence dominated their parties and party machines.

But other forces, as yet hardly recognized, were beginning to stir in the nation. New ideas were fermenting—ideas which found no place in the traditions of either party. Lord Randolph Churchill had sensed their beginning when he launched his slogan of "Tory Democracy" and started his Fourth Party. Winston made direct contact with them when he fought alongside a Socialist in his first election contest. It was the rousing of the masses of the nation, educated and self-conscious for the first time (the 1870 Education Act had been in force for just a generation) to share responsibility for their country's policy, not merely to leave it to their masters.

ADDRESSING AN OPEN-AIR ELECTION MEETING AT

Very soon after his entry into politics, Churchill, in spite of his extreme youth, made his presence felt. His radicalism reminded people of his father's "Fourth Party." His view that Free-traders of all parties should form one line of battle against the common foe was regarded as dangerous and he was disowned by the Conservatives of Oldham. One

MANCHESTER EARLY IN HIS POLITICAL CAREER

evening in March, 1904, when he rose to speak, Mr. Balfour, the Prime Minister, together with his party left the Chamber. Sir William Harcourt, the veteran Member of Parliament for West Monmouthshire, said deprecatingly of Churchill at this time, "the want of judgment of the fellow is despairing but there is a good deal of force in his oratory."

As yet the movement was in its early, unformed childhood. Two significant portents had appeared as far back as 1892. One was Keir Hardie, arriving at Westminster in fustian and cloth cap among the frock coats and silk toppers, as a Socialist and Labour M.P. In 1893 he founded the Independent Labour Party. Another was the election of John Burns as Labour member for Battersea. The 1900 Parliament contained a new symbol—the return of two members standing for the Labour Representation Committee; a body which six years later was to change its name and become known as the Labour Party.

TALK OF SOCIALISM

The air was full of talk of Socialism. No one quite knew what the term meant, for every self-styled Socialist put his own interpretation on it. But all theories alike pointed towards a new attitude to society, differing from the old feudalism and nineteenth-century individualism. They expressed a conviction that neither land nor money, but human life and happiness were the first concern of the State.

Having won his seat in Parliament, Winston had to collect the money to enable him to devote himself to what were then the unpaid duties of an M.P. So he spent a couple of months carrying out lecture tours, first in Britain, then in America, and delighting big audiences with vivid accounts of his South African experiences. The lectures were both a popular and a financial success, and with several thousand pounds in hand, he got back to England and took his seat in the new Parliament towards the end of February, 1901.

Four days later he made his maiden speech. As usual, he prepared carefully and learned by heart everything he meant to say. He followed that fiery Welsh lawyer, David Lloyd George, who was already one of the most effective orators on the opposition benches. L.G., after making an impassioned attack on the Government for the inhumanity of its treatment of the Boers, cut his own speech short to give way to Winston, who scored parliamentary success in this first effort.

Yet even here his frank and unorthodox honesty alarmed his leaders. "If I were a Boer fighting in the field," he said, "—and if I were a Boer, I hope I should be fighting in the field—I should not allow myself to be taken in by any message of sympathy." And again, "I have often myself been very much ashamed to see respectable old Boer farmers—the Boer is a curious combination of

82

DAVID LLOYD GEORGE

Many famous people have been caricatured in the pages of "Vanity Fair," from which source both the cartoons on this page are taken. That below shows David Lloyd George as seen by "Spy." This most influential member of the Liberal Party was a determined Anti-Imperialist and Free-trader who exercised a considerable influence on Winston Churchill, particularly in his early years in politics.

WINSTON CHURCHILL

The cartoon above is by "Nibs"; like that of David Lloyd George it was drawn in the early years of the twentieth century, when Winston, still a newcomer to politics, was establishing a reputation as an orator. He then held the view that Free-traders of all parties should join forces.

the squire and the peasant, and under the rough coat of the peasant there are very often to be found the instincts of the squire—I have been ashamed to see such men ordered about by young subaltern officers as if they were private soldiers."

It was the essential chivalry of the young man speaking. But old Tories glowered. It ill befitted any government supporter to have a good word for the Boers. "That's the way to lose seats!" muttered Joseph Chamberlain forebodingly from the Treasury bench.

Soon he was to cause them greater alarm. He took up his father's lost cause, and tried to swing his party into a line of Tory democracy. He attacked a Government proposal to increase the standing army, arguing far-sightedly that the increase suggested would be far too small to make it capable of fighting a European war, while it was needlessly large for the task of fighting savages.

SHOCKING THE CONSTITUTIONAL CLUB

Presently he was shocking the Constitutional Club by telling its members that they ought to adopt Gladstone's slogan: "Peace, Retrenchment and Reform!" as the Tory motto. He gathered round him a group of the abler young Conservatives, who were nicknamed "The Hooligans," and carried on a guerilla warfare against the die-hards. The Liberals watched his development with delight, and Massingham, their leading journalist, wrote that Churchill would one day be Prime Minister—he hoped, a Liberal Prime Minister.

Party discipline was far less rigorous in those days than it came to be from the nineteen-thirties onwards, when the Government whips established a tyrannical control over private members. Men could and frequently did speak and vote in opposition to their party if they disagreed with it about some issue. Winston might have remained in the Tory fold, despite his rebellious criticisms of Government policy, but for a sudden new twist of events. In May, 1903, Joe Chamberlain raised the banner of Protection and summoned the Tories to a fight for "Tariff Reform."

We need not question Chamberlain's sincerity, though he had previously been a fierce opponent of protective tariffs. Anyhow, the South African War had to be paid for, and income tax already stood at the "crippling figure" of elevenpence in the pound. Next year it would rise to a shilling. (There was as yet no supertax.) Besides, the party was in the doldrums. Winston was vainly trying to enliven it with a cry of social reform. Chamberlain adopted the alternative programme of "making the foreigner pay" by a system of protective tariffs, as a means of reviving the spirits and fortunes of the party.

Chamberlain won. Winston lost. He and a band of Tory Free-traders fought the tariff issue up and down the country, following Chamberlain round, holding Free Trade meetings to answer his Protectionist rallies. Winston even invaded Birmingham itself, where the angry mob gathered to tear him apart, as it had sought to do to Lloyd George during the South African War. But at the sight of the bright-faced, boyish figure, standing superbly confident in an open carriage, they broke out instead into cheering.

In Parliament Churchill and his allies assailed the Government in an effort to find out where it stood on this issue. Balfour was adroitly non-committal, but the bulk of the Tories took up the new policy. Those who did so whole-heartedly became known as the "whole-hoggers," while those who temporized with Balfour were called the "little-piggers." But the Tory Free-traders were a small minority.

ON THE LIBERAL BENCHES

Winston soon found himself fighting shoulder to shoulder with the Liberals. "Thank God for the Liberal Party!" he exclaimed when speaking at a Free Trade meeting at Halifax. The Oldham Conservative Association promptly disowned him. Back in the House he rose to speak, and the whole Tory party, led by Mr. Balfour, the Prime Minister, got up and walked out. It was a schoolboy insult; but political conflict was growing bitter and unscrupulous. The sequel was inevitable. On 31 May, 1904, Winston Churchill crossed the floor of the House, and took his seat beside Lloyd George on the Liberal benches.

It has been suggested that Winston's change of party postponed by twenty years his rise to the premiership; that if he had remained in the Tory ranks he would inevitably have led the party during the war years, and become Prime Minister when the war was over, rather than Bonar Law or Baldwin. More spitefully, it was suggested that Winston always changed to the winning side—to the Liberals when they were marked out for victory, and back to the Conservatives when their star was again in the ascendant.

But his change of party was the result neither of calculation nor

85

of miscalculation. Winston was never a tortuous schemer. He acted always with a large-handed impulsive daring upon his clear vision of the big, essential facts of the matter. In this critical hour his intelligence, his conscience and his human sympathies all impelled him to adopt the Liberal attitude toward the burning issues of the day. He did not stop to ask whether it would pay him better in the long run to stick by the Tory Party. Winston made many mistakes, but never the big mistake of acting insincerely in the hope of personal advantage. He flung himself exultantly into the task of denouncing those reactionary Government policies which had irked and outraged his conscience when he had been on the Conservative side. These were the handling of the South African question, the treatment of the natives, the introduction of Chinese labour, the muddle over army reform, the Licensing Bill, and the fiscal controversy over Chamberlain's tariff proposals.

FRONT RANK REPRESENTATION AS AN ORATOR

On all these issues Churchill found himself more in sympathy with the Liberal outlook than with the views and actions of his old party. Still more, his generous spirit warmed to the temper of zeal for social improvement, the earnest eagerness for progress and reform, that stirred the Liberals and Radicals with whom he was now linked. These were worth-while causes for which to fight, and Winston was ever a bonny fighter. Soon he had established for himself a front-rank reputation as a Liberal orator, and a welcome among the inner councils of the Liberal party.

The Edwardian Age, 1901-10, can be seen today as an age of revolution—a subconscious revolution. In the Victorian era a big new class of wealthy manufacturers and mine-owners had arisen, which presently rivalled in money-power, though not in social standing and influence, the great traditional aristocracy of landowners. The rise of these lords of commerce and industry was marked by a pitiless exploitation of the workers, who were herded into the slums of new industrial cities, or the foul hovels of mining villages, to slave through a brief and sickly life to pile up wealth for their masters.

"Grouse and black-cock—so many brace to the acre, and men and women—so many brace to the garret," wrote John Ruskin bitterly in the 1860s; and the forty years that followed saw a vaster

MR. LEWIS HARCOURT AND MR. CHURCHILL

Mr. Lewis Harcourt, seen above walking with Mr. Churchill, later became Viscount Harcourt. He was First Commissioner of Works from 1905 until 1910 and again from 1915 until 1916. He also served as Colonial Secretary under Asquith from 1910 until 1915. He withdrew from active politics in 1916 and died on 24 February, 1922.

growth of those slums. Industrial towns were deliberately built as slums. Leeds, for example, consisted mainly of back-to-back houses, of which nearly half were two-roomed brick hovels, crammed seventy and eighty to the acre, with the most primitive and appalling communal sanitary arrangements. Even in Edwardian times the stock jest about the Glasgow slums was the tale of the room shared by five families—one in each corner, and one in the middle—who lived happily until the centre family took in a lodger.

TACKLING A SOCIAL EVIL

The Factory Act of 1833 had forbidden the employment in factories of children under the age of nine, but throughout Victorian times such children continued to be set to work in factory or field. By the end of the century this evil was being cleared up through the activities of the School Board inspectors; but there were still many sweated industries where women and children, protected by no trade union, worked long, hopeless hours for less than starvation wages. Outdoor relief was sparingly given under the Poor Law. The workhouse was held to be the proper place for paupers. If a worker lost his job or fell sick, it was the workhouse for him and his family. There was no unemployment benefit, sickness insurance or old age pension.

For the workers crowded in these foetid back streets there were but two avenues of escape. One was the public house, where with beer at twopence a pint, and spirits at three-and-six a bottle, they could quickly drug their ill-nourished bodies into intoxication and a brief illusion of well-being. It was a regular practice with many workmen to get drunk on a Saturday night; almost a point of honour. The fouler the local housing conditions, the richer the harvest of the gin palace.

The other refuge was religion. In the Victorian age Nonconformity grew to great strength. For in his chapel the working man laid aside his slavery and slumdom, and gained the worth and dignity of a Child of God. His chapel became his club and his university. It set him thinking and discussing. This led on to politics.

It was inevitable that men who had risen in their chapels to a sense of human dignity, which was but ill reflected in their daily conditions, should begin thinking in terms of social reform. In late Victorian times the chapels became centres of Radical enthusiasm.

Their members revered Gladstone, High Churchman though he was, because he abolished the last of the religious disabilities under which Nonconformists laboured. Their antagonism to their deadly rival, the gin palace, and the human degradation it fostered, made them fanatical teetotalers. The Nonconformist vote was a valuable asset to the Liberal party. The Nonconformist conscience was an insistent if uncomfortable voice in its counsels.

Politics and religion: these were the most active intellectual interests of the more thoughtful among the middle and lower classes. Religious weeklies had a wide and influential circulation. Daily papers filled columns with parliamentary debates and political articles. The growing earnestness for social reform sought political expression. Only a minority were entitled to the vote, for this was confined to male adult householders and male adult lodgers renting premises worth ten pounds a year or more unfurnished. There were still in existence parliamentary constituencies with fewer than five thousand electors. The political leaders, up to 1906, were drawn almost entirely from the higher circles of Society—and Society spelt with a capital S had then an exclusive meaning which it has long since lost.

When Winston Churchill joined the Liberal party he found himself in a very mixed body of people, the lower ranks of which were heaving and straining with half-realized desires for economic and social reforms. They wanted the abolition of class privileges, the liberation of the worker; while the more affluent were thinking mainly in terms of the party fight with their political opponents, and were concerned to attack Tory blunders and advocate traditional Liberal policies.

POPULAR INDIGNATION AGAINST THE GOVERNMENT

The Government had aroused popular indignation on several counts. There was its record of mismanagement of the South African War; and worse, its introduction into the Transvaal of Chinese coolies, at the bidding of the Rand mine-owners, to give them cheap labour in the mines. Hopes of a vast new field for British emigration and employment in South Africa, as some return for the recent conflict there, had given place to the spectacle of something unpleasantly near to slave conditions on what was now British soil. For the coolies were strictly confined in compounds at the mines.

Tariff reform, which Chamberlain was preaching as the new gospel, attracted plenty of support from those merchants and manufacturers who saw a hope of commercial profit to themselves from its adoption. On the other hand, the fact that, as Chamberlain bluntly declared, Colonial Preference meant a tax on food roused a warning and sinister cry of "Dear Food!" which immediately made the policy unpopular with the masses.

NONCONFORMIST OPPOSITION

Two measures of the Government particularly angered the powerful Nonconformist voters. The first was Balfour's Education Act of 1902, which transferred the Church schools to the rates, while leaving them under their Anglican Management Committees. Echoes of the old Tithe War were roused by the measure, and a campaign was started against paying rates for sectarian education. So violent was the feeling that it took shape in a "Passive Resistance" movement. All over the country men refused to pay the education rate for Church schools, and suffered distraint of their furniture by the authorities. Dr. Clifford, the venerable Baptist divine, thundered against the Act from his pulpit at Westbourne Park, while Sylvester Horne, the brilliant pulpit orator of Whitefields Tabernacle, carried the conflict up and down the country at a series of great meetings.

The other measure, the 1904 Licensing Act, annoyed Temperance enthusiasts by providing compensation for licensees if their licence were not renewed. True, the compensation was to come from a fund raised by the trade itself, but a legal vested interest was created in what had been no more than an annual and terminable concession. Licences, once granted, now became valuable properties. Brewers set to work to buy them up and "tie" the public-houses to their breweries. Thereby the liquor trade became far more centralized, organized, and powerful. Whatever the intrinsic merits of these two Acts, they certainly lowered still further the declining popularity of the Government with a large part of the electorate.

CHAPTER V

CHURCHILL AS A SOCIAL REFORMER

B Y the end of 1905 the Tory Government could no longer hold
together. The long succession of defeats at by-elections, and
the open quarrels within its ranks between Chamberlainites,
Balfourites and Free-traders, had created an impossible situation.
Adroit to the last, Balfour would not himself dissolve Parliament and
appeal to the country; he resigned office, so that the Liberals should
be forced to form a Cabinet and put out a programme on which the
election would be fought. The Tories confidently asserted that the
Liberals could neither agree on a political programme nor produce
a Cabinet that would command public confidence.

Both predictions were falsified. Campbell-Bannerman, the
Liberal leader, gathered a body of ministers that even its enemies
admitted to be a formidable team. It included experienced statesmen
and administrators such as the Marquess of Ripon, the Earls of Elgin
and Crewe, Earl Carrington and Lord Tweedmouth; national figures
such as Asquith, Haldane, Sir Edward Grey, Augustine Birrell and
John Morley, and that rising young Welsh solicitor, Lloyd George;
and in the junior ministerial ranks Herbert Samuel, McKenna,
Runciman and, by no means least, Winston Churchill. A significant
appointment was John Burns, the Labour member, the first Labour
M.P. to enter a Cabinet.

Campbell-Bannerman's programme included, of course, undertakings to stop recruitment of Chinese labour for the Rand; to reduce
taxation; to uphold Free Trade. Free Trade versus Protection was in
fact the biggest single issue in the election. Ireland was to be given
Home Rule. But the most important new feature in the programme
was the insistence on constructive social reform—slum clearance in
the towns, restoration of the countryside, reform of the Poor Law,
the tackling of the unemployment problem and the abolition of
restraints on Trade Unionism. This was the voice of a New Age,
breaking through the stale blether of nineteenth-century political
disputation.

In January, 1906, a general election was held. The Free-trade issue was debated from platform and press all over the country. Posters of the "Big and Little Loaf"—the Free-trade and the Protectionist Loaf—appeared on all the hoardings. A loaf of German black bread was put in a shop window in St. Pancras to show what protectionist countries ate. A sanitary inspector entered the shop and condemned the loaf as unfit for human consumption, and a roar of laughter rose all over the whole country.

CHINESE SLAVERY AS AN ELECTION CRY

Chinese slavery came a good second as an election cry, and the education controversy and Irish home rule were noisily debated. But the instinctive groping of the masses after a better social order furnished a heavy ground-swell to lift the tide. The issue was an overwhelming victory for the Liberals. In a parliament of 670 members the Tories and Unionists held only 158 seats. The Liberals, with their 390, had a clear, independent majority over all the other parties combined. In addition, they could count on the support of the 83 Irish Nationalists and of the 39 Labour members who at that time formed a semi-detached left wing of Liberalism.

Churchill fought the North-west Manchester constituency. It was a Tory seat, and his opponent was a clever young solicitor, Joynson-Hicks—to be known to a later generation as "Jix." The fight was fierce and spirited. At one meeting held in a covered-over public swimming bath, the floor gave way and dropped the audience into the empty bath. "Let justice be done, even though the floor falls in!" cried Winston, and the dawning panic changed to a roar of laughter. He was returned at the head of the poll, with a majority of 1,241. This was a striking victory, all the more remarkable in a constituency which at the previous election had returned a Tory candidate unopposed.

Although so recent a recruit to the Liberal ranks, Winston Churchill had already made such an impression that office was found for him in the new Government as Under-Secretary for the Colonies. Since the Secretary, Lord Elgin, was in the Upper House, Churchill was responsible in the Commons for explaining and defending the Government's policy in Colonial affairs (which at that time also included the Dominions). The most important and controversial issues in this policy concerned the newly-acquired Boer territories.

MEMBER FOR NORTH-WEST MANCHESTER

Winston Churchill successfully fought North-west Manchester in the General Election of 1906. This contemporary drawing (by courtesy of the "Illustrated London News") was made when Churchill spoke at the Reform Club at Manchester after his election.

There were two main issues: the Chinese labour question, and the grant of full self-government to the Transvaal and the Orange River Colony.

"Chinese Slavery" having been a charge against the Tories at the election, the Liberals promptly took steps to stop further recruitment of coolies, and to improve the conditions under which those already on the Rand were living. On 5 June, 1906, Churchill announced in the House that "Holding of trials within the mine premises, deduction of fees from wages, fining the head boy for not reporting offences, and collective punishments . . . have ceased to be operative." The immediate repatriation of the coolies could not be carried out without disaster to South African employment and finance; but they were sent back as fast as their indentures could be terminated, and in a little more than three years the last of them had gone.

"TERMINOLOGICAL INEXACTITUDE"

It was in this connexion that Churchill coined a phrase which many still remember with delight. Challenged as to whether the indentured labour was really "slavery," he answered that it could not be so classified without "some risk of terminological inexactitude." "Terminological inexactitude" passed at once into political currency; and while Winston's foes flung it at his head as a reproach, the public relished it as a merry jest.

Although Winston had fought against the Boers, he had always respected them, and he greatly enjoyed the task of carrying through Parliament the grant of full self-government to the conquered territories. Perhaps he enjoyed it the more because of the rage with which the Tories attacked him. Balfour denounced the concession of self-government to the Boers as "the most reckless experiment ever tried in the development of a great Colonial policy," and hinted darkly that it would be bound to result in another Boer war.

It is now a fact of history that the grant of self-government to the Boers of the Transvaal and Orange Free State proved to be the noblest action in our Imperial record, and one that has been more than justified by its results. It turned enemies such as Botha and Smuts into loyal friends. It kept South Africa faithful to the British Commonwealth, alike in 1914 and in 1939, thus frustrating the hopes and the designs of Germany.

Churchill had urged as early as 1902 that self-government should be accorded to the Boers as soon as circumstances would permit, so he had a particular satisfaction now in putting his principle into practice. His speech to the House of Commons, introducing the resolutions for the Transvaal constitution, reflected his generous and progressive spirit. Picturing "a tranquil, prosperous, consolidated Afrikander nation under the protection of the British Crown" as the result of this policy, he added: "The cause of the poor and the weak all over the world will have been sustained; and everywhere small peoples will have more room to breathe and everywhere great Empires will be encouraged by our example to step forward—it needs only a step—into the sunshine of a more gentle and more generous age."

In 1909, this policy of trust and fair play was consummated in the Act for the Union of South Africa, which was passed amid the plaudits of all parties. Mr. Balfour, eating his former words, called it "one of the most important events in the history of the Empire, one of the great landmarks of Imperial policy . . . the most wonderful issue out of all those divisions, controversies, battles and outbreaks, the devastation and horrors of war, the difficulties of peace. I do not believe the world shows anything like it in its whole history!"

By this time Churchill was no longer at the Colonial Office. He had moved on to new tasks of reform.

FEMININE INFLUENCE ON HIS CAREER

It would be an absorbingly interesting task to trace the influence that has been exerted upon the careers of great statesmen by the women in their lives. Behind the history of many a fine achievement, and of many a national disaster, there lurks—often unwritten—the tale of fair women, helpful or fatal.

For long it has been a firm tradition in British public life that those who would fill the highest offices of State must not be involved in any public scandal. Private gossip has, however, bandied about many disreputable stories about some of the men who have in the course of the past century held prominent positions in this country. Some of the stories may have had a foundation of fact; some have been mere scurrilous mud-slinging—a contemptible weapon of underhand party warfare.

It is immensely to Churchill's credit that no such whispered scandal ever succeeded in clinging to his name. Attempts to

GERMAN EMPEROR ENTERTAINS WINSTON

In 1906, Winston Churchill, as Colonial Under-Secretary, was invited to Germany by the Emperor William II to see the "Kaisermanoever" in Silesia. In this photograph he is talking to his host, while a group of German staff-officers are in attendance. Churchill was interested in the perfect evolutions of the German troops but was doubtful of how they

CHURCHILL AT THE "KAISERMANOEVER" IN SILESIA

*would stand up to musketry. At the same time, Churchill saw demonstra-
tions of all the latest German weapons. The Emperor obviously regarded
his guest as a coming man and was desirous of impressing him. He was
entertained at lavish banquets and had several confidential talks with his
host upon colonial questions, even then matters of increasing moment.*

blacken his reputation, as well as those of his colleagues, were indeed made in the worst bitterness of the party fights that raged round the Liberal reform measures of the period between 1906 and 1914. But the slanders withered and died, for they were so patently devoid of foundation. His record is clear of errant gallantries and philanderings.

The women who have figured in his career may be straightforwardly divided into two groups. First come the enemies. These were the suffragettes. From 1906 to 1914 they badgered and pursued him unmercifully.

The same tide of progressive reform which swept the Liberal Government forward into the social legislation of those crowded years roused the female half of the population to a new impatience for political equality; an impatience which was no longer content to keep to the conventional track of agitation, of public meetings, pamphlets and orderly deputations, but broke out in the militant suffragette movement.

WOMEN AS POLITICAL HECKLERS

It began with boisterous interruption of Government spokesmen in the 1906 election. People were, of course, used to interruptions at political meetings by men of the opposing side, but not to this shrill and persistent heckling by white-faced women, desperately, viciously in earnest. Then came vast importunate processions, seeking to invade the House of Commons and assailing the police who barred their progress. Prisons began to fill up with arrested demonstrators, and with women caught smashing shop windows with hammers, pouring acid into letter-boxes, and otherwise making themselves as troublesome as possible. A poem by Rudyard Kipling, entitled "The Female of the Species," appeared in the *Standard,* pointing out that she was more deadly than the male. One desperate enthusiast even flung herself to death beneath the horses' hooves at the Derby in 1913.

It was all very disturbing and inconvenient. The British male, his mind still crackling with the starch of the Victorian age, fulminated against the unwomanly conduct of the suffragettes, and wondered why they could not stay at home, darning socks and rearing large families like their grandmothers, instead of trying to meddle with politics which they weren't fitted to understand. "These militant tactics won't do their cause any good," he grunted savagely and with

MRS. PANKHURST ARRESTED OUTSIDE BUCKINGHAM PALACE (1914)

From 1906 until 1914, Winston Churchill was perpetually bothered by the Suffragettes. They often demonstrated during his political meetings. The leader of the Suffragettes movement was Mrs. Emmeline Pankhurst (1858-1928) who later became a member of the Conservative Party.

COLONIAL CONFERENCE, 1907

Winston Churchill was present at the Colonial Conference of 1907 as Under-Secretary of State for the Colonies. This conference resolved to become thenceforward an "Imperial Conference." Statesmen present, reading from left to right, were: (Standing) Mr. Winston Churchill, Sir, F. Hopwood, Sir W. Baillie Hamilton, General Botha, Mr. T. W. Holderness, Sir J. Mackay, Mr. C. W. Johnson, Mr. H. W. Just, Sir W. Lyne, Hon. L. P. Brodeur, Mr. W. A. Robinson, Sir R. Bond. (Seated) Mr. Asquith, Sir T. Ward, Sir W. Laurier, Lord Elgin (President), Hon. A. Deakin, Hon. R. R. Moor and Mr. David Lloyd George.

determination. "We won't be bullied into giving that sort of woman the vote!"

There will perhaps always be debate whether in the changing temper of the time a less violent method of agitation would have been more successful. Peaceful methods had been futile in the past, and certainly the militants made Women's Suffrage an issue that could no longer be ignored. But in the end it was the part played by women in the First World War that actually silenced their opponents and gained them the vote.

What annoyed the Liberals, many of whom were supporters of votes for women, was the fact that the agitators made a dead set at the Liberal leaders, whose meetings they systematically broke up. Even an enthusiastic pro-suffragist like Lloyd George suffered from

them as severely as Asquith, whose opposition to them was mainly responsible for the refusal of the Government to move in the matter. It looked suspiciously as if these women were tools of the Tories; and, indeed, certain of their leaders may have nursed party sympathies that made them enjoy harassing the Liberals. But they justified their course, and with good show of reason, as being based on the strategy of attacking the government in power, since it alone was in a position to grant them their demand.

No one suffered more from the attentions of the suffragists than Winston Churchill, though he professed sympathy, if not quite passionate enthusiasm for their cause. They started on him in Manchester during the 1906 election. Manchester was a stronghold of the militants. They failed then to bring about his defeat. But in 1908, when

WINSTON CHURCHILL'S ENGAGEMENT

In 1908, at the age of 33, Winston Churchill married Miss Clementine Hozier, the daughter of Colonel Sir H. M. Hozier, of the 3rd Dragoon Guards. In this picture, which was taken during his engagement and just before his marriage, he is seen with his fiancée.

on taking a new office—the Board of Trade—he had to seek re-election, they played a noisier and more effective part. This time he was defeated, and when the result was announced, a woman grabbed his arm and shouted: "It's the women who have done this!" He shook her off and growled impatiently "Go away, woman!" His exasperation was natural; but the women didn't go away. At Dundee, where he retrieved his failure, his meetings were deafened by a pretty Irishwoman named Maloney, who came to them with a bell and rang it hard and long.

They pestered all the Cabinet, but they pestered Winston most of all. He attracted them, no doubt, because he was such a brilliant and flamboyant figure that everything about him was news, and their attacks on him were sure to hit the headlines. He roused their venom because he seemed a rather half-hearted supporter, needing to be chastened into full surrender. But perhaps it was the schoolboy quality in Winston, which he was never entirely to lose, that

WEDDING AT ST. MARGARET'S, WESTMINSTER

Mr. and Mrs. Churchill were married in September, 1908, in St. Margaret's, Westminster, the parish church of the House of Commons. The best man was Lord Hugh Cecil, who had been one of the leading Conservatives when Churchill was a member of that party. Mr. Churchill is shown arriving at the church with Lord Hugh Cecil.

awakened in some of these earnest amazons a maiden-aunt complex, which made it their duty to keep the unruly boy in his place.

These, then, were the unfriendly women in his career. They bothered him a lot, but they did not seriously mar his progress.

The friendly women? Two have already been mentioned, his mother and his nurse. Now the third came on the scene—his wife.

His romance had that crystal simplicity which is so much lovelier than some tortured, soul-straining drama. In his busy political life Winston had little time to spare for social gaieties. He was no addict of the ballroom or the banquet, and match-making mammas spread their nets for him in vain. But one day, in a friend's house, he met Miss Clementine Hozier, who was a granddaughter of the Countess of Airlie, an important figure in his new constituency of Dundee.

The two fell in love with one another at first sight. There was nothing to hinder or delay the match, and in September, 1908, they were married at St. Margaret's, Westminster, the parish church of the House of Commons. Lord Hugh Cecil was best man, and a huge crowd gathered to wish them well.

Churchill himself, writing of this event twenty-two years later, in his autobiographical fragment *My Early Life,* could state simply and sincerely: "I married and lived happily ever afterwards." His most intimate friends attest that this is no more than the truth. He and his wife were to remain lovers through all the following years. Their loyalty left no room for the intrusion of rivals. Mrs. Churchill's gracious, poised personality was to prove the ideal complement to Winston's impulsive restlessness. As wife and mother, as hostess and companion, building for him a happy home life and fostering his friendships and social contacts, sharing his joys and sorrows, his disappointments and successes, her shining example stands. If Winston Churchill well served his country and his age, she can claim no small share in the credit.

FRIENDSHIP WITH DAVID LLOYD GEORGE

Probably the biggest formative influence on Winston's political outlook in those years was his close friendship with David Lloyd George, the Welsh Radical. It began on the evening when Churchill made his first speech in the Commons, attacking L.G., who had shortened his own speech to make way for him. It persisted unbrokenly through the succeeding forty-odd years, whether they were allies or opponents in politics.

The two men had as many points of contrast as of likeness. One was reared in the heart of Society, heir of an aristocratic name and tradition, educated at a famous public school. The other grew up in a remote Welsh village, went to a National school, was articled to a local solicitor, and won his first successes defending poachers in the county courts. One was a typical John Bull, the other a typical Celt. Yet this strangely dissimilar pair had much in common. Both were always intensely, rebelliously alive overspilling with energy, gluttonously eager to be up and doing. Both had keen, fresh, active intellects, brilliant oratorical gifts, and both were intensely pugnacious, fighters to the core.

Above all, both had a warm and generous love of the common man, and a passion to secure justice and fair play for the under-dog. In Winston this perhaps sprang mainly from his English love of fair

MRS. CHURCHILL DEPARTS FOR HONEYMOON

In his book, "My Early Life," Mr. Churchill wrote: "I married and lived happily ever afterwards." This was no more than the truth. In fact he and his wife were to remain lovers through all the following years and Mrs. Churchill's gracious, poised personality was to prove an ideal complement to Winston's impulsive restlessness.

play, and distaste for hitting a man when he is down. L.G. had a more intimate understanding of the under-dogs. He grew up among them, and championed them against oppression by the privileged and highly placed. He shared his interest and experience with his younger ally, and found him a quick learner.

The swing-over of Churchill's mind to these problems of social reform is well illustrated by a speech that he made on unemployment in February, 1908. "In my opinion," he told his audience, "the question of unemployment is the greatest of the day. The people never complain without terrible cause, and we have to solve the question of the crying need of a man who finds himself unable to get employment. I am not one of those who say that everybody should be equal, but what I do say is that no one should have anything unless everybody has something. The general trend of Liberal policy must be increasingly to build up the minimum standards of life and labour in this country. Below a certain limit men should not be allowed to labour."

Lloyd George, as President of the Board of Trade, had put in hand various measures to improve trade and industry and working conditions. Among them were the Merchant Shipping Act, the Patents Act, the securing of better conditions for railwaymen and the negotiations for setting up the Port of London Authority. Winston followed these moves with keen interest; and thus it came about that when, in April, 1908, Campbell-Bannerman resigned the premiership and was succeeded by Asquith, Winston entered the Cabinet, not as First Lord of the Admiralty—the post which Asquith first suggested to him—but as L.G.'s successor at the Board of Trade. L.G. himself moved to the Exchequer.

In the lively years that followed, L.G. and Winston were the two outstanding figures in politics, both working, speaking and leading the campaign for reform. Cynics tried to hint at rivalries and jealousies between them. But, in fact, their genuine friendship was too firm for any such rivalry to spring up. They were partners, not competitors.

PRESIDENT OF THE BOARD OF TRADE

To those who think of Churchill only in his later and more familiar role of our fighting Premier, his choice of the Board of Trade in 1908 in preference to the Admiralty may well sound incredible. But there was fighting to be done then in that office, too—more fighting than seemed likely at the Admiralty. It was the fight against unemployment. This was the struggle which Winston made peculiarly his own. In more modern days we have witnessed unemployment on a bigger and grimmer scale than existed at that time. But there have been means to combat and alleviate it which did not then exist. We owe them to Winston Churchill.

His general aims were indicated in a speech on the Government's Licensing Bill which came before the House in July, 1908. Though he supported the Bill, he urged that it was not the only road to temperance reform. "Shorter hours of labour, healthy conditions of industry, greater opportunities for leisure and commonsense forms of diversion, the wide extension of education—all these are sure, direct roads to the diminution of the evils of intemperance." In

106

ASSOCIATION WITH LLOYD GEORGE

In 1905, Balfour's Conservative Government was superseded by a Liberal Government under Campbell-Bannerman. Churchill, now a Liberal, took office as Colonial Under-Secretary in this Ministry and his friend Lloyd George was President of the Board of Trade; Winston himself succeeded Lloyd George in the same office in 1908.

October he was already denouncing the evils of casual labour, and especially the wasteful use of boy and girl labour in blind-alley jobs.

In 1909 he brought in a Bill to set up Labour Exchanges, and carried it triumphantly to the Statute Book. It was the preliminary step to the introduction of Unemployment Insurance, on the planning of which he was busily engaged. Lloyd George, who had made a study of workers' insurance schemes in Germany, was preparing a big National Insurance measure for Britain; and while he worked out the Health aspect of it, Winston at the Board of Trade took charge of the Unemployment section. In 1909 he also carried through the Trade Boards Act, the object of which was to put a stop to the sweating of labour in trades whose workers were not effectively organized for their own protection.

Some people are puzzled at the way in which, during the years before the Second World War, Churchill was so persistently and deliberately cold-shouldered by his own party leaders; why Neville Chamberlain showed such bitter and implacable hostility to him; why the Conservative Central Office even contemplated putting up a rival candidate to him in his constituency.

ADVOCATE OF SOCIAL REFORM

The answer to this problem is to be found in Winston's activities during those years, from 1906 to 1911, when he was in the forefront of the battle for social reform, and of the savage struggle with the Conservative party into which it developed. A brilliant and effective orator, he was one of the main spokesmen of the Liberals, and plunged joyfully into the fray.

Bill after Bill in this social programme was fought through the Commons. The Tories, powerless to defeat them there, fell back on the expedient of getting the measures they found most obnoxious thrown out by the Lords. Many peers who had never taken any real interest in politics—"backwoodsmen" they were dubbed—were dragged up from their country estates to crush the Liberal legislation. They destroyed three Education Bills, a Licensing Bill, a Plural Voting Bill, a Scottish Small Landowners' Bill, and a long list of other measures. They barely held back from killing the Old Age Pensions Bill—though in the end they let it through with a resolution of protest. Tempers rose above boiling point.

Finally Lloyd George brought the issue to a head. Social reform

MR. AND MRS. CHURCHILL AT AN AIR-MEETING AT HENDON

Being enthusiastic about all forms of endeavour, Mr. Churchill
followed the progress of the flying machine with interest. He travelled
by air from the early days of flying and during the First World War
was one of the first to realize the great importance of aerial warfare.
During the Second World War he travelled thousands of miles by air.

—pensions, insurance, school meals, and so on—cost money, which as Chancellor he had to find. Matters of finance and taxation were by constitutional tradition the province of the Commons. But when in 1909 L.G. brought in a Budget which provided for raising money by a series of duties on the increment value of land, the Tories, livid with fury, flung discretion to the winds and got the House of Lords to throw it out.

Tactically it was a disastrous blunder, for without the money voted yearly by the Commons the Government cannot be carried on. The constitutional fight that followed was waged with an acrimony unparalleled in more recent politics. It was the death-struggle of the old order against the new; of the relics of the feudal caste system, of class privilege and domination, against the rising surge of a newly self-conscious democracy. The power of the peers to veto popular legislation, and the less creditable aspects of land and property ownership which that veto had been used to shield in its rejection of the "People's Budget," provided a broad and vulnerable target for attack.

BATTLE WITH THE PEERS

Lloyd George revelled in the fight, and assailed the Lords with thrusts that made them squirm. Did the mere fact that they were "the first of the litter" in their families, he asked, make these hereditary peers supernormally capable legislators? At Limehouse he made a speech on landlords which the present-day reader would find witty, pungent and forceful but by no means scurrilous. But hitherto the class he attacked had regarded itself as too lofty for criticism, and it was horrified at being thus held up to scorn and ridicule. The term "Limehouse" became a label for political abuse that passed all gentlemanly limits.

Churchill himself was the scion of a ducal house of ancient lineage, and at first must have found his position embarrassing. His family traditions and social connexions pulled him to one side, his political comradeships and his progressive spirit to the other. He decided to stand for progress, and took the field as a champion of the rights of the Commons.

It was unforgivable. In some die-hard quarters it never was forgiven. Lloyd George was the bugbear of Society circles, and it is history that fretful children in aristocratic nurseries were scared to sleep by the warning: "If you aren't good, Lloyd George will get you!" But Winston was detested even more savagely, as a traitor to his class. He was regarded as a completely unworthy person whose every action was suspect. In Mayfair drawing-rooms a reputation was built up for him which was a grotesque travesty of his character, and it passed into currency, not only in the quarters where it was invented, but by degrees in a much wider circle. Right up to 1939 the legend of his clever unreliability handicapped and stultified his efforts to serve his country.

PEERS' RIGHT OF VETO ABOLISHED

The battle with the peers fell into two campaigns. In the first, the passing of the Budget was the main issue; in the second, the limitation of the Peers' veto. On the rejection of the 1909 Budget the Government appealed to the country, and was returned to power at a general election in January, 1910, amid scenes of wild excitement. Night after night dense crowds thronged Trafalgar Square and other centres of the great towns, singing "God made the land for the people," and yelping with delight as election results came in and were thrown on screens by magic lanterns.

The Lords let the Budget pass. But it was followed by the Parliament Bill, abolishing their power to amend or reject any financial measure, and authorizing the Commons to override their veto in regard to any Bill which the lower chamber should pass in three consecutive sessions. This was too much for them.

In May, 1910, King Edward VII passed away; and it is characteristic of the bitterness of the political strife at that time that the Globe newspaper roundly accused the Liberals of having been the cause of his death! The Tories openly hoped that as Edward had been regarded as friendly to the Liberals, his son and successor, George V, would incline to the Conservatives, and this hope doubtless stiffened their resistance to the Parliament Bill. They threw it out, and Mr. Asquith once again appealed successfully to the verdict of the nation—two General Elections being thus held in a single year, and both yielding practically the same result.

Whatever King George thought about the Parliament Bill, he acted with the greatest wisdom and constitutional orthodoxy in this extremely painful crisis that confronted him so soon after his accession. The Parliament Bill was again sent up to the Lords, and Asquith

111

was able to inform Lord Lansdowne, the Tory leader there, that His Majesty was ready, if need be, to create enough new Liberal peers to secure its passage, should the Lords again reject it.

It is perhaps hardly to their credit that while the national will, as expressed in two General Elections, moved them not at all, the prospect of a flood of three or four hundred jerry-built Liberal peerages desecrating their order proved decisive with the Tories in the Upper Chamber. A group of "Ditchers" (Die in the last ditch!) still wanted to throw out the Bill and damn the consequences. But the "Hedgers" under Lord Lansdowne decided on abstention, and the measure was passed.

It marked the culmination of a very important, though bloodless revolution, which had been in the making all through the ten years since Churchill entered parliament. Prior to the present century effective political power rested with an oligarchy, Whig or Tory, which held the democracy in leading strings. Lord Randolph Churchill, very much in advance of his own generation, had felt the stirring of the new democracy a quarter of a century before; and his son Winston took a leading share in freeing it from its trammels.

MOVED TO THE HOME OFFICE

In Asquith's new Cabinet, formed after the election of January, 1910, Churchill moved up from the Board of Trade to the Home Office, where he threw himself with his usual energy into the task of improving the lot of the coal miners. He carried the Mines Accidents Act, 1910, to compel provision to be made on mines for appliances for rescue work, first-aid training, and so on. Next year he carried the Coal Mines Act, to secure more stringent inspection of mines, precautions against gas and coal dust, and the provision of pit-head baths. The Act also prohibited the employment underground of boys under fourteen years old. That such a provision became law only as recently as 1911 is a rather revealing sidelight on the need for social reform which existed on all sides at that time.

But Winston's crowning act of reform was his scheme for Unemployment Insurance, which became law in 1911. He had worked out its details when he was President of the Board of Trade and, though he had now left that office, he watched and assisted the passage of the measure through Parliament.

It appeared as Part II of Lloyd George's National Insurance Bill

OPENING OF A NEW REIGN

This photograph of Mr. and Mrs. Winston Churchill was taken on 22 June, 1911, at the Coronation of King George V. Owing to bad organization, there had been disastrous crowding at the funeral of King Edward VII on 20 May, 1910. In order to avoid a recurrence of this mishap the procession was held on two days and over a wider area.

—the biggest piece of social reform in all those busy reforming years, and one of the best hated and most fiercely contested. The Conservatives opposed it tooth and nail. Society raged at the notion of having to pay contributions to the insurance of their domestics. "What! Me lick stamps?" a cartoon depicted an irate duchess as exclaiming, and the phrase, which aptly hit off the attitude of certain people, passed quickly into currency. Balfour argued disingenuously that it would ruin the trade unions—for which his party had not up to then showed marked solicitude. Scott Dickson, a former Lord Advocate, declared that it would do "a monstrous amount of mischief." But it was L.G.'s "ninepence for fourpence" health insurance scheme which came in for all this hostility. Winston's unemployment insurance got a much calmer passage.

Since then it has been extended by many further Acts, but its foundations were well and truly laid. Until Churchill took the matter in hand, a workman who had lost his job had no way of knowing where to look for another, and no means of support for himself or his family except the pawnshop while their few effects lasted, and then the workhouse. A quite incalculable sum of human misery has in recent times been averted as the result of the work done

FIGHTING FOREIGN GANGSTERS IN LONDON

On 3 January, 1911, Churchill was present at the so-called Sidney Street siege in his capacity as Home Secretary. A gang of Russian criminals under the leadership of "Peter the Painter" (Jacob Peters) had taken refuge in a house in Sidney Street, Whitechapel. In this photograph, Churchill is taking cover with Scots Guards and armed policemen who

AT THE SIEGE OF SIDNEY STREET

were called in to eject the gang. He suggested a frontal attack upon the building behind a sheet of metal obtained from a local foundry but the plan was rejected and artillery was brought upon the scene. Before it could be put into action, however, the gangsters set the building on fire and two of them were found dead in the ruins. Peter the Painter escaped.

by Winston in creating Labour Exchanges and Unemployment Insurance.

For ten years Churchill had immersed himself in the warfare of politics. But he could not entirely suppress his love of physical combat and military operations. Happily for him, even the Home Office managed to provide him with occasions to gratify this passion.

THE SIDNEY STREET SIEGE

In January, 1911, a party of alien gangsters, led by a Russian anarchist known as "Peter the Painter," tried to raid a Houndsditch jeweller's shop, and shot and killed three policemen who interrupted them. They were traced to a house in Sidney Street off the Mile End Road, where they were surrounded by a police cordon. But when an attempt was made to arrest them, they shot and killed another constable. The military were appealed to, and some Scots Guards came along from the Tower, erected a barricade at the end of the street, and opened fire on the house.

It was a fabulous occurrence in those peaceful days for a real war to break out in London, with a gang of bandits, armed with automatic pistols, shooting police and fighting soldiers. Churchill, as Home Secretary, felt entitled to hurry to the scene and supervise operations. A field gun was brought to reinforce the attack, and Winston, who was exposing himself recklessly to the fusillade of the bandits while he made suggestions for advancing on the house behind a metal shield, was with difficulty induced to take cover.

Crowds assembled at vantage points and looked on enthralled by the unfamiliar spectacle of a Cabinet Minister conducting a real war in person. At last the house was set on fire, and Winston had to use his authority to keep the Fire Brigade from acting on their standing orders to extinguish any fires in the metropolitan area without delay. They would only have been shot. Peter the Painter himself somehow managed to elude the police cordon and get away, to reappear years later in other dubious circumstances; but the corpses of his associates were found in the smouldering ruins of the house when the blaze subsided. People thought that Winston's debonair conduct was vaguely unseemly in a Home Secretary; but he himself enjoyed it all immensely. Fights drew him like a magnet.

Perhaps Sidney Street whetted his appetite for military operations. In August a railway strike broke out. The railwaymen had

116

genuine grievances. But the strike was called at twenty-four hours' notice, and threatened to bring all national industry to a standstill. Riotous crowds assailed trains run by non-strikers. Churchill, fearing sabotage of the lines, immediately called out a big force of military to guard stations, signal boxes and railway works. His promptness no doubt averted real danger, and the large scale on which he used soldiers kept down to a minimum the need for them to employ force, as their strength made resistance vain. In some places shots had to be fired at violent rioters, and men were killed. Most people agreed that Winston had done the right thing, though they were again somewhat shocked at his promptness in turning to arms, and his enjoyment of the opportunity to engage in military manoeuvres.

What many failed to recognize in those pacific years was that it takes a fighter to be an effective reformer. The Liberal Governments between 1906 and 1914 were flowing with noble ideals and reforming enthusiasm; but it is doubtful if they would have achieved a tithe of the flood of daring progressive legislation which made that epoch famous, if they had not had two such doughty fighters to lead their van as Winston Churchill and Lloyd George. Give such men a worthy cause for which they can fling themselves into battle, and they will work miracles.

Winston's pugnacity was to be displayed in many arenas for the benefit of his country. His years as a reformer were far from being the least warlike in his career, and Britain for years has reaped the fruits of the victories which in those years crowned his efforts on her behalf.

TROUBLE IN BELFAST

In 1912, the Irish Home Rule question assumed dangerous proportions.
Mr. Churchill regarded the passage of the Home Rule Bill as necessary
to avoid a civil war and so strongly did he feel that he went to Ulster
to address a meeting on Home Rule. In this drawing by Cyrus Cuneo,
reproduced by courtesy of the "Illustrated London News," Mr.
Churchill is shown driving through a hostile crowd of Ulstermen.

CHAPTER VI

FIRST LORD OF THE ADMIRALTY

T HE year 1911 was a year of harvest. During that hot summer and painted autumn, twentieth-century Britain took the shape familiar to the present generation, and the revolutionary developments at work in its social and political structure reached their fulfilment. At the same time, within the Empire the modern pattern of the British Commonwealth of Nations began to appear and, in the diplomatic world, the shadows cast by international alliances and groupings darkened heavily with the presage of approaching war.

The motor-car had by now come into its own, and motor-buses were sweeping their horse-drawn predecessors from the streets of London and other cities. The cinema, too, had flaringly arrived, and in almost every town there were "picture palaces" where motion dramas and slapstick comedies flickered, a bit jumpily and as yet silently, across the screen. Telephones had become more common. The aeroplane was no longer a mere dream of scientific inventors, for in 1909 Blériot had flown the Channel, and in the coming year, 1912, the Royal Flying Corps would be founded.

The passing in 1911 of the National Insurance Act put the wage-earners on to something more like their present-day footing, compared with their insecurity and abasement in Victorian times: while the abolition of the House of Lords veto and the introduction of payment for Members of Parliament marked the year as one that saw a revolutionary broadening of the basis of British democracy. The Labour Party, which had won forty-two seats in the election of December, 1910, was growing less dependent on the Liberals under whose wings it had sheltered. Asquith and his cabinet were laying plans for the introduction of full manhood suffrage, although votes for women were still toughly opposed.

In June the first Imperial Conference was held, and resolutions were adopted which were precursors of the Statute of Westminster. Botha appeared at this conference as Premier of the Union of South

Africa. During its course, the Dominion Premiers attended for the first time in history the meetings of the Committee of Imperial Defence.

Abroad, the aggressive intentions of the German Empire became clearer. The German Fleet was being rapidly expanded. German diplomacy was adopting a new truculence. As far back as 1904 Britain, misliking the Kaiser's naval policy, had established an "Entente Cordiale" with her ancient enemy, France. By 1911 this was being hammered under the menace of German policy into a virtual alliance. Military discussions which had been pursued for some years between the French and British war offices reached the formulation of definite plans for combined action in the event of war.

Most people as yet did not take seriously the talk of a possible war with Germany, though Lord Roberts and the National Service League made great play with it as an argument for compulsory military service. A melodrama entitled "An Englishman's Home," depicting a German invasion, had been drawing crowded houses. But this year the Agadir crisis drove home to two very important members of the Cabinet the reality of the threat, and set them thinking in a new way about problems of national defence. It would hardly be untrue to say that 1911 was the first year of that conflict between Germany and the Western civilized world which was to continue intermittently until 1945.

CRISIS AT AGADIR

It was the Agadir crisis which put an abrupt end to Winston's career as a domestic politician. So far he had been absorbed in projects of social reform. Agadir spun him round to concentrate on those problems of military strategy and Imperial defence which were more native to his temperament and his experience.

France had been accorded a sphere of influence in Morocco at the Algeciras Conference of 1906. She was bent on developing this into a protectorate, and in 1911 took the cue of some trouble in that restless country to send a military expedition to Fez. The Kaiser decided to muscle in on the game, and to secure a slice of Morocco for Germany. With this object he dispatched the gunboat *Panther* to the Moroccan port of Agadir, to stake out his claim.

While not an act of war, this was an unmistakable threat of war, and it set the chancelleries of Europe humming. Britain sent a Note

EARLY FLIGHT IN A HEAVIER THAN AIR MACHINE

The aeroplane is such a recent invention that Winston Churchill watched its development from the earliest days. This photograph, like that on page 122, was taken in 1910 on the occasion of a race from London to Manchester, a distance of 186 miles. Churchill is here seen talking to Lord Northcliffe before the contest started.

to Germany, asking the meaning of the visit of the *Panther*. No answer came, but France reported that impossible claims were being pressed on her by Potsdam, and the *Panther* was replaced at Agadir by the cruiser *Berlin*.

Lloyd George, who as Chancellor formed one of a small inner circle of the Cabinet, had not previously given much time to foreign affairs, but he, too, realized the gravity of this new situation. With his pro-Boer record, he was commonly counted a pacifist, though in fact he was temperamentally as pugnacious as Winston himself, and in his own way fully as patriotic. Speaking at a Mansion House banquet on 21 July, he uttered a grave warning to Germany that this country would be no mere spectator in the development of the affair. The Kaiser was furious; he even tried to get Asquith to sack L.G.! But he

GRAHAME WHITE AND MR. CHURCHILL

The race was for a prize of £10,000 offered by the "Daily Mail." The contestants were Grahame White, an English aviator (second from the right in the photograph) and Louis Paulhan, a Frenchman. Both airmen were forced down by cold and darkness. M. Paulhan landed at Trent Valley, near Lichfield, 117 miles from London, while Grahame White came down at Roade, 57 miles behind his rival. M. Paulhan's speed was 40 miles per hour; Grahame White's 43 miles per hour.

was unready just then to meet France and Britain together, so terms were patched up, and he gained a small part of the French Congo as compensation for leaving Morocco alone.

Winston, of course, got the full story from his crony Lloyd George, and Sir Edward Grey confirmed it with particulars of the military conversations that had been going on between the French and British army authorities. Here was something after Winston's own heart! Like Job's war-horse, he sniffed the battle from afar, and turned his magnificent intellect, so razor-keen when well set, to the problem of how to meet the German war menace.

His first action had rather a school-boy flavour. He discovered that as Home Secretary he was responsible for the safety of certain naval cordite stores, which were guarded only by the police. Off he hurried to take more serious steps for their protection, and when the Admiralty pooh-poohed his anxiety and refused to provide marines to stand sentry over the stores, he got Haldane to lend him troops for the purpose.

This was spectacular rather than serious. But his further actions had a more solid quality. He managed to get himself included in the Committee of Imperial Defence, and quickly familiarized himself with the military problems then being studied. He then proceeded to put in a paper to the Prime Minister setting out his view as to the probable course which the opening stages of a war between France and Germany would follow, and the part that a British force should be prepared to play in it. The paper was laughed to scorn by the War Office experts of the General Staff. "Ridiculous—fantastic—a silly memorandum!" ejaculated Sir Henry Wilson. But in truth it was quite uncannily discerning. Written in August, 1911, it described almost as exactly as if written after September, 1914, what actually took place—even to predicting that "By the fortieth day Germany should be extended at full strain both internally and on her war fronts. . . . If the French Army has not been squandered . . . the balance of forces should be favourable after the fortieth day, and will improve steadily as time passes." Germany in fact lost the Battle of the Marne on the forty-first day!

CHANGES NEEDED AT THE ADMIRALTY

The new urgency given to defence questions by the Agadir incident brought to light a curious situation. Haldane had done wonders at the War Office, creating not only the Territorial Army but a General Staff and a War Plan. The plan was co-ordinated with the French War Office down to the smallest details of the constitution and dispatch of an expeditionary force. But no similar intelligence had been displayed by the Senior Service, and no arrangements existed for the sea transport of the force! McKenna, the First Lord, was no strategist. He served his admirals loyally, and he had put up a good fight for more battleships at their bidding. But they disapproved of the idea of an expeditionary force, and he backed them. Clearly, if Britain was to be put in readiness for war, there were half-sunken hulks in the Admiralty fairway that must first be removed.

Haldane suggested that he should himself change places with McKenna, and repeat at the Admiralty his work of reorganization. It would have been a rather open affront to the Senior Service, and

Asquith hesitated. Lloyd George urged him to put Winston there. He pondered the advice. Finally, in October, while on a holiday in Scotland, he invited both Haldane and Winston up to see him, discussed the matter with them, and got Haldane to consent, rather dubiously, to Winston changing places with McKenna. The young man was inexperienced: but he was eager to co-operate with Haldane, and he clearly had the root of the matter in him.

The change was made, and, in November, Winston became First Lord of the Admiralty, with a special instruction from the Prime Minister to develop a War Staff and generally reform the organization. He himself felt the appointment to be of the nature of a divine call to fulfil a mission hidden in the purpose of Providence, and he dedicated himself to the task with the zeal of a devotee.

ADVICE FROM ADMIRAL FISHER

To support his own inexperience, he at once sought Admiral Fisher, who had retired a year before from the position of First Sea Lord. Winston had struck up a friendship with him four years earlier at Biarritz. Admiral Fisher was a type of Englishman not unknown in this island: clear-thinking, endowed with an abundance of practical horse-sense; a man of terrific energy and drive, of violent individual opinions, forcibly expressed; sometimes pig-headedly right, at other times no less pig-headedly wrong, but always positive and unfaltering; with beneath it all the heart of a little child, and a devout religious faith, which took, like so much else about him, an unconventional twist, for he was a convinced British Israelite.

In his stormy six years as First Sea Lord, Fisher had largely created the British battle fleet, and had taught the Navy to shoot. Now he took the young First Lord under his wing, and counselled and admonished him by speech and letter. "Yours till Hell freezes," he would sign himself: "Yours till charcoal sprouts." The two had much in common, and during the years that followed they quarrelled and made friends again, and argued and disagreed, and reached fresh understandings. Fisher was a stimulating, if difficult, colleague.

Tutored by this Mohawk-faced sage, Winston carried through drastic reforms—not all of them approved by his mentor. To Fisher's delight, he appointed Jellicoe as second-in-command of the Home Fleet. "That means," gloated Fisher, "that he will be in command of the Home Fleet before October, 1914—the date of Armageddon."

124

LAUNCHING OF H.M.S. "IRON DUKE"

This photograph of Mr. and Mrs. Churchill was taken at the launching of H.M.S. "Iron Duke" in 1912. During the years immediately preceding the First World War, the Kaiser was frantically expanding the German Fleet, and it was due to Churchill's insistence that British naval superiority was not lost.

It was a shrewd forecast to make in 1911, for Fisher was only a couple of months out. Winston brought in Beatty as his Naval Secretary—another notable selection. He had met Beatty on the Nile, thirteen years before. He set up a Naval War Staff, and cleared out a good deal of dead wood at the Admiralty. His supreme aim was to put the fleet in complete readiness for instant action in the event of war.

Churchill's achievement in persuading Fisher to work with him was the more remarkable because their views on the role of the Navy in the approaching war differed sharply in important respects. Winston had been put into the Admiralty by Asquith to carry out two tasks on which the Prime Minister had already decided—tasks which were opposed by McKenna, Winston's predecessor, and by the naval chiefs; and, in particular, by Fisher. One was the transport of an expeditionary force to support the French in continental war; the other, the creation of a Naval War Staff.

Fisher held by the traditional strategy of Britain, which regarded the Navy as our real arm, and treated our small army as a projectile to be flung by the fleet here and there at vulnerable points to harass the enemy while sea blockade wore him down. He objected to any engagement by Britain in continental war. He would have held the seas and flung raiding parties at Antwerp or Pomerania. He also disliked the notion of setting up a War Staff on the Army model. He had a poor opinion of the Army and of its commanders.

TROUBLES WITH ADMIRAL FISHER

The first big breach between Fisher and Winston came, however, not in regard to these matters, but over the appointment to naval commands of three admirals of whom Fisher strongly disapproved. He wrote to Winston in high indignation, severing their relations. "I consider," he said, "you have betrayed the Navy by these three appointments, and what the pressure could have been to induce you to betray your trust is beyond my comprehension." With that, he packed his bags and retired to Naples.

It is not Winston's habit to take "No" for an answer when he wants anything. He wanted Fisher, and he refused to leave him in idle relaxation. He pelted him with requests for his advice on this matter and that, and persuaded his colleagues to do the same. Finally, he went after him.

In the spring of 1912 Winston persuaded Asquith to come for a cruise with him to the Mediterranean, in the Admiralty yacht *Enchantress,* in order to visit Malta and talk over the problems of Mediterranean strategy with Kitchener there. For Kitchener was at this time British Agent and Consul-General in Egypt, in succession to Lord Cromer. During the trip Winston saw to it that they called at Naples, where the Prime Minister reinforced Winston's appeal to Fisher to return to England.

Fisher was no respecter of persons, and Asquith's plea seemed unavailing. But Churchill secured a more telling advocate. On the Sunday morning they all went to the English service. Whether Churchill had primed the chaplain beforehand is not recorded. What is historic is that the chaplain, in the course of his sermon, looked hard at the Admiral and said: "No man possessing all his powers and full of vitality has any right to say 'I am now going to rest, as I have had a hard life,' for he owes a duty to his country and fellow-men!' "

Fisher's conscience was stirred. He came back to Britain. Once again, he and Winston were putting their heads together to plan daring improvements to the Navy. It was on the advice and with the backing of the old Admiral that Winston secretly ordered 15-in. guns for his new battleships in place of the 13·5-in. guns which had been thought the last word in giant naval artillery. For Fisher never stood still. He was always trying to go one better than before. When he joined the Navy, all its ships still carried sails, and many had no auxiliary steam. None was armoured. The transformation to the modern battle fleet as we know it was Fisher's work. In Winston he found a kindred spirit, as eager as himself to improve, to experiment, to seize on and develop any daring new idea.

FACTIONS AT THE ADMIRALTY

The antagonism which Winston constantly evoked whenever he engaged in vigorous and picturesque activities was not lacking during his tenure of the Admiralty. He came to a house divided against itself—split into factions between the Fisher school and the Beresford school.

His hearty alliance with Fisher did nothing to heal the split, and his changes came under heavy fire. He had innumerable enemies, for his scarifying eloquence on behalf of the Parliament Bill and his presidency of the Budget League, which advocated Lloyd George's Land Value Duties, had made him the best-hated member of the Cabinet in those Tory circles to which he had once belonged. The criticisms of his naval reforms made by Lord Charles Beresford and others of the anti-Fisher school were avidly seized on by them. Here was a stick with which to beat the renegade! A tradition was sedulously built up that Churchill had wrecked the Navy; that in flamboyant egotism he had deliberately reversed the wise policy of McKenna, and imposed a War Staff and other novelties quite unsuited to the Navy's special character and functions.

Winston also annoyed the Kaiser, although at first his appointment had been welcomed in Germany. His record as an opponent of inflated army estimates, and his close association with Lloyd George in social reform, made Berlin hope that he would soft-pedal on naval policy. Bitterly were the Germans disappointed when they found that, on the contrary, he was using his powerful influence to compel the Cabinet's support for naval expansion. In his very first naval estimates, in 1912, he lifted the rate of battleship construction from two a year to four, and presently raised it to five.

He explained to the country with complete frankness that this programme was imposed on Britain by Germany's insistence on a big navy—an unnecessarily big navy. Speaking at Glasgow on 9 February, 1912, he said :

"The British Navy is to us a necessity and, from some points of view, the German Navy is to them more in the nature of a luxury. Our naval power involves British existence. It is existence to us: it is expansion to them. We cannot menace the peace of a single Continental hamlet, nor do we wish to do so, no matter how great and supreme our Navy may become. But, on the other hand, the whole fortunes of our race and Empire, the whole treasure accumulated during so many centuries of sacrifice and achievement, would perish and be swept utterly away if our naval supremacy were to be impaired. It is the British Navy which makes Great Britain a Great Power. But Germany was a Great Power, respected and honoured all over the world, before she had a single ship."

In his naval estimates he laid down the formula of a sixty per cent superiority over the German Navy in capital ships with higher ratios for smaller craft, as the necessary minimum safety level for Britain. But Germany's fury at this arrogant British insistence on maintaining naval superiority was as nothing to her Teutonic rage at his description of her Imperial Navy as a "luxury fleet!" The name seemed to hint that it was the Kaiser's toy: in fact, it was just that—but a very dangerous toy.

At home, Winston's naval policy came under fire from both sides of the House. If the Tories watched him with bitter scepticism, convinced that this Radical with his parsimonious attitude to the Services was bound to be letting the Navy down, the Liberals were rather shocked at the militant delight he seemed to take in polishing and expanding a powerful fleet. Even within the Cabinet his zeal found little answering sympathy. Lloyd George wanted for purposes of social reform all the revenue he could get, and argued that a number of cheaper and smaller craft, such as destroyers and light cruisers, would be more valuable than these extremely costly capital ships.

CHURCHILL AS AN AIRMAN

Churchill was one of the earliest statesmen to realize the potential importance of air power. He discussed the question with Kitchener and was able to infect him with his enthusiasm. His was the inspiration which conceived and created the Royal Naval Air Service (as a means of defence) and the Royal Flying Corps (as a means of attack).

This controversy over the relative importance of big and little ships went on for many years, and only quite recently ceased to be a debated issue. But Winston, following the advice of Fisher, insisted on his battleships: and, at the cost of very considerable ill-feeling, he got them.

Since Britain was utterly determined to maintain a definite ratio of naval superiority over the German fleet, it seemed obvious to the Cabinet, anxious to use its revenue for more beneficial kinds of construction, that both countries would be better off if they agreed to limit the size of their navies.

LORD HALDANE'S UNSUCCESSFUL VISIT TO GERMANY

Early in 1912, Lord Haldane went over to Germany to see what he could do to promote such a plan. He was of all men in Britain the best qualified for the task. He knew Germany well, had studied in Göttingen, was steeped in German philosophy, and indeed could think inside the German mind, so to speak—at least, the minds of those German philosophers, poets and scientists who form the finer and really valuable part of the complex German nation. A friend once asserted of him that Germany was his spiritual home—a statement that would later be twisted to his unmerited ruin. It was from Germany that Haldane had gathered many of the notions which enabled him to reform the War Office, establish the Territorials and devise the Expeditionary Force: just as it was from Germany that Lloyd George collected his ideas for Trade Boards, Labour Exchanges and National Insurance.

Haldane found, however, that at Potsdam he was dealing not with German philosophers, but with Prussian Imperialists. So he brought back with him, not terms for a truce, but a copy of the new German Navy Bill with its expansionist programme. Winston framed his naval estimates accordingly, but he continued to plead for a mutual slowing-down. On 18 March, 1912, when moving his estimates, he said: "Let me make it clear that any retardation or reduction in German construction within certain limits will be promptly followed here, as soon as it is apparent, by large and fully proportionate reduction." He suggested that in 1913 both countries should take a holiday from naval shipbuilding. But there was no response from Germany.

In March, 1913, he repeated the offer in set terms. "No one builds

WITH GENERAL FRENCH AT ARMY MANOEUVRES, 1912

When he was First Lord of the Admiralty, Churchill continued to retain a keen interest in the doings of the Junior Service, in which he had started his career. General French is standing on Mr. Churchill's left next to the umpire with the white armlet.

Dreadnoughts for fun," he claimed, and urged the mutual abandonment in 1914—if only for one year—of "a wasteful, purposeless and futile folly." He again reiterated the proposal at Manchester a few months later, but to no purpose. Von Tirpitz went on with his building, while the officers of the Germany Navy toasted "Der Tag!"

The effort to secure a naval truce was a failure. But in another direction, Winston's work at the Admiralty bore lasting fruit, not only for the Navy, but for the resources of Britain in other fields of defence. He changed the Navy over to the use of oil as fuel, making sure of a supply of oil for the purpose by securing for the British Government a controlling interest in the Anglo-Persian oil-fields.

"OIL MANIAC"

It was Fisher who persuaded him to switch the Navy over from coal to oil fuel. Fisher was regarded as an "oil maniac." Fanatical in everything he took up, he pursued his hobby of oil-firing with relentless persistence. On its superior merits to coal he had an unanswerable case. It was quicker and more convenient to take aboard, handier to transport and store, and it gave men-of-war a higher speed. In sea warfare, that last factor might be decisive. But the diehards shook their heads. They distrusted this new-fangled fuel, just as their grandfathers had raged against the iron ships that displaced the good old "wooden walls" of England. Coal was British and far more reliable than this alien oil. What would happen in a war, if we had abandoned coal and were cut off from our oil supplies?

There was some force in that last argument, and as Winston was busily proceeding to adapt all the Navy's most powerful vessels for oil-burning, he looked round for ways of meeting it. The obvious remedy, he decided, was to have our own oil supply. The Scottish shales would not nearly suffice for that purpose, and the production of oil from coal was still in the early experimental stage. So he decided to buy an oil-field.

The American fields were not for sale, nor were those of the Caucasus, which in any case would be inaccessible in war. The Dutch East Indies were too remote, even if they were purchasable. But the Persian wells filled the bill admirably. Accessible, just outside the war zone of any European conflict, little developed as yet, but capable of great expansion, and in need of capital for the purpose, they were exactly what was wanted.

WINSTON CHURCHILL AND GEORGE LAMBERT

Above, Mr. Churchill is seen at Sandwich in 1912 while he was First Lord of the Admiralty. With him is the Right Honourable George Lambert, Liberal M.P. and Civil Lord of the Admiralty from 1905 until 1915. Mr. Lambert was an authority on naval questions and was a member of the Royal Commission on Fuel and Engines for the Navy.

Winston had the fields very carefully examined by experts, and on getting their report he obtained Cabinet authority to negotiate a contract with the Anglo-Persian Oil Company, whereby the British Government would invest some two million pounds in the venture, thus getting control of it and securing a first call on all its production for the British Navy.

BRILLIANT STROKE OF NATIONAL COMMERCE

The scheme finally came before the House of Commons for confirmation on 17 June, 1914. A whole day was spent in debating it, and opposition was at first strong in some quarters. But Winston scored a personal triumph, answering his critics, silencing objections, and finally carrying the project by 254 votes to 18.

It was a brilliant stroke of national commerce, not unworthy to rank close behind Disraeli's purchase of the Suez Canal shares. Financially, the tax-payers' holding in the company has repaid them many thousand per cent on the sum invested. Strategically, it has furnished an expanding and invaluable supply of oil for the naval, military and air services. Churchill can hardly have foreseen quite how vital a part oil would come to play in modern warfare during the next thirty years. But his instinct was sound, and he built even better than he knew. The action of the Persian Government in 1950 and 1951 in repudiating its agreements with the Anglo-Persian Oil Company, and expelling it from the country, has meant a heavy setback. To Churchill, the spectacle of this melancholy end to the scheme he had engineered so successfully some forty years ago must have been particularly bitter.

By 1912, the Golden Age of social reform was nearing its close, and the bill was being presented. The Liberal Government, which in 1906 had so overwhelming a majority, suffered the inevitable swing of the pendulum. The election of December, 1910, left the Liberals with a majority of only two over the Tories. They had in addition the support of the 42 Labour members, but the casting vote was in the hands of the 84 Irish Nationalists. It was given to the Government to enable them to carry the Parliament Act and National Insurance, but a price was demanded for this assistance. That price was Home Rule for Ireland.

Lloyd George was impatient to carry on with the next stage of his programme of social reform—his schemes for the land: for

AT THE EARL'S COURT EXHIBITION

This photograph of Mr. and Mrs. Churchill was taken at Earl's Court on 6 May, 1912, when Mr. Churchill was First Lord of the Admiralty. Mrs. Churchill is on her husband's right. Trade exhibitions were held almost continuously each year at Earl's Court until the outbreak of the First World War in 1914 made their continuance impossible.

reviving agriculture and embarking on housing and slum-clearance. But the next two years had chiefly to be sacrificed, so far as parliamentary time was concerned, to the tedium of carrying repeatedly through the House of Commons the two highly controversial measures of Welsh Disestablishment and Irish Home Rule.

Both were anathema to the Conservatives, who used their majority in the House of Lords to block them, so both had to rely for their ultimate enactment on the provisions of the Parliament Act. By these a Bill carried through the Commons in three consecutive sessions and rejected each time by the Lords could, despite that veto, receive the Royal assent. Between 1912 and 1914 each of these measures was thrice pushed through all stages in the House of Commons, with a wearisome reiteration of the same arguments, and was thrice opposed by the Lords. The advent of the First World War put both bills into cold storage.

IRISH HOME RULE CONTROVERSY

Welsh Disestablishment was not an issue that held Churchill's interest, and he took no part in that controversy. But Irish Home Rule was another matter. Here was a good, fiery, swashbuckling struggle, with more than a threat of actual military operations in the background. Besides, Winston was delighted to take the opportunity which the Home Rule struggle provided of showing himself to be an indispensable champion of the Party's measures. At the time he was spending large sums on the Navy in a way which alarmed his Liberal colleagues, who held war to be an anachronism that could not really happen now, and disapproved of bloated armaments. But they conceded to him what they might have refused to another, because of his value in the Home Rule debates. He found the cause a lively one in which to break a lance, and the tourney was not the less attractive for helping him to push his naval plans through in the heat of this most furious mêlée.

It must be admitted that for the mass of the public in Britain, the Home Rule controversy which filled so big a place in politics during the years before the First World War roused perplexity rather than enthusiasm. So far as the Liberals were concerned, the flag of Home Rule had been nailed to their masthead by Gladstone in 1885, and the nails had split the flagstaff. The Liberal Unionists had broken away, Chamberlain and Carson among them. Those who were left

136

WITH KING GEORGE V AT MILITARY EXERCISES

This photograph of Winston Churchill talking to George V was taken in 1913, the year before the First World War. Churchill had kept closely in touch with Continental military matters and in consequence his judgments about them were well-informed.

continued to salute the flag, but they supported Home Rule more
through principle than through passion.

Advocates of liberty for small nations, they could not deny liberty
to a country which demanded it so persistently. They acknowledged
the justice of the claim, but they were less sure of its wisdom. The
Nonconformists in particular, who provided so large a body of support for the Liberal Government, were made uneasy by the threat
that "Home Rule is Rome Rule!" They had a hereditary horror of
Rome.

Winston suffered from neither of these complexes. He was not a
theologian—and he had not been a Liberal at the time of the party
split. As he had shown over South Africa, he liked making a generous
settlement with the opposing side, and in 1913 this meant Home
Rule for Ireland.

THE IRISH CONTROVERSY GROWS MORE SAVAGE

The Irish controversy grew more and more savage, till it
harrowed the King's Peace in Britain with a violence unknown since
the Chartist riots. Winston spared it what time and effort he could
from his Admiralty work, and it provided him with a lot of fun.

With characteristic daring he set out for Belfast, the stronghold
of Irish Unionism, in February, 1912, to address a big meeting on
Home Rule. The Orangemen threatened to wreck his meeting, and
refused to let him engage the Ulster Hall. Eventually he had to speak
in a big marquee, in the teeth of noisy opposition—though the
suffragettes and their male supporters caused him more trouble than
the Orangemen.

At the end of April he moved the second reading of the Government's Home Rule Bill. From that point on he was continually
engaging in the fight. He and Lloyd George were the star debaters
on the Government side, and had to keep at it, in Parliament and in
the country, week by week. For this conflict went on without a break
until it was at last interrupted by the First World War.

The wordy battles were as savage as parliamentary etiquette
would permit. Not infrequently they passed that limit, and debates
broke up in disorder. Nor did the strife stop at words. On one
occasion, when the Tory opposition, ravening with fury, raised such
a storm that the Speaker suspended the sitting, Winston had to pass
his opponents on his way out, and when he smiled benignly at their

IRISH ANTI-HOME RULE PARTY

When the question of Irish Home Rule came before the Commons in 1912, a party in Ulster under Edward Carson, threatened to use force to oppose it. In this cartoon by Sir Bernard Partridge, reproduced by permission of the proprietors of "Punch," Edward Carson is engaged in defending the Ulster Hall against Winston Churchill.

yelled insults, Ronald McNeill, one of the Ulster members, flung a book at his head and hit it. The blood of the Churchills was roused, and only the massed intervention of the spectators kept him from trying to tear McNeill apart. But a full apology was offered him next day. Red heads, if quick to flare, are not lacking in generosity, and the insult was forgotten.

VERGE OF CIVIL WAR

Meanwhile, Ireland was on the verge of civil war. Carson openly set about raising an army in Ulster to defend it against control by Dublin. It was characteristic of the tragi-comedy of that contradictory island that the "loyalists" showed their loyalty to the British connexion by preparing to maintain armed rebellion against the King's government, and even hinted openly that they would break away and join with Germany sooner than accept Home Rule; while the Nationalists, after long ages of rebellion, were by contrast meekly entrusting their cause to the peaceful arbitrament of constitutional procedure.

Carson's army, in defiance of the law, ran in a big store of rifles, machine-guns and ammunition, acquired from Prussia. The southern Irish, whose nationalism was rapidly changing into a Sinn Fein movement, started to enrol their own force, the Irish Nationalist Volunteers. They tried to emulate the Ulstermen's gun-running feat, but were stopped by the police and military, not without bloodshed. The officers in charge of the British troops stationed at the Curragh threatened to resign their commissions if they were sent to keep order in Ulster. The whole island was on the boil, and it seemed that civil war could not be averted.

The sober English looked on bewildered. *The Times* solemnly rebuked the warmongers; *Punch,* in a vigorous cartoon, warned Carson not to fight. Peaceable, kindly, law-abiding, the English could not see the sense of men actually killing one another to settle whether the Irish Members of Parliament should sit in Dublin or in Westminster. They did not share the fanaticism of the Celt, and were mostly ignorant of the long bitterness that is Irish history.

Although Winston was bent on giving the Irish the Home Rule for which they had so long and passionately struggled, he had no desire to see the country plunged into that most pitiless and unchivalrous of all conflicts, a civil war. Surely a pacific settlement of

140

the Ulster problem was not impossible? As early as January, 1913, he was pointing out that the exclusion of Ulster from the Home Rule Bill was practicable, if both sides could agree to it. Before the end of the year, he was quietly trying to negotiate with the Conservatives for an agreed solution of the difficulty, and suggesting the setting up of a Coalition to put it through.

The negotiations broke down with the growth of Carson's army and the gun-running episode. The Home Rule Bill was duly pushed a third time through the Commons, with the knowledge that it would once more be rejected by the Lords. But Asquith took up the plan that Winston had suggested, and offered to bring in an amending Bill in the Lords for the exclusion of Ulster from the operation of Home Rule. On 1 July, 1914, the Bill came before the Lords, who proceeded to amend it almost beyond recognition. That the Nationalists would accept it in its changed form was unthinkable, and on 21 July the King summoned a conference at Buckingham Palace, to see if any agreement were still possible. On 24 July the conference broke up in failure. Rioting promptly started in Dublin. The second reading of the Amending Bill was due to be debated in the Commons on 30 July. But when that day came, the age-old vendetta of Dublin and Belfast had been swept off the parliamentary slate by the first waves of a vaster flood of war.

THE BRITISH FLEET WAS READY

Winston Churchill has been charged with many and various blunders and indiscretions by his enemies, during his animated and gladiatorial career. But none has been able to deny him full credit for one supreme achievement that was of crucial service to his country. The British Fleet was ready at the outbreak of the First World War.

It was ready as the result of three years of eager and imaginative work by the First Lord, urged on by the radical zeal and blistering tongue of his counsellor, Lord Fisher. Winston might spread his activities into many fields—Home Rule debates, the Trade Unions Bill, the continued defence of National Insurance, Land Values Taxation, Free Trade and all the other issues he had championed hitherto—but the Navy was his chief enthusiasm. It was well for the Navy that Winston had the overspill of energy to spare for these other causes, so that by his services for them he could purchase

141

acceptance of naval plans and estimates that would have been granted to no one else.

Although Lloyd George by his Agadir intervention had first roused Winston to study the foreign situation, the Welsh wizard had soon reverted to concentrating on matters of domestic policy. For despite their close friendship he had little sympathy with the younger man's eagerness to spend lavishly on the fleet. On social reform they had hunted together like a leashed couple, but now they drew farther apart. However, L.G. still maintained a judicial and seemingly detached support for Winston in the Cabinet, which modified the opposition to his naval projects of the more extreme pacifist wing.

Winston Churchill was one of the first British politicians to visualize the possibilities of aircraft and to anticipate their use in war. When the Royal Flying Corps was established in 1912 he promptly developed a naval wing, the Royal Naval Air Service, as a semi-independent arm. The first year's estimates for it were £141,150. For 1914 the initial estimate was £900,000. The result was that when war came our fleet and coastal defences had eyes in the air that proved invaluable for their effectual activity.

The Navy grew in size, potency and efficiency under Winston. He spent much time with it, going hither and thither in the Admiralty yacht *Enchantress,* and studying his charge at first hand. He had the German naval programme as his justification for his expenditure on it. When he spoke at the Lord Mayor's banquet at Guildhall on 10 November, 1913, he warned his audience that:

> "Next year it will be my duty—if I should continue to be responsible for this important department of the State—to present to Parliament estimates substantially greater than the enormous sum originally voted for the present year. . . . We shall not hesitate for a moment, once we are satisfied of the need, to go to Parliament boldly for the supplies of men and money which the House of Commons, whatever its party complexion, has never refused to vote in living memory for the vital services of the State."

He was as good as his word, and in 1914 he submitted the largest estimates for naval expenditure ever presented to the House of Commons up to that time. The figure was £51,550,000. (In 1931 the Naval Estimates were only £51,605,000—at the post-war value of the pound.) It would have been fully a million more, but Winston

FIRST LORD OF THE ADMIRALTY AND FIRST SEA LORD

Prince Louis of Battenberg, here seen in 1914 on Horse Guards Parade with Winston Churchill, was of German origin and bore a German title. As First Sea Lord he had shared with Winston Churchill the responsibility for keeping the Fleet mobilized up to the outbreak of war. This was not known generally, and his origin was enough to start against him ill-informed murmurings which led to his retirement.

had been forced to fight desperately in the Cabinet for his estimates, and eventually had to forgo the luxury of naval manoeuvres in the summer, thus cutting off the million they would have cost.

The summer came. Instead of the manoeuvres, Winston carried out a mobilization exercise, which involved putting not only the main fleet but the second and third reserve fleets—ships and men—on an active service footing. This exercise was timed for mid-July.

A lucky accident? Rather a remarkable piece of prescience, inspired by a watchful eye on foreign affairs, an attentive ear, and perhaps a stirring of that instinct which will sometimes warn a man of danger when he is moving in the dark. For in the spring of 1914, when the movement was planned, the sky still wore a deceptive morning brilliance, and relations with Germany seemed easier than they had been for long. But below the horizon a storm was lurking, marshalling its fury to sweep across the firmament. Even if there had been no pistol shot at Sarajevo, some other incident would have been found to loose the hurricane.

As it happened, the bullet of a Bosnian patriot, which struck down the Archduke Franz Ferdinand, heir to the Austrian crown, gave their cue to the military plotters of Berlin. The shot was fired on 28 June. Few foresaw that it might start a European war. Indeed, it was not till nearly a month later, on 23 July, that Austria used the assassination as a pretext for sending an ultimatum to Serbia, making demands that amounted practically to annexation.

But Winston had his ear near the ground. His test mobilization had culminated in a grand review of the Fleet at Spithead by the King on 17 and 18 July. After that the normal course would have been for the Fleet to have dispersed, the reserves to have gone home, and some well-earned leave to have been granted to the serving crews. Instead, on Monday, 20 July, the Press carried a notice, authorized by Winston after consultation with the First Sea Lord, Prince Louis of Battenberg:

> "Orders have been given to the First Fleet, which is concentrated at Portland, not to disperse for naval leave for the present. All vessels of the Second Fleet are remaining at their home ports in proximity to their balance crews."

For the next week, statesmen and diplomats were busy night and day all over Europe, some of them trying to stave off the war which could now be seen approaching, others carefully blocking the efforts of the peacemakers. On 28 July, Austria declared war on Serbia. Next day, Russia started to mobilize on the Austrian frontier. On 31 July, Germany sent an ultimatum to Russia calling on her to abandon her mobilization. On 1 August she invaded France and Belgium, in advance of any declaration of war, hoping to catch them napping. The British Government, more or less bound in honour to France through the Entente, and explicitly bound to the defence of Belgium, sent its ultimatum to Germany on 4 August, demanding her withdrawal from Belgium. By 11 p.m. that evening Britain, too. was at war with Germany.

The Germans had tried to rush matters at the last, for they pinned their hopes of victory on a swift and crushing blow that should finish off France before the Russians were ready. But whoever was surprised by their *blitzkrieg*, the British Navy was not: for Winston followed up his first order by issuing instructions on Sunday, 2 August, for the completion of naval mobilization. He did so without Cabinet authority: the Cabinet was still debating the issue of peace or war.

But Winston had passed beyond the debating stage. He saw the inevitable, and acted with characteristic impulsiveness on his vision. It mattered not at all to him that by his unauthorized action he jeopardized his whole political future. War was upon the country, and there was no longer room for argument. The national interest came first, as in the ultimate resort it always was to come first with Winston Churchill. The British Navy had to be ready for its duty. It was ready.

BACK INTO THE ARMY

In November, 1915, Churchill was commissioned a Major in the Oxfordshire Yeomanry and in this photograph he is seen in the uniform of this regiment. He was transferred to the Grenadier Guards and later promoted Lieutenant-Colonel in the 6th Royal Scots Fusiliers.

CHAPTER VII

WAR STATESMAN

MUCH ink has been spilt since 1914 in reviews of the origin of the First World War, and in efforts to apportion the guilt for it. By the Treaty of Versailles the Germans were required to admit their responsibility for the launching of the conflict. They signed; but ever since their apologists have exhausted their ingenuity in patching up arguments to show that they were innocent—that the Russians, the French and the British were the real plotters of the war!

We will not waste time over those arguments here. The common sense of the ordinary man always recognized, until befogged by this gas-attack of propaganda, that Germany and Austria started the war. They started it by declaring war and opening hostilities against Serbia, Russia, France and Belgium; and their war aims, published continually till almost the end of the struggle, showed their object to be the conquest and annexation of their neighbours' territory. Doubtless it is true that all men, and all nations, are sinners, and that errors by other Great Powers contributed to the international relations in which the war was born. Nevertheless, it is as plain as any fact of history can be that the war was actually begotten by German militarism.

Russia, maybe, included in her calculations certain gains she might hope to secure *if* a European war came, as there was always the chance that it might. But she was not prepared to start a war for the purpose. France muttered *"Revanche!"* when she thought of Alsace-Lorraine, but had no intention of loosing war to recover her lost provinces. Britain had in prospect no gain at all for which she could contemplate a war. War talk in Britain up to August, 1914, was entirely about the danger of suffering an attack, not the advantages of making one. Norman Angell's book, *The Great Illusion,* had a wide vogue, and confirmed public opinion here that war would be such an economic disaster to victor and vanquished alike that no intelligent person could conceivably embark on such a folly.

In Germany, however, other counsels prevailed. War was held in high esteem as the proper expression of national strength, and those responsible for the nation's policy were determined to secure at any cost certain prizes which could not in fact be gained without war. No doubt they would have liked their victims to give in quietly, so that war might change to a victory march: but, if necessary, they were resolved to use military force as their instrument.

THAT "PLACE IN THE SUN"

The writer himself spent the two years prior to 4 August, 1914, in Germany. Coming from peace-minded Britain, it was amazing to find that throughout the country, among students and professors, members of the governing classes, law, medicine, commerce, those who led or voiced German opinion were looking forward with unconcealed eagerness to the day of reckoning with Britain. Britain had that "place in the sun" which by merit should belong to Germany! Britain must yield place to Germany, if not quietly, then by force! To the mischief with Norman Angell and his commercial arguments! Germany had always made war pay. If Britain were foolish enough to fight, she would be crushed. In any event, she was doomed, for the future of the world belonged to Germany!

This seething belligerency had been taught to the nation by her military leaders (all the youth of Germany had to pass through the army), by her university professors, and by her popular writers. In 1914 Germany was agog for war. Admiral Fisher expected the crisis then, for the Kiel Canal would be ready for use. The German war party wanted it then, before the French law extending the service of her conscripts took effect. A further reason was provided by the swift expansion inside Germany of the Social-Democratic party, which threatened the power of the Junkers. A war—a victorious war, of course—would settle the governing classes afresh in the saddle. The summer of 1914 seemed finally the right moment, because England had her hands full with the Irish trouble. "England can't join in this war," said a member of the *Herrenhaus* (German Upper Chamber) to me on 2 August, 1914. "If she does, Ireland will stick a dagger in her back!" When I assured him that the Irish would rather fight the Germans than the English, he was frankly incredulous.

So the assassination of an Austrian Prince by an Austrian subject was seized on by the German warmongers, and worked up into a pretext for a campaign which was bound to bring Russia and her ally

France into the field. If Britain kept out at first, as Germany hoped she might, that would make the war all the simpler. With France and Russia crushed, the reckoning with Britain would be an easy affair.

Knowing what some of us knew at the time (and the world came later to know) of Germany's aggressive intentions, it seems incredible that anyone in Britain should have hesitated whether to support France from the outset, or whether passively to watch her destruction, knowing that Britain herself was marked down as the next, in fact, the chief victim. Yet not only in the country at large, but in the presumably better-informed circle of the Cabinet, men were actually divided in opinion as to the course Britain should follow.

DIVIDED COUNSELS

Those who had been watching the foreign situation with clear-eyed intelligence—Asquith, Grey, Haldane, Churchill—saw unhesitatingly that we must stand by France if she were attacked. Sir John Simon, John Burns, Lord Morley and some other Ministers were for peace at any price, and threatened to resign if we went to war. In the event, Burns and Morley did resign, but Simon, after some uneasy sitting on the fence, decided to leave his letter of resignation in his pocket.

Between these two extremes was a group, of which the chief figure was Lloyd George, who were prepared to fight in certain eventualities. They held that we were not definitely committed by the Entente to support France, though the naval and military understandings entered into with her might have morally involved us. In particular, we had undertaken the naval policing of the Channel and the Atlantic, while the French moved the bulk of their fleet into the Mediterranean. We must honour that arrangement unless Germany would guarantee to make no naval attack on French shipping or ports in the north and west. But the crucial issue was Belgium, which we were bound by treaty to defend. Would Germany pledge herself not to invade that country?

By her ruthless outrage on little Belgium, Germany settled the issue for Cabinet and nation alike. Britain might quite justifiably have gone to war in 1914 in self-defence, since if Germany had crushed France our own turn would not have been long delayed. She might have chosen war as an effective way of repressing a country that was becoming a powerful trade rival. She might, with a divided

AT MILITARY MANOEUVRES

In this photograph, Major Churchill is with General French who is in the foreground facing the camera. While in the army, Churchill prepared a valuable memorandum, which advocated the use of massed tanks, as a master weapon to beat machine guns and barbed wire.

mind, have fought because she had become entangled in secret understandings with the French. In fact, she fought for none of these things. The decision to fight was reached by the bulk of the Cabinet and by the all but unanimous voice of the nation outside, neither for gain nor for safety, but because we were pledged to the defence of Belgium, and must unquestionably honour our word.

On Sunday, 2 August, 1914, powerful voices were still demanding peace, and were publicly warning the Cabinet of bitter opposition to any attempt to plunge the nation into war. By Tuesday those voices had swung swiftly to the other side. Sir Edward Grey, the Foreign Secretary, had made on Monday a statement about the course of the negotiations and the vain efforts of this country for peace, which left doubts in very few minds where Britain's honour and duty lay. Ramsay MacDonald, it is true, still urged neutrality; but the Labour

Party which he led did not follow him here, and he resigned his leadership next day. Redmond, on behalf of the Irish, offered unhesitating support. "You may withdraw tomorrow every one of your troops from Ireland," he assured the Government. "The coast of Ireland will be defended from foreign invasion by her armed sons, and for this purpose armed Nationalist Catholics in the South will be only too glad to join arms with the armed Protestant Ulstermen in the North!" Bonar Law, for the Conservative Party, pledged their whole-hearted aid to the Government in the crisis.

THE BRITISH PEOPLE RALLIED AS ONE MAN

The fierce political strife, the dawning Irish rebellion, on which Germany had counted to cripple any war effort by Britain, were swept aside when the Huns crossed the Belgian frontier. The people cheered all along Whitehall, sang *God Save the King* and started to mob the recruiting offices in a business-like fashion. This was no predatory venture like the Boer War, but a fight for the liberty of small nations. The British people rallied to it as one man.

Winston, with his Fleet all ready and mobilized, opened the innings for Britain. The Navy, our first line of defence, was by far the most powerful in the world and the only arm always equal to meeting any foe. Our professional army was for its size the superior of any other fighting force in existence, but in numbers it was insignificant compared with the vast continental conscript armies. The German Kaiser had that much excuse for jeering at it as a "contemptible little army"—though he later had cause to regret that sneer, for the "Old Contemptibles," as they joyously dubbed themselves, taught the Germans to hold them in an anxious respect and very great fear.

The Navy's first tasks were four in number. Our island shores had to be guarded against any attempt at invasion. The German battle fleet had to be bottled up in its bases or destroyed if it attempted to come out and fight. The seas had to be swept clear of German naval and merchant craft. The British Expeditionary Force had also to be transported to France and protected in transit.

Britain's first blow in the war was struck by the Navy, when on 5 August, 1914, the German minelayer, *Königin Luise,* was sunk while on duty in the North Sea. The Germans knew well that their *Luxus-Flotte* was no match for the British Navy, and from the outset they relied on mine and submarine as their chief weapons. Our fleet patrolled the North Sea, trying to tempt the German Navy to come out and give battle, but without success. When on 29 August enemy cruisers ventured to attack our light craft nosing into the Heligoland Bight, Beatty came up with his battle-cruisers and sank the *Mainz* and *Köln*. After this the enemy was more cautious than ever. Lord Riddell recorded in his diary a jesting description by Lloyd George of Winston, as First Lord of the Admiralty, "like a dog sitting on the Dogger Bank, looking at a rat who has just poked his nose out of the hole at the other side of the water!"

All the oceans of the world were scoured for German craft, and hundreds of merchantmen were rounded up and made prizes. A hunt was made, too, for enemy cruisers, which were acting as commerce raiders. Winston himself made a special effort to catch the *Goeben* and *Breslau,* a German battleship and cruiser in the Mediterranean. But these vessels managed to dodge their pursuers and get to Constantinople, with disastrous results for us, as their menace proved a powerful argument in persuading the Turks to join with Germany.

EARLY NAVAL ENGAGEMENTS

The most formidable German naval force at large was her Pacific fleet. On the outbreak of war two of its cruisers, the *Königsberg* and *Emden,* wriggled into the Indian Ocean, where they sank a number of merchantmen, before the *Königsberg* was trapped in an East African river, while the *Emden* was caught and destroyed in November, 1914, off the Cocos Islands by H.M.A.S. *Sydney.* The remainder of the German Pacific Fleet, under Admiral von Spee, made its way down the coast of South America. Off Coronel it met and destroyed Admiral Cradock's British squadron of old and slow vessels—the worst defeat that the Royal Navy suffered during the whole war.

Von Spee's triumph was, nevertheless, short-lived. At Valparaiso he got orders—forged in Berlin, so the story goes, by a British secret agent on instructions from Admiral Sir Reginald Hall, the head of the Naval Intelligence Service—to attack the Falkland Islands. A British squadron was meantime sent off post-haste from Britain to the same rendezvous, and got there on 7 December, a day before von Spee. That was the end of von Spee. His whole squadron was sunk except the *Dresden,* which was caught and sent to the bottom three months later.

CHURCHILL VISITS THE SOMME BATTLEFIELD

In this group, taken in 1915, Churchill is standing beside General Emile Fayolle, Commander of the French Sixth and First Armies in the Battle of the Somme. In the following year, Churchill left the Army for good, since his command had disappeared with the amalgamation of the 6th Royal Scottish Fusiliers with another battalion.

Therewith all German naval craft outside their home bases were accounted for. The German High Seas Fleet stayed cautiously within the defences of Kiel and Heligoland, to the intense annoyance of Winston, who declared in a moment of intemperate boasting that if it would not come out to fight we should "dig the rats out of their hole!" He may later have somewhat regretted this extravagance.

The Navy's fourth task, the transport and protection of the Expeditionary Force to France, was faultlessly accomplished in the first fortnight of August, and Winston looked about him hungrily for other ways in which to advance the nation's war effort.

There was to his hand, a new and as yet untried weapon—his Naval Air Force. The military air arm, the Royal Flying Corps, had gone to France with the Expeditionary Force. Churchill talked things over with Lord Kitchener, who had to the great delight of the nation been appointed War Secretary by Asquith as soon as hostilities opened. On 3 September Kitchener agreed that the Royal Naval

Air Service should undertake the air defence of Britain. On the theory that attack is the best defence, Winston sent out raiding sorties to harass the enemy positions in Belgium and the Zeppelin sheds at Cologne and Friedrichshafen. He also sent a miniature expeditionary force of his own to Dunkirk.

During those early weeks of the war the military situation across the Channel was confused and unsettled. The Germans had swept round through Belgium and northern France, thrusting for Paris, and driving before them the French Fifth Army and the B.E.F. The Allies were pushed back step by step from Mons, from Le Cateau, past Villers Cotterets and across the Aisne, and ultimately beyond the Marne, where at last the German pursuit met with a fateful defeat, North of this sweep, wandering troops of German Uhlans were raiding up toward the Belgian and French coasts.

THE "DUNKIRK CIRCUS"

About the end of August, Winston dispatched a squadron of R.N.A.S. planes under Commander Samson, the "Captain Kettle" of the Air Service, to Dunkirk, to give air protection to the Channel from that side. Samson was a free-lance of immense energy and initiative. To safeguard his base from raiding enemies, he collected cars, put protective armour on them, and scoured the country. He rounded up German Uhlans and cycle troops, rousing the French and Belgians to rally against the invader. Reinforcements of Marines and Yeomanry were sent to join him, and his highly unorthodox force became known as the "Dunkirk Circus."

Trivial though it was in numbers, the "Dunkirk Circus" played quite a useful role in that opening phase of the First World War. Winston often went over to visit it and to witness its unconventional campaigning. Its raids harassed the line of communication of the German forces as they drove westward. Every hour of delay caused to the enemy in those critical days was a victory.

The Germans tried to restrict the operations of these restless armoured cars by digging trenches across the roads. Churchill promptly suggested that the cars should be equipped with portable bridges, which they could let down to cross ditches and trenches, and then pick up again. One such car was in fact designed and constructed. Thus the "Dunkirk Circus" helped to give birth to the idea of the tank, which was later to prove so important.

Other minds, too, were working in that direction from various angles. Colonel Swinton was pressing on the War Office his notion for an armoured vehicle on caterpillar tracks, to crush out machine-gun nests. The War Office dropped the idea after a few perfunctory tests. In December, 1914, Colonel Hankey, however, brought it before the Committee of Imperial Defence, and Winston saw at once how it linked up with his bridge-carrying armoured car. He set his engineers of the R.N.A.S. to work, and in March, 1915, without any Treasury sanction, he daringly ordered the construction of eighteen "landships." Mr. Balfour, who succeeded him at the Admiralty in May, promptly cut down the order to one. But that one was made, the landship H.M.S. "Centipede," and she was the mother of all tanks. She showed her paces at a trial demonstration before Lloyd George and Kitchener in February, 1916, and a few days later a hundred more were ordered.

Today the whole world is aware of the immense military value of the tank. But to Winston goes the credit for having foreseen its possibilities when the military wiseacres were shaking their reactionary heads, and for having taken the risk of ordering its construction on his own responsibility—a somewhat characteristic step, typical of Churchill, never afraid to trust his own judgment.

DEFENCE OF ANTWERP

A curiously perverse fate seems often to have dogged Winston's best achievements. Time and again he became the object of abuse for bold and imaginative strokes, which history was to pronounce to be deserving of high praise. If the "Dunkirk Circus" played a useful part in hampering the German sweep towards Paris, it did little to increase Winston's reputation. Its joyous filibustering seemed far too irresponsible for his credit as a reliable statesman. His defence of Antwerp was a stroke of vastly greater value to the Allied cause, for there can be little doubt that it saved the Belgian Army and the Channel ports, and made possible the British victory in the First Battle of Ypres. But at the time, and for long afterwards, it dragged his name in the mud, and was twisted by his detractors into a reproach and a proof of his reckless incompetence.

The Antwerp story is now fully recorded, but so slow is truth to catch up with misrepresentation that even today one may find people who, remembering only the slanders it once inspired, shake their heads at the mention of it, as an instance of Churchill's headstrong and costly folly.

The facts are these. When the German armies began falling back after the Marne the question where their northern flank would rest became of crucial importance. The Belgian southern army had been overwhelmed at Namur, but the main Belgian force had retreated to cover Antwerp. If the Franco-British armies could link up with it they would pen the Germans back into eastern Belgium. But if the Germans could crush it and sweep round on the north quickly enough they could hold all France down to the line of the Seine. The Channel ports of Dunkirk, Calais, Boulogne, Dieppe, Le Havre, would all have been lost to us, and our only lines of communication with the French and with our own B.E.F. would have had to run through Cherbourg, Brest and the harbours in the Bay of Biscay. A race northward for the coast began between the contending armies, while German forces began to smash at the Belgians covering the city of Antwerp, the strategic gateway to North-west Europe.

On 2 October Winston set off in a special train to visit the "Dunkirk Circus." Twenty miles from London his train was stopped and sent spinning back again. Kitchener wanted him. In the presence of Sir Edward Grey he told Winston that the Belgians were on the point of surrender. British reinforcements would take some days to arrive. Could Winston go to Antwerp and rally the Belgians to keep up the fight until help reached them?

COLOURFUL AND DRAMATIC ARRIVAL

Winston could. At midnight he set off again, this time for Antwerp. His arrival there was colourful and dramatic. An American correspondent on the spot described how his car dashed up to the hotel, and Winston, in the uniform of an Elder Brother of Trinity House, jumped out and charged through the crowded lobby with out-thrust hands. "It was a most spectacular entrance, and reminded me for all the world of a scene in a melodrama where the hero dashes up bare-headed on a foam-flecked horse, and saves the heroine, or the old homestead, or the family fortune, as the case may be."

Doubtless Winston thoroughly enjoyed the drama. But it was introduced, not for mere amusement, but for a purpose—to rouse and stimulate the flagging spirits of the Belgians. De Broqueville, the Premier, was stirred and impressed. The fight went on. Kitchener

156

sent out the Naval Division—three brigades without supporting arms —to help in the defence of Antwerp, and Churchill wired to Asquith, offering to resign his post as First Sea Lord, and stay on in command of the troops. He was in his element, for above all things he dearly loved a fight. Lord Mottistone, sent across by Sir John French, reported that when he got to Antwerp he found Winston in complete charge of everyone—King, ministers, soldiers, sailors: and that if only he could have been given 20,000 British troops he could have held Antwerp against all comers.

But he had only 8,000 men of the Naval Division—some of them young and untrained, and the Germans had brought up their heavy siege artillery and had begun to smash the ring of defences. Not until the siege of Stalingrad in the Second World War did generals conceive it possible to keep up a fight in the ruins of a great city when it came under devastating fire by heavy artillery.

BARRED BY A SHEET OF WATER

On 7 October the Belgian and British forces started to evacuate the town, and on the 10th the Germans entered a deserted city. Part of one brigade of the Naval Division was driven into Holland, where it was interned for the duration of the war; but the bulk of the Belgian troops, and what was left of the British, retreated along the coast. As they went they opened the sluices of the Yser, and flooded the country behind them. At Dixmude the pursuing Germans were faced by a sheet of water which barred their advance to the Channel ports.

Meantime the British, racing north to make contact with them, had got to Ypres, where a confused battle raged for weeks. The British line only just held, with cooks and batmen thrown in and no reserves at all left to support it: but it held. Had Antwerp fallen a week earlier than it did—nay, a couple of days earlier—the Battle of Ypres would have had a different ending and the Germans would have pushed on to the Channel.

Winston's dramatic soldiering at Antwerp badly damaged his reputation at home. Asquith was impatient of his readiness to desert the Admiralty for a military command, and his enemies put round the story that he had thrust himself into his mission to Antwerp against Kitchener's wishes, and was solely to blame for the dispatch of the under-equipped Naval Brigade on a wild and foolish errand. In fact, the mission was thrust upon him by Kitchener, who was responsible for the sending of the Naval Brigade: and Winston's personal work at Antwerp was of quite incalculable value to the subsequent course of the war.

The British do not show up to the best advantage when they are shaken by a spy scare. The suspicion of German or pro-German sympathies was roused from some base quarters early in the First World War to damn two men who had taken leading parts in making those preparations for her defence which saved Britain from calamity in her hour of peril—Lord Haldane, Secretary of State for War, and Prince Louis of Battenberg, First Sea Lord.

EXIT HALDANE AND PRINCE LOUIS

Though party strife was outwardly stilled by the war, party hatreds survived and worked their mischief throughout its course. They found a victim in Haldane, the man who had reformed the Army and the War Office and had done more than anyone since Cardwell to promote military efficiency. The Expeditionary Force was his idea, and its faultless planning was his work. But his political enemies remembered that Germany had once been called his "spiritual home," and that he had dined with the Kaiser. They pursued him with cries of "Traitor!" till they hounded him out of public life. Winston, a far more hated political figure, had given no such handle to his enemies, but he had a colleague, the First Sea Lord, Prince Louis of Battenberg, who was of German origin and bore a German title. Away with him! Was the fleet, our first line of defence, to be left in such treacherous hands?

Prince Louis had shared with Winston the responsibility for keeping the Fleet mobilized up to the outbreak of war—a step which saved us from the peril of a disaster akin to what the Americans were to suffer in more recent days at Pearl Harbour. But the mutterings against him grew swiftly in volume, and by the end of October, 1914, he felt his position to be intolerable, and resigned office.

Winston decided to take a very bold and hazardous step, which was presently to lead to his downfall. He recalled Lord Fisher to be First Sea Lord.

Fisher was still the most capable and dynamic figure in the higher ranks of the Navy, with an unequalled capacity for getting things done, and a fertile and inventive mind. Unhappily, he also had a long-standing feud with half the Admiralty, and a violent and tenacious devotion to his own ideas and plans which their merits were not always sufficient to justify.

Winston, too, had his own ideas and inspirations. In many ways the two resembled one another, particularly in their strong individuality, self-assertion and conviction of a mission to save the country. They were too much alike to run for long in double harness, for each was bent on taking his own course.

At first, however, they worked together as gamely as twins. One or other of them was continually on duty at the Admiralty, Churchill working till the small hours and Fisher rising early to take over from him before dawn. The plans for the destruction of von Spee's squadron off the Falkland Islands were among the first results of their co-operation. Only Admiral Fisher, with his immense drive and energy, could have driven the Devonport dockyard authorities to get the *Inflexible* to sea in time for that important operation.

Friction gradually developed as Fisher began to chafe at his subordination to a younger and less experienced man. At the War Office, Kitchener, a soldier, was in supreme command. At the Admiralty, Fisher, the expert, was subject to Winston, the greenhorn. He resented this extremely. The final cleavage came over the Dardanelles affair. Fisher was as ready as Winston for unorthodox ventures: but they had to be his own. He had a pet scheme for an attack on the German coast in the Baltic. He at one moment consented to the Dardanelles plan, but repented when he realized that it would interfere with the prospect of his own scheme being carried out. As Winston pushed ahead with the attack, Fisher's baffled fury mounted till it nearly choked him. Combined with his vexation at Winston's independent ways it finally provoked him into an explosive resignation which brought down not only Winston but the whole Government.

THE DARDANELLES CAMPAIGN

The story of the Dardanelles campaign is one of the most glorious and most bitter in the First World War. It was magnificent for the reckless heroism and steely determination of the men who took part in it: tragic for the blunders which dogged alike its planning and its execution. Historians have put it under the microscope. Their verdict is that it was a strategically sound conception; that it could and should have succeeded; that its success would have shortened the

CHURCHILL AND FISHER AT THE ADMIRALTY

In this contemporary drawing by S. Begg, Admiral Fisher is seated on the left. Fisher had been in retirement since 1910 but became Churchill's guide and mentor when he was First Lord of the Admiralty. He was recalled in 1914 at the age of 73 to the post of First Sea Lord. Strongly opposed to the Dardanelles campaign, he quarrelled with Churchill over

...URING THEIR STORMY COLLABORATION

Having largely created the British battle fleet, Fisher fought steadfastly against the risking of his beloved ships in attacks upon the Turkish and forts. He often threatened to resign but was persuaded to refrain until May, 1915, when he precipitated the fall of the Government. The drawing is reproduced by courtesy of the "Illustrated London News."

war by years. But some inscrutable destiny ruled that it should be frustrated by human frailty, hesitation and errors of judgment.

At the beginning of November, 1914, the Turks, awed by the menacing guns of the German battleship *Goeben* trained on Constantinople, entered the war on the German side. Turkey was in a very vulnerable situation, for Greece and Rumania were inclined to the French and British, and together with Serbia could isolate Turkey from the Central Powers. Turkey and the Balkans were a favourable ground for British operations, since the hilly country, where only small, lightly equipped forces could be deployed, resembled the Indian frontier regions where our troops had gained most of their battle experience.

Success against Turkey would also have brought in Bulgaria to our side, for she was still swaying between her ancient friendship with Russia and her recent quarrel with Serbia and Greece. Further, the defeat of Turkey would open the Dardanelles and give us direct access to Russia. Serbia was at the time more than holding her own against Austria, and if supported by a solid Balkan bloc, by Russia and by Britain, she could have begun the break-up of the "ramshackle Empire," whose diverse elements were so uneasily held together.

WHEN TURKEY WENT TO WAR

When Turkey went to war with us Winston proposed a combined naval and military attack on Constantinople. Lloyd George preferred the idea of a thrust up through the Balkans from Greece, with Greek and Rumanian co-operation, combined with another stroke in Syria that might cut off and destroy those Turkish forces which were assembling in Palestine to attack the Suez Canal. At the beginning of 1915 Kitchener also was favouring a stroke through the Balkans, and two of the ablest French generals, Gallieni and Franchet d'Esperey, were also advocating this course. Thus the strategic wisdom of a "backdoor" attack on the Central Powers had the highest expert support.

Russia was appealing to us for help against Turkey, which was attacking her in the Caucasus. But she would not hear of the Greeks getting to Constantinople, so the idea of a combined Balkan operation against Turkey fell through. Kitchener received an urgent appeal from General French for more troops for the Western Front, and decided that he could not spare men for a joint naval and military attack on the Dardanelles. He welcomed, however the notion of a naval assault. Fisher also expressed approval of the idea of forcing the Dardanelles with the Navy, while the Army launched an assault on Alexandretta. Old-fashioned, superannuated men-of-war could be used for the naval attack, and detailed plans for it were worked out by Admirals Carden and Sir Henry Jackson.

KITCHENER COULD NOT SPARE TROOPS

Since Kitchener could not spare troops and the Russians were clamouring for help, Winston urged this operation, though it was so much less than his original plan, and the Cabinet finally approved it. By this time Fisher was again in opposition, as he wanted all our battleships for an attack on Schleswig-Holstein—his latest scheme. He even tried to resign, but Kitchener, who wanted the Dardanelles attack, talked him round.

So a squadron of ancient battleships was dispatched under Admiral de Robeck, with our latest and most powerful super-Dreadnought, *Queen Elizabeth,* to support them at long range with her powerful guns. There was a successful preliminary bombardment in February, which destroyed the outer defences of the straits, and on 18 March the main onslaught began. Unfortunately our ships encountered an unsuspected minefield, and three battleships were lost and three more damaged. Admiral de Robeck broke off the engagement. The Turks and their German advisers were astonished. As we now know, they had used up most of their ammunition, and were thoroughly demoralized. Had the British fleet come on next day, it would have been almost unopposed. But it did not come on. After consultation with General Sir Ian Hamilton, who was observing for Kitchener, de Robeck decided to wait till the army could co-operate.

In vain Winston waited and pleaded for a fresh attempt. Kitchener was now disposed to send troops, and Admiralty opinion rapidly hardened against fresh purely naval attempts. Fisher insisted on the return of the *Queen Elizabeth.* Asquith, who was preoccupied at the time with certain private worries, could not be induced to give the matter his attention, and the whole enterprise hung in the balance for more than a month. That delay was fatal.

Kitchener sent out the 29th Division, but it was shipped in such confusion that it had to go to Egypt to sort out its stores and equipment. Eventually, on 25 April it made a landing on the Gallipoli Peninsula, along with the "Anzacs" (the name given to the Australian and New Zealand Army Corps). But the Turks had received by now the fullest advertisement of what to expect, and had heavily reinforced their position. The British force might have been ample in February or even in March. At the end of April it was too small to make headway. A month later, the dispatch of more troops was sanctioned. They arrived in late July—again too late for the growing strength of the defence. Even so, at one moment they almost won a decisive success: but the nerve of an elderly general failed at the critical moment, and against Ian Hamilton's instructions he ordered his men back, when an advance would have brought victory. At the close of the year, the costly and futile expedition was abandoned.

Before the evacuation was carried out, Winston left the Government. Long since he had been cast out of the Admiralty, when in mid-May the Cabinet was reconstructed as a coalition of Liberals and Conservatives.

A number of causes contributed to break down the Liberal Cabinet under which the war had begun. It had to bear the blame for all the mishaps and setbacks experienced by a nation entering on a gigantic conflict for which neither civilians nor soldiers were prepared. War did not turn them all into able warriors, and people sensed a certain amount of nervelessness and lack of grip, alike among some ministers with no talent for war, and among elderly and crusted minds at the War Office. There was the great "Shell Scandal," exposed by the *Daily Mail,* which printed Colonel Repington's account of our army's deplorable lack of artillery ammunition. The opposition press kept up a ceaseless sniping, despite the nominal party truce. But the dissensions of Churchill and Fisher, particularly about the Dardanelles venture, finally pulled down the pillars.

MORE TROUBLE WITH ADMIRAL FISHER

The Dardanelles brought to head the inevitable rivalry between Fisher and Churchill as to which of them should control the Fleet. Fisher regarded that as his special duty, and grew slowly frantic at the high-handed way in which Churchill, as First Lord of Admiralty, dared to issue orders for its use. Pinpricks can vex more than sword-thrusts. He said little. Inwardly he was boiling. Finally his rage boiled over.

On 15 May Fisher sent his resignation to Asquith. He then bolted himself into the Admiral's House, pulled down the blinds and refused to see visitors. McKenna managed to speak with him, but without success. Anyhow, McKenna was not best qualified to bring him to reason, for McKenna was jealous of Winston, his successor at the Admiralty. Winston pleaded with him by letter. Asquith ordered him in the King's name to stay on the job. The old man was immovable.

News of his resignation soon leaked out to the Tories. Bonar Law was informed by Fisher himself in a curious anonymous note. There can be little doubt that the Admiral hoped to get their support in his feud with Churchill, and to return to the Admiralty with a dominating status. He had made no secret of his differences with the First Lord. For some time past he had been dropping his terse and explosive notes—he was very fond of letter-writing—to friends in the Tory ranks, whenever he had a disagreement with his political chief. Detesting and distrusting Winston, the men who got these notes took it to be axiomatic that Fisher was right and Winston was wrong —a vain and headstrong fool who thought he knew better than the expert. So when Fisher resigned in protest against Winston's conduct, they felt that the cup of the Liberal Government was full. After consulting with his party colleagues, Bonar Law informed Asquith that the Conservatives could no longer support the Government in its present form.

Two days later Asquith announced in the House of Commons that a Coalition government would be formed: and a busy week was spent sorting out the new Cabinet. The Tories were adamant on two points. Haldane must go. Churchill must not stay on at the Admiralty. Fisher, peering round his drawn blind, could see his vengeance overtake the fellow who had dared to ride rough-shod over him.

CHANCELLOR TO THE DUCHY OF LANCASTER

Winston was offered, and accepted, the post of Chancellor of the Duchy of Lancaster—a sinecure without duties—virtually a ministry without portfolio. As Lloyd George afterwards pointed out, the degradation was needlessly severe. He might well have been returned to the Colonial Office. The Admiralty passed to Arthur Balfour.

Fisher now tried to cash in on his rebellion. He wrote another note to Asquith, offering to continue in office on his own terms, which

BACK IN ENGLAND AGAIN

*In March, 1916, Mr. Churchill was back in England and in this photo-
graph, he is riding in Rotten Row, Hyde Park, with Mrs. Churchill.
The same month, he appeared in the House of Commons to speak on
the Navy Estimates and in his speech was very critical of the work of
his successor and of the general sloth of British naval strategy.*

were those of complete dictatorship over the Admiralty. Churchill must leave the Cabinet. Balfour must not get the Admiralty, which must be given to someone who would be willing to act as Fisher's mouthpiece and henchman. There must be an entire new Board of Admiralty, and Fisher must have sole autocratic command of the Fleet and all its officers, as well as of all naval dockyards, shipbuilding, and civil establishment of the Navy. Asquith replied: "I am commanded by the King to accept your tendered resignation of the office of First Sea Lord of the Admiralty." It was the only answer possible.

A TIME OF BITTER FRUSTRATION

The months that followed were for Winston a time of bitter frustration. True, he was still in the Cabinet: but he was without a department or executive power. He wrote memoranda, setting out his views on war policy, but their source discounted their merits. The common impression was that he had made a mess of the Admiralty, and although the Gallipoli campaign was the sole responsibility of the War Office, people blamed him rather than Kitchener for the delays and muddles which dogged that ill-starred venture.

Presently his resilient spirit found distraction in a novel direction. The sight of a lady painting stirred him to try his own hand in this unexplored territory. He started with the paint-boxes of his children. As his speeches and writings had already shown, Winston had the artistic temperament—the passion to give in elegant and picturesque shape an expression of his ideas and perceptions. To this he now proved to be able to add a gift of really competent manual dexterity.

He was quite untutored: but before long he got advice from Lady Lavery, from Orpen, and from other professional artists. In the following summer, when Lavery was painting his portrait, his interest grew so keen that he spent some time working as a pupil in Sir John's' studio. His work has strength, quality and originality. Indeed, the time came when he exhibited his paintings in Paris, under the name of "Charles Morin." They were bought, too, by strangers who knew nothing of the identity behind the alias. One of his paintings, a remarkably chosen view in the Landes of south-west France, hung in the office of Earl Lloyd George's house at Churt, and the then Father of the House of Commons was fond of showing it to visitors and quizzing them on the identity of the artist.

When winter came, Churchill found his forced inaction unbearable. He was a soldier. He would return to the Army! The decision became final when in November, 1915, Asquith prepared to form a small War Council, and found the opposition to Churchill's inclusion too strong for him. In a letter dated 11 November, Winston sent in his resignation of his Cabinet post. "I could not accept a position of general responsibility for war policy without any effective share in its guidance and control," he wrote. "Nor do I feel able in times like these to remain in well-paid inactivity. I therefore ask you to submit my resignation to the King. I am an officer, and I place myself unreservedly at the disposal of the military authorities, observing that my regiment is in France."

He made one final appearance in the House of Commons on 15 November. In a powerful speech he reviewed his record at the Admiralty, dealing extensively with the story of the Dardanelles operation and the part he had played.

> "I did not make a plan. Not a line, not a word, not a syllable that was produced by naval and expert brains have I combated with the slightest non-expert interference. But I have approved of the plan, I backed the plan, I was satisfied that in all the circumstances that were known to me, military, economic and diplomatic, it was a plan that ought to be tried, and tried then."

For the subsequent military operations he had no personal responsibility. As for Fisher, the Admiral might have disapproved of the Dardanelles, but he never said so in Council, or offered any criticism of the definite method of attack proposed. Fisher in fact neither gave the clear advice before the event nor the firm support afterwards which Winston had a right to expect. Both Asquith and Bonar Law paid tributes to him. Bonar Law admitted that, starting with strong prejudices against him, he had learned to value his qualities. "In mental power and vital force he is one of the foremost men in our country!"

His swan-song sung, Winston left for the front. A few days later Major Churchill of the Oxfordshire Yeomanry disembarked at Boulogne. After visiting Sir John French at his headquarters, he was attached to the 2nd Grenadier Guards to gain some practical experience in the art of modern warfare.

CHAPTER VIII

MINISTER OF MUNITIONS

T HE formation of the first Coalition Cabinet in 1915 put an end to the incessant party sniping which had previously hampered the Government in its conduct of the war. It is doubtful, however, whether any other marked advantage accrued to the direction of the war effort. The new men who were brought into the Cabinet were little better qualified to wage war effectively than those they displaced. The squeezing out of Winston robbed the country of a far more potent personality for war, alike in his vigour, resource, initiative and military knowledge, than any who succeeded him.

The new Cabinet, like the old, consisted of twenty-two civilized, highly intelligent controversialists. Most of them were so saturated with distaste for war that they could not fling themselves whole-heartedly into the task of waging it. But if they could produce little initiative for war-making, they loved argument and discussion, and could pick holes in any plan with masterly skill. Asquith, the Prime Minister, was a benevolent and judicial chairman of this debating society. He himself rather recoiled from making decisions; so, as matters were never put to the vote, it is not surprising that decisions were deferred interminably.

As a result, the history of the years 1915 and 1916 is a dismal record of Government delay, nervelessness, muddle and indecision: of vain heroism and futile sacrifice on the battlefield, of blunder and incompetence in the Council chamber. Lloyd George pronounced the epitaph of 1915 in his speech on 20 December, when he defined its story in the words "Too late!" "Too late in moving here, too late in coming to this decision, too late in starting with enterprises, too late in preparing! In this war the footsteps of the Allied Forces have been dogged by the mocking spectre of 'too late,' and unless we quicken our movements, damnation will fall on the sacred cause for which so much gallant blood has flowed."

Tragically, that same story was continued into 1916. The "victories" of 1915 at La Bassée and Loos, which achieved next to nothing at enormous cost, were succeeded in 1916 by the bloody holocaust of the Somme campaign, with its six hundred thousand casualties. Here fell in vain the flower of Britain's manhood, those who should have been our national leaders in the succeeding years. In the next two decades British statesmanship and British social and political life were inevitably to be the poorer for such grievous loss.

THE WAR GOES BADLY

In the Balkans, an Allied force was landed at Salonika in September, 1915, too late to save Serbia or to prevent Bulgaria from joining the enemy. In Mesopotamia, 1916 saw the first British expedition collapse in the surrender at Kut. In August, 1916, Rumania was encouraged to declare war on Austria and was then left to be overrun and wiped out by the Germans in a three months' campaign.

In Ireland an extraordinarily stupid mishandling of the situation, by Kitchener and by the "Blimps" who were sent to conduct recruiting campaigns, succeeded in destroying the effect of Redmond's noble initiative, and at Easter, 1916, the Sinn Fein rebellion broke out. Thenceforward Ireland was a liability, not an asset, to the Allied cause and remained for seven years a scene of tragedy.

At sea the Navy played for safety. Balfour at the Admiralty was not the man to encourage any daring adventure. Jellicoe, oppressed by his heavy responsibility for protecting our island home, dreaded taking risks. The year 1916 saw the one big fleet action of the war, the Battle of Jutland. It was indecisive, because Jellicoe feared to force the issue. The Germans, however, thereafter avoided a repetition of the surface challenge and bent their energies to the submarine campaign. In that campaign they achieved marked success and, before the end of the year, the outlook for Britain was becoming dark and dispiriting, both on the land and on the sea.

Winston had no share in the responsibility for this wretched story. It is one of the ironies of the First World War that the soldier-statesman who by heredity, training, experience and natural capacity was better equipped than any other to take a leading part in guiding the nation's destinies in such a conflict was so early thrust aside and driven into semi-obscurity. The statesman was edged out of office. The soldier was firmly barred from all high command.

On his return to the Army in November, 1915, Winston spent a month with the 2nd Grenadier Guards. It is a curious illustration of

WITH DAVID LLOYD GEORGE

In 1916, Lloyd George became Prime Minister on the resignation of Asquith. Asquith disliked Churchill and blamed him for the failure of the Gallipoli campaign. The final findings of the Committee of Investigation appeared soon after the fall of Asquith but Lloyd George did not at first dare to include Churchill in his government. Above, Winston Churchill and Lloyd George are seen together in Whitehall in 1917.

the brevity of human fame that he, who fourteen years earlier had been the idol of the British public for his martial gallantry in the South African War, was at first viewed by his new mess-mates with sour disfavour as a "damned politician." The colonel greeted him with a long, cold silence, which he broke after half-an-hour to say: "I think I ought to tell you that we were not at all consulted in the matter of your coming to join us!" Another officer spitefully remarked to Major Churchill, "We want no politics here, you know!"

DISTRUST AND DISLIKE OF POLITICIANS

The Army had a profound distrust and dislike of politicians—an attitude that one finds faithfully reflected by Kipling, who soaked in their prejudices in boyhood. In Kipling's tales and verses, politicians are habitually sub-human meddlers. This cleavage between the military and the civil authorities was a repeated source of weakness to Britain all through the First World War. Without mutual confidence and complete frankness, there could be no full co-operation.

The suspicion felt by high officers for Winston the politician was not unmixed with curiosity. On one occasion this saved his life. A General summoned him to a rendezvous, where Churchill vainly waited for an hour. The General failed to arrive. He had in fact only wanted to encounter and to be saluted by that fabulous monster, a Cabinet Minister. But when Winston returned to his dug-out, he found that in the interval it had been wiped out by a shell.

The Commander-in-Chief had promised him a brigade : so after a month, spent in learning the ways of trench warfare, Winston asked Sir John French to fulfil his promise. But Asquith vetoed the appointment. He had developed an active dislike of his young colleague, and did not intend to let him climb up the rival ladder of military command. This attitude was somewhat surprising in one so generally fair-minded as Asquith, and it is hard to avoid the suspicion that he was subconsciously influenced by the antipathy which men often feel for those they have wronged. Winston had been made the scapegoat for the failures at the Dardanelles and at Gallipoli, for which, as history has shown, Asquith was really to blame. An instinct of self-defence may have bred in the Premier a conviction that Winston was not to be trusted with authority.

Sir John French was not able to press the matter further, for at

IN HYDE PARK WITH THE CROWN PRINCE OF SWEDEN

Winston Churchill is here seen watching a military review in Hyde Park in 1917 in company with the Crown Prince of Sweden. Although Churchill had left the Army, he still retained great interest in military questions, particularly in the proper equipment and arming of the troops overseas. His first-hand knowledge stood him in good stead.

this stage he, too, was removed from his post, to be replaced by Sir Douglas Haig. So Churchill only achieved the rank of a colonel in the 6th Royal Scots Fusiliers.

It was a cruel blow. The pathway to high military command was also to be barred to him. But Churchill was not the man to sulk, like Achilles, in his tent. He took up his new post with unquenchable high spirits. Trench warfare at that time could be a deadly dull affair. It was not dull for the Royal Scots while Winston was their colonel!

CHURCHILL AS A FIGHTING OFFICER

His first campaign was launched the day after his arrival. He announced to the assembled officers: "War is declared, gentlemen, on the lice!" Thereafter for days there was great work with thumb-nail and hot iron, till for the time at least the battalion was clear of those subtle vermin. He followed this domestic war with a shake-up of the offensive against the German trenches in front, making the night hideous with fusillades and barrages till the enemy were in a jumpy state of nerves, anticipating incalculable attacks.

He worked hard at his job. Three times a day he went round his front line, wearing a French steel helmet—his passion for bizarre headgear was growing on him—and cheered up his men or ordered a fresh spasm of "hate" against the enemy. Fearless of personal danger, he revelled openly in the hazards and excitement of battle. Before long his men came to adore him. His frank friendliness and warm interest in them, joined with his readiness to share their dangers and discomforts to the full, quite won their hearts.

His friends in London were less happy about him. Lloyd George openly mourned his loss. "Like a political Mrs. Gummidge, he still hankers after Winston," recorded Lord Riddell. Sir F. E. Smith (later Lord Birkenhead), the Attorney General, seized the occasion when Bonar Law and Lloyd George were visiting Paris in January, 1916, for a conference with the French, to slip over with them and look up Winston. This led to a grotesque incident. The Army G.H.Q. refused F.E. a permit to visit the front. One can almost hear the mutter of a choleric "brass-hat." "Some damned politician wanting to visit another! Certainly not!" F.E. went without a pass and the Provost-Marshal ordered his arrest. He was dragged out of bed at Winston's dug-out, and carted off ignominiously to G.H.Q., where he was placed in custody. Only the indignant protests of L.G. and

OFFICIAL VISIT TO FRANCE

On 16 July, 1917, Churchill became Minister of Munitions. While in this office, he paid many official visits to France in order to obtain first-hand knowledge of the requirements of the army and to ensure they were met without delay. He is here seen, during one of these official visits to France, having a talk with a British Army officer.

INSPECTING AN ARMS FACTORY

Before he had been in office many months, Churchill was questioning the steel consumption of the Royal Navy and was suggesting the reorganization of purchases from America. Above, he is searching out for himself details of an armaments factory. As Minister of Munitions, he did much to simplify the organization of his department.

Bonar Law saved him from compulsory deportation. The gem of the situation was that, as Attorney General, F.E. was the ultimate court of appeal for all court-martial cases, and thus the superior of those who sought to discipline him. The affair was another illustration of the Army Staff's ingrained antipathy to politicians.

In March, 1916, Winston revisited the House of Commons to speak on the Navy Estimates, and to urge greater energy in the task of new construction.

Unhappily he marred his speech by ending with what he meant for a generous gesture. He urged the recall of Lord Fisher as First Sea Lord. The generosity was characteristic. For Winston did not hug vendettas, and was quick to seek friendship with former antagonists. Though Fisher was the prime cause of his fall from office, Winston knew him to be capable of driving forward a construction programme more effectively than any man alive. The essential tact, on the other hand, was sadly lacking: for if there had been any possibility of Fisher's recall, it was destroyed by the fact that Winston proposed it. The Government could not adopt the advice on Admiralty organization of one who was popularly regarded as having left the Admiralty in disgrace.

Winston went back to his regiment. Here, too, frustration soon overtook him. In May his battalion was amalgamated with another and he was left without a command. Politics seemed to offer the only hope of a sphere where he could render outstanding war service. He returned to London.

Lloyd George's great fight for the introduction of compulsory service was just over when he arrived. All through the winter the Welshman had been fighting fiercely for this measure, not against public opinion, but against the opposition of his Liberal colleagues in the Cabinet—Simon, Runciman, McKenna—and against Asquith's indecision. Finally he carried his point with the aid of Bonar Law. Sir John Simon resigned, thinking the country would be with him in abhorring conscription. But he soon found that it was not, and to his bitter disgust his allies in the Cabinet sat tight.

THE BATTLE OF JUTLAND

Soon after Winston's return there was fought in the North Sea, on 31 May, 1916, the one big naval engagement of the war—the Battle of Jutland. It was a confused affair, because actual British losses were greater than those of the German Navy, our battle-cruisers under Beatty having borne the burden of conflict with the German battle fleet before our own battleships arrived. Also, the enemy were subsequently allowed to slip off before getting the full hammering that could have been given them. Both sides later claimed the battle as a victory: and we had this justification for our claim, that our fleet was left in command of the sea.

When the first reports from the battle came in, with their tale of British losses, Balfour, the First Lord, published them with philosophical nonchalance. No comment was added that might prevent the impression that we had sustained a major defeat. The effect on public opinion was most unfortunate. So the Chief Censor at the

177

Admiralty, Sir Douglas Brownrigg, hit on the bright idea of getting Balfour to ask Churchill to write a semi-official "appreciation" of the battle which would set the facts in their true perspective. Winston accepted the task joyously, and did it with gusto. Himself devoid of cunning, he probably never realized that this move had a double purpose. It gagged the most dangerous potential critic of the Admiralty, who with his inner knowledge of naval affairs could have exposed alike the folly of the Balfour communiqué and the weakness of the Jellicoe strategy and tactics.

DEATH OF KITCHENER

Hard on the heels of the Jutland affair, the country was plunged into mourning by the loss of Kitchener. On 5 June, H.M.S. *Hampshire,* taking him to Russia for a consultation with the military authorities there, struck an enemy mine off the Orkneys. This is not the place for a detailed estimate of Kitchener's work in the First World War. Some things he saw clearly, such as the probable long duration of the war. Some things he did well, such as the raising of the new armies. But despite flashes of insight and moments of greatness, he was in many ways a calamity as a War Minister. He could not delegate. He would not communicate. He had great experience, but not of the complex tasks of the War Office, nor of the need for working with his fellows in a Cabinet. After the Dardanelles campaign he seemed to lose his nerve entirely, and the nation's war effort floundered and halted in consequence.

Lloyd George, whom Asquith had first intended to send to Russia, had been kept back to deal with the situation resulting from the Easter rebellion in Ireland. He now inherited the War Office, a thankless post with shrunken and equivocal powers. In view of Kitchener's growing inertia, most of his authority had recently been transferred by Order in Council to Sir William Robertson, the Chief of the Imperial General Staff.

The Munitions Ministry, which L.G. left, was now running well and turning out goods in abundance. L.G. urged Asquith to appoint Winston to the vacancy, but the Prime Minister refused. His antipathy to Winston had not weakened. Montagu was moved across to Munitions. Winston was left to paint landscapes and make occasional speeches.

It was a soul-shattering position for him. The greatest war the world had yet seen was being fought, and Britain's part in it was being run far from well. Weak fumbling characterized the Government's handling of its many problems, for Asquith refused to face unpleasant facts and reckoned he had sufficiently disposed of them if he successfully glossed them over in a powerful speech. Yet Winston was condemned to be a mere spectator—

> "Like a sea-jelly weak on Patmos strand
> To tell dry sea-beach gazers how he fared
> When there was mid-sea, and the mighty things."

The war dragged on through the summer and autumn of 1916. Haig launched his big Somme offensive, with the preliminary warning of a vast and prolonged artillery barrage that left the Germans unharmed in their deep dug-outs, to pour forth and massacre our men when they advanced to the attack. After weeks of appalling casualty lists, Haig seized on Churchill's tanks as an expedient which might break the deadlock. Churchill pleaded with Asquith not to allow this petty and premature disclosure of the new weapon, before it could be used in mass formation and with decisive effect: but he pleaded in vain. The soldiers were permitted to play with their new toy, and used a handful of tanks for the first time on 15 September. Conditions were far from ideal, yet the effect was certainly startling, and rattled the enemy considerably. People read with delight in their papers next morning correspondents' accounts of the monsters, and an eye-witness's declaration that "A tank is walking up the high street of Flers, with the British Army cheering behind!"

It was just a local success. No real break-through was achieved. Haig and Robertson, who now and later controlled the use of the British forces, were men of great military efficiency and experience, but without strategic vision or genius. Their idea of waging war was to get a bigger army than the other fellow, fling it at his forces and overpower them (God being on the side of the big battalions) on the theory that if the two sides killed each other off, the bigger side would still have some men left alive at the end. This was the strategy of "attrition," and was openly advocated by them. It cost us millions of casualties, and nearly lost us the war.

At home, the shipping and the food situation were both growing more and more serious. The Cabinet could be brought to no decision on any topic. There was a babel of argument and counter-argument on every issue, ending in its adjournment for later review. Lloyd George had been girding and chafing at this aimless mismanagement for a long time. Finally, in December, he could stand it no longer. He demanded an Inner War Council, working full time, to determine war policy. Asquith rejected his proposals, and he resigned. Bonar Law backed him, and the Government broke up. Bonar Law refused the premiership, and Lloyd George had to take it over himself.

LLOYD GEORGE BECOMES PRIME MINISTER

Asquith had been confident that no government could be formed without him—especially as most of the other Liberal ministers promised him not to serve under any other Premier. But L.G. formed a strong ministry despite their non-co-operation. There were other able Liberals outside the ranks of the pledged Asquithians, and the Conservatives were under no pledge to Asquith. All the same, the strain of ensuring adequate support for the new Government was anxious and acute, and Lloyd George had at first to watch his step carefully.

Churchill suffered from that fact. L.G. wanted to bring him in, but some of his new colleagues would not have Winston at any price. The shadow of the Dardanelles and Gallipoli still lay dark across his reputation, and his energy and flashing intelligence were taken by them as so many symptoms of reckless and dangerous brilliance. L.G. pleaded with Bonar Law. "The question is," he urged, "whether, although you distrust him, he would not be more dangerous as a critic than as a member of the Government?" "I would rather have him against me, every time," replied Bonar Law, voicing perhaps less his own prejudice than that of his party.

The Second Coalition, as Lloyd George's Government was called, took charge at a time when the country was nearing the lowest point of its fortunes in the First World War. The Home Front was still unorganized. Ireland was in turmoil. The "attrition" policy of the military leaders in France had cost the British and French two casualties for every one inflicted on the enemy, and the flower of our nation had been slaughtered on the Somme. In the Balkans, Rumania had fallen. The King of Greece was intriguing with Germany. Russia was nearing collapse. We had been defeated by the Turks in Mesopotamia, and were menaced by them on the Suez Canal.

180

SPEAKING AT ENFIELD MUNITIONS WORKS, 1917

Although Churchill was now a Minister, he was not a member of the War Cabinet. He bitterly complained that although "not allowed to make the plans, I was set to make the weapons." He remained sternly critical of the conduct of the war by the War Cabinet and several times asked unavailingly to be informed about its war plan.

Worse was yet to come. In February the Germans launched their ruthless submarine campaign and proceeded to sink every ship, Allied or neutral, in the sea approaches to Europe. They calculated by this means to bring Britain to her knees in a few months, and at first it looked as if they would succeed. Sinkings rose astronomically; at one period one out of every four vessels that put to sea was sunk.

In March the Russian Revolution broke out. At first it was a revolt of the army commanders and progressive-minded statesmen in Russia against the utter corruption and ineptitude of the Tsar's misrule and that of the Grand Dukes. As such, it was welcomed in Britain as holding out a hope both of political reform and of increased military efficiency. But in fact, once the flood-gates of revolution were opened, those who had loosed the tide found themselves powerless to control it. One by one they were swept away, as all the forms of discipline and order dissolved and the nation drifted into chaos and anarchy and civil war. By autumn the central government had been gripped by the firm hands of Lenin and Trotsky, who had no interest in the national war with Germany: they thought only in terms of an international war of the proletariat against the capitalist. Russia ceased to count as an effective ally in the First World War.

AMERICA BECOMES A BELLIGERENT

On the other hand, Germany's U-boat warfare finally shattered the long patience of the United States, and in April, 1917, President Wilson announced that a state of war existed between the two countries. In the end, this change of partners—the gain of America to compensate for the loss of Tsarist Russia—would prove a good bargain, but for some months the military help forthcoming from the other side of the Atlantic was very limited and America was not to make the Germans feel her full strength for some time to come.

At home, too a new spirit of confidence stirred in the nation as the direction of the war was being more firmly handled. At long last, Britain began to be properly organized on a war footing.

Ministries of Shipping and of Food were set up. Agricultural production was tackled in earnest. Lloyd George and his inner War Cabinet sat continuously, giving immediate attention to each important issue and reaching prompt decisions upon it. The convoy system was introduced to deal with the new submarine menace and an Air Ministry was organized to make fuller use of the new weapon of war which the invention of flight had placed in our hands.

Unhappily, the new regime failed to exercise effective control in the military field. There Haig and Robertson had managed under the former Cabinet to establish their pontifical authority in matters of strategy. Though Lloyd George might not respect it, his colleagues did and he was unable to over-rule them. In consequence, the bankrupt policy of "attrition" still held the field, and reached its full horror in 1917 in the appalling crime of Passchendaele. Here Haig squandered half a million men in a futile effort to plough through a muddy swamp which in the whole course of the battle neither he nor his Chief of Intelligence ever troubled to visit and inspect.

If Lloyd George was not at first able to bring Winston into his new Government, he could at least do him one signal service. He published the Report of the Dardanelles Commission.

Asquith had steadily refused Winston's demand that the papers about the Dardanelles and Gallipoli campaigns should be published, and had finally side-tracked the issue by appointing a Commission to go into the whole matter, both of the origin and of the conduct of these campaigns. The investigation rolled leisurely on, and it was not until February, 1917, that the Report was finally ready.

REPORT OF THE DARDANELLES COMMISSION

The volume of evidence submitted to the Commission could not of course be published during the war, as it included matters of military secrecy. But the Report itself was not thus handicapped, and Lloyd George decided to publish it forthwith. Asquith protested strongly, and his protest was easy to understand when the document came before the public. For the Commission's conclusions were, in effect, a severe condemnation of Asquith's handling of the issue, and of Kitchener's yes-and-no attitude about the supply of troops. Winston's part in the affair, however, showed up by contrast as having been far from discreditable.

The Commission, hand-picked by Asquith and by no means composed of pro-Churchillians, admitted that Winston had expert opinion to support his proposal for a naval attack on the Straits, even if it was somewhat half-hearted, and that no expert voice had been raised in opposition. They judged that the amphibious operation originally urged by him was the right one, and blamed Asquith's War Council for not pressing Kitchener for the troops to conduct it—troops which in fact he later produced in a dilatory and ill-organized manner. The Report also condemned in strong terms Asquith's failure to call any meeting of the War Council between 10 March and 14 May—the period within which came the first belated military attempt on the Gallipoli Peninsula.

The publication of the Report was followed by howls of anger in certain quarters, particularly in the many powerful journals at that time controlled by Lord Northcliffe. "Impeach the Old Gang!" cried the *Evening News,* while the *Weekly Dispatch* suggested the Old Bailey. The influence of Northcliffe during the First World War on public opinion and on statesmen themselves was at times considerable, and not always beneficial. A man of violent likes and dislikes, he had immense personal ambition and aspired to the role of a king-maker. His dislike of Churchill was one of the hindrances to

47TH DIVISION MARCH PAST

At the end of hostilities 900,000 men were required for the Army of Occupation. These were selected out of the 3,500,000 men on the strength of the British Army. Mr. Churchill is here at the Grande Place in Lille in 1918, watching a march past of Allied troops before the problems of demobilization and occupation were settled.

Lloyd George's efforts to bring his friend back into the Government. But on this occasion his main attack was launched against Asquith and the late Lord Kitchener, who had been shown by the Report to be primarily responsible for the Gallipoli fiasco. Elsewhere, public opinion came reluctantly to recognize that Churchill was not so much to blame as people had been led or allowed to believe.

Winston's stock began to rise. It went up higher in May, when, at a secret session which he had persuaded the Government to hold, he gave a remarkably powerful review of the war situation and displayed his mastery of current issues. By 16 July, Lloyd George had been able to win Smuts' support and Bonar Law's acquiescence for the appointment of Winston as Minister of Munitions. His long exile from office was ended.

It felt good to be back in office again; but at first Winston must have thought somewhat ruefully of the proverb, "It is better to travel hopefully than to arrive!" For a departmental ministry no longer carried with it membership of the War Cabinet, which Lloyd George had reduced to an inner group of four or five men. Winston found himself in the irksome situation of having to co-operate in the execution of policies, for the framing of which he did not share responsibility. Still, he had his kingdom, and the Dundee electors duly returned him with a big majority over Scrymgeour, the prohibitionist, who alone ventured to contest the seat with him. Dr. Addison, his predecessor at the Munitions Ministry, moved on to take charge of Reconstruction Plans.

CHURCHILL AT THE MINISTRY OF MUNITIONS

There were plenty of problems for Winston. His Ministry had no long traditions. It had been built at top speed by Lloyd George two years before, and a large array of separate departments—some fifty in all—had clustered round their creator. Satisfactory enough as an emergency working arrangement in the early days, this uncoordinated collection of separate groups no longer functioned well when its central figure was removed and a stranger to the departments took his place. So Churchill set to work to combine and integrate them into an organic structure, in which the fifty groups were sorted into a dozen departments with a central committee over all.

Labour troubles supplied him with another set of problems. As the country entered the fourth year of the war, with victory apparently no nearer, war weariness became a growing danger. It was accentuated by food shortages and rising prices. A commission of inquiry into industrial unrest was appointed in June, 1917, and reported on 17 July—the day after Winston's appointment to Munitions. It advanced some fourteen recommendations about wages, prices, and the representation, organization and transfer of the workers.

By the summer of 1918 unrest among the workers had risen to danger level, and in July of that year a series of strikes broke out among munition workers. Most were settled quickly, but one at Coventry threatened to take a revolutionary character. It was no time for fumbling, for the war just then was looking its blackest, with the Germans again advancing on the Marne. With the backing of the Prime Minister, Winston gripped his nettle unhesitatingly. He told the munition workers that they could go back to work or be forthwith conscripted and sent to the front. The strike collapsed.

As Minister of Munitions Winston had the rich satisfaction of being able to produce in abundance the tanks he had taken so large a share in creating.

Tanks had been prematurely and inefficiently used on the Somme. They were fatuously flung into the mud of Passchendaele. Orthodox military opinion viewed them with grave suspicion and thought that they were of little real value—a low estimate which their poor showing in the Flanders quagmire tended to reinforce.

TANK ATTACK AT CAMBRAI

But at last, in November, 1917, they were deployed as Winston had always urged they should be, in the surprise mass attack at Cambrai. More than four hundred tanks swept upon the enemy, who broke and fled in disorder. Had there been troops to follow through and exploit the success, a great and perhaps crucial victory might have been gained. But those reserves were lacking: they had been sunk in the slime of Passchendaele. Presently the Germans recovered from their fright and came probing back, to find small and unsupported forces holding the area they had abandoned. They retook it, and Cambrai became the symbol of a lost victory. But Churchill went on turning out tanks. They had proved their possibilities and, at any rate, our armies now knew how to use them. Their day would come.

It came in the summer of 1918. That spring had seen Ludendorff's last great series of desperate offensives, which smashed back the British on the Somme and in Flanders, and then swung south to drive the French almost to the gates of Paris. In those months, from March to July, it looked as if Germany would yet win the war outright. Yet in little over three months more the Kaiser's armies were to scurry back towards their own frontiers and lay down their arms. In the military operations which brought about that swift transformation, tanks played a decisive part.

Their work began on 18 July, when Foch used a vast fleet of

186

"mosquito" tanks to lead his flank attack at Villers-Cotterets, which smashed the head of the German thrust and started the Allied counter-offensive. They reached their full glory on 8 August—the "black day for the German Army," as Ludendorff called it—when, on the Somme front, the British went over to the offensive. The German line crumbled under the stroke: the German Army never recovered its morale.

That attack was headed by four hundred and fifteen tanks, which broke through an enemy smoke-screen and blasted him into flight or surrender. "The nerves of our fellows could not stand the strain," said a German staff officer, explaining their defeat to the politicians at home. "They broke through our forward lines, cleared the way for their infantry, appeared at our rear, produced local panics, and broke up in confusion the system of battle control." Ludendorff frankly admitted that it was not the growing weakness in man-power of the German armies, but the incalculable menace of the British tanks, which reduced him to despair and made him insist on appealing for an armistice.

Happily for the Allies, the German High Command despised the tank till too late. Ludendorff preferred good old-fashioned cannon-fodder. His German soldiers must not learn to skulk forward behind iron monsters! Winston had an unorthodox preference for using steel to economize flesh and blood: he saved untold thousands of British troops from butchery on the battlefield by the tanks he turned out to smooth their pathway to victory.

Churchill's tanks were vitally important tools for the Allied triumph. But it was the reinforcement of the Allies' fighting strength through the advent of the American armies in 1918 which effectively turned the tide and gained the victory.

WHY GERMANY DISCOUNTED AMERICAN INTERVENTION

When the United States entered the war in April, 1917, the German High Command did not take this new adversary very seriously. Ludendorff knew how totally unready the Americans were, and reckoned on finishing the war before they could intervene in force. For some time it seemed that he had calculated correctly: it was nearly seven months after America's declaration of war before her first division entered the front line, and her organization of equipment for her troops was even more chaotic and inefficient than that

187

of Britain had been before Lloyd George's creation of the Ministry of Munitions. When Ludendorff's great offensive was launched in March, 1918, there were about 300,000 American troops in France, of which a third were non-combatants. Only four American divisions were sufficiently trained and equipped for use in the battle-line.

DEFEAT OF LUDENDORF'S LAST OFFENSIVE

At that time the French and British forces, wasted in the fatuous strategy of "attrition," were outnumbered by the Germans, who had been able, now that the Russians were knocked out, to bring large formations from the Eastern Front. Lloyd George made an urgent appeal to President Wilson to send over all the men he could. Britain would provide shipping, arms and equipment. A plan for dispatching 300,000 a month was agreed upon and carried out. There were two million Americans in France when the Armistice was signed in November. It was their presence as a reserve, even more than their actual fighting contribution—considerable though this was—that enabled Foch and Haig to venture their full forces in the big offensives which finally crumpled the German line and flung it back in defeat.

Those were busy days for Winston at the Ministry of Munitions. The German break-through in March cost us a heavy loss of equipment. Our Chief of Staff estimated that we might have lost a thousand guns. Winston was able in a day or two to promise two thousand in their place, along with all spare parts, ammunition and so on. In a very short time he had more than made good all the losses in munitions and stores inflicted by the enemy.

But the arrival of the American troops in their hundreds of thousands placed a bigger strain on his Department. It became his job to furnish all equipment of which they were short, including the whole of their requirements in medium artillery. It was a job after his own heart : not for nothing was he half an American by birth. He established the most cordial relations with his opposite numbers in the States, so that the British and Americans shared one another's stores—to use his own phrase—"as easily as two friends might share a luncheon basket!" His work in this field was monumental, and did very much to promote the good fellowship and effective co-operation of the two nations during the closing phases of the war.

His position as Minister of Munitions gave Winston a good

excuse for indulging in his passion for experiencing the thrills of battle. It was obviously important for him to know at first hand how the goods he provided were doing their work, and what else might be wanted. So he would "flip" over to France, day after day, in an aeroplane, and visit Headquarters or call on the troops in the line. He would even watch the fighting from an observation plane, patrolling above no-man's land. The French Government presently furnished him with headquarters at the Château of Verchocq, to which he would fly after a morning's work at the Ministry. Then he would go on to watch the fighting: he saw nearly every major battle in France during this period.

Though he was not a member of Lloyd George's Inner War Cabinet, the friendship between the two men grew closer than ever in those strenuous days. The Premier talked over all his problems with Winston, and got the full benefit of his advice and his alert, quick-thinking mind. Together they had entered on the war. Together they saw it end. On the evening of 11 November, 1918, while the streets of London were jammed with delirious mobs, Winston and his wife drove down Whitehall amid their deafening cheers to join Lloyd George for dinner at No. 10 Downing Street. Grievously though Churchill had been buffeted by fate and fortune, he finished the voyage in triumph at the end.

WITH SIR HENRY WILSON ON THE RHINE

In 1919, Churchill became Secretary of State for War. In this photograph, he is on the Rhine, inspecting troops before their demobilization, in company with Sir Henry Wilson, Chief of the Imperial General Staff. Wilson did not altogether approve of Churchill's appointment and his comment in his diary was only one word—"Whew!"

CHAPTER IX

BACK TO THE TORIES

THE two decades which followed the signing of the Armistice in 1918 were an unhappy period of turmoil and uncertainty. People were groping in a strange new world. The familiar political alignments had been broken up. The old economic formulas no longer worked. Traditional social customs and moralities had lost their binding force. The confident assurance of the Victorian age had long ago vanished, and men wandered, afraid and bewildered, into an uncharted territory.

Bankers wanted to restore the Gold Standard. Exporters dreamed of recovering the former world markets for their goods. Manufacturers for the home market revived their schemes for protective tariffs. Politicians hankered after the old two-party duel of Liberals and Tories. Employers wished to check the growing independence of labour. Abroad, Americans sought to recover their old isolation from Europe and its quarrels. The French aimed at the economic devastation of Germany; and the newly constituted states of Central and Eastern Europe showed an imperialistic greed for territories and a repressive tyranny over minorities and subject races, copied from the bad features of old autocracies.

Those who might have led the march forward were frustrated by all these reactionary tendencies. Their plans miscarried. Their policies were broken off long before they reached fruition. In short, the post-war years became a graveyard for the hopes of mankind, littered with broken ideals.

In Britain the end of hostilities was the signal for a General Election. The old Parliament, elected in 1910, had already outlived its legal span by three years, having been prolonged to avoid holding an election in the middle of war. The Prime Minister felt, not unnaturally, that before setting out to conduct the peace negotiations, or engaging in the big tasks of domestic reconstruction, he ought to have a mandate from a chamber truly representing the national will on these issues. Besides, the Representation of the People Act had been passed in the spring of 1918, widely extending the franchise and giving votes to women. There was impatience to put this reform into practice.

These were, in fact, excellent reasons for holding the election without delay. But the event showed that this haste was disastrous. A moment when the Armistice shouts were still echoing round the country was not one to expect a balanced and considered judgment on post-war issues. Alike in the way in which it was fought and in its results, this election proved the first of a series of post-war calamities.

Lloyd George himself was fully occupied in conferences with the Allies and in preparations for the peace negotiations. The business of the election he left to the "whips" and to the party machinery. While the Conservative party machine supported the Government, that of the Liberals remained with Asquith in opposition, and the Labour Party resumed its independence. So, though the Coalition Liberals improvised an emergency machine, the Conservative Central Office was the dominant organization on the Government side—a fact of which Sir George Younger, its astute chairman, took full advantage.

GENERAL ELECTION OF 1918

The Government, being a coalition with no approved party programme, appealed to the country on its war record and its purpose to effect peace and reconstruction. It asked candidates, whatever their party, to pledge their full support to Lloyd George and his administration. L.G. stood for the moment on a dizzy pinnacle of popular acclaim as the "man who won the war"; and it was arranged that letters of commendation, signed by him and Bonar Law, should be sent to approved candidates. Younger saw to it that most of these "coupons" went to Tories. Of four hundred and seventy-one issued, three hundred and twenty-two were given to Conservative candidates.

In the existing state of popular feeling, the "coupon" was all but a guarantee of election for its recipient. The Coalition scored a sweeping majority—roughly three to one, or, if the Sinn Fein Irish members are omitted, nearly five to one over the rest. The Liberal Party was hopelessly split. Great parliamentarians such as Asquith disappeared, and the newcomers to the House were described by a discerning spectator as a gang of hard-faced men who looked as if they had done well out of the war. Such a body was hardly likely to

ROYAL TANK REGIMENT IN GERMANY

A leading part in the evolution of the tank was played by Churchill, and he was also very largely responsible for inspiring the idea of the armoured car. He is here inspecting some British armoured cars shortly after the close of the First World War in 1918.

display the vision, balanced judgment and unselfish purpose needed in the architects of a new Britain.

At the Ministry of Munitions the Armistice was the signal for closing down war production. Plans for this had been worked out in advance, and were set smoothly in motion. Meanwhile Winston looked round impatiently for a more promising post. Indeed, he demanded one from Lloyd George in rather threatening fashion!

Dundee returned him to Westminster with a sweeping majority, though in the course of the election campaign he suffered, like his chief, from the mob frenzy of the moment, which expressed itself in frantic demands for hanging the Kaiser and making Germany pay. Unhappy concessions were made to that mood, though both Lloyd George and Churchill shrewdly surmised that the hope of recovering any substantial payment from Germany was remote—as, in fact, it later proved to be. But what was the strength of shrewd common sense against a popular demand backed by the weighty pronouncements of leading bankers and reputed economic experts? Not for the last time in the post-war period did those so-called "experts"

COLONIAL TROOPS MARCH THROUGH LONDON

In this photograph, taken in 1919, Mr. Churchill is watching Colonial troops march through London. Field-Marshal Haig is on his left and next to him is Field-Marshal Plumer. King George V is taking the salute. Queen Mary is seated behind Churchill, and behind her to the right is the Prince of Wales.

lead the country into economic folly and disaster. A dozen years later they were to do it again.

The election over, Winston was promoted to the War Office, with which he combined the Air Ministry. He would have liked the Admiralty, but the War Office was the more critical job, with the problem of military demobilization immediately ahead.

Here, too, the plans had been worked out on paper. On paper they seemed excellent. The "pivotal men" for industry were to be released first, so that the wheels of industry could be promptly restarted; the remaining men were to be absorbed by it as they in turn were released from military service. But the planners had forgotten human psychology. The "pivotal men" were in general the latest conscripts, not those with long battle experience behind them. Men who had been years "in the line" were not going to tolerate the newest recruits getting out the Army ahead of them. There was very nearly mutiny. Men who had come home on leave flatly refused to return to the Continent, and riotously besieged the War Office. Troops abroad swarmed into Calais, demanding to be taken home, and got completely out of hand. This was the situation which Winston found awaiting him when he took over his new office.

As usual, he acted promptly. A bare fortnight after his appointment he had completed consultations with the military authorities and with the Prime Minister. Fresh orders were issued abolishing the old plan and giving first release to the men with longest service and to those with most wound-stripes. An army was still needed for the occupation of Germany, and this was made up from the newer recruits, reinforced by the sixty-nine "Young Soldier" battalions of the 18-19-year-olds, who had been training in Britain when the fighting ended. Serving soldiers retained in the Army of Occupation were given extra pay and bonuses to gild the pill.

These new orders allayed all the discontent, and within the next six months some three million men were demobilized without further trouble. Not a few of them, indeed, were but a short time back in civilian life before they began to think with regretful longing of the army life which they had been in such haste to leave!

ADVENTURES IN THE AIR

Those who cherish a conviction of Churchill's preservation through his adventurous career being ordained by Providence, so that he might become the leader of this country in its darkest hour and carry it on to victory, can find ample evidence to support their belief in his numerous hairsbreadth escapes from death while flying, He ought to have been killed a dozen times. That he survived suggests very strongly that Providence had further use for him.

He had a passion for flying—for its risk and adventure. As First Lord of the Admiralty before 1914, when aviation was in its infancy, he could not keep away from the primitive flying-machines of the time. A seaplane in which he was travelling broke down. It floated. He was towed to shore in it, and flew on in another machine. Another seaplane once took him on a trip from which he left it by a tug to hurry back to London. There he heard that on its further flight it had perished with all hands. Asquith was vainly entreated to keep his First Lord from killing himself in these reckless adventures in the air.

As Minister of Munitions, Winston was constantly in the air, flying to and from France. He began to pilot his own machine. Planes, when compared with present-day aircraft, were then gimcrack contraptions. One crashed as he was taking off; another caught fire in the Channel. Yet another broke down over the water, and he barely managed to glide as far as the beach. His last attempt to pilot himself was in 1919, when he crash-landed at Croydon. Even then he escaped unhurt, though the airman with him was badly injured. The accident put him out of conceit with piloting, but not with flight. No statesman has made more various and persistent use of aircraft, nor to greater purpose, than Winston Churchill. From the First World War onward the plane was to be his favourite conveyance for foreign travel.

MILITARY COMMITMENTS IN RUSSIA

One of the tasks which Churchill inherited at the War Office was that of clearing up the situation in regard to military commitments in Russia. His activities in this field are held by many, not without reason, to have been the most ill-advised in his career. Certainly he paid the penalty for them in political discredit at the time, and in lasting suspicion and animosity thereafter in certain quarters.

At the time of her revolution Russia was our ally in the war against Germany. The first revolutionaries continued that war, and when the nation became split into factions, and the Bolsheviks gained control of the central government, some of the factions were still anxious to continue that fight. The Allies naturally encouraged them to do so, and Britain, which during the Tsarist régime had been pouring munitions into Russia via Murmansk, Archangel and Vladivostok, continued to send them. But after the Bolsheviks signed the Treaty of Brest-Litovsk with the Germans in March, 1918, an immediate danger arose that the two million tons of military stores we had heaped up at Murmansk and Archangel, and the further vast dumps at Vladivostok, might fall into German hands.

British troops were dispatched to protect these stores and either to bring them away or to effect their delivery into the hands of those groups of Russians who were still keeping up the fight against the Germans. At that time, though Lenin and the Bolsheviks were in power in the capital, none could foretell if they would endure, or be displaced by another turn of fortune's wheel. The White Russian armies of General Anton Ivanovich Denikin and his Cossacks in South Russia, and Admiral Alexis Kolchak in the east, with the

196

WITH GENERAL DIAZ AND FIELD-MARSHAL HAIG

On 23 October, 1919, General Diaz visited England and was met by Churchill and Lord Haig (who is standing next to General Diaz). After the Battle of Caporetto in 1917, Diaz became Commander-in-Chief of the Italian Armies and Austria's final defeat was largely due to his skill. Above, the arrival of Diaz at Victoria Station.

Czecho-Slovak brigade, were still active and forceful against German and Bolshevik armies alike.

By 1919, when Churchill arrived at the War Office, the war with Germany was over, and there was no further justification on that score for supporting these pro-Ally factions. Should the Allies continue to support them against Lenin and the Bolsheviks? Churchill grew eager to do so, and pressed the Allied Supreme Council for authority. Lloyd George was opposed to such a policy, for he held that nations must be left free to settle their own form of government, and that if Russia chose Bolshevism, we must try to establish friendly relations with it. He banned absolutely any military intervention, and ordered the withdrawal of the British garrisons in Russia. But the Supreme Council had consented to arms and money being furnished to Deniken and Kolchak, and Churchill proceeded to pour credits

197

TANK INQUIRY AT LINCOLN'S INN

Shortly after the end of the First World War, a Tank inquiry was held at Lincoln's Inn. Churchill is seen in the witness box. In this inquiry it was emphasized that it was largely owing to the courage and driving force of Winston Churchill that the idea of a tank as an instrument of warfare was converted into practical shape.

and munitions into anti-Bolshevik Russia to a nominal value of nearly a hundred million pounds.

Deniken was defeated. Kolchak was defeated. The British garrisons at Murmansk and Archangel had definitely to be withdrawn. Churchill was advised that it would be necessary to send out a covering force to secure their withdrawal. He called for volunteers, and thereby roused a widespread suspicion that he aimed at plunging the country into war with Russia. His inclination that way was well known. However, he raised and sent out a force of 8,000 men, which effected a diversion and secured the evacuation of our troops.

If Lloyd George had not forbidden him to do so, Winston would have dashed across to Russia to inspect the situation. The Prime

Minister feared, perhaps, that once on the spot his pugnacious War Minister might take the bit between his teeth, repeat his Antwerp activities, and conduct a vigorous campaign against the Bolsheviks!

Winston's attitude to Russian affairs, and his eagerness to carry on the war there, did much to damage his reputation, still smirched in the public view by the legends of Antwerp and the Dardanelles. Left-wing Labour, which looked on the Bolsheviks, despite their barbarities to the aristocracy, the Church and the bourgeoisie, as champions of the worker and the under-dog, denounced Churchill as a reactionary enemy of the proletariat. Even those on the Right, who shared his views about Bolshevism, were angry with him for trying to involve the country in another war, just when it was settling down again to peace. Winston could no doubt argue a powerful case for his attitude; but the instinct and common-sense of the nation were opposed to him. It was not Britain's business, they felt, to impose a particular set of rulers on the Russian people, regardless of their wishes.

MODERATE TERMS OF THE VERSAILLES TREATY

During the first half of 1919 the Paris Peace Conference was drafting the peace terms for Germany, embodied in the Treaty of Versailles. That Treaty was eventually signed in June, and, considering the speed with which it was drawn up and the atmosphere of passion still prevailing among the belligerent nations, it was in the main a quite remarkably fair and reasonable settlement. A time was to come later on when German propaganda would direct an incessant stream of abuse and denunciation against the treaty, and promote a flood of criticism against it from every angle and through many well-camouflaged channels. It is scarcely surprising that the ordinary man then began to repeat parrot-fashion what he so constantly heard: that the Versailles Treaty was a monstrous document, responsible for all the ills in Europe.

In fact, its terms were so moderate that the British House of Commons, pledged though it was to unflinching loyalty to Lloyd George, grew rebellious under the impression that he was letting the Germans off too lightly. He had to dash back from Paris in the middle of the negotiations to defend himself. So much for the pledges of the "hard-faced men"!

The one major defect of the treaty was that it provided for an

ARMY OF OCCUPATION: CHURCHILL INSPECTS

*In January, 1919, Mr. Churchill said, "The new Armies of Occupation
will begin forming from 1 February and it is hoped that in three months
they will be completely reorganized." He stated that volunteers for one
year's service at a time would be accepted from men who were eligible
for release if they were physically fit. "In particular," he added, "69*

TROOPS OUTSIDE COLOGNE CATHEDRAL, 1919

attalions of young soldiers of 18 years of age and upwards, who are
ow at home, will be sent at once to help guard the Rhine bridgeheads."
his new policy helped to demobilize the men with longest service and
layed a good deal of discontent. Above, he is inspecting some of
he troops paraded on Cathedral Square at Cologne in the Rhineland.

unspecified total of reparations payments by Germany—a provision which was to lead to prolonged economic chaos on the Continent. The defect was inevitable, since the only figures to which the French and Belgians would have consented were fabulous and impossible, and the one way to sidetrack that folly was to leave the total for later settlement when the difficulties of extracting money across a frontier had been learned by practical experience. None the less, the delusive hope of "making Germany pay," sustained by this part of the treaty, was later the cause of the French invasion of the Ruhr and of Germany's currency collapse, of fatuous war-debt settlements, and finally of the great economic depression and the rise of Hitler.

The treaty settled the new map of Europe on the basis of giving independence to the various nationalities. It set up the new or revived Succession States of Poland, Czecho-Slovakia, Austria, Hungary, the Kingdom of the Southern Slavs (Yugoslavia), Estonia, Latvia, Lithuania; it restored Alsace-Lorraine to France and gave the Trentino to Italy. On the whole, the new frontiers drawn at the Peace Conference were as fair and appropriate as the tangle of races on the Continent permitted. Here and there strategic or economic considerations modified the strict racial principle, as when Italy was given the South Tyrol with a frontier on the Brenner, or the Saar was detached from Germany and placed under League of Nations control for fifteen years, in the hope of assimilating it to France. Germany's colonial possessions were taken away, as were the Arab territories held formerly by Turkey. Most of them were placed, as mandated territories, under the guardianship of one or other of the victorious Allied Powers.

COVENANT OF THE LEAGUE OF NATIONS

The part of the treaty on which rested the highest hopes was the Covenant of the League of Nations. All nations were henceforward to consult together to keep the peace, and act jointly to stop aggression. The League would adjust frontier problems, revise obsolete treaty provisions (including any in the Treaty of Versailles itself), protect minorities, promote economic co-operation and clear away social evils and abuses. Had the League in fact done what was entrusted to it, the world might have been on the high road to Utopia. Unhappily, the U.S.A., whose President, Woodrow Wilson, had made himself the arch-priest of the League, refused to ratify the

AT NUMBER 10 DOWNING STREET

Above is a group taken at Number 10 Downing Street on the occasion of a luncheon given in 1922 to M. Raymond Poincaré, French Prime Minister from 1922 till 1924. Sitting in the front row, reading from left to right, are:—Mr. Winston Churchill, Earl Balfour, M. Poincaré, Mr. David Lloyd George and Marshal Philippe Pétain.

treaty or to join the new world order. That withdrawal hamstrung the whole scheme. Without America no resolute joint action by the other Powers could be assured. So the new Palace at Geneva became, not the hub of a world order, but a hotbed of national rivalries.

Another international body set up by the peace settlement had a happier fate—the International Labour Office. While the truncated League reeled and staggered through the following years until after two decades it finally collapsed, the I.L.O. jogged quietly along. It built up an understanding among the industrialists and workers of different countries and, moreover, secured a measure of American co-operation denied to the League. During the Second World War the I.L.O. took refuge across the Atlantic and later affiliated to the United Nations Organization.

MR. AND MRS. CHURCHILL IN THE EARLY 'TWENTIES

In 1922, Churchill resigned his post as Secretary for the Colonies after holding it for a year and nine months. He was then out of office for two years before becoming Chancellor of the Exchequer in 1924. In the photograph above, he is seen with Mrs. Churchill in 1923.

The Versailles Treaty was warmly welcomed by all parties in Britain, though doubts were expressed by some about the reparations clauses, and about the provision for trying the Kaiser in London. In the event, we hardly got any reparations from Germany, as practically all she nominally paid was financed out of loans advanced to her by her former foes under the Dawes and Young schemes. Neither was the Kaiser ever brought to trial.

Indeed, the succession of disasters which befell the world in the years between 1919 and 1939 was due, not to the defects in the Versailles Treaty, so much as to the failure of statesmen to live up to its principles and carry out its conditions. It was faulty, of course; but it was a courageous and imaginative attempt to build a just and peaceful world society.

When the peace terms had been settled and our troops were withdrawn from Russia, the War Office palled on Churchill. The visible future held out no prospect of new wars. The tasks at the moment were those of peace. So when Lord Milner resigned his post as Colonial Secretary at the beginning of 1921 Winston moved across to succeed him.

Peace-making was in fashion, and he found a job of peace-making awaiting his attention in the Middle East. Here the Arabs of Mesopotamia, of which Britain held the mandate, were restless and dissatisfied. He promptly went east, true to a life-long preference for going to deal at first hand with any situation, instead of sitting in a Department reading and writing memoranda about it. In Irak he added T. E. Lawrence to his train, and that strange self-torturing genius, with his intimate knowledge of the Arabs and their ways, helped him to achieve a satisfactory settlement at a conference in Cairo. He appointed the Emir Feisal as ruler of Irak, and cut the heavy expense of the British Army there by the novel plan of policing the country with an Air Force. Thereby he reduced our bill for keeping order in Irak from forty million pounds to five million pounds a year!

Lawrence notes in *The Seven Pillars of Wisdom* that:

"Mr. Winston Churchill was entrusted by our harassed Cabinet with the settlement of the Middle East; and in a few weeks, at his conference in Cairo, he made straight all the tangle, finding solutions fulfilling (I think) our promises in letter and spirit (where humanly possible) without sacrificing any interest of our Empire or any interest of the peoples concerned."

205

ON HOLIDAY WITH HIS SON IN ITALY

Churchill is seen here with his only son Randolph, who was later to become prominent as one of the younger Conservative members and M.P. for Preston. When the Second World War broke out he joined a "Commando," a type of unit named after the Boer formations with which his father had come into contact years earlier in South Africa.

But Mesopotamia was child's play to the next task of peace-making in which Winston was involved. Ireland was still in a state of savage civil war. The Chief Secretary, Sir Hamar Greenwood, had adopted a stern policy of repression, and in his efforts to stamp out the elusive Irish Republican Army, had reinforced the police with the "Black and Tans" and the Auxiliaries. They met savagery with savagery in a campaign of ruthlessness unpleasantly akin to the methods of the Nazis later in the countries they overran. The British conscience was horrified by all the terrible tales that filtered back of the deeds of these ruffians, and in 1921 Greenwood resigned and Lloyd George decided to make an earnest bid for a peaceful settlement with the Sinn Fein leaders.

In the absence of an Irish Secretary, Churchill at the Colonial Office became the departmental minister associated with the Premier in these negotiations. They were tedious, fragile and extremely difficult. Probably no other two men could have carried them through; but Lloyd George with his Celtic *finesse* and sensitive understanding, and Winston with his hearty English frankness and sincerity, made a good team.

De Valera went with Michael Collins, Arthur Griffith and other Sinn Fein leaders to discuss the treaty terms. They were nervous, suspicious, as men might well be who had spent the last years "on the run," hunted for their lives by the Government into whose citadel they were now venturing for the conference. On one occasion Michael Collins, visiting Churchill's house for some conference, complained testily that the British had put a price of £5,000 on his head. Winston cheerfully countered this by producing the Boer proclamation offering £25 for his own capture, alive or dead, and pointed out that Collins evidently was two hundred times as valuable as himself. The thought cheered Michael wonderfully, and thereafter the negotiations made far better progress.

FORMATION OF THE IRISH FREE STATE

At length a treaty was signed, whereby Southern Ireland accepted the severance of Northern Ireland and the maintenance by the Imperial Government of naval bases at certain Irish ports, as the price of peace and self-government. The practical common-sense of Griffith and Collins warned them that since these were conditions which the might of Britain could enforce, with or without their con-

207

sent, it was better to accept them and secure peace than to defy them and continue the horror and devastation of civil war. They induced Barton, Duggan and Gavan Duffy, their fellow-delegates, to join them in signing the terms. De Valera, however, who had slipped back to Dublin, denounced the Pact, and branded his fellow-negotiators as traitors.

The Dail ratified the treaty and set up a constitutional government; but a dissenting minority, headed by De Valera and supported by a section of the Irish Republican Army, carried on a rebellion against their own government. In August, 1922, Michael Collins was shot by some of his former associates. He had expected and foretold it when he signed the treaty.

Outrages continued throughout 1922 along the Ulster border, and England had a grim reminder of the trouble still seething across the Irish Sea when, in June, Field-Marshal Sir Henry Wilson was shot in London by a couple of I.R.A. assassins. But by degrees the Irish Government established its control of that fevered and distressful country. At last, after seven hundred years of strife and barbarism, Ireland saw the dawning of peace and progress.

EMERGENCE OF KEMAL ATATURK

The Treaty of Versailles between the Allies and Germany was the first of a series of instruments of the peace settlement. It was followed, nearly a year later, by the Treaty of Trianon with Hungary, and in August, 1920, the Treaty of Sèvres set out the Allies' peace terms for Turkey. But Mustafa Kemal, the Turkish general and leader of the National Party, refused to accept this treaty, or the concession of Smyrna and all Thrace to the Greeks. He took up arms again, and a fresh war broke out in Anatolia between Turk and Greek.

Kemal was by far the ablest Turk brought to the front by the war. A strange, original personality, he was strong, ruthless and entirely competent. He had a passionate love for his nation and a determination to turn it into a modern civilized and prosperous people. But for him, the British Gallipoli expedition would almost certainly have been successful. But for him, at this new crisis in his country's history, Turkey might have shrunk to a weak, lethargic, backward nation, living meanly in the Anatolian hinterland, while its commerce and resources were exploited by Greeks and Armenians.

ADDRESSING A PUBLIC MEETING AT FINSBURY PARK

Winston Churchill's speeches as Chancellor of the Exchequer were among his most brilliant orations. His great opponent, Philip Snowden, his predecessor as Chancellor of the Exchequer, who was in office in 1924, wrote of him in his autobiography: "He learnt to rely less on careful preparation of his speeches and more on spontaneous effect."

He was content that Turkey should abandon her former ramshackle Empire, which had once spread over all the Middle East. But her own homeland must be preserved intact, including Constantinople and her foothold in Europe on the west of the Dardanelles and Bosphorus, which the Allies proposed to place under international control. His struggle with the Greeks swayed back and forth, and at last the issue turned in his favour. His forces routed the Greek Army, and swept on to sack and burn Smyrna amid scenes of carnage and horror that shocked the civilized world.

Flushed with triumph, Kemal advanced against the neutral zone of the Straits, which had been internationalized and was policed by a small force of British, French and Italian troops. There seemed little chance of stopping him from crossing the Dardanelles and carrying fire and sword into Thrace. The situation was complicated by bad faith among the Allies, for when the Treaty of Sèvres came to nothing, both France and Italy had entered into secret understandings with Turkey behind Britain's back. France was actually supplying Kemal with arms to fight the Greeks, whose campaign against the Turks had been authorized by the Allies!

THE CHANAK INCIDENT

Lloyd George, who was strongly pro-Greek, determined to use every effort to keep the Turks from invading Thrace. So critical was the position that, on 15 September, Winston sent off a telegram to the Dominions, appealing to them to furnish contingents to defend the Straits. On the next day a communiqué drafted by him was issued by the Cabinet, announcing this fact and declaring that the Allies had been called on to support the British in using military and naval forces "to oppose by every means any infraction of the neutral zones by the Turks, or any attempt by them to cross to the European shore."

This bellicose utterance produced a wide variety of effects. The French promptly left the British in the lurch and ordered their troops in the Neutral Zone to withdraw. The Italians also "ratted." Australia and New Zealand promised help, but Canada and South Africa were dubious and asked for fuller information. Kemal, however, was checked by the Note's determined tone. He did not want to fight the British Empire. He halted on the fringe of the Neutral Zone, close to Chanak, where the British garrison was posted, and awaited developments.

General Harington, in charge of this force, acted with great tact in negotiations with Kemal, and open hostilities were averted. The Allies suggested a Conference to reach a peaceful settlement of the new situation. This duly met at Lausanne in November, and ended by producing the treaty which settled the future of Turkey on lines with which the world has since then been familiar. But it was a new British Government that sent representatives to Lausanne.

The Chanak incident gave Lloyd George's Administration its death-blow. Public sentiment had caught its breath at the threat of the country being landed in a new war. Winston's manifesto no doubt checked the Turks and averted a grave disaster in the Balkans, but it wrecked the Government. The Labour and Independent Liberal parties had long been bitter opponents of the Coalition, which depended mainly on Tory support. But the Tories were unhappy about Lloyd George's incurable Liberalism and his imperious domination; for he was no tame captive of his Tory following. Chanak snapped the last bonds of their allegiance. Even Garvin, the editor of the *Observer*, who had faithfully backed Lloyd George through thick and thin, now parted from him in sorrow. Resolutions and protests in favour of Tory independence poured in from local Conservative associations.

On 19 October, 1922, a meeting of Conservative Ministers and M.P.s was held at the Carlton Club. Stanley Baldwin, a junior Minister, adroitly sensed the current of the moment and tried to harness it, working hard behind the scenes to secure the fall of the Coalition. He persuaded Bonar Law, who had retired some time previously on account of ill-health, but was now partially recovered, to come and back this movement. Bonar Law's intervention was decisive, and by a majority of more than two to one those present resolved to end the Coalition. Lloyd George at once resigned, and Bonar Law was invited by the King to form a government.

ELECTION DEFEATS FOR CHURCHILL

A General Election followed forthwith. It was a confused fight. While the Conservatives stood clearly for themselves alone and their right-wing policy, the Liberals were split into Independent Liberals and National (formerly Coalition) Liberals, and there were Labour and Communist parties also in the field. All these central and left-wing groups were fighting one another as well as the Tories, and the result was disastrous to them. The Tories, with only 40 per cent of the total votes cast, got a clear majority in Parliament. Labour moved up to second place across the broken ruins of the once mighty Liberal Party. Baldwin got the Chancellorship of the Exchequer, carrying the succession to the premiership, which fell to him in the following May, when Bonar Law's health finally broke down.

It was a disastrous election for Winston. He was overwhelmed by a series of calamities. Shortly before the election he was bowled over by an acute attack of appendicitis, and was rushed off for an operation. He had to send his election address from a nursing home, and he only appeared in his constituency of Dundee—still weak and an invalid—two days before the poll.

He found the electorate, with its left-wing traditions, aggressively hostile to him. He tried to address a meeting on the eve of the poll, but was howled down by a noisy mob of hecklers. Scrymgeour, his old prohibitionist opponent, was standing on the Labour ticket, along with E. D. Morel, the pacifist. They easily defeated him together with his "National Liberal" colleague by a three-to-two majority.

Churchill felt himself in the following months to be politically in the wilderness. For eighteen years he had been associated with the Liberal Party—one can never say of Winston that he "belonged" to any party—but the National Liberal group to which he was now attached was clearly a party without a future. Intermediate between Tories and Liberals, it was foredoomed to disintegrate and to divide itself to right and left.

Foreseeing that danger, Winston had tried in 1921 to get support for the setting-up of a Centre Party, which could make permanent the temporary alliance that existed in the Coalition between Liberals and the progressive wing of the Tories. The centre was his natural place. He had started as a Tory Democrat. He had blossomed forth as a warm-hearted Progressive. But with his roots deep in aristocratic soil, he was at no time tempted to regard the proletariat as divinely inspired rulers and was a vigorous opponent of Socialism and the Labour Party. His Centre Party, however, never showed any hopeful signs of life, and the 1922 election swept it right off the map. It had no solid political body of support.

AN ENEMY OF SOCIALISM

Winston's dislike of extreme left-wing politicians and their antagonism to him had been accentuated by his experiences of labour troubles at the Ministry of Munitions, and by the bitter hostility he aroused with his anti-Bolshevik policy in Russia. The attitude of the British Labour Party to Russia has varied a good deal during the past three decades, but in the early twenties it was strongly sympathetic, and the *Daily Herald* was rumoured to be subsidized with Russian money. To Winston, Bolshevism seemed at that time to be the deadliest of menaces, and the political left wing, with its tendency to drift towards Communism, seemed a national danger.

In the autumn of 1923, Baldwin, who had now succeeded Bonar Law as Prime Minister, decided for some obscure reason to appeal to the country on a programme of protective tariffs. He thereby achieved the seemingly impossible task of bringing the scattered

DECLARING THE POLL AT EPPING

The Conservatives of Epping in 1924 elected Mr. Churchill as a Constitutionalist and anti-Socialist candidate, with a majority of 10,000. This General Election put the Conservatives under Baldwin into power and, in their government, Churchill became Chancellor of the Exchequer. Above, he is seen with Mrs. Churchill listening to the official declaration of the poll. He had been without a seat since the defeat of Lloyd George's government two years before.

relics of the Liberal Party together. He also gave Churchill a cause for which he could fight whole-heartedly. Yet it is indicative of the way Winston's thoughts were turning that, of the many seats he was invited to contest, he chose that of West Leicester, where his chief opponent in a three-cornered contest was not a Tory Protectionist, but Pethick Lawrence, the Socialist.

The Socialists were uninterested in his diatribes against Protection. They, too, supported Free Trade. But they recognized him as an enemy of socialism, and used every effort to discredit him. In particular, they dragged up the old, futile charges about Antwerp and the Dardanelles. At the poll he was defeated.

In the new Parliament, Liberals and Labour between them formed a majority against Baldwin and Protection. As Labour was the larger party, it was almost inevitable that Asquith, the Liberal leader, after fighting the election principally against Tory policy, should offer to support a Labour rather than a Tory administration. Churchill, now an onlooker, was profoundly shocked, for he had developed an exaggerated dread of socialism. The arrangement, he declared, was not fair to Labour, which must take office on condition that it did not carry out its Socialist policy, nor fair to the country, which would be ruled by a frustrated government. Protection having been killed by the election, he held that there was now no difference of principle between Liberals and Conservatives, which were both anti-Socialist. He now definitely broke off his last links with liberalism and called himself a Constitutionalist.

Under this new label he intervened in February, 1924, in a by-election held in the Abbey Division of Westminster. It was a lively contest, and many of his old friends rallied round him. Balfour sent him a letter of commendation. He had, of course, no party organization to back him, and the time available proved just too short for him to dominate the contest. The official Conservative candidate beat him by the narrow margin of 47 votes in a four-cornered contest.

It was Winston's last defeat. On 22 September he was adopted by the Epping Conservatives as Constitutional and Anti-Socialist candidate. At the beginning of October the Labour Government fell, nominally on its mishandling of the prosecution of Campbell, a Communist, who had been charged with inciting the armed forces to mutiny, but actually because of a treaty it was proposing to conclude with Russia. In this election Churchill was at last returned triumphantly to Parliament, and Baldwin signalized his re-admission to the Tory fold by making him Chancellor of the Exchequer in the new Administration.

CHAPTER X

CHURCHILL AND THE BRITISH GAZETTE

THE Baldwin administration which Winston now joined was one with which he can have had only mixed sympathy. Baldwin, apart from his incurable hankering after the Tory policy of protective tariffs, was in his general political temper a Whiggish Liberal. He was willing to adopt cautious progress and moderate reform. Indeed, one of his first measures was the Widows', Orphans' and Old Age Contributory Pensions Act, which carried forward and rounded off the National Insurance scheme that Lloyd George had introduced in 1911.

But Baldwin was no Radical. He had a profound distaste for any daring changes and experiments. As far as possible, he preferred to leave things alone. The keynote of his administration was sounded in his words to the Birmingham Conservatives on 5 March, 1925: "If I have a message to you tonight, and to the people of this country, it is just this: I would say to England, 'Steady; look where you are going!'" Next day after he had spoken in Parliament he added as a footnote the prayer: "Give peace in our time, O Lord!"

The general aim of Baldwin's Government was counter-revolutionary. In that postwar period all kinds of hopes and dreams of a new and juster order of society were stirring in the minds of the British people. The Liberals, whose parliamentary representation had been almost extinguished in the 1924 election, turned to the planning of reform, and Lloyd George assembled committees that produced schemes for the revival of agriculture, the improvement of towns, and the re-organization of industrial relations. Among those farther to the political left, the ferments of the Russian revolution were working yeastily in many minds, brewing much restless talk of Communist revolution, of "direct action" and of the need to "liquidate" the reactionary capitalists. In opposition to all these plans and theories, the Baldwin administration exerted its weight to swing the country back into the familiar, conventional paths.

With the counter-revolutionary trend of his chief Churchill was in

HONORARY DEGREE AT OXFORD

Winston Churchill (left) received the honorary degree of Doctor of Civil Laws at Oxford University in 1925. Some of those honoured by the University are seen above with Stanley Baldwin in the centre. Baldwin was then Prime Minister, a post he was occupying for the second time and which he held from 1924 until 1929. He later became Chancellor of the University of Cambridge. On the right is Admiral Jellicoe, Commander-in-Chief of the Grand Fleet from 1914 until 1916. In 1916 he became First Sea Lord and in 1918 he was raised to the peerage as Viscount Jellicoe of Scapa.

full sympathy. He had an exaggerated dread of extreme socialism. Democrat and reformer he might be, but his veins ran true blue with the Tory dye of his ancestry and of his early training. Yet the Baldwin method of dealing with these dangerous tendencies must have irked his restless and vigorous temperament.

CONTRAST BETWEEN CHURCHILL AND BALDWIN

They made a strangely contrasted pair—Churchill quick, lively, utterly frank and open, ever eager to be up and doing; Baldwin leisurely, reserved, discreet, placid behind his pipe. Churchill, not content with handling all the work of his own Department, was continually writing long, brilliantly argued memoranda on each and every current problem of politics or diplomacy. Baldwin could not be relied on even to read the essential documents for his Cabinet meetings. Their very relaxations were typical of their difference. Churchill had a passion for polo. Baldwin was reputed to be never happier than when contemplating his pigs.

Their association lasted for just over four and a half years. When his Government fell in 1929 Baldwin may have well sighed with relief at the consoling reflection that he need not invite Winston again to join any administration of which he was a member. He never did.

At the Treasury Winston found waiting for him the various financial problems resulting from the First World War; in particular, the astronomical total of war debt, and the depreciated exchanges produced by wartime inflation.

In theory, the external war debt to America was a self-balancing item. Britain was a net creditor as regards international war debts, though in accordance with a declaration of policy in a Note issued by Balfour in 1922, she had decided to ask her debtors to pay her only what she herself had to pay to the U.S.A. In practice they never fully did so, and Britain was a steady loser in war debt and reparation payments up to the world-wide depression of the early thirties, when all those payments vanished together down the drain of economic chaos.

The internal debt was an ever-present strain on the Budget, the more so as most of it carried the high interest rate of five per cent. Since financial orthodoxy demanded a balanced budget, the watchword of the day was "retrenchment." In handling his accounts Churchill had to find some way of keeping within his income. This was difficult for on the one hand, cheeseparing was not congenial to his nature, and on the other, the country was being carried forward with an expanding economy and an insistence on a rising standard of living. That meant inevitable additions to the scale of national expenditure.

He met these difficulties by a series of adroit financial improvisations. When revenue failed, he patched up his defective resources by raiding funds which had been accumulated for specific purposes— such as the Road Fund, in which motor taxation was set aside to pay for road improvements. By one device or another he always made his Budgets balance. But it must be admitted that these devices were in the nature of emergency measures which could not be repeated, nor form the basis of a permanent policy. He left his successors an Exchequer in which all the hen-roosts had been stripped bare, and no reserve hoards remained for some future Chancellor in financial difficulties to loot.

RETURN TO THE GOLD STANDARD

Winston's first Budget was awaited with keen speculative interest. What surprises might this wayward genius spring upon the country?

He opened it on 28 April, 1925. He began by announcing the decision to return forthwith to the Gold Standard. This important step had been generally forecast. He then dealt with the financial outlook. The past financial year had closed with a credit balance, and on the old basis of taxation and expenditure there was a prospective surplus of some twenty-six millions in 1925-6. This surplus Winston proceeded to give away in reductions of income tax and super-tax and increased preferential concessions to dutiable Empire imports.

He paused. "It is imperative that I should refresh the revenue!" he declared, and raising a glass, drank appreciatively some liquid which some thought to be stronger than water. The House chuckled. Winston was at his tricks again! But the mirth of Liberal and Labour members turned to growls when Winston went on to reimpose the McKenna duties on motor-cars, watches, films and musical instruments, and added new protective duties on hops, silk and rayon. Winston was turning Protectionist! And indeed these taxes were hardly consistent with the pure doctrine of Free Trade orthodoxy.

The return to the Gold Standard which Churchill announced in

218

HOUSE OF COMMONS v. HOUSE OF LORDS

Winston Churchill never lost his early love for polo and was still playing it late in life. This photograph was taken in 1925 (when he was 51 years old) and shows him playing in the annual match between the House of Lords and the House of Commons. In this particular match, held at Ranelagh, the House of Commons team was victorious.

CHURCHILL IN BELFAST AGAIN

In 1926, Mr. Churchill re-visited Belfast and received a very different welcome from his stormy one in 1912 when the Anti-Home Rule Party refused him the use of the Ulster Hall. In this photograph he is being driven to the Ulster Hall in a jaunting car. This time, instead of hooting him, an enthusiastic crowd cheered him through the streets.

his Budget speech was the first task laid upon him as Chancellor of the Exchequer.

In the happy pre-1914 era, a British pound sterling had been a sovereign—a coin of 22-carat gold, weighing about 123 grains. Well-off people carried about pocketsful of them. Anyone who was owed pounds sterling, in any part of the world, was entitled, if he chose, to get them in gold. The City of London, which was the hub of world finance and of international exchange, was convinced that its business depended upon the operations of this system, and that the restoration of the Gold Standard was essential to the revival of pre-war prosperity.

During the First World War the Gold Standard had been suspended and the sovereigns and half-sovereigns in people's pockets had gradually been replaced by currency notes. The vast scale of war expenditure compelled the issue of far more of these notes than could have been redeemed by gold at the bank; and as goods at the same time got scarcer, prices went up and wages followed after, so that the pound sterling had a lower purchasing value. This was "inflation," and it took place in varying degrees in most if not in all countries. The French franc slumped to about a quarter of its pre-war value, while the German mark entirely collapsed. Millions of marks were needed to make the smallest purchase, and presently a new currency of Rentenmarks, and later Reichsmarks, superseded the old, worthless money.

ORTHODOX FINANCE

The purchasing power of the pound sterling fell, not only in terms of the goods and services it could buy in Britain, but in the amount of gold, or of goods measured in terms of gold-price, that would be given for it abroad. This external fall in value was in 1924 about 10 per cent greater than the internal fall. So the restoration of the Gold Standard meant that the purchasing power of the pound must be pushed up by 10 per cent. This involved the process of "deflation" —squeezing down the price of British goods and the level of British wages.

As soon as the First World War ended, British financial authorities had set themselves, first, to check the growth of currency inflation, and then to deflate the pound. They did this by restricting bank credit, calling in advances, reducing the amount of money in circulation and thus giving money a scarcity value. By 1925 this process had been pushed far enough for the final step to be taken of wiping out at a blow that last 10 per cent of inflation and re-establishing the international gold value of the pound. There was no talk of returning to gold sovereigns and half-sovereigns for daily use. The proposal was to authorize the Bank of England to sell gold bullion on demand in exchange for sterling, in the form of bars of 400 oz. Gold could thereupon be exported when necessary to correct an adverse movement in the foreign exchange rate of the pound.

All the orthodox economists and financial experts were agreed as to the necessity of this return to gold. Not till years later would the country find how vain were its sacrifices to the golden calf! Winston was neither orthodox nor an economist, but he of course felt bound to accept their judgment. Besides, a Select Committee of financial experts, appointed by the former Labour Government, reported in February, 1925, in favour of an early return to the gold basis, and this was the general view, accepted by all parties. Lloyd George, however, urged further delay to enable trade and employment to accommodate themselves more gradually to the drastic change in prices and wages which would be caused.

KEYNES' FORECAST OF FAILURE

The one clear voice raised against the proposal was that of the somewhat heretical economist, Professor (later Lord) Keynes. In a series of articles in the *Evening Standard*, later reprinted as a pamphlet entitled *The Economic Consequences of Mr. Churchill*, he pointed out that a 10 per cent rise in the world value of the pound sterling, while its domestic value for buying wages and materials remained unaltered, meant that our exports would at once become 10 per cent dearer and less saleable in the world market. This could only be remedied by reducing production costs; and as wages would not fall automatically, people would have to be driven to accept a wage reduction of two shillings in the pound by the deliberate intensification of unemployment. "We are depending for the reduction of wages on the pressure of unemployment and of strikes and lock-outs," wrote Keynes. "Deflation does not reduce wages 'automatically.' It reduces them by causing unemployment." He pleaded for an easy credit policy as a better way of reviving industry and promoting prosperity.

It was a voice crying in the wilderness. Winston carried through his policy, and Keynes' forecast was promptly and shatteringly verified by the subsequent course of events.

The effect was felt immediately by the coal-mining industry. After cotton, coal was our most valuable export, and for some time past had experienced the greatest difficulty in maintaining its overseas markets. The automatic rise in its world price, caused by the return to the Gold Standard, was a crushing handicap to its sale abroad.

The background of the industry was already troubled. Relations between owners and workers had been uneasy ever since, in 1921, the Government abandoned its wartime control. The Sankey Commission, which carried out an investigation of the coal-mining industry

BUDGET DAY, 1928

The Chancellor of the Exchequer, Winston Churchill, is here seen crossing to the House of Commons, followed by his eldest daughter, Diana (who married Mr. Duncan Sandys, M.P., in 1935). As Chancellor (1924 till 1929), Churchill restored the gold standard and showed great ingenuity in balancing budgets without imposing fresh taxes.

in 1919, had found it in grave need of reform. The Commission recommended various measures, such as the seven-hour day and a two-shilling increase in wages per shift, which were enacted by the Coalition Government. But the nationalizing of coal ownership, which it advised, and of the mining industry itself, which a majority of the Commission strongly favoured, were not then carried into effect.

Government de-control in 1921 had been followed by a coal strike, as owners and miners could not reach agreement on wage rates and working conditions. Eventually terms were settled, which were superseded in 1924 by a new agreement. But in 1925 the industry, hampered by its clumsy and uneconomic organization and its uncertain foreign markets, was hardly paying either workers or owners. There was much short time, and wages earned were in some

223

districts inadequate for the decent support of miners and their families. Unemployment was increasing. The owners had sandbagged all efforts to induce an efficient reorganization of the mines, and there was an atmosphere of unconcealed antagonism between many of them and their workers.

WAGE CUTS PROPOSED

The owners now decided that with the return to gold they must cut down their costs or lose their markets. As wages were about 80 per cent of costs, the simplest way was to reduce wages and lengthen hours. They gave notice to terminate the 1924 agreement, and offered continued employment on new terms, which included abandoning the guaranteed minimum wages and the seven-hour day, and reverting to district wage agreements involving cuts varying, so the miners contended, from 13 to 48 per cent.

The miners flatly refused to consider such an offer. Sympathy with them was very widespread. The Trades Union Congress and the Labour Party guaranteed them full support in their fight, even if this involved a General Strike.

Baldwin tried to mediate, after announcing emphatically that in no circumstances would he consider subsidizing the industry. The Mining Association, representing the owners, and the Miner's Federation for the men could not be brought into a joint conference, but in the closing days of July he saw them both separately. (The old agreement ended on 31 July.) At the last minute he offered a subsidy from August till the end of the following April, while a Royal Commission looked into the whole matter.

The Samuel Commission—so called because its Chairman was Sir Herbert (later Lord) Samuel—duly met, inquired, deliberated and reported. Its impartial, constructive proposals were distasteful to the Government, which, however, gave a rather vague promise to implement them if the parties to the dispute agreed. The mineowners rejected them, and so did the miners, who could not agree to the temporary reduction of wages which the Commission recognized as necessary—as J. M. Keynes had predicted from the beginning.

The miners' mood was by now one of downright uncompromise, and their leader, A. J. Cook, was burning with revolutionary zeal for a fight. No accommodation between miners and owners could be reached, and when the Government subsidy ended on 30 April, 1926, and Baldwin sent the miners the final terms offered by the owners for future wages and hours, the miners refused flatly to accept any wage reduction. A national coal stoppage began at midnight.

Next day the Trades Union Congress met in earnest conclave to consider how to help the miners, and in the afternoon Bevin announced the decision to call a strike of vital services—transport and the staple industries. The Government started anxious negotiations with the T.U.C., but broke them off when news arrived that the compositors of the *Daily Mail* had refused to set up a leading article condemning the threat of strike action This, they declared, was an assault on the freedom of the Press! Tempers, it was evident, were getting short.

GENERAL STRIKE

On 4 May, 1926, the General Strike came into force. Transport of all kinds closed down. So did the Press, the iron and steel trades, building, electricity and gas-power plants. Work everywhere came to a standstill, and the Government called for volunteers to act as special police, engine drivers and so on. Pools of motor transport were formed to distribute food. Lorries travelled about with military guards and escorts, and with festoons of barbed wire round their chassis and bonnets to keep the excited mobs from crippling their works.

The General Strike was fore-doomed to failure because it antagonized a large section of the public. There had been wide and general sympathy with the miners; but the idea of unconstitutional methods of coercion being employed by one section of the community to force the hand of the elected Government exacerbated middle-class feeling already inflamed by a bitterly partisan Press. The strikers' cause might be sound; the remedies advised by Royal Commission might have been perversely rejected by the Tories, but the T.U.C. must not override Parliament.

The Government could therefore count on substantial backing. Its problem was how to keep in touch with the people, furnish them with news and instructions, and thus maintain the administration. Today the radio would amply serve the purpose, but in 1926 the radio was far from universal and many of these who had by then taken it up possessed only some primitive apparatus of crystal and cat's whisker, through which by earphones a faint, intermittent murmur could be heard.

Winston came to the rescue. Alone among Cabinet Ministers he possessed among his innumerable qualifications considerable experience as a journalist—even if he lacked a proper apprenticeship. He had never yet edited a newspaper, unless you count a single manuscript effort which he once brought out at school, when a small boy; but he had often longed to do so and now, with the permission of the Cabinet, he asked the proprietors of the *Morning Post* to lend their idle plant and offices for the issue of an official news sheet, to be called the *British Gazette*.

WINSTON CHURCHILL AS A NEWSPAPER EDITOR

They said "No" at first, but changed their minds an hour later. He was welcome to use their premises and presses if he could find any compositors and printers to set up and run off his paper. As for their own staff, it was all away on strike.

At this point Churchill's friend, Lord Beaverbrook, took a hand. His newspaper presses, too, were silent; but his technical expert had once been a working compositor, and undertook to do Winston's type-setting. He came, and brought two assistants with him. These three men, with the amateur aid of Winston and other volunteers, including some students, saw the whole job through.

The main task of Winston's *British Gazette* was to carry the Government's messages and instructions to all parts of the country. For the rest, it gave news of the events of the day, incidents of the strike and of anti-strike developments, and vigorous propaganda comment, attacking the authors of the upheaval and all who assisted them. It was in fact an avowedly partisan, pugnacious broadsheet. What else would one expect from Winston? Later on, Labour spokesmen complained that it was biased. Of course it was. So was the *British Worker,* brought out by the T.U.C. One can hardly fight without taking sides.

Winston derived rich satisfaction from the fact that his editor's chair was that of the *Morning Post.* In earlier years, before the Liberal interlude in his career which for the time made his name a byword and a hissing to that high Tory journal, the *Morning Post* had employed him as a special correspondent and had printed his articles. Now, as an editor, he dwelt in its inner sanctum, choosing

or rejecting material for his own paper. There can be no denying that as an editor he achieved the most phenomenal success of his generation. His first issue, on 5 May, ran to fewer than a quarter of a million copies. Eight days later, when the strike ended, the circulation of the *British Gazette* had risen to over two and a quarter millions—a 1,000 per cent increase in a week! It was in fact the daily paper with the largest circulation on record in the United Kingdom.

The Times also managed in some marvellous fashion to keep a four-page edition going all through the strike, and the T.U.C. had its own broadsheet. But the *British Gazette* carried off the journalistic honours of the day. It was a typical expression of Winston in his most conspicuous qualities.

The General Strike ended on 12 May, and may claim, therefore, to have been a real nine days' wonder. Much fault may be found with both sides for the causes which led to it and the wrong judgment which loosed it. But the conduct of all sections of the nation under the stress of its operations was beyond praise.

There was a good deal of mob excitement and some scenes of rioting and violence. But Americans present in the country were astounded to observe that there was a complete absence of killing. As one of them later put it, the British managed to carry out their General Strike—nine days of intense turmoil, high passions and social upheaval—with fewer fatal casualties than would occur in the course of any average Fourth of July celebration in the States.

Those who disapproved of the strike, even though many of them sympathized with the grievances that provoked it, were active in helping to keep order and maintain essential services. Food distribution was kept going, and so was the supply of milk, even in the vast urban wilderness of London. Men got somehow to their offices, and even furtively enjoyed the element of adventure which brightened this normally prosaic journey.

THE STRIKE CALLED OFF

Motor transport and volunteer help were forthcoming on a scale which can hardly have been foreseen by the leaders of the T.U.C. It soon became clear to the majority of them that as a weapon of political compulsion the General Strike had proved a failure. Further, a judgment elicited by the National Sailors' and Firemen's Union from Mr. Justice Astbury pronounced the strike to be illegal and outside the protection of the Trade Disputes Act. This meant that the funds of the Unions on strike were in jeopardy. The T.U.C. looked round for a way out. Baldwin told them that the door to negotiations about the mining dispute was still open, and Samuel produced a memorandum making proposals for a basic settlement, which it was hoped the Government might be ready to consider. Thereupon the T.U.C. decided to call off the strike.

So, on 13 May, men went back to work all over the country, though in some industries a few days elapsed before employers and employed came to terms about resumption of work. But the mining stoppage dragged on. The miners had rejected the Samuel memorandum, and the mine-owners on their side dug in their heels and refused to offer anything but their own terms.

By the autumn the resistance of the miners was being broken

down. Dire want forced many of them to drift back to work on the owners' terms, until more than three hundred thousand were again in the mines. The Union leaders faced an all but impossible task, and in November they accepted terms submitted by the Government on behalf of the mine-owners—terms substantially the same as those originally offered by the owners and rejected by the miners' leaders as unjust and intolerable.

LOSS OF FOREIGN MARKETS

The coal stoppage was over. But the foreign market for coal, already crumbling, had been further dissipated during the dispute. The industry became permanently depressed, and some two hundred thousand miners found their occupation gone. Nor were other industries unaffected by the whole affair. They, too, were sufferers through the interruption of trade, and large-scale unemployment settled down as a permanent feature of the social life of Britain.

When the negotiations were ended. Churchill went off for a holiday in sunnier climes. He visited Egypt, taking his paint-box with him, and the public were tickled to hear that he had tried to paint a picture of the pyramids while sitting on a camel; but the sulky brute had thrown him off into the sand! He travelled back through Italy, and on 15 January, 1927, he had an interview in Rome with Mussolini. Because of his strong anti-Socialist feelings, Churchill was disposed to sympathize with the Duce's method of rule by the strong hand, particularly after his own recent experience of the General Strike. But that part of the Fascist creed which denied political liberty to the rest of the community was by no means to his taste.

He came back to England for a parliamentary session in which the outstanding feature was the Government's Trade Disputes Bill—Baldwin's retort to the General Strike. The aim of this measure was to cripple or at least to circumscribe the power of Trades Unions, which Baldwin declared were now becoming organized, not in regiments or brigades, but in armies. The Bill made general strikes and sympathetic strikes illegal, restricted the right of picketing, and handicapped the collection of political funds by compelling subscribers to "contract in" for the purpose, instead of leaving on them the onus of contracting out if they did not want to subscribe. Unions of Civil Servants were also prohibited from affiliation to the T.U.C.

The outlawing of general strikes was no doubt inevitable. But public opinion was divided about the rest of the bill, which many felt to be a vindictive reprisal on trade-unionism, and an effort by the victors of the moment to crush the growing strength of the Labour vote. Churchill himself took little part in the debates on the Bill. Undoubtedly he approved its prime object of outlawing direct action, and accepted its other provisions as being warranted and justifiable. But, never fond of harassing a defeated foe, he could take little joy from advocating the measure, however much he might have considered it necessary. His budget and financial policy were the main themes of his speeches in 1927.

PREPARING TO GO TO THE COUNTRY

A new General Election was due to take place at latest in December, 1929. Baldwin decided not to hang on till the last moment, when chance might present him with an unfavourable set of circumstances, but to go to the country in May. There had been by now a large measure of recovery from the setback of 1926; indeed, trade and industry reached in 1929 the highest level of prosperity they had known since the war, though the numbers of the unemployed still obstinately topped the million mark.

Winston prepared the ground for an election contest by bringing in a "Prosperity Budget," in which he showed a surplus of nearly twelve million pounds, and distributed two-thirds of it by remitting the tea duty, lowering railway fares, reducing the licence rates on motor-cycles, goods vehicles and taverns, and abolishing the unpopular betting tax, which he had introduced in 1926 as one of his bright ideas for money raising.

Baldwin went to the country on a programme of increased protective duties and other proposals for the benefit of industrialists, and also promised a number of social reforms. It was, in fact, an election of generous promises from all parties. Over the problem of persistent unemployment the Prime Minister skated lightly. He always preferred to ignore unpleasant issues.

It was this matter of unemployment which took first place in the election programme of the Liberals, who now made one last desperate effort to recover their old place in Parliament. Lloyd George, who was now leading the party, had summoned well-known experts in many fields into conclave. They brought forth a bold pro-

HUNTING WILD BOAR IN FRANCE

Besides being an enthusiastic polo player, Mr. Churchill developed a keen love of other equestrian sports. Above, he is shown ready to follow the hounds at a wild boar hunt in the Forest of Eu at which he was present in company with the Duke of Westminster at Foncarmont, in the Seine-Inferieure Department of Northern France.

gramme of agricultural revival and capital expenditure on public development and reconstruction, on roads and harbours, land drainage and housing, electricity and telephones, whereby employment could be found for all who were employable in the lost million of the workless. He published this programme in a pamphlet entitled *We Can Conquer Unemployment,* and poured out money like water from the residue of the old Coalition Liberal Fund, which was still considerable, to place five hundred Liberal candidates in the field to continue the struggle.

The Labour Party benefited to no small extent by that propaganda, for they too announced their determination to deal with unemployment by similar methods. In addition, they could rally support on the strength of bitter memories of the coal stoppage and the Trade Disputes Act, and from the widespread discontent over meagre pensions and unemployment grants and dear food.

The election was fought out in a warm and sunny May. At its close, Labour emerged as the largest single party with 289 seats. The Conservatives were reduced to second place with 260, while the Liberals, despite their strenuous campaign and the five million votes polled by their supporters, came last, with a derisory total of 58 seats.

The Liberals now held the balance of power, as they had done in 1924, and they again offered to support a Labour Government on condition that Labour would set to work to carry through those policies which the two parties shared in common. Baldwin resigned, and once more Winston found himself out of office. A black chapter in British history was to be written before he was again summoned to fill a place in the national administration.

CHAPTER XI

A REBEL IN EXILE

D URING the first two out of the ten years from 1929 to 1939 a
Labour Government managed the country. Then came the
financial crisis of 1931. The leaders of the Labour Cabinet
threw over their colleagues and followers and joined with the Con-
servatives and some Liberals to form a National Government—in
which no place was found for Churchill. For the next eight years
Britain was ruled by governments that continued to use the title
"National," though their majorities consisted overwhelmingly of
Conservatives. They retained token groups of former Labour and
Liberal M.P.s in order to preserve the façade of national unity.
Eventually the Second World War compelled this counterfeit unity
to give place to a genuine coalition of all parties, of which Winston
Churchill was the successful architect.

The domestic history of those ten years was dominated by what
was happening in the rest of the world. A universal economic collapse
that smote first America and then Europe sent Britain sliding down
into a pit of economic depression, out of which she climbed slowly,
dragging after her a heavy load of increased permanent unemployment. For the rest of the decade Britain confronted a world in which
international chaos reigned, where the bonds of law, order and good
faith were snapping, one by one; where in open contempt for cove-
nants and treaty pledges, violent acts of aggression were being perpe-
trated by nations on their neighbours and feverish preparations were
being made for total war.

For Britain, the history of that decade will make bitter reading
in after years. It is a record of dismal and disastrous futility, first in
domestic and then in foreign affairs. The economic crisis was deplorably mishandled, and its victims, the workers in those once thriving
areas of massed industrial activity where our national wealth was
created, were left to rot for years in hopeless unemployment. Abroad,
the nations that were our friends and fellow-members of the League
of Nations—peoples to whose defence we were solemnly pledged

TRAVELLING BY AIR

Mr. Churchill, always fascinated by air travel, yet complained that in the beginning he was conscious of a "a dread of going into the air for the first time." Later, he gained greater confidence and used aircraft for all his urgent journeys. Above, Mr. and Mrs. Churchill are embarking in an Imperial Airways aircraft.

under the Covenant: China, Abyssinia, Spain, Austria, Czecho-Slovakia, Albania—were in turn abandoned or betrayed to their enemies by the recreant weakness of the League, in which Britain and France were playing a dominant part. Our diplomacy gradually became sullied by timidity to an extent that bred among Allies and enemies alike a belief that the British had grown decadent. Our responsible leaders appeared to be satisfied if they could blinker the nation, and conceal from it alike their failure to preserve the peace and their lethargy in preparing for war. So, encouraged by Britain's policy of appeasement, and unchecked by her pretence of re-arma-ment, the aggressor nations grew from weakness to strength, like a neglected sore that festers and corrupts the whole system, until their deadly menace was all but incurable.

IN OPPOSITION

Throughout those doleful years the voice of Churchill was con-tinually raised, faithful and unfaltering, to urge more vigour in organizing peace, more energy in arming against the danger of war. His warnings went unheeded; worse, they were mocked and scorned by the supporters of the Government, who denounced him as a war-monger. So at the last, unarmed, untrained, unorganized, Britain was flung into the most desperate conflict she had ever faced. In that furnace the results of a policy of feebleness and vacillation by which she had been trammelled and shamed during the past dreary decade were scorched away, and her true manhood showed itself once more still valiant and sound of heart.

The defeat of the Baldwin Government in 1929 had put Winston on the Opposition front benches, and restored to him that individual freedom which is impossible for a Cabinet Minister, fettered by the principal of collective responsibility.

The result, with a man of his strong individuality and indepen-dence of mind, was the gradual development of a rift between him and his former colleagues. Baldwin in opposition was bent on rallying the Tories round a policy of protective tariffs, including taxes on food, with which Churchill had no sympathy. He himself was always ready to attack the Government for its Socialism and for any move it made toward left-wing policies, but not for being Free-Trade. In a characteristic speech in Scotland on 6 September, 1930, he said:

> "Some of our friends think that the question of food taxes to unite the Empire ought to be made the main and almost the sole issue upon which the Conservative Party will appeal to the country at the next election. I do not agree. I think the first object should be to turn out this wretched Socialist minority Government which is hampering business and enterprise and breeding unemployment at home, and is rapidly liquidating many of our most important interests abroad."

Seven weeks later, in his own constituency, he hinted his impatience with the confusion of Tory policy and its vague drift toward tariffs in the remark:

> "I am not going to make any declaration on staple food taxes tonight. Our policy changes so rapidly, almost from day to day, that it is difficult to keep pace with all the things one has to believe in and to which one has to be loyal!"

The Labour Government's attempt to amend the Trade Disputes Act of 1927, which had so painfully clipped the wings of the unions, gave Winston a theme for an attack on the Prime Minister, of which he made brilliant use. By this time MacDonald's growing lack of sympathy with his trade-union supporters was becoming well known behind the scenes, so that when he surrendered to their pressure and brought in this bill his display of mental elasticity excited some contempt among those "in the know." Winston attacked him joyously:

> "What is the Prime Minister going to do? I spoke the other day, after he had been defeated in an important division, about his wonderful skill in falling without hurting himself. He falls, but comes up again smiling, a little dishevelled but still smiling. But this is a juncture, a situation, which will try to the very utmost the peculiar arts in which he excels. I remember, when I was a child, being taken to the celebrated Barnum's Circus, which contained an exhibition of freaks and monstrosities, but the exhibit on the programme which I most desired to see was the one described as the 'Boneless Wonder.' My parents judged that spectacle would be too revolting and demoralizing for my youthful eyes, and I have waited fifty years to see the Boneless Wonder sitting on the Treasury Bench!"

He went on to suggest that MacDonald had said privately to Lloyd George, whose support was necessary to carry such a measure: "Just look at the monstrous Bill the trade unions and our wild fellows have foisted on me! Do me a service and I will never forget it. Take

236

WITH THE PRIME MINISTER OF CANADA

Mr. Churchill and his son Randolph are standing on either side of Mr. Mackenzie King, Prime Minister of Canada. A frequent visitor to this country, Mr. King received the freedom of London, Manchester, Sheffield, Edinburgh and Aberdeen, and honorary degrees from Oxford and Cambridge Universities. Photograph taken in 1929.

it upstairs and cut its dirty throat!" (The Bill was being referred to a Standing Committee.)

The "Boneless Wonder" epithet stuck painfully. MacDonald never forgot or forgave it. Churchill was not among those he sought to draw into collaboration when he set up his National Government.

But before that Government was formed Churchill had also become estranged from Baldwin, his own party leader. They took opposite sides over the question of the treatment of India. Winston's intense Imperialism was strongly coloured by the Kiplingesque tradition of the "White Man's Burden," and by the outlook of the officers'

LORD RECTOR OF EDINBURGH UNIVERSITY

Many have been the honours bestowed on Mr. Churchill by British Universities. Prominent amongst these was his selection as Lord Rector of Edinburgh University from 1929 to 1932. In this photograph, he is being chaired by enthusiastic Edinburgh undergraduates from Mac-Ewen Hall to the Union Club on the day of his election as Rector.

messes in India, where his early manhood had been spent. He could be sympathetic and generous when it came to giving self-government to South Africa or Ireland. But Indians, he felt, should be ruled by the British for their own good.

Baldwin, however, had appointed a Commission under Sir John Simon in 1927, to recommend further extensions of responsible self-government in India. They spent two and a half years in investigations and discussions, and their final conclusions were published in March, 1930. In the autumn a Round Table Conference assembled in London, to discuss how far agreement could be reached for carrying into effect the Commission's proposals for Indian self-government.

Baldwin supported this step; but the die-hard Tories regarded the Conference as a shameful device for handing over our Indian

Empire to Gandhi and a lot of Hindu agitators; and Churchill, who took the same line, found himself for once lined up with the die-hards. Churchill's attitude at that time was opposed to the broad liberal sentiment of the nation, which favoured a fair and generous settlement—if one could be found—that Indians of all the various groups would accept and in which they would co-operate. This problem, indeed, in 1947 found a hopeful solution through the setting up in that vast sub-continent of the Dominions of India and Pakistan.

By January, 1930, Churchill's violent opposition to Baldwin on this issue led to his resignation from the Tory "Shadow Cabinet" in which the Conservative leaders discussed and agreed their party line on current issues. He retained his seat on the front Opposition bench and his chairmanship of the Conservative Finance Committee. But on 4 April a letter from him to Baldwin appeared in the Press, saying:

> "I read in the newspapers that you wish Mr. Neville Chamberlain to conduct the opposition to the Finance Bill in my stead. As a matter of purely private courtesy, I should have expected a letter from you to this effect."

Thereupon Churchill resigned his last official position in the party organisation, and became entirely free to take his own line.

The Labour Government which took office in June, 1929, was acutely aware both of its inexperience in the conduct of the national administration and of the profound distrust and antipathy felt for it by the country's powerful business and financial interests. So it started out with the determination to prove that Labour could be as discreet and statesmanlike in office as the older parties.

It had been elected on a policy of finding work for the unemployed, who had persistently numbered over a million for the past eight years. It had promised valiant and heroic measures to remove this evil; but it actually started with quite a modest programme of expenditure on public works, loans to Public Utilities and other devices to stimulate industry.

Churchill compared this favourably with the Liberal Party's "expensive and audacious plans," and promised it the support of the Conservatives.

But the Government soon found itself facing a crumbling dam, which these modest patches were inadequate to reinforce; and Philip

Snowden, the Chancellor, who inclined to a rigid economic orthodoxy, was chary of embarking on bigger schemes. MacDonald, jealous of Lloyd George's prestige, disliked doing anything that might appear to be copied from the Liberal programme of unemployment removal. The City, alarmed at the advent of Socialists to power, tightened the money market and was timorous of financing expansive operations which might have stimulated trade and industry. The numbers of the workless, instead of diminishing, slowly rose.

STOCK MARKET COLLAPSE OF 1929

Then in October, 1929, the great stock exchange boom, which had been flourishing in America, suddenly ended in a yet greater crash. All through the summer there had been an orgy of speculation in the United States, which had sent stocks up far above their real value. Speculators had borrowed every cent they could get hold of to invest in stock-buying on margins. Then, abruptly, the bottom fell out of the market. Stock prices came tumbling down from their fantastic heights; tumbling far too swiftly for speculators to get away from underneath. Some much-boosted securities became worthless. Others, though intrinsically sound, fell to far below their proper value. The provincial U.S.A. banks, which had advanced money to the limit on the security of these inflated stocks, failed by the hundred all over the country, leaving their clients penniless and bankrupt. Many industries were ruined and came to a standstill. Unemployment rose to most appalling heights, and workers by the million shambled about in idleness, and lined up in bread queues or hunted for employment. It was a catastrophe quite without parallel and beyond description.

Its effects were felt far beyond the borders of the United States. Europe staggered under the shock. Germany, which had been paying reparations with money borrowed from America and Britain, could pay no more, now that the source had dried up. Thereupon her European creditors, France, Belgium and Britain, had to abandon their war-debt payments to the U.S.A. London's financial houses, which had fatuously been borrowing on short-dated loans from France and Holland and other foreign lenders to use in long-term investments in America and Germany, found themselves insolvent when these loans fell due, and the Government had to come to their aid to prevent national disaster.

When so much had been lent and lost, money grew tight everywhere, trade became slack and industry slowed down. With nothing in the till, the British Government's programme of work for the swelling army of unemployed could not be maintained if the budget were to be balanced out of revenue. We later became quite familiar with the idea of an unbalanced budget in war, when current revenue went only halfway or less to meet current expenditure, the remainder being piled up as an addition to the National Debt. But the notion of leaving the budget unbalanced in peace—of borrowing on the future to finance recovery, as one borrows in war to finance victory—was then regarded as outrageous by the pundits; though it was adopted a few years later to pay for rearmament. So unemployment grew and the Unemployment Fund ran into debt. MacDonald looked round for some way of shaking off his embarrassing Labour supporters, who inspired such lack of confidence in the City, and of standing in with more elegant and credit-worthy allies.

BACK-STAIRS INTRIGUES BY MACDONALD

Early in 1931 it began to be whispered that back-stairs intrigues were on foot. The Londonderrys were maintaining an informal liaison with MacDonald on behalf of Tory interests, and Hore-Belisha was sounding Liberals to gather those willing to form, under Sir John Simon's banner, a group that would co-operate with the Conservatives. The industrial depression was growing apace, owing in large measure to the action of the City in restricting credit and strangling enterprise—as the Macmillan Committee presently pointed out. Intentionally or otherwise, the banks and financial interests of the City were working most effectively against the Government, and bringing its policy into discredit. Labour and Conservative leaders alike began to talk in public about the duty of all parties to co-operate in getting the country out of its difficulties.

In March, 1931, MacDonald set up the May Committee on National Expenditure, composed mainly of very right-wing leaders of banking and big business, to propose economies in Government expenditure. At the end of July it reported, and duly advised drastic reductions in the cost of social services, including big cuts in unemployment benefit and increases in unemployment insurance contributions. These proposals were of course regarded by the Trades Union Congress as utterly intolerable; but MacDonald saw in them a tool

241

to snap his Labour fetters. By accepting them he could on grounds of financial orthodoxy make a dignified and blameless shift to the right, abandoning the intransigent Union leaders and their extravagant ideas.

Luck was with him. Lloyd George, his most dangerous rival in popular appeal, and the most stubborn champion of the unemployed, had to undergo a serious operation and vanished for a time from the scene. MacDonald seized this golden opportunity and precipitated a Cabinet crisis, in the conduct of which his own course was later alleged to be more tortuous than honest. The foreign exchange value of sterling had been badly shaken by the international financial slump, particularly as London acted as the central clearing-house of world monetary transactions. The gold standard to which we had climbed back at such cost in 1925 was imperilled, and the Government appealed to America and France for credits with which to buttress the pound. The credits were forthcoming, but MacDonald managed to give the bulk of his Cabinet, most of whose members were stubbornly opposed to cutting down the unemployment benefit rates, the impression that the American bankers made such cuts a condition for their loan. It was untrue, but it enabled him to collect the resignations of his Cabinet to lay before the King. Then, to their complete stupefaction—for they took it for granted that he was coming out with them—he proceeded to form a new "National" Government, keeping with him three of his Labour colleagues and completing his Cabinet with Conservatives and a couple of Liberals.

MACDONALD'S PLEDGE BREAKING

MacDonald gave an explicit pledge that this was solely an emergency Government, set up to deal with the financial crisis and carry the economy measures that had been recommended, and that it would not go to the country at the next election to seek a continuing mandate, but break up and restore the party *status quo* as soon as its urgent task was accomplished. Meantime he appealed to Parliament and the country to support this temporary administration in the drastic economy programme it put forward.

Financial orthodoxy was his battle-cry. The wicked Labour Party wanted to nationalize the banks, a measure he had himself long supported. The country was in danger of being driven off the gold standard, and that meant bankruptcy. In one of his speeches MacDonald

242

CHANCELLOR OF BRISTOL UNIVERSITY

*In 1930, Mr. Churchill was again honoured by the academic world
when he was chosen to be Chancellor of Bristol University. He is
here seen wearing his Chancellor's robes at his installation on
3 January, 1930. With him is Professor Thomas Loveday, Vice-
Chancellor of Bristol University and a distinguished scholar.*

waved at this point a German billion-mark note of the inflation
period—a worthless bit of paper—as a warning. The people's savings
in the Post Office would be squandered by being lent to the Unemployment Fund and paid away in doles—this was Snowden, viciously
trading on the ignorance of the masses, who pictured the Savings
Bank Fund as an actual store of money, not knowing that it existed
only as a figure in a balance sheet, and that by banking practice all
their deposits were lent out as soon as made, either to the Treasury
or to other credit-worthy borrowers.

These appeals were successful, and an emergency budget and an
Economy Bill were quickly rushed through Parliament, which
drastically slashed expenditure on social services—on education,
health, wages and pensions, road improvements and, above all,
unemployment benefit, while raising unemployment insurance con-

tributions by £10 million. At the same time the gold standard, the maintenance of which had been the ostensible reason for the National Government's formation, was light-heartedly abandoned.

No sooner was the Budget passed than MacDonald, in defiance of his pledge, dissolved Parliament and held a general election to establish his new administration in power. The result of the election was a sweeping victory for the Conservative Party, which collected more than three-quarters of the seats in the Commons. Labour, bereft of its leadership and taken at a complete disadvantage, was reduced to impotence. Liberals were unready, without funds, and split into three sections: the Simonites, who pledged support to the Government with its Tory majority; the Samuelites, who gave it qualified support; and little more than a family group rallying round the sick-bed of Lloyd George, who denounced the election and all those who had consented to it, and withdrew all countenance from the National Government.

RUIN OF A LIFE'S WORK

The new administration promptly set to work to clap protective tariffs on a large range of imported goods, though Snowden had assured the public that protection was not an issue at the election; and in fulfilment of its economy policy, the dole of the workless and the pay of the workers were both cut to the bone, while public works for relief of unemployment were shut down. This policy of restriction, the exact opposite of the expansionist programme which had been recommended by the Macmillan Committee on Finance and Industry, sent the number of the unemployed rocketing upward to three millions. Only the essential toughness of the nation's industrial and commercial structure enabled it to survive the quack doctoring it suffered at the hands of MacDonald's new Government and its unenlightened advisers.

The disaster suffered by the Labour Party in 1931 was in a special sense the personal tragedy of Ramsay MacDonald, though he may at the time have mistaken it for his triumph. He seemed to himself to have stepped up from being the worried driver of a team of restless Labour ministers, despised and disliked by the wealthy and socially elegant, to being the titular head of a government which all these superior beings were proud to serve; and he occupied that position for the next four years. This, surely, was success?

On the contrary, it was the ruin of his life's work. The Labour Party, as it emerged after the First World War to become the second largest party in the Commons, was very much MacDonald's creation. He had built it up from being little more than a handful of representatives of organized labour, into a national political body including Socialists and former left-wing Liberals and many other supporters far beyond the ranks of the trade unions. The Cabinet which he disbanded in August, 1931, consisted not only of manual workers, but of members of the aristocracy, distinguished intellectuals and prosperous heads of business undertakings.

Ramsay MacDonald was a romantic and spectacular figure. Son of a working girl on a Scottish farm, he had climbed up by ability, grim hard work and the spur of unquenchable ambition to the leadership of the Labour Party. As writer and orator, as an exponent of Socialist policy, as spokesman and ruler of his turbulent following, he was in his prime a formidable personality.

MACDONALD "WAVERED AND HESITATED"

As a Labour Prime Minister, however, the weaknesses and limitations of his character and temperament revealed themselves. He was a man of words rather than deeds. All his experience had been gained and his work done in the role of head of a minority movement, opposed to the Government. When he found himself in the highest post of responsibility, called on not to challenge others' actions but to decide and act himself, he wavered and hesitated.

He was handicapped by his character. Proud, thin-skinned, secretive, intensely suspicious of his colleagues, he withheld his confidence from his Labour team, and still more from the Liberals whose support kept him in office, and by whom a share of the credit might be claimed for anything he did to implement those policies which were common to Labour and Liberal parties. He suffered acutely from what we have learned to call an "inferiority complex." As a young man he was stung by it to a heightened passion of Socialist revolt, an impatience with those who appeared serene and secure in the possession of superior wealth and culture. But when at length he himself reached the high places his zeal for Socialism faded, and he yearned to escape from his old associates and be accepted as an equal by the cultured aristocrats he had envied and anathematized.

245

Poor Ramsay! He gained what had become for him the whole world. Was the prize worth the price? As the prisoner and puppet of the Tory Party he continued to call himself a Socialist, but the name was all that was left to him of a creed once passionately held. Losing the faith which had once spurred him on, he presently began to crumble mentally, and the last days of his premiership were pitiable. The fine presence, the rolling voice remained, but all that came forth were meaningless jumbles and inconsequent phrases. And poor Britain, too, that in her vital years of crisis had as her spokesman and Premier this fading simulacrum!

Churchill had been Chancellor of the Exchequer under Baldwin up to 1929, and was thereby next in succession for the Party leadership. But when the Tories returned to power with an overwhelming majority under the label of "National" Government in 1931 no place was found for him in the new cabinet. He had quarrelled with both Baldwin and MacDonald, and they left him to cool his heels in the back-yard. For the next eight years, while remaining a member of the Conservative majority on which the Government rested, he acted as an independent critic, and at times as a one-man opposition to the activities of its leaders.

He gave guarded acceptance to the Government's initial policy, including its introduction of tariffs. The country had apparently decided to have them: let it! Only he sounded a warning note that tariffs must not be carried to a point where they hampered our external trade. As unemployment deepened, he waxed impatient with the apathy of the Government. Neville Chamberlain at the Exchequer was determined to do nothing that cost money. In February, 1933, when the total of the workless touched three millions, Winston attacked this feeble attitude to the problem facing the nation.

> "What is the picture that Mr. Chamberlain puts before the House?" he demanded. "What is the proposition? It is that everything is being done that can be done and that all is proceeding satisfactorily and in due course, but that in spite of all this, many years must pass before the figures of unemployment can be reduced to—I think he said—a small figure. . . . If this that we have heard today is the last word that the Government have to speak upon this problem, then indeed the outlook before us is grave and lamentable."

It was an heretical speech; for the National Government had

ON BOARD THE "EUROPA"

*Winning fame as a lecturer on his South African experiences while
still young, Churchill continued to lecture from time to time throughout his life. He delivered the Romanes lecture at Oxford in 1930.
Above, he is talking to reporters on board the German ship S.S.
"Europa," at New York before the start of an American lecture tour.*

taken office to put a stop to the spending of money for the reduction
of unemployment, and was firmly resolved not to be lured into any
activity on behalf of the workless. Every device had been adopted
to cut down the dole and to limit the payment of public assistance.
The allowance to a workless home for each child, to cover the cost
of all its food and clothing, was limited to two shillings a week!
MacDonald vowed the country could afford no more, though at the
same time he sought to win a reputation for culture by handing out a
hundred thousand pounds to buy for the British Museum the Codex
Sinaiticus, which Russia was at that time offering for sale.

Employment problems had long interested Churchill; but his
natural instincts always tended to draw him more to Imperial and
international issues than to domestic affairs, and it was to those

issues, which were rapidly growing more serious and menacing, that he came to devote most of his attention during the life of the National Government.

Here, too, he found himself out of step with the official policy. He was a strong advocate of the ideals and principles of the League of Nations, while insisting that Britain could only make those ideals effective if she were powerful enough to support them by her arms. The Government, in common with other States, was very lukewarm and half-hearted in its allegiance to its pledges under the League Covenant, as it showed only too clearly in its attitude to Japan's invasion of Manchuria. It certainly had no intention of using arms to uphold League policy. The mass of the nation failed to realize that there was or could be any serious menace of war, if only the League policy of all-round disarmament could be achieved. So for some time it was rather impatient of Churchill's appeals for strengthening our armed forces.

WINSTON BECOMES A SYMBOL

At the outset, therefore, Winston was at loggerheads with both the Government and the nation. As time went on the nation began to give him an ever more attentive hearing, but the Government, writhing under his attacks, still clung to a policy of inaction which he truthfully denounced as a betrayal of the country's safety. It used the nation's will to peace as an excuse for a passivity which wrecked the League on which the hope of that peace was founded, and it then tried to palliate its feebleness by alternatively blaming the public for pacifism, and upbraiding them for advocating bold action which might result in war.

Towards the end Winston became for the mass of the nation a symbol of that practical and courageous attitude and outlook which they failed to find in their official leaders. All along he had represented their real purpose better than they knew.

It is a bitter commentary on the impression created abroad by the setting up of the National Government that its immediate effect was to loose the forces of aggression.

The new administration was formed in August, 1931. In September the Japanese launched their attack on Manchuria. They judged that the new Government, dominated by the business interests of the City, and with the motto of "Safety First," would risk no bold course to check them. They judged rightly. The first reaction of the British Government was to recommend China to give way to Japan. When the U.S.A. issued a Note in January, 1932, warning Japan that they would not recognize the fruits of any aggression in Manchuria, and invited Britain to join them in this attitude, Sir John (Lord) Simon, the Foreign Secretary, said he preferred to trust to Japan's assurances.

A year later the League of Nations unanimously denounced the Jap aggression, whereupon Simon, who had already declared in March, 1932, that Britain—the only League member that was a first-class power in the Far East—was resolved not to lift a little finger to oppose Japan's action, now put an embargo on the sale of arms, not only to the Japanese aggressor, but also to her Chinese victim.

Under the Covenant of the League of Nations all its members were bound to make common cause with any one of them attacked by an aggressor. The skilful glozing of Simon's lawyer tongue could not really disguise the fact that when in face of Japan's attack on Manchuria—presently extended to Jehol and Shanghai—the British Government declared it would have nothing to do with the imposition of sanctions against the aggressor, it was flatly breaking faith with a fellow-member of the League.

DISARMAMENT CONFERENCE AT GENEVA

Four and a half months after the Japanese started their invasion of Manchuria the Disarmament Conference opened at Geneva. Years had been spent in preparations for it, and elaborate paper schemes had been prepared for World Disarmament, which was one of the prime objectives of the Versailles Treaty and the League Covenant. If all nations disarmed, as Germany was already presumed to be disarmed, none would have the means to start a major war, or to resist the judgment of its neighbours acting in concert, and thus peace would be secure. All-round disarmament was in fact the keystone of collective security for the whole of Europe.

But from the start this conference, on which such immense hopes were centred, was a dismal and hypocritical farce. How could it be otherwise, when one of the League members was already waging aggressive war on another, while the rest stood and gaped? In truth, the world was far from ready for disarmament, for no nation could

WORKING AT CHARTWELL MANOR

In this picture Mr. Churchill is seen working at his home at Chartwell Manor, Westerham, during the time he was out of office. At this period he wrote an average of one book each year. Among these volumes were: "World Crisis" (1929), "My Early Life" (1930), "The Eastern Front" (1931), and "Thoughts and Adventures" (1932).

trust the rest to "play the game," so none would abandon its favourite weapons. Britain suggested abolishing big tanks—the French had much bigger tanks than the British—and submarines, of which the French had a formidable fleet; but insisted on retaining the right to bomb from the air, as this was a handy way of inflicting reprisals on tribesmen on the Indian frontier and in Irak. Germany demanded that either the pledge of all-round disarmament in the Versailles Treaty should be honoured, or that she should be allowed to rearm. France would not hear of this unless Britain would very explicitly bind herself to the defence of France; for the general pledge of the Covenant was evidently regarded by the British Government as not binding. Manchuria had shown that.

The German delegates withdrew, and Bruening, the last peace-seeking Chancellor of the Reich, fell from office. In fact, the one positive achievement of the Disarmament Conference was to help Hitler and the Nazis to seize power. Germany was coaxed back for a time, but to no purpose. In October, 1933, Simon proposed that the armed powers should put off disarmament for four years and see how Germany behaved. At that, Germany finally left the conference and resigned from the League. Hitler began at once to rearm on a big scale, at first secretly, then openly and defiantly.

"YOU CANNOT STOP HIGH EXPLOSIVES WITH A PHRASE"

The empty shell of the conference rattled about for a little longer in the streets and halls of Geneva. Arthur Henderson, its chairman, who had brought to his task a passionate devotion and unfaltering faith, wore himself out in vain efforts to lay there a foundation for world peace through disarmament. Less than nothing of positive value was accomplished to reward his labours, and the records show that Britain herself bears a heavy share of the blame for the disastrous issue. You cannot hope for agreement to disarm unless you can ensure general disarmament and give the disarming nations the protection of absolutely trustworthy pledges of mutual support against aggression. Universal disarmament was clearly out of the question when one of the Great Powers, Japan, was actually engaged in aggressive war. Britain was condoning her misdeeds while stubbornly refusing to give any firm pledge of aid to her neighbours if they, too, were attacked. Britain's spokesmen at the conference offered on behalf of collective security nothing more costly than smooth phrases

251

and evasive eloquence. It was not good enough. You cannot stop high explosives with a phrase.

The logical conclusion to be drawn from Manchuria and Geneva was that since the National Government would not support League action against aggressors, and had abandoned the cause of all-round disarmament, it should at once set about renewing its own defences against any potential enemy.

BITTER TRUTH SUPPRESSED BY BALDWIN

But the Government did not dare to confess that bitter truth to the nation. Indeed, Baldwin would later boast of having won the 1935 election by suppressing the truth about the need for rearmament. People were still hoping for world peace through the League; and indeed, if the League had been a reality, as with determined backing from Britain it might yet have been, despite the defection of Japan and Germany, it would at that time have been strong enough to crush any aggressor. But even with a real League the utter collapse of disarmament made it essential for the members to keep up and increase their fighting strength to match the growth of armaments in states that were potential peace-breakers. The nation did not realize this, and the Government were in no hurry to enlighten them, or to admit the worse-than-failure of Geneva.

Churchill saw things more clearly. He still held stoutly and sensibly by the idea of a real collective security through the League, though the hope of general disarmament was dead. In a broadcast address on 16 January, 1934, he said:

> "I don't agree with those who say the League of Nations is no use, and can never prevent another European war. It might be the only chance of preventing one; or, if it can't prevent it, of making sure that the guilty disturber of the peace has the worst of it. If the League of Nations is not broken up by wrangles and intrigues about disarmament it may still remain an august tribunal to which not only Great Powers but small peoples might look. . . . We must take our place there and bear our share in building up a confederation of nations so strong and sincere that in Europe at least no aggressor will dare to challenge them."

But Winston nursed no illusions about the value of Geneva resolutions with no armed force behind them. Six months later, in a speech at Wanstead, he attacked the Government for its lack of progress in air plans for defence:

"We are told that plans are being made and that paper work is proceeding. All that ought to have been done long ago. We ought to have a large vote of credit to double our Air Force—we ought to have it now, and a larger vote of credit as soon as possible to redouble the Air Force. We ought to concert plans for mutual protection with the French and with other peace-loving powers which are in danger from what is happening and what may happen in Germany."

His attitude was well summarized by himself in a speech in the House on 24 October, 1935, when, after referring to Germany's rearmament and Italy's attack on Abyssinia, he said:

"Some people say 'Put your trust in the League of Nations.' Others say 'Put your trust in British rearmament.' I say we want both. I put my trust in both. . . . It is quite certain that the British Empire will never fight another war contrary to the League of Nations. Any attempt to embark upon a war of aggrandisement, or pride of ambition, would break the British Empire into fragments, and any government that was even suspected of such a motive would be chased from power long before its machinations could become effective. Therefore, if ever the British Empire is called upon to defend itself, its cause and the cause of the League of Nations will be one.
"If I were asked how far I am willing to go in support of the Covenant of the League, I would reply that we ought to go the whole way with the whole lot. . . . If there is one moral to be drawn from our experience, it is that we must without delay and apart from any obligations that arise in the North Sea, provide for the security and lasting command of the Mediterranean."

At Bristol, on 4 July, 1936, he said:

"If the idea of force, force in the extreme, be excluded from the procedure of the League of Nations, it is naught but a sham. There is, I conceive, no hope for the prevention of war except in the banding together of many nations, great and small, against an aggressor, whoever he may be. This has hitherto failed because those who sought to restrain the aggressor were not prepared to suffer and die for their convictions, because they were not united into a strong enough confederacy, and because, in a particular instance, the occasion was not one which united the vital interests of powerful States."

Churchill's view was not in keeping with the policy of the Government, but it accurately voiced the convictions of the people at large. At the end of 1934 and in early 1935 a big unofficial referendum was organized through the League of Nations Union to sound popular opinion. It was called the "Peace Ballot"; and though the Government and the officials of the Tory Party tried to throw cold water on the scheme, it was carried through on a big scale. The votes of nearly eleven million people were collected on a series of questions as to their readiness to support the League, and the control of armaments and their manufacture. Ninety-seven per cent of the answers were in favour of Britain standing by the League, and over 87 per cent supported international economic action against an aggressor. Sixty per cent further agreed—very significantly—that military action should, if necessary, be taken to stop an aggressor nation.

Later it became the fashion for apologists for the National Government to allege that the Opposition parties and a large part of the nation had been so pacifist-minded, as shown by the Peace Ballot and the Fulham bye-election (where a candidate standing on a programme of full support for the League was returned), that they prevented the Government from rearming or presenting a firm front to would-be aggressors. In fact, as the answers to the Peace Ballot showed, the people were pacific but not pacifist. They wanted peace to be maintained by resolute collective action through the League—maintained, if need be, by force of arms. But they still hoped that agreed all-round disarmament might reduce the danger of war to trivial proportions, and therefore looked somewhat askance on suggestions for increasing armaments.

The responsibility for this last notion lay with the Government, which flinched from telling the nation plainly that with the collapse of the Disarmament Conference and the rapid growth of military power in Germany and Italy all hope of general disarmament was dead, and we must rearm if we would defend the peace. They feared that if they made such an admission they would be turned out by an indignant nation for the bungling incompetence which had destroyed its hopes of peace. "Supposing I had gone to the country and said that Germany was rearming and that we must rearm," said Baldwin, in November, 1936, excusing with appalling frankness the false and misleading statements he had made to win the 1935 election, "I cannot think of anything that would have made the loss of the election from my point of view more certain."

The Government abandoned so completely all thought of disarmament that in June, 1935, they concluded behind the back of

AT A PUBLIC DINNER AT THE CONNAUGHT ROOMS

On 20 November, 1934, Mr. Lloyd George and Mr. Churchill both attended a dinner at the Connaught Rooms, in aid of the Printers' Pension Almshouse and Orphan Asylum Corporation. They are here reading its record. Lloyd George was at this time out of office but had just completed the first two volumes of his important War Memoirs.

France a rearmament naval treaty with Germany, by which she was authorized to build up a navy 35 per cent the size of the British fleet, and submarines up to 100 per cent of our submarine fleet. In retrospect, that treaty appears as fatuous as it was treacherous. It facilitated the construction of the U-boats that were to form the most persistent and deadly menace to this country during the Second World War, causing the loss of thousands of our seamen's lives and millions of tons of shipping. It raised a wall of distrust between France and Britain. But while German rearmament was encouraged, the British were not told that our own armed strength was rapidly becoming unequal to the task of defending either the League or our own Empire. They were allowed to live in a fool's paradise.

WITH KING EDWARD VIII

In the constitutional crisis of December, 1936, the King had asked permission to see Churchill as a private friend. Mr. Churchill had been his staunch supporter in the events leading up to the abdication, and he tried to persuade Mr. Baldwin to take no irrevocable step without first giving a formal statement of events before Parliament.

CHAPTER XII

THE AGE OF APPEASEMENT

BALDWIN took over the Premiership in June,1935, from Mac-Donald, whose intellectual powers were now obviously failing. He was as lacking as his predecessor in zeal for the League of Nations. He was, however, a subtle politician, adroit to profit by the mood of the moment. He had taken note of the popular sentiment in favour of the League evinced by the Peace Ballot, and he watched for a chance to capitalize it to his advantage.

The chance was not long in coming. Mussolini had for some time been planning to seize Abyssinia, the only territory left in Africa, except Liberia, which was not already owned or protected by some European Power. He had bargained with France for a free hand there, and MacDonald's Government, which was well aware of his intentions, had carefully refrained from comment and by its silence implied acquiescence. So in the summer of 1935 the Duce started to pick a quarrel with Abyssinia and to move troops and munitions to Eritrea and Italian Somaliland in readiness to cross her borders.

Abyssinia appealed to the League to arbitrate, and Sir Samuel Hoare, the British Foreign Secretary, went to Geneva and made a valiant speech in which he asserted Britain's resolve to fulfil her obligations under the League Covenant. But at the same time, with a strange inconsistency, the British Government had placed an embargo on the export of arms, not only to Italy, which was well armed, but to Abyssinia, which was almost weaponless. Abyssinia was told: 'Don't bother about arms. Trust in the League!"

In October, despite the League's efforts to negotiate a settlement, Mussolini launched his attack; and Geneva, hopeful for once in view of Britain's apparent determination, denounced the aggressor and voted for combined action to be taken against him, beginning with economic sanctions. The British people were delighted at this firm stand. Churchill declared: "The whole world has been astonished at the energy and vehemence displayed by His Majesty's Government, and I think we have been astonished ourselves!"

Baldwin promptly held a General Election in November, so that this wave of popular approval should be cashed as a fresh mandate to the "National" Government and its Conservative majority for a further term. "The League of Nations," declared his election manifesto, "will remain, as heretofore, the keystone of British foreign policy." The manoeuvre was highly successful. The Government obtained 70 per cent of the seats, 60 per cent being secured by Conservative candidates. In the light of its later history it is a somewhat curious reflection that the 1935 House of Commons which subsequently perpetuated its own existence by its own votes without securing any fresh mandate from the nation, till it lasted longer than any Parliament in our history since the "Long Parliament" of Stuart times, was originally elected to uphold the League of Nations and stop Mussolini from seizing Abyssinia.

THE HOARE-LAVAL PACT AND ITS EFFECT

Hardly had Parliament reassembled in December, 1935, than Sir Samuel Hoare went to Paris and there signed with Laval the infamous Hoare-Laval Pact, whereby all the best parts of Abyssinia were to be handed over to Mussolini. Baldwin and his Cabinet promptly endorsed this pact; but the next day the British Press got hold of the story, and a veritable roar of public indignation went up. Baldwin was quite taken aback. He at once called for Hoare's resignation, offering up his Foreign Secretary as a scapegoat for the Government's sin. The Cabinet's agreement with the Pact was, he confessed rather shamefacedly to the House, "an error of judgment." They had not the slightest idea that they were being untrue to their election pledges. "I was not expecting that deeper feeling which was manifested by many of my hon. friends in many parts of the country on what I may call the ground of conscience and honour."

But though the pact was thrust aside, the mischief had been done. Mussolini realized that Britain and France had no intention of letting the League press on to any really effective action; and the other League members became aware that Hoare's valiant declarations of the previous summer were nothing more than window-dressing for the British election. So the League's one effort to stop aggression came to naught. Though some economic sanctions had already been imposed, the British Government refused to agree to extending them to the stoppage of Italy's oil supplies—the one measure which would really have interfered with her war on Abyssinia—and six months later they were all called off." "The imposition of oil sanctions," declared Neville Chamberlain, "would be the very midsummer of madness." Meanwhile, with the aid of poison gas which she was solemnly pledged not to use, Italy had defeated the Abyssinian forces and annexed the country.

Winston was abroad at the time of the Hoare-Laval Pact incident. But he told a foreign correspondent that he was opposed to the British Government's proposals, and that in his opinion and in the eyes of the British people the Government were not fulfilling the obligations they had contracted to carry out at the general election.

FAILURE OF THE LEAGUE OF NATIONS

There is no doubt that the League could have prevented this triumph of Fascist aggression, had its leading members so willed. Fifty nations agreed to impose sanctions against Italy. Thirty-four were ready to go the whole way in mutual military support of the strongest action to stop Italy from continuing the war. The British Fleet, single-handed, could have effectively barred the Red Sea to the convoys of Mussolini's troops and their supplies—but Baldwin had taken care to send it to the Mediterranean without adequate ammunition! Abyssinia's fate showed the world that the French and British Governments had no intention of standing by their pledges under the League Convenant if serious risk or cost to themselves were involved. Hitler read the omens, and forthwith thrust his troops into the demilitarized Rhineland in defiance of the Locarno Treaty. The French wanted to drive him out again; and, as was later learned, he would have withdrawn quickly in face of a show of force. But Britain, despite her Locarno pledge, refused to support such firm action. Firmness never had been the most outstanding characteristic of the National Government.

Winston was an impotent spectator of this nauseating episode, so fatal for Abyssinia, shameful for Britain and France, and catastrophic for the League of Nations. He was frank in his criticisms of the bungling insincerity of Baldwin's tortuous course. "I have tried to support the Government and Mr. Baldwin upon the League of Nations and about Abyssinia," he remarked in a speech at Chingford, "but I found it very difficult to keep in step with all their zig-zags." He drew two morals from the dismal story. First, "we should be scrupulously

259

careful not to involve the word and honour of Britain upon the Continent of Europe in any business which we are not prepared, if the worst comes to the worst, to carry through, whatever the cost, with all our force and strength." And second, that the cause of our dishonour was "the lamentable weakness into which our defences have been allowed to fall. Errors, feebleness, vacillation there have, no doubt, been in the current policy of the government, but the underlying cause of our impotence is the improvident neglect of our defensive strength in years when every other great nation was arming sternly and resolutely."

Winston has never been one to accept idleness with meekness, and he had long been weary of his banishment from office when in 1935 Baldwin replaced MacDonald as Prime Minister. It was not unnatural for him to hope that this elevation of his party chief and former Cabinet colleague would soon open the door for his return to a ministerial job.

Baldwin and his cronies had in fact not the slightest intention of admitting into their nest so restless and untamable a colleague as Winston. But there seemed to them no point in telling him so. On the contrary, hints and rumours were adroitly conveyed to him through friendly channels that if he would only be patient and carefully avoid criticising the government, a post might presently be found for him. Winston, himself completely devoid of chicanery, unsuspectingly allowed himself to be taken in by these bogus suggestions. As a result, he was for a time muffled and enmeshed by them into political inaction.

WRITING, PAINTING AND WAITING

But Winston was constitutionally unable to sit still and do nothing. Both his brain and his hands had to find employment, and so it came about that these years of official exile yielded a rich production of literary masterpieces.

During his previous short spell of freedom from office in 1923-4 he had begun a monumental work on the events leading up to the First World War, and the progress of that struggle as he had witnessed and shared it—a work which he managed to complete during his tenure of the Treasury. It came out between 1923 and 1929 in four massive volumes entitled *The World Crisis*. He now added a fifth volume, as a pendant to the others, on *The Eastern Front*, giving a detailed account of Russia's part in the First World War, of the breakdown of the Tsarist Empire and the subsequent chaos and civil strife, out of which the Bolshevist Government arose. He also published in 1931 an autobiographical fragment, written in a racy, whimsical style, entitled *My Early Life,* recounting his reminiscences of childhood and early manhood, and ending with a reference to his happy marriage.

In 1933 came a volume of miscellaneous writings called *Thoughts and Adventures*; and then he started work on what is perhaps his masterpiece—the life of Marlborough, his famous ancestor. For this he had a mass of material in the family papers and records preserved at Blenheim Palace, and hitherto unpublished, with which to complete and correct former histories. In his own florid, oratorical, entertaining style, reminiscent of Gibbon and Macaulay, he paints a favourable and perhaps flattering portrait of his hero, who in fact, for all his courage and ability, was cold, treacherous and unscrupulous— blemishes which Winston most emphatically did not inherit.

Churchill's paint-brush, too, was kept busy. Every holiday trip abroad yielded its crop of boldly coloured oil paintings of landscape scenes. A typical instance of this activity occurred in the winter of 1935, when he was spending a few weeks in Morocco. A day or so after his arrival in Marrakesh he sallied forth into the street to paint. But he had hardly set up his easel before he was mobbed by such a throng of Moors and Arabs that he had to retreat to the hotel and content himself with sketching the view from his balcony. But, never accepting defeat, he went afterwards by car to a village a few miles away, where the denizens were scanty and he could capture undisturbed the startling reds and purples, ochre and orange of a Moorish street scene.

INCIDENT AT MARRAKESH

A characteristic incident enlivened this visit to the ancient capital of Morocco. Al Glaoui, Lord of the Atlas, the Pasha of Marrakesh, invited Winston and Lloyd George to a banquet. The feast was served in Arab style, the diners squatting on low divans, before great brass dishes and pots in which roast mutton, pigeons, fowls, cous-cous and other courses in endless procession were set before them. There were neither plates, knifes nor forks, the eater's right hand—or rather the thumb and first two fingers of it—being expected to do all the work of

PAINTING IN FRANCE

Mr. Churchill's painting started in a small way by the annexation of his children's water-colour paint-boxes. He was encouraged by his work and bought more ambitious apparatus the very next day. It soon became an absorbing interest with him and, in the photograph above, he is shown painting in oils while spending a holiday in France.

tearing portions of chicken carcass and mutton joint, digging out tit-bits from the stews and messes, and conveying them to the mouth. Winston was at first distinctly embarrassed and awkward at this un-familiar game. Then, flinging himself almost excessively into the spirit of the occasion with a sudden schoolboy outburst, he cried: "To hell with civilization!" and plunged his hand up to the wrist in the dish before him.

Another of his active recreations was building. He started this in 1928, while still in office as Chancellor of the Exchequer. Some con-struction was being done on his little estate at Chartwell, Westerham, and he decided to take on the building of a wall himself. He soon mastered the art of brick-laying, but found that he was incurring liability to a mock charge of employing scab labour, and George Hicks, the Secretary of the Amalgamated Union of Building Workers, jocularly invited him to regularize his activities by joining the Union.

Winston, no laggard at a jest, promptly accepted and sent a cheque for 5s. for his registration as an "adult apprentice." The laugh was on Hicks, for a number of the more humourless among the members of the Union were highly indignant at this "buffoonery," which they felt cast a slur upon their dignity. But Winston kept his membership card, and could with full orthodoxy indulge in his new passion for brick-laying. During his years of political unemployment he added additional structures to his property.

The year 1936 saw the throne of Britain twice vacated.

On 20 January King George V passed away in his seventy-first year, after a life of faithful and sincere service to his people which had won their abounding love and admiration. He was succeeded by Edward, the Prince of Wales, who possessed great personal charm, marked energy and ability, and a progressive outlook which some quarters felt to be embarrassing. During his very brief reign the active interest and sympathy he showed for the unemployed in the depressed areas, and his impulsive pledges that something should be done for them, profoundly disconcerted Whitehall, which had no intention of doing anything. This may, in fact, have contributed not a little to his final undoing.

CONSTITUTIONAL CRISIS

At his accession he was a bachelor, but had lost his heart to an American lady, Mrs. Simpson, who was already married for the second time, having divorced her first husband. A second divorce followed, which set her free to marry Edward. This produced an acute crisis. It was impossible to regard her as an acceptable Queen Consort; and morganatic marriages, though they had historic precedent, were not recognized by English law. The Church, with its growingly hostile attitude to divorce, was horrified at the notion that the King, its constitutional head, should contract a marriage, morganatic or otherwise, with a party to two divorce cases.

Whether or not some compromise solution of this impasse could have been reached if on other grounds the leaders of Church and State had been acutely anxious to keep Edward on the throne, it is impossible to say. But in fact they were already afraid of what he would do or say next, and they appear to have welcomed the opportunity afforded by this social and religious problem to compel him to abdicate.

It was a painful situation for those who, like Winston and Lloyd George, were personal friends of the King. They were torn between their affection and instincts of loyalty on the one hand, and their sense of the unfitness of marriage between the King and Mrs. Simpson, on the other. Churchill, to whom Edward appealed for advice, worked very hard to obtain delay and a postponement of any final and fatal decision; but Baldwin and those around him had steeled their resolve that Edward must go, and pressed the crisis unrelentingly to a swift culmination. On 10 December, 1936, Baldwin read out in the Commons the King's message announcing his abdication.

"THE ACME OF TRAGEDY"

So rapidly and secretly had the whole affair been managed by Baldwin that Parliament had been denied any statement on the constitutional issue, or any opportunity of debate, till the final act of abdication was laid before it. Churchill's efforts on Edward's behalf were thus bereft of any support which might have been forthcoming for them from public opinion. The nation was left in ignorance till the very last moment of what was happening, and then was presented with an accomplished fact which it must, perforce, accept.

History will no doubt decide that Baldwin's subterranean strategy, whether or not it was constitutionally sound, was justified by its results. The throne that Edward vacated was filled by his brother George, Duke of York, who with his gracious Consort, Elizabeth, upheld the finest traditions of our Royal House, and inspired the deep and devoted loyalty and affection of the whole nation. Alike in his public conduct and in his family life the King was a model to his people and fulfilled the highest standards of kingly dignity. Yet one could hardly fail to mourn the ignominious fall of the brilliant young Prince on whom so many bright hopes had been set. At the announcement of his abdication Churchill voiced the feeling of many when he said in the course of his speech on this stunning calamity:

"In this Prince there were discerned qualities of courage, of simplicity, of sympathy and, above all, of sincerity, qualities rare and precious which might have made his reign glorious in the annals of this ancient monarchy. It is the acme of tragedy that these very virtues should, in the private sphere, have led only to this melancholy and bitter conclusion. But although today our hopes are withered, still I will assert that his personality will not go down uncherished to future ages, that it will be particularly remembered in the homes of his poorer subjects, and that they will ever wish from the bottoms of their hearts for his private peace and happiness."

In May, 1937, King George was crowned at Westminster, and Baldwin, having reached his triumphant hour, resigned the Premiership and retired with an earldom to the House of Lords.

His successor was the Chancellor of the Exchequer, Neville Chamberlain. Had Baldwin and Churchill not fallen out it would have been Winston, and the history of Britain would have been less spotted, and that of Europe less tragic.

CHAMBERLAIN AS PRIME MINISTER

Chamberlain was a good man of business and had been a competent and energetic Lord Mayor of Birmingham before turning to national statesmanship. Ignorant of all countries but his own, incapable of understanding alien mentalities, devoid of imagination and lacking any popular appeal, he might yet have achieved a moderate and undramatic success as a Prime Minister in jog-trot times of orderly peace. But these were not jog-trot times. Vision, moral courage, extreme mental alertness and a profound understanding of alien minds were essential to cope with the dangerous international situation which it was his hard lot to face. These were not qualities to which he could lay claim; and the old breach between Baldwin and Churchill which diverted the succession to Chamberlain at this juncture was to prove a disaster for Britain and for the world.

Needless to say, Chamberlain did not invite Winston to join his new Cabinet. Instinctively he knew that beside Winston he would have dwindled to a minor role. Moreover, he had determined on his line of policy, and it was not that which Winston advocated. Chamberlain had no use for the League of Nations or collective security. He was a matter-of-fact business man, and could not conceive that any responsible person should be anything else. He would "talk turkey" with Hitler and Mussolini. Sensible fellows, they would of course be ready to behave decently if dealt with on a business footing. He could make bargains with them as one business man to another, and the world would be able to get on peacefully with its own business.

So, if Baldwin's policy had been one of lethargy and drift in foreign affairs, of accepting the popular cry while failing to act upon it, Chamberlain set about more definitely to "appease" the potential aggressors, to do as much business as he could with them, and to ignore, as far as public opinion would let him, their ways of meddling with other countries. Had they also come from Birmingham the policy might have succeeded. But as things were it was as inappropriate as an attempt by a cow-herd to make a business settlement with a pair of very hungry tigers. It was a policy which was regarded by them only as weakness.

Chamberlain had inherited from Baldwin the policy of standing aloof from the Spanish Civil War, which broke out in 1936. "Non-Intervention" was the label for this policy, to which all Europe nominally subscribed. But as the struggle proceeded the intervention of Germany and Italy on the side of the Fascist rebels became more and more open and insolent. In fact, they used Spain as an experimental station to try out their latest weapons and battle tactics in readiness for aggression elsewhere. Chamberlain strained and broke his moral integrity in trying to deny the patent facts of this breach of pledges. He was determined to make friends with Italy, and when Eden, the Foreign Secretary, urged a firmer line, Chamberlain forced him to resign and pressed forward with his appeasement plans. Winston openly deplored this action. Eden's resignation, he said, would rejoice the enemies of Britain and discourage their friends. The dictators would rejoice, and the free peoples of Europe would hear it with foreboding and dread.

FOREIGN POLICY TAKEN OVER BY CHAMBERLAIN

Chamberlain now took the control of foreign affairs into his own hands. In April, 1938, an Agreement was signed in Rome by which Britain acknowledged Italian rule over Abyssinia, undertook to give Italy a share in the control of the Suez Canal—Britain's lifeline—to exchange military information with her about all troop movements and dispositions round the Mediterranean and Red Sea, and to establish no new naval or air bases there without first telling her. Our plans for developing a strong base at Cyprus were of course abandoned.

Churchill protested vainly against this move, saying:

"We are now choosing—and it is a very vital choice that we have to make—between two broad lines of policy. On the one hand, we

266

ADDRESSING A FRENCH AUDIENCE

Churchill often lectured in France and in this photograph, taken on 24 September, 1936, he is speaking before a distinguished audience at the Ambassadeurs Theatre in Paris. On many occasions his addresses to the French people were in their own language.

may buy a few years of peace at the cost of the people of Spain and Abyssinia, and at the cost of abandoning the effort to organize security on the basis of equal justice for all nations, and of surrendering strategic positions, or of enabling the Italian Government to establish strategic positions which would be of vital importance in war and would greatly strengthen its diplomacy in peace; or, on the other hand, we can organize a defensive system which would be able to resist aggression and thus avert war, provided at the same time we make it clear that we are willing to contribute to the satisfaction of genuine national grievances of other countries on the basis of disarmament and third-party judgment.

"This last is the only possible peace policy—the policy which preserves the foundations of international law and order, upon which alone peace can be secured."

But Chamberlain had already decided against that second, saner alternative. He had resolved to "buy a few years of peace"—how few he did not realize; for, in fact, all that he got was a year and a half.

Winston's prophecy was swiftly fulfilled. Eden's resignation occurred on 20 February, 1938. Within three weeks, on 12 March, Hitler marched his troops into Austria and annexed it to the Reich. If Chamberlain was proposing to "appease" the dictators, the Fuehrer would start showing him the size of their appetite. Chamberlain sent a formal protest and was bluntly and rudely told to mind his own business by his confident adversary.

GROWING MENACE OF GERMANY

France, alarmed at the growing menace of Germany, gave a pledge to Czecho-Slovakia—obviously the next victim—to come to her assistance if she should be attacked. Chamberlain refused to associate himself with this pledge, but went so far as to give an undertaking to support France if she were involved in war.

Hitler was quite unperturbed by these warning noises. He knew the rotten condition of French politics, where Laval and Flandin were more than ready to sell out to him, and Bonnet was balancing on the fence. He had seen that Chamberlain was prepared to go to almost any lengths of wilful blindness to the facts in order to cling to his creed that there could be no real danger of anything so unbusinesslike as war. He was well aware that numbers of Chamberlain's principal supporters were heads of the big financial trusts and holding companies of the City, which were closely—and, for the moment profitably—co-operating with the German combines and cartels. The popular view in the City was that it did not matter if Hitler took control of all central and eastern Europe, so long as the commercial transactions of those regions continued to be discounted in London. Besides, Ribbentrop had assured him that the governing circles of Britain were so terrified of Bolshevism that they would stand anything from Germany rather than impair her value as a bulwark against the Soviets; and that, anyhow, the English were hopelessly decadent, morally degenerate and sheep-hearted.

NOTHING BUT APPEASEMENT

It must be confessed that in the conduct of British affairs during the years before September, 1939, there seemed no lack of evidence to support that impression. Hitler's purposes were plain for all to see. Had he not set them down with but little concealment in his book, *Mein Kampf,* which he had made the substitute for Holy Writ in Germany? He had published a map showing the course and dates of his prospective conquests of his neighbours. Britain appeared on that map, with the date when she was due to perish. Yet Chamberlain could talk of nothing but appeasement, brag that his policy of refusal to honour Britain's pledges under the League Covenant was keeping the country out of war, and flatly refuse to credit or even hear the warnings which well-informed observers brought back from the Continent about Hitler's preparations for aggression. During these years, Chamberlain, like a waterman, was looking one way and rowing the other; gazing at peace, but steering his craft to disaster.

True, he had announced a programme of rearmament, but he was failing to put it into effect. The sums voted for it were only partially spent, and their product in weapons was still more meagre. It was the deliberate policy of the Government, announced as such by Sir Thomas Inskip, Minister for the Co-ordination of Defence, to do nothing in the way of rearmament which would impede the course of normal trade, and munitions factories did not even get priority for the machine tools they needed. So, for all her paper programme, Britain was falling farther and farther behind Germany every month in her comparative weapon strength. Churchill pleaded constantly for a more determined drive, both for arms and for allies; but he met with such mulish obstinacy that he was driven to urge that Chamberlain should not refuse to do what was wanted merely because he, Churchill, had proposed it!

Three months after snatching Austria, Hitler prepared to seize Czecho-Slovakia by a similar swift stroke. But the alert and well-armed Czechs got wind of his troop movements and carried out a lightning mobilization and manned their frontiers. Finding that his attack was certain to run up against powerful resistance and involve him in a general war, Hitler called it off and set to work to foment disorder in the Sudetenland, the fringe of Czecho-Slovakia, which had a considerable German population. He backed this up with threats and fulminations which made clear his intention to use the disturbances as a pretext for invasion and annexation.

But if Czecho-Slovakia resisted him and war followed, France was pledged to come to her aid, and Britain would have to come to the aid of France. Chamberlain worked desperately to avoid this. At the beginning of August he sent Lord Runciman to Prague, nominally as an "independent mediator and investigator," in the hope of finding some plausible grounds for the surrender of the Sudetenland to Germany. True, he induced the Czech Government to furnish an invitation for the visit, which they could hardly refuse; and he also got Runciman an invitation from Henlein and his pro-Nazi movement among the Sudetens, who were well aware of the real object of the mission. The Runciman report was curiously contradictory. Honesty compelled him to admit that economically as well as historically the Sudetenland was an inseparable part of Czecho-Slovakia, and also that the offers of local autonomy made to the Sudetens by the Czech Government were very fair and adequate as a settlement of their alleged grievances. But he said that the extremist Nazi group among the Sudetens were so violent and intractable that the only way to keep the peace was to hand over the predominantly German-speaking parts of the country to Hitler.

GERMAN TROOPS MOVE TOWARD THE FRONTIER

Meantime the Fuehrer, determined that there should be no question of the reasonable offers of the Czech Government being accepted, set these Nazis to work to start bloody incidents along the frontier districts, and on 12 September made a fiery speech at Nuremberg, declaring that his patience was exhausted.

On the day after this speech the Sudeten leaders broke off negotiations with the Czech Government, and Hitler began to move troops toward the frontier. War became nearer.

MR. CHURCHILL IN HIS STUDY AT WESTERHAM

Between 1933 and 1938, Churchill published his masterpiece, "Marlborough," a life of his famous eighteenth-century ancestor, in four large volumes. Meanwhile, in 1937, he had collected a number of personal sketches on "Great Contemporaries," in which he had written anecdotes about a diverse collection of celebrities of all nations.

Chamberlain could not face the idea of war, though nothing was plainer, or had for years been plainer, than that unless a firm stand were made against Hitler, even at the cost of fighting, all Europe and Britain herself would pass under the heel of the Nazis. This was a truth that Chamberlain flatly refused to admit. Completely unwarlike in temperament, he was ready to make any sacrifice to avoid a conflict. So he promptly sent word that he would come to Germany to talk things over, and on 15 September he flew to Berchtesgaden to beg the Fuehrer to stay his hand.

Hitler's first terms were the cession of the Sudetenland. Chamberlain hurried back to London and summoned the French Premier and Foreign Minister, MM. Daladier and Bonnet, to get them to agree to

271

this. After prolonged discussions, the French leaders consented to the issue of a joint memorandum to the Czech Government, calling on them to accept Hitler's demand, and backing this with the threat that if the terms were refused, the French would repudiate their treaty pledge of military aid for the Czechs under their treaty.

It is noteworthy that although Russia was linked with both France and Czecho-Slovakia by treaties of mutual defence, and was pledged to come to the aid of the Czechs if France did so, she was carefully excluded from this and all subsequent negotiations. She announced her readiness to stand by her treaty pledges, but this offer was studiously ignored by both France and Britain.

SCANDAL AND CORRUPTION IN FRANCE

The position of France throughout this crisis calls for some comment. On paper her military strength was formidable, and, as she was much more intimately menaced by Germany than Britain, she must have realized more fully than Chamberlain did what danger lay in postponing the inevitable struggle, and forfeiting the by no means inconsiderable fighting strength of her Czech ally. Up to the time of Chamberlain's visit to Berchtesgaden the French leaders seem to have been fully ready to act on their treaty obligations. But their talks with Chamberlain convinced them that the British Government was not in a position to give them any effectual backing; that even if it did not leave them entirely in the lurch, as at the time of Hitler's military occupation of the Rhineland, it was too ill-equipped with arms and too determined not to fight to be a useful ally.

Their own administration was rotten with scandal and corruption. Many of the leading French industrialists and financiers were supporters of the Fascist "Cagoulard" plot, and pro-Nazi influences had also infected the officers of the French Army to an extent which became tragically evident to the world in 1940. So the visit of Daladier and Bonnet to London swung them round to a determination to keep out of war at all costs, and to bring the utmost diplomatic pressure to bear on the Czech Government to compel agreement with the Berchtesgaden terms.

Deserted by their allies, the Czechs reluctantly gave in, and Chamberlain flew back to Germany—this time to Godesberg—to give Hitler the news and discuss the arrangements for putting the Anglo-French plan into effect. To his horror and disillusionment he was

272

subjected to a savage bullying and presented with a fresh set of demands which he knew that neither the Czechs nor the British public could stomach.

War now seemed unavoidable, and gas-masks were issued and trenches dug in the parks. On the advice of the French and British, the Czechs proceeded to mobilize their army, and Britain mobilized her fleet. On 26 September Hitler made another speech, again announcing that his patience was exhausted. Next day, Chamberlain broadcast his willingness to visit Germany again if it would do any good, and followed it with a letter to Hitler offering to come and see him. Hitler, delighted to get his triumph cheaply, invited Chamberlain to Munich.

MUNICH

The British and French leaders went there on 29 September, determined to find some excuse for a settlement. At this later stage of the crisis the French Premier was even more desperately resolved than the British to postpone a war, and had resorted to unscrupulous misrepresentation of the advice of his own army chiefs in order to convince the British Government that some accommodation with Hitler must at all costs be reached.

At Munich the Godesberg terms were presented in a slightly modified form. The alterations made little difference to their scope, and less still, in the actual event, to the way in which they were carried out. But Chamberlain and Daladier grasped eagerly at the pretext afforded by the concessions, and signed on the dotted line. The Czech leaders, who had been excluded from the negotiations, were then brought in and made to do the same. Chamberlain flew back exultantly to London, waving in triumph a scrap of paper bearing Hitler's autograph and announcing that he had brought peace. He even called it "Peace with Honour!"

When the film of his return with his brandished paper was shown in German cinemas, eye-witnesses report that the audiences broke into loud and irreverent guffaws. He had become a figure of contempt.

Winston summarized the matter during the parliamentary debate that followed in these words:

> "I will begin by saying what everybody would like to ignore or forget, but which must nevertheless be stated, namely, that we have sustained a total and unmitigated defeat and that France has suffered even more than we have."

273

He declared that we had not merely given away the interests of Czecho-Slovakia, but deeply compromised and perhaps fatally endangered the safety and even the independence of Great Britain and France. We might desire friendship with the German people. We could never have friendship with the Nazi Government—"that power which spurns Christian ethics, which cheers its onward course by barbarous paganism, which vaunts the spirit of aggression and conquest, which derives strength and perverted pleasure from persecution, and uses, as we have seen, with pitiless brutality the threat of murderous force. That power cannot ever be the trusted friend of British democracy."

The British people, he asserted, should know that there had been gross neglect and deficiency in our defences, and that we had sustained a defeat without a war, the consequences of which would travel far with us along our road. "Do not suppose this is the end. This is only the beginning of the reckoning. This is only the first sip, the first foretaste of a bitter cup which will be proffered to us year by year unless by a supreme recovery of moral health and martial vigour we arise again and take our stand for freedom as in the olden time."

SHAMEFUL AND MISTAKEN EPISODE

Munich, though not quite the last act in the National Government's appeasement tragedy, was its culminating point. France and Britain had joined hands to play false to a solemn undertaking given to a loyal ally and neighbour, precisely at the moment when the situation arose against which that undertaking had been given. They postponed for eleven months a war which there was clearly no chance of avoiding, at the price of sacrificing a sturdy democratic country that might have been their war ally, and handing over its up-to-date arms and equipment and its munitions factories that made the finest big guns in Europe to their enemy.

In Britain the first feeling of immense and natural relief at the passing of the immediate threat of war was soon followed by acute uneasiness about the price of weakness and dishonour by which the brief peace had been bought. Later, when the postponed war broke in magnified disaster, the nation realized unmistakably that Munich had been a shameful and mistaken episode.

Apologists there will always be for Munich, who will advance the arguments which were pleaded at the time by the Premier, and will urge that his course, even if ill-fated, was justified by circumstances. Germany was already powerfully rearmed, whereas the French military equipment was rapidly becoming obsolete and the British was contemptibly small. Time for warlike preparation had to be bought, even at the expense of the Czechs. Britain, unlike France, had no specific commitment binding her to defend Czecho-Slovakia —only her general pledge under the League Covenant, which had lost all force since the desertion of Abyssinia. The French, Russians and British had no common frontier with Czecho-Slovakia, across which they could join forces with her for her defence. And, anyway, how was honest Chamberlain to know that Hitler was lying when he protested that he only wanted the German-speaking parts of the country?

ORIGINS OF APPEASEMENT

There are others, however, who after reviewing all the publicly known facts, hold that these excuses do not palliate the betrayal, for as the pace of German rearmament was vastly greater than that of France or Britain, the eleven months' delay only made Germany yet stronger in proportion in 1939 than in 1938; and besides, the first-class equipment she obtained by the Czech surrender was itself far greater than all the production of our munition factories during that dearly bought interval. Time was on the side of the Nazis, not of the Allies. If we had no special treaty with the Czechs, we were morally bound to support them as a State set up by us at Versailles, with frontiers defined by British experts. We had given a guarantee to France, and it was our threat to back out of that guarantee if the Berchtesgaden terms were not accepted which was used by the French to compel the Czechs to their first surrender. None but a wilfully blind man could be unaware that Hitler intended to seize all Czecho-Slovakia, once he gained entry into the Sudetenland and firm control of that area.

But the Munich surrender had its roots deeper than in the immediate circumstances of September, 1938. It went back to the Anglo-German naval treaty, to the side-stepping of the need for re-armament in the interests of electioneering tactics in 1935, to the break-up of the League over Abyssinia and the repudiation of the Locarno treaty by refusing to back France in stopping Hitler's troops from occupying the Rhineland. It was linked with the failure of the

Government to carry out their rearmament programme, despite Churchill's protests, their complaisance at the Italian and German interventions in Spain, their placid acceptance of Hitler's annexation of Austria.

Perhaps most of all, Munich should be traced to the effect of Hitler's subtle and persistent propaganda on the theme that Russian Bolshevism was a vast and insidious danger, against which the only safeguard was a strong Nazi Germany that could protect Western Capitalism from the menace of Communism. It was this last notion, by which many intelligent and high-minded people became infected, that induced them to shut their eyes to the blatant facts about Hitler's ambitions and preparations for world conquest, although these preparations formed an immediate, not a remote menace. It was this which, after Munich, held the Western democracies back from any honest effort to establish relations with Russia, and half-paralysed their rearmament against the German peril. The political ideas and financial interests of the City were allowed to take precedence over the claims of national defence and national honour, and even right up to the outbreak of war London merchants were pouring military supplies into the Reich, while the Government, which had powers to stop that traffic, was too deeply imbued with the tradition of tenderness to Hitler to lift a finger.

DEATH BLOW OF THE APPEASEMENT POLICY

There is no doubt that Chamberlain was badly scared and shaken by the ravings of Hitler at Godesberg, and realized most unwillingly that there were unbusinesslike people in the world who would not stand by a proper bargain. He found, too, that when the cheering died down responsible opinion in Britain was beginning to despair of a settlement. Even the City was not too happy about the commercial transactions of the Nazis, and their treatment of the financial trusts in which British business was interested.

But it was not until March, 1939, that the policy of appeasement received its death-blow from Hitler. The British and French Governments had cloaked their retreat at Munich with a promise to guarantee Czecho-Slovakia's new frontiers. On 15 March Hitler completed the outrage begun at Munich by seizing the rest of the unlucky country, incorporating Bohemia and Moravia in the Reich and setting up a puppet government in Slovakia.

Chamberlain made a formal protest—he could hardly do less. But he at last realized that Hitler was not to be held by appeasement methods, and that perhaps a firmer line was needed. So on 31 March he announced a pledge of military support for Poland if Hitler should attack her.

CHAMBERLAIN'S CURIOUS GESTURE

This was a curious gesture. What did Chamberlain expect from it? Defending his recreant attitude over Czecho-Slovakia, he had whimpered that it was "incredible" that we might be involved in war "because of a quarrel in a far-away country between people of whom we know nothing!" Poland was farther, even less familiar, and quite inaccessible to British aid. Was Chamberlain trying to bluff Hitler into quiescence by making this threatening gesture? Or was he trying to recapture the respect of the disillusioned British public?

Had he any intention, when he gave the pledge, of implementing it if the occasion arose? There was little clear evidence to furnish the answer. The work of rearmament went leisurely forward, and the Government still resisted all urging by Churchill and others to set up a Ministry of Supply. The outlook of the Government still seemed to resemble that shown a few months previously by W. S. Morrison, when as Minister of Agriculture he had rejected proposals for increasing food production. "What fools we should all look if we interfered with the industry," he had cried petulantly, "to guard against a war that never happened!"

On 7 April—Good Friday—Mussolini invaded Albania and proceeded to annex it. When asked if a British protest had been made, Chamberlain plaintively answered: "We would send a protest if it would do any good!" But he refused even to denounce the Anglo-Italian Agreement, which fettered our defence preparations in the Mediterranean.

It was pointed out by Lloyd George, and Churchill repeatedly urged the same counsel, that if we were to act in defence of Poland we must make an alliance for that purpose with Russia. After they had hammered away for a couple of months, Chamberlain consulted with the French, and finally sent a belated offer to Moscow of a Tripartite Pact. The offer was presently followed by a political Mission, headed not by the Foreign Secretary but by a subordinate official of the Foreign Office. Dilatory discussions followed, with

Russia asking and Britain refusing inclusion of the Baltic States among those for which a joint guarantee was to be issued.

Churchill declared in a speech on 29 June:

> "A full and solid alliance should be made with Russia without delay. The Russian claim that we shall all stand together in resisting an act of aggression upon the Baltic States seems just and reasonable, and I cannot understand what we have been boggling at all these weeks."

Chamberlain went on boggling. A military mission was sent to discuss defence plans, but went unprovided with any full information about British equipment or strategic prospects. At last Stalin wearied of the futile talk. Clearly the British did not mean to do real business, while the Germans had long been secretly urging an arrangement with themselves. On 23 August he signed a pact of mutual non-aggression with Germany, and Hitler, his patience once again exhausted, at once mobilized to attack Poland. He marched into that country on 1 September, 1939.

When Chamberlain met the House of Commons, eye-witnesses reported that he seemed embarrassed at the whole-hearted assurances he received from all sides of the nation's determination not to back out this time on his announcement of the dispatch of an ultimatum to Germany. On 2 September, when he was found to be still angling for a renewal of negotiations through Mussolini, he faced an angry sound of criticism. Why were we still sitting on the fence? He earnestly disclaimed any such intention, and at 11 a.m. on Sunday, 3 September, Britain declared war on Germany. At five o'clock the same afternoon France very reluctantly followed the British lead, and the world entered upon what was to prove the most disastrous and terrible war humanity had ever waged.

CHAPTER XIII

FIRST LORD AGAIN

THERE was no cheering this time. Twenty-five years earlier, when the First World War broke out, excited throngs had set Whitehall ringing with their wild huzzas. But now half the nation remembered vividly the long weariness and tragedy of that struggle, and all were educated in the fear of war.

Propaganda for disarmament and support of the League had painted the horrors of modern weapons of destruction—especially of gas warfare, whose threat was brought home to everyone by the gas-masks distributed at their doors. The Government had sought no less persistently to justify its appeasement policy by stressing the gruesome suffering which war would entail. Bombing from the air, it was realized, would be on a far vaster scale than in 1918. People had read accounts of the smashing of Guernica in Spain by German bombers, and cinemas had shown news-reels of Japanese air attacks on helpless Chinese.

The outbreak of war, it was assumed by many, would forthwith be followed by the devastation of London and other big towns: and a great exodus of government offices, commercial concerns and private citizens began. Schemes of evacuation of school-children and mothers with little ones were at once put in hand. Nearly a million and a half were moved in the first three days, and the quiet country-side sustained an invasion by swarms of town-bred youngsters who had much to learn and often much to unlearn in their new environment.

These feverish precautions against the anticipated perils were carried through with grim faces and without exultation. The nation knew that it was facing a foe who had the amoral ruthlessness of a wild beast; who would be unrestrained by any stirrings of humanity, any instinct of fair play, any solemnly given pledges, any limits imposed by the rules of civilized warfare. It was total war—war in which the civilian no less than the soldier, the women and little children no less than the men, might expect to suffer.

Yet, for all their set seriousness, the people were uplifted in heart. It had come at last, this terrible thing which had scared them for years: come, and they had not run away, but had faced it. The long shame of appeasement was over. "Safety First" was dead. Churchill put their mood into words when, on Chamberlain's announcement of the outbreak of war, he said:

> "Outside, the storms of war may blow and the lands be lashed with the fury of its gales, but in our own hearts this Sunday morning there is peace. . . . It is a war, viewed in its inherent quality, to establish on impregnable rocks the rights of the individual, and it is a war to establish and revive the stature of man."

About this the nation was of one mind. If any excuse is found by future historians for Baldwin's lethargy and Chamberlain's surrenders, it will be that by going to the farthest limit—and beyond it—in their effort to keep out of war, they left no room for question that this conflict was not of Britain's seeking. There was no peace party, charging the Government with reckless bellicosity. The Government itself had been a peace party till the national conscience could brook that policy no longer.

What heartened the country more than anything else at this hour of crisis was the fact that Chamberlain forthwith reconstituted his Government, bringing in Anthony Eden as Dominions Secretary and Winston Churchill as First Lord of the Admiralty. Eden had earned the respect of the nation by losing office rather than be a party to appeasement. As for Winston, the country had for months been clamouring for his inclusion in the Government. At the beginning of July papers as different as the *Daily Telegraph* and the *Manchester Guardian* were urging Chamberlain to bring him in. Now that Lloyd George was in semi-retirement, Churchill symbolized the warrior temper of Britain more than any other statesman, and he had had a wide experience of high office in the previous war. With Winston at long last in the Cabinet, there was some hope that greater vigour and vision might be infused into our fighting effort.

Hard worker though he was, Churchill found during those opening weeks of the war that his hands were full, with a job which kept him busy all day and all night. There were convoy arrangements to plan and set in motion; ships to requisition and adapt for naval use; mine-sweeping to organize; defensive patrols to institute; a new and

THE ORIGINAL WAR CABINET, 1939

*When the Second World War broke out on 3 September, 1939, Mr.
Neville Chamberlain, the Prime Minister, formed a special War
Cabinet, shown in this photograph. Reading from left to right (stand-
ing) are:—Sir John Anderson, Lord Hankey, Mr. Leslie Hore-Belisha,
Mr. Winston Churchill, Sir Kingsley Wood, Mr. Anthony Eden, Sir
Edward Bridges. Seated (left to right) Lord Halifax, Sir John Simon,
Mr. Neville Chamberlain, Sir Samuel Hoare and Lord Chatfield. Mr.
Churchill was again at the Admiralty.*

intensive drive to start in Admiralty shipyards and every other
available shipyard in the country for augmenting the strength of the
Navy. Enemy merchant shipping had to be swept up, and enemy
submarines and commerce raiders hunted down. A blockade of
Germany must be established, and all neutral vessels searched for
contraband.

The sea was at first Britain's only battlefield, as her navy was her
only potent war weapon. Despite all the talk of rearmament, the
warning of Munich, and the pleadings of Winston, not enough use
had been made of the time bought so cravenly for defence preparations. The Royal Air Force expansion had barely begun, while the
Luftwaffe was a balanced force already blooded in Spain. The Army
was no less weak in comparative numbers and backward in training.

British air design was no doubt superb, as subsequent air conflicts were to prove, and British courage was of the old, unquenchable quality. But we were unready to take on our ruthless and highly equipped foe.

Contrary to the nation's fears, however, Hitler did not immediately launch a military campaign in the west, or order big bombing attacks against our cities. Following his method of dealing with one foe at a time, he sent his Luftwaffe east, to support his armies in their blitzkrieg on Poland. Nazi bombs rained down on Warsaw, on Krakow, on Gdynia, Lwow, Poznan and scores of other open towns and defenceless villages. In the first three days over one thousand five hundred Polish civilians were killed, and many thousands more were injured by this pitiless total war.

EARLY STAGES OF THE WAR AT SEA

But if Poland was receiving the full attention of Hitler's land and air forces, his navy was free to devote all its efforts to attacking British shipping. It embarked on this task with ruthless vigour.

In the First World War Germany had slowly intensified her frightfulness at sea, and only after two years did she openly announce unrestricted submarine warfare. This time the real Nazi intention was precipitated by the action of a U-boat commander in sinking, without warning, the S.S. *Athenia*, a passenger liner, off the north coast of Ireland, on the very day that war was declared. Goebbels bluffed, the German Admiralty subsequently court-martialled the U-boat commander, but the gloves were off. Unrestricted war at sea had begun.

During the first fortnight of the war, German submarines that had been posted in advance on our sea routes sank 111,000 tons of British shipping, and also sank indiscriminately the merchantmen of neutral countries—Finnish, Dutch, Norwegian, Swedish, Greek and Belgian ships. The United States, mindful of the way in which German submarine frightfulness had entangled her into the First World War, made a prohibited zone around the British Isles and the northern and western waters of Europe, which American vessels must avoid: she also forbade her nationals to travel in the ships of belligerents.

But if Hitler remembered the lessons of 1914-18, so did Churchill. He at once put in hand a system of convoys, and all other proved devices against submarines, together with the improved methods

LEADER OF THE NATION

*This camera portrait of Winston Churchill by Yusuf Karsh is an
excellent character study of a frank and outspoken statesman. In
times of peril, he never understated the seriousness of the situation and
yet his broadcast speeches, vivid and powerful in their delivery, always
had a heartening and invigorating effect upon the people.*

CHURCHILL AND CHAMBERLAIN

*On 23 February, 1940, the crews of the cruisers "Ajax" and
"Exeter," which gained fame in the "Graf Spee" action, marched
through the City of London to Guildhall, where they were entertained
to lunch. Afterwards the King decorated some of the men on the
Horse Guards Parade. Mr. Churchill and Mr. Chamberlain watched.*

since planned by the Admiralty. German merchantmen on the seas were rounded up and captured by the Navy. In the first month the German merchant ships captured exceeded our own losses due to submarine sinkings by 150,000 tons. Thereafter the enemy developed a policy of scuttling his ships when they could not escape, relying on British chivalry—not in vain—to rescue the crews.

The U-boats were remorselessly hunted down, and Winston was able to announce that by the end of 1939 the Germans had lost half the number with which they entered the war. Two U-boats, however, scored definite successes against us. One torpedoed the old aircraft-carrier *Courageous,* while another daringly slipped inside the boom of Scapa Flow and sank a battleship, the *Royal Oak.* Another German success was the sinking near Iceland of the armed merchant cruiser *Rawalpindi* by the *Scharnhorst* and *Gneisenau,* on 23 November, 1939.

DEFEAT OF THE "GRAF SPEE"

The Navy was not long in bringing off a brilliant counter-stroke. On 14 December the "pocket" battleship, the *Admiral Graf Spee,* which had been commerce-raiding in the Indian and South Atlantic Oceans, was intercepted off the River Plate by three British cruisers, *Achilles, Exeter* and *Ajax.* In theory their armament was no sort of match for the 11-in. guns of the *Graf Spee,* but with what the German commander of the battleship later described as "inconceivable audacity" they dashed in to the attack, poured shells into the enemy and hammered her until she took refuge in Uruguayan territorial waters off Montevideo. There, on Hitler's orders, she scuttled herself, and her commander committed suicide.

It was an inspiring action, in the true Nelsonian tradition of the British Navy. Churchill could well say, when a short time later the City of London was doing honour at Guildhall to men of the *Exeter* and *Ajax*: "The battle of the River Plate, in a dark cold winter, has warmed the cockles of our hearts."

The incident was not yet over; for some three hundred of the British seamen taken by the *Graf Spee* from vessels she had sunk in her raiding career were imprisoned in a supply ship, the *Altmark,* which eluded pursuit and tried to wriggle back to Germany through Norwegian territorial waters.

But Churchill was at the Admiralty. Aircraft were sent prowling, and when the *Altmark* was located destroyers hunted it. It slunk up a narrow fiord and Norse naval craft guarded the entrance. On Winston's express orders, H.M.S. *Cossack* thrust past them, grappled with and boarded the *Altmark,* and British seamen, prisoned in the depths of an empty oil-tank, heard a shout "The Navy is here!" There were yells of delight as the men greeted their rescuers and were brought off home in triumph. Hitler, who had planned quite a different triumph—the dragging of the prisoners through the streets of Berlin—was furious; but the outside world looked on with sympathy and chuckled at his discomfiture.

Whether or not Winston's action was formally correct in international law, everyone recognized it as sound sense, especially when dealing with a foe who daily tore international law to tatters, and then frothed with cries of "Piracy! Roguery! Deeds unworthy of humanity!" on having his prey snatched from his clutches. The *New York Herald-Tribune* found humour in the "wild cries of anger, pain and outraged moral virtue" that issued from the Nazis, and remarked:

> "They come from a nation whose governors have made brute force their deity, which has torn up one treaty obligation after another, with no weak regard for law or decency, which has butchered the Polish civil population without compunction, which has torpedoed crowded liners without warning, which has strewn the murderous and illegal contact mine in the shipping lanes without a thought of the rights either of humanity or neutrality, and which has never admitted that any feeble consideration of 'plutocratic ethics' could stand in the way of its sacred ambitions."

The German assault on Poland was a brilliantly successful first trial of Hitler's blitzkrieg strategy. Starting on 1 September, it utterly shattered the Polish forces in a fortnight, swept round Warsaw and on into eastern Poland. The Polish Government fled toward the Rumanian frontier. By 16 September the Germans had reached Brest-Litovsk in the north and Lwow in Polish Ukraine.

Then Russia took a hand. Eastern Poland contained large Russian and Ukrainian populations and had originally been assigned at the Paris Peace Conference to Russia, though Poland subsequently annexed it in 1921. Stalin had no intention of letting this territory fall into German hands. The Russo-German non-aggression pact of August, 1939, had a secret protocol, by which the spheres of influence in Poland of Germany and the U.S.S.R. were recognized as bounded approximately by the Rivers Narew, Vistula and San. The disappearance of the Polish Government gave Stalin his chance. He announced that the treaty of non-aggression with Poland had lapsed, and sent his troops into the country to "protect the life and property of the population of Western Ukraine and Western White Russia." They met the German forces who fell back to the agreed line. On 29 September a treaty was signed by which Poland was once again partitioned. Russia recovered her lost territories of Byelo-Russia and Western Ukraine, while central and western Poland fell into German hands.

With the liquidation of Poland, Hitler suggested that there was now no point in Britain and France keeping up their war with him. They had gone to war for Poland's sake, but had done nothing to save her. Not a single formation of British or French troops had appeared on the Polish battlefields, nor had a single flight of aircraft from the Western Democracies been interposed to prevent the Luftwaffe from wrecking Poland's cities. Clearly, their guarantee to Poland had been only a formal gesture. As there was now no Poland, couldn't they call it off?

"Why should there be any war in the West?" Hitler asked in a speech to the Reichstag on 6 October. Poland would never rise again. If war went on, millions of lives would be sacrificed, and the conflict would spread far overseas.

> "I make this declaration only because I very naturally desire to spare my people sufferings. But should the views of Churchill and his following prevail, then this declaration will be my last. We should then fight. . . . Let those repulse my hand who regard war as the better solution!"

The views of Churchill and his following did prevail. The country had utterly shed the spirit of Munich, and spoke that name only with shame and abhorrence. Its new temper was defined by Winston in a broadcast on 12 November:

> "You may take it absolutely for certain that either all that Britain and France stand for in the modern world will go down, or that Hitler, the Nazi régime, and the recurring German or Prussian menace to Europe will be broken and destroyed. That is the way the matter lies, and everybody had better make up their minds to that solid, sombre fact."

INSPECTING COASTAL DEFENCES

His appointment to the Committee of Defence in 1940 meant further responsibilities for Mr. Churchill. When Lord Chatfield, Minister for Co-ordination of Defence, resigned from the Committee, his post was abolished and Churchill became a dominant figure in the control of the armed forces. Above, he is inspecting coastal defences.

Stalin had studied *Mein Kampf*. He was perfectly well aware that, whatever designs Hitler might have on western Europe, he quite definitely intended, sooner or later, to seize western Russia, the Ukraine and the Caucasus. When he judged that the time was ripe, the Fuehrer would sweep aside like chaff the treaties he had signed with the Soviet and the professions of friendship he was now making.

Against that day it would be well to deepen a cushion between the German Army and Russian territory. The strip of eastern Poland would be useful for this. So, too, would the Baltic States. On the same day as the treaty partitioning Poland was signed with the Reich, a Treaty of Mutual Assistance was signed with Estonia, by which Russian forces were allowed to establish naval and air bases in that State. Three days later the Latvians were summoned to Moscow to negotiate a similar pact, and within a week Lithuania had to follow suit.

Finland was the next to be invited to furnish Russia with defensive bases against the coming struggle. But here the process did not run so smoothly. The dominating personalities in Finland were anti-Russian. Their central figure, Field-Marshal Mannerheim, was strongly pro-German, and had brought Finnish forces into the field on the German side in the First World War. Stalin's pressure met with a determined refusal, and at the end of November, 1939, the Russians set out to gain their ends by force of arms.

At first they put into the field what can have been only a token force, for they seem to have expected that Finland would put up no more than a token resistance. Obviously she could not hope to hold off a full-scale attack by her giant neighbour, and Russia's demands upon her, if unpleasant, were limited. But the little country maintained a stout and most embarrassingly resolute defence. The Russians were held and at points defeated, much to the surprise of the general public.

RUSSIA'S DILEMMA OVER FINLAND

Stalin faced a delicate situation. He particularly did not want to unmask his full military strength, for he was anxious that Hitler should not suspect its formidable character. The more Hitler underrated it, the better the chance Russia would have of meeting successfully the first onset of German arms. But the Finnish affair was dragging on, and rousing widespread sympathy throughout the world with the gallantry of the little country. Italian airmen came to her aid, and Swedish volunteers. Britain poured in arms and equipment, and finally began to press Norway for permission to send an expeditionary force. Very luckily for us, Norway refused it passage.

The war had to be finished quickly: so in February, 1940, Stalin turned on some of his heavy artillery and blasted away the Finnish defences. On 12 March peace was signed. Russia got her naval and air bases in the Gulf of Finland and the strip of the Karelian isthmus running to within gunfire of Leningrad, possession of which by a potential enemy had been a continual menace to Russia's northern capital.

The Finnish war was destined to have results of critical importance. Russia's initial failure confirmed the widely held notion that her military forces were a hollow pretence, and that she would crumple up if resolutely attacked. Churchill, always a bitter enemy of Communism, in a broadcast on 30 March, suggested that the apparent failure of Russian arms was the result of a weakening of the fibre of the nation under Communism. If Churchill was misled, so was Hitler. No doubt a similar underestimate of Russia's strength influenced his decision to turn east before attempting to finish his fight with Britain. But if Germany and the Western Powers were deceived by the initial weakness of the Russian forces, Stalin was not. He set about remedying the failures in command and equipment that had been made apparent in the Finnish campaign.

Hitler was absolutely right when he singled out Churchill as the central figure in the war against Nazidom. For, truth to tell, the rest of Chamberlain's Government, made up as it was in the main of the same people who had been associated with him in his appeasement policy, was pitiably deficient in the martial spirit.

Only at sea, and in the air over the sea and over German naval bases, did Britain pursue any active hostilities during the first months of the war. Our aircraft, it is true, made flights over German cities, but they dropped there, not bombs, but only pamphlets! Within a week of the declaration of war a British Expeditionary Force had once more been landed in France. It joined its French comrades holding the much-publicised Maginot Line, and the two armies sat still, making a few trivial raids on the enemy and waiting for him to start the fighting. Their aircraft made reconnaissance flights into Germany, but they were careful to drop no bombs.

BUILDING OF THE SIEGFRIED LINE

Hitler hurried on the building of the line of fortifications along the German frontier—the Siegfried Line. His workers toiled at it day and night, labouring through the dark with the aid of arc lights. They formed a magnificent target for bombing attacks, but not a bomb was dropped on them. The British were allowed to sing about "hanging out the washing on the Siegfried Line." They were not allowed to damage it. The theory of both the British and French Governments seems to have been that if they didn't hurt Hitler, he wouldn't hurt them!

They misjudged him. If for a time he left the West alone, it was not out of kindness, nor fear. He was preparing his stroke. But in Britain, though we were committed to a fight to the death with the most formidable military power in the world, the Government

FEEDING ROTA, THE "PINNER LION"

Rota, the lion who had acquired some notoriety by being kept in a back garden in Pinner, Middlesex, was presented by his owner to Mr. Churchill. He was handed over to the Zoological Gardens and, in this photograph, he is shown being fed by Mr. Churchill. Mr. Churchill also visited a black swan presented to him by Australians.

meandered along with its preparations, making no serious effort to speed up the output of munitions or to mobilize the whole nation for war. In fact, the figures of unemployment increased between August and October, 1939, by more than half a million!

Neutral countries looking on grew contemptuous, and began to jeer. Britain and France had so valiantly declared war to save Poland. But they had done nothing whatever to help her, and seemed quite incapable of fighting. Americans began to dub the affair a "Phoney War"! Were British and French statesmen in the pay of Germany? Or did they think Hitler could be scared by heroic speeches and crushed by showers of pamphlets? The British were restless and uneasy. Reports about their army in France told only of the visits of concert parties and the unbroken morale of men bivouacking in mud and rain. That sort of thing could not hope to defeat Hitler.

The truth was that Chamberlain was utterly unwarlike. Not without reason did he protest when announcing the outbreak of war: "Everything that I have worked for, everything that I have hoped for, everything that I have believed in during my public life, has crashed into ruins!" He could not bring himself to order real acts of war, and eagerly seized on any excuse for postponing the actual clash of arms.

Churchill, who had no such inhibitions, did what he could to maintain a real war in the naval sphere, but despite his efforts to be loyal to his Cabinet colleagues, he found it hard to muzzle his impatience at their passivity. Speaking in the Commons on 27 January, 1940, he hinted his restlessness, and urged a more energetic national effort:

> "We must plough up the land, we must organize agriculture upon at least the 1918 scale. We must grow more food and accommodate ourselves as much as possible to eat the kind of food we can grow.... In this way, also, we may lighten the task of the Navy, increase its mobility, and free its striking forces for offensive action. We do not wish indefinitely to continue merely awaiting the blows which are struck at us. We hope that the day will come when we shall hand over that job to Herr Hitler, when he will be wondering where he is going to be struck next."

Britain, Churchill asserted, had much slack to take up, and had not yet done this or there would not be 1,300,000 unemployed (actually there were over 1,500,000), of whom at least half could play their part. She had to make a huge expansion of her labour forces, and bring women into war industry. Otherwise "we should fail utterly to bear our fair share of the burden France and Britain have jointly assumed and which we must now carry forward together to the end or perish miserably in slavery and ruin."

But Winston's protest passed unheeded. When on 19 March Chamberlain reported the progress of the war, he had practically nothing to say about operations against the Germans, whom we were fighting, but much about the munitions we had sent to Finland, and the hundred thousand men we had intended to send, if the war had not terminated there so soon. It might have been Russia, not Germany, with which Britain was at war! He declared that the Government would not let itself be hustled into adventures which appeared to present little chance of success and much chance of danger or even disaster, in response to the demands of those who urged a more vigorous policy to secure the initiative. At the end of the debate he admitted that our organization was still faulty in many respects, and recognized that there was room for improvement in the matter of transport and shipping. He had no rigid mind upon matters of administration and the machinery of government, and it would be his endeavour so to change that machinery from time to time as to correct deficiencies and create efficiency!

END OF THE "PHONEY" WAR

This dilatory dithering, this readiness to consider anything except fighting the enemy, was no way to win a war. Early in April Chamberlain's complacency even led him to make the amazing assertion that Hitler had "missed the bus"! It was a statement that showed an utter inability to understand the nature of Hitler, and of the war to which the country was committed. Hitler promptly retorted by invading Denmark and Norway, and thereafter the war lost its "phoney" character and started in real earnest.

During those dreary months, the spirit of Britain found expression, not in the procrastinations of its Government, but in the militant utterances of the First Lord. Winston had the right to speak thus, for his own department was really fighting. He put into words what the nation was feeling. He became the people's spokesman, the clarion of their purpose.

At the outset of war Churchill's Admiralty duties left him little time for speaking. But on 1 October, 1939, he gave the first of a series of broadcasts on the progress of the war. The world was then to discover that he had an effective radio delivery. His rich, oratorical style, tinged with humour, suited the microphone well and the people enjoyed his blunt, forthright manner of speaking.

In this October broadcast, he said that the question of how soon victory was gained depended upon how long Hitler and his group of wicked men, "whose hands are stained with blood and soiled with corruption," could keep their grip on the docile, unhappy German people. The war began when Hitler wanted it, and it would end when the Allies were convinced he had had enough. "Now we have begun : now we are going on; now with the help of God, and with the conviction that we are the defenders of Civilization and Freedom, we are going on, and we are going on to the end."

In a second broadcast on 12 November he breathed a defiant response to "the bloodcurdling threats which the Nazis exude

293

through every neutral country and bawl around the world by their propaganda machine." Hitler, "that evil man over there," might be preparing violent and dire events. The Nazis were looking with hungry eyes at some small countries in the West which they could trample down and loot. But the victory of the Allies would at the last decide the fate of Holland and Belgium. It might well be that the final extinction of a baleful domination would pave the way to a broader solidarity of all the men in all the lands.

If there was little to boast about in respect of our deeds on the Continent, the exploits of the Navy gave Winston heartening themes, alike for Parliament and for public speeches. In a broadcast on 20 January, 1940, he was able to report that the protection afforded to our convoys was so adequate that the odds against a convoyed craft being sunk were five hundred to one. The U-boats were turning in despair to easier prey and sinking the ships of neutral countries—Dutch, Belgian, Danish, Swedish and, above all, Norwegian—"not only by the blind and wanton mine, but by the coldly considered, deliberately aimed torpedo."

He expressed his concern for these unfortunate neutrals. "Whether on sea or on land, they are the victims upon whom Hitler's hate and spite descend. . . . Every one of them is wondering tonight who will be the next victim on whom the criminal adventurers of Berlin will cast their rending stroke." He advised them to fulfil their pledges under the League Covenant and stand together with Britain and France against aggression and wrong.

> "At present their plight is lamentable, and will become much worse. They are bowing humbly and in fear to German threats of violence, comforting themselves with the thought that Britain and France will win, each hoping that if he feeds the crocodile enough, the crocodile will eat him last! All hope that the storm will pass before their turn comes to be devoured. But the storm will not pass. It will rage and roar, ever more loudly—ever more widely. It will spread to the South. It will spread to the North. There is no chance of a speedy end, except through united action."

The warning was prophetic. But, as he has done again and again, Winston displayed uncanny foresight in his predictions. Before a dozen weeks had passed, the crocodile would open his jaws, and one by one the states which had vainly thought to hide themselves in the dim shadows of neutrality would vanish into his maw.

Very early on 9 April, 1940, in the dark small hours of a moonless night, German troops landed from transports at the main harbours of Norway, while a big convoy sailed up the Oslo fiord, escorted by powerful naval forces. At the same time, great numbers of troops poured across the Danish frontier, and German warships drove into the great port of Copenhagen.

INVASION OF DENMARK AND NORWAY

The treacherous attack effected a complete surprise, for if the Governments concerned had heard advance rumours of it, they had refused to credit them, wishfully thinking: "It can't happen to us!" Chamberlain, with his recoil from any thought of warlike operations, had been similarly incredulous, though Churchill had persuaded the British and French Governments to lay minefields off Norway's western coast. These minefields were announced on 8 April. The German Press raved against this "dare-devilry of Churchill," although for more than a fortnight their own troops and transports had been secretly in motion for their attack on Norway.

Denmark, unarmed and powerless, surrendered to the German ultimatum, and accepted her "protection." The Norwegian Government resisted, but discovered to its horror that the country was riddled with treachery. Nazi sympathizers and German agents everywhere were co-operating with the invaders and opening the gates to them, while the Norwegian Army and populace, taken completely by surprise, at first gaped in bewilderment. By the time that resistance was organized, the main harbours and all the scanty airfields were in German hands. The King and his counsellors were hunted by German bombers from village to village, and an *ersatz* Norse government was set up under the Norwegian Nazi leader, Colonel Quisling, whose name became a synonym for treachery.

Hitler's purpose was clear. He knew that the British were his ultimate enemy, and that if he was to defeat them, he must hem them in at sea. His harbours on the continental mainland were few, dependent on the tides, easy to blockade. But Norway had, up the fiords of her serrated coastline, numerous blue-water harbours, capable of entry at all states of the tide, from which the German Navy could get free access to the Atlantic Ocean and maintain a constant watch on the British Isles. Indeed, if Hitler could also gain control of Denmark's possessions, the Faroe Islands, Iceland and South Green-

MR. CHURCHILL WITH THE R.A.F.

The photograph on the opposite page was taken aboard the Boeing 314 flying boat "Berwick," with Mr. Churchill at the controls, when he made his trans-Atlantic flight. Above, Mr. Churchill in the uniform of Air Commodore of the R.A.F. in the mess of 615 Fighter Squadron. He became honorary Air Commodore of the unit.

land, he would be able to enclose Britain from the north and west.

Winston was alive to the danger. The Navy struck, and on the very next day, 10 April, warships went to the Faroes and established a British garrison there to hold it against any German attack. Our fleet scoured the North Sea. On 9 April the battle-cruiser *Renown* engaged and damaged the *Scharnhorst* off Narvik; and on the next day five of our destroyers struck at six German destroyers, escorting transports in the Narvik fiord. For the loss of one destroyer and another run ashore, they sank all six transports and an ammunition ship, sent one enemy destroyer to the bottom and damaged and set on fire three more. Three days later our destroyers returned to the attack, swept right up the fiord and sank seven German destroyers right in the very harbour of Narvik itself.

Meantime our submarines, too, had been busy in the Kattegat, smashing at the stream of German transports carrying troops and equipment to Oslo, and at their protecting warships. Our bombing aircraft were out on the same task, and so was the small Norwegian Navy. The carnage was terrific. Thousands of corpses from sunken transports were washed up on the coasts of Norway and Sweden. Such damage was inflicted on the German Navy during the operations that she was for some time able to make only limited use of the ports she had acquired. She was in no fettle for striking across the sea to Iceland, which at once severed its connexion with Denmark; and before a German expedition could be organized, the British had established a garrison and naval base there.

BRITISH BASE ESTABLISHED IN ICELAND

Churchill had done a good job with the Navy in the face of this crisis. But on land the British performance was no theme for boasting. Six days passed before the first British troops arrived in Norway to help its hard-pressed forces. Without air cover they were at a heavy disadvantage. Chamberlain would not listen to bold spirits who urged a direct assault on Trondhjem. Certainly this meant taking big risks, but it was the only line of attack that could have given us a first-class naval and air base, and thereby a chance of success. Instead, the Germans were allowed to hammer their way through to Trondhjem and to link up with the small advance force already occupying it. All hope of frustrating them in Norway disappeared.

On 2 May—less than three weeks after their first landing—the British expeditions at Namsos and Andalsnes were withdrawn "with complete success," and all Norway was abandoned to the Nazis except for the extreme north, where a British force hung on at Narvik for another five weeks before pulling out.

The timid inadequacy and the dismal failure of the British effort to help Norway filled to overflowing the cup of public disgust and anger at the incapacity of Chamberlain and his "old gang" to lead the nation in war. Whatever his virtues and talents might be, they certainly were not of the kind needed to deal with Hitler. Were the nerveless surrenders of appeasement to be followed by nerveless

TRYING OUT A TOMMY-GUN

In April, 1940, there was a minor reconstruction in the Government and Neville Chamberlain took the opportunity of putting Mr. Churchill at the head of a Committee of Service Ministers for the purpose of guiding the conduct of the war. His energy and military knowledge made it a very popular appointment. Above, Mr. Churchill is examining a tommy-gun during a visit to North-East England.

surrenders of retreat? Would the capitulation of Munich be crowned by the capitulation of London?

On 7 and 8 May a very hostile House of Commons met to debate the collapse of the Norwegian effort. The Prime Minister tried with poor success to excuse the blunders and unreadiness that had wrecked the campaign. It was not only the Liberal and Labour Oppositions that rose in criticism. Some of the most scathing denunciations came from Government benches.

Sir Roger Keyes announced that the Navy had been let down by Whitehall. It would have seized Trondhjem and changed the whole face of the campaign if it had been allowed to carry out its plans. One of the bitterest assaults came from Amery, who dealt faithfully with Chamberlain's record as autocrat of national policy in peace and war. He rounded off his peroration by quoting Oliver Cromwell's biting words to the Rump of the Long Parliament:

> "You have sat here too long for any good you have been doing. Depart, I say, and let us have done with you! In the name of God, GO!"

Even more devastating was the attack of Lloyd George, who spoke with the authority of one who had in his day been Britain's most resourceful and energetic war statesman. A vote of censure had been moved, and Chamberlain, in accepting the challenge, had called on his "friends in the House" to save him from defeat. Lloyd George said:

> "'It is not a question of who are the Prime Minister's friends. It is a far bigger issue. The Prime Minister must remember that he has met this formidable foe of ours in peace and in war. He has always been worsted. He is not in a position to put it on the ground of friendship. He has appealed for sacrifice. The nation is prepared for every sacrifice so long as it has leadership. I say solemnly that the Prime Minister should give an example of sacrifice, because there is nothing which can contribute more to victory in this war than that he should sacrifice the seals of office."

Churchill, who replied for the Government, loyally tried to save his chief by himself accepting responsibility for the course of events —a gallant effort which drew from Lloyd George the protest that "he would not allow himself to be converted into an air-raid shelter to keep the splinters from hitting his colleagues." Winston's main argument was that the fault really lay in our failure in the last five years to maintain or regain air parity in numbers with Germany—a failure which "has condemned us and will condemn us for some time to come to a great deal of difficulty and suffering and danger." But if that was some excuse for the failure in Norway, it was none for the ineptitude of the National Government which had been responsible for the wasted five years.

IN DEFENCE OF THE NAVY

In defence of the Navy, Churchill had to admit that all plans were made for a landing a Trondhjem of a force superior to that of the enemy, but the Government had preferred to make an indirect attack which they hoped would be cheaper. "I must make it perfectly clear that the Admiralty never withdrew their offer, nor was it considered impracticable in the naval aspect."

The House drew its own conclusions. Indeed, it had no notion of crediting Churchill with the choice of a nerveless or faint-hearted course. It knew him too well for that!

When the division bell rang no fewer than thirty-nine supporters of the Government, including thirty-three Conservatives, went into the opposition lobby—an unprecedented event at that time, because of the strict discipline maintained by the Tory whips. The Government majority, normally about two hundred, fell to eighty-one, and Chamberlain could not mistake the meaning of the red light.

On 9 and 10 May he summoned the Labour and Liberal leaders, and invited them to join in a coalition government. They both declined to do so if Chamberlain were the Prime Minister. The news which came through on the morning of the 10th, that Germany had invaded Holland and Belgium, added the finishing touch. Chamberlain resigned that evening, and advised the King to send for Winston Churchill. At last Britain's warrior statesman entered into his long-postponed inheritance as leader of the British nation.

CHURCHILL AS PRIME MINISTER

In April, 1940, the Nazis swept through Denmark and from there occupied Norway. It was a great blow to the dwindling prestige of Neville Chamberlain and he resigned. On 10 May, Mr. Churchill was summoned to Buckingham Palace and invited to succeed Chamberlain. He is here shown leaving No. 10 Downing Street as Prime Minister.

CHAPTER XIV

CHURCHILL TAKES THE HELM

I n May, 1940, the British nation passed through the refining fire of a spiritual purge; experienced a change of heart; and came forth high tempered, stern in courage, ready for sacrifice. Its material fortunes struck bottom, but its feet braced themselves on a rock. The people realized afresh what their fathers had once known, that honour is more to be desired than safety, and that until a man has found something worth dying for he has not entered into life.

They took Winston Churchill to their hearts because they recognized in him a man who incarnated those principles; who had kept faith with them through the days when they were forgotten or condemned. "The nation is prepared for every sacrifice," Lloyd George had declared, "so long as it has leadership." In Winston the people of every party and class realized that they had exactly the leader they wanted for the grim days of life-and-death struggle which now loomed ominously ahead. Even before the war began a large and swiftly growing number had come to look to him as their hope. In 1940 the whole nation was of the same mind. It was the warrior-statesman's hour.

The Labour and Liberal Parties, which had declined to serve with Chamberlain, promptly accepted Churchill's invitation to unite in a Coalition Government. The day after his appointment as Prime Minister he was able to announce the formation of an Inner War Cabinet of five members, which included Attlee and Greenwood; and two days later, on 13 May, he met the House of Commons with his new Government substantially complete—an omnibus assembly in which members of the "old gang" rubbed shoulders with those who for five years had been their bitter critics. Winston's incapacity to bear malice, always one of his most attractive characteristics although arousing acute impatience among those more under the influence of their long memories, led him to act with instinctive generosity, in the hour of victory, to those over whom he triumphed. He would have no vendettas. Lamentable though the record of the

CHURCHILL AT WORK

It was at the most critical hour in the history of Britain that Mr. Churchill became her Prime Minister. Belgium and Holland were overrun and then followed the heroic disaster at Dunkirk. In June, 1940, France surrendered. "I have nothing to offer," said the recently appointed Prime Minister, "but blood, toil, tears and sweat."

appeasers might be, this was a new start. If they were ready to serve the country loyally in the spirit of the new era they should have their chance to do so.

What this new era betokened Winston put into memorable words in his first statement to the House as Prime Minister, on 13 May. He declared:

"I would say to the House, as I said to those who have joined this Government: 'I have nothing to offer but blood, toil, tears and sweat!'

"We have before us an ordeal of the most grievous kind. We have before us many, many long months of struggle and of suffering. You ask, what is our policy? I will say: It is to wage war, by sea, land and air, with all our might and with all the strength that God can give us; to wage war against a monstrous tyranny, never surpassed in the dark, lamentable catalogue of human crime. That is our policy. You ask: What is our aim? I can answer in one word: It is Victory! Victory at all costs, victory in spite of all terror, victory, however long and hard the road may be: for without victory there is no survival. Let that be realized—no survival for the British Empire, no survival for all that the British Empire has stood for, no survival for the urge and impulse of the ages, that mankind will move forward towards its goal. But I take up my task with buoyancy and hope. I feel sure that our cause will not be suffered to fail among men. At this time I feel entitled to claim the aid of all, and I say: 'Come then, let us go forward together with our united strength!'"

It was the call that the nation had been longing to hear. "Blood, toil, tears and sweat!" The people were ready for sacrifice, if the cause was worthy. And the cause was indeed worthy. They could not easily twist their tongues round phrases with a religious flavour, because for so long that sort of expression had ceased to be as habitual as it had been to their Victorian forefathers. Yet at heart the nation knew that they were fighting for Right against naked Evil, and they were content. They shared their leader's mood of "buoyancy and hope."

It was needed; for Churchill took the helm at the blackest hour of mortal danger this country has ever known since the barbarous hordes of Teutonic heathen swept into it with fire and sword in the Dark Ages of the sixth and seventh centuries. Even the Napoleonic menace, a century and a quarter before, was not so deadly, for Bonaparte's rule was neither pagan nor lawless, as was that of Hitler. The Frenchman was no mere gangster. But the Nazis had no use for either justice or mercy; and for Britain, the penalty of defeat would have been nameless horror and savagery and practical obliteration. When Churchill took charge that fate was drawing very near.

ATTACK ON HOLLAND AND BELGIUM

Hitler's attack on Holland and Belgium had been long foreseen and foretold by competent observers. Ostrich-like, the Dutch and Belgian Governments had refused to admit what was coming or to prepare for it by uniting with France and Britain for common defence. By clutching round them the flimsy veil of neutrality, they bought a few months of nominal peace at the price of certain defeat when Hitler should reach them in his time-table of conquest.

His invasion started at 3 a.m. on 10 May, and just after 6 a.m.

the Dutch Minister and Belgian Ambassador called on Lord Halifax, the Foreign Secretary, to implore Britain's aid. Measures were taken at once to help them. British and French troops left the shelter of the lines they were holding along the Belgian frontier and pushed forward into Belgium and Holland to reinforce the local troops in their vain effort to stem the Nazi advance. Hitler had no doubt anticipated and planned for precisely this move, and flung the main weight of his thrust farther south, through Luxembourg and the Belgian Ardennes—a hilly, wooded region which the French strategists had dismissed as unsuited to offer passage to a modern army—thus cutting down behind the forces which had gallantly but incautiously spread themselves across the Low Countries.

CAPITULATION OF THE DUTCH AND BELGIANS

At the same time Hitler flung those countries into confusion by the intensity of his bombing attacks, and by dropping innumerable parachute troops on aerodromes and other key points. Rotterdam was bombed by a savage raid by the Luftwaffe, a third of the city was destroyed and many thousands of people were killed. The Dutch Queen took refuge in England, and on 14 May, just four days after the war began, the Dutch commander ordered his troops to lay down their arms. The capitulation of the Netherlands Army was signed next morning.

In Belgium the fighting continued for nearly another fortnight. There the left wing of the British Army was in contact with the Belgian forces. But on 16 May the German drive enveloped Brussels, and next day Antwerp was abandoned. The "impregnable" Liége forts fell to paratroops who dropped on their roofs and clambered through their casements and ventilation shafts. Namur fell. The Louvain library once again went up in flames. The Belgian Army was hemmed against the coast, and, on the evening of 27 May, King Leopold sent to German Army headquarters his offer of surrender.

Meantime, farther south, the Germans had forced the crossing of the River Meuse near Sedan with their tanks and motorized columns. They drove straight ahead, right across north-eastern France; through the old Somme battlefields—St. Quentin, Bapaume, Amiens, Abbeville—in a long corridor which seemed to be asking to be cut off. But somehow the French were powerless to sever it, and fresh troops streamed along, to strengthen and widen the channel, while

ON THE SOUTH COAST DURING THE BATTLE OF BRITAIN

This picture shows Mr. Churchill while on a visit to the South coast during the Battle of Britain. He inspected air-raid damage at Dover and Ramsgate and other towns, and talked to A.R.P. workers. He witnessed an aerial battle in which two enemy machines were shot down. He replaced his usual headgear by a steel helmet.

its tip bent up north to circle round on Boulogne, Calais and Dunkirk. The British Army and the First French Army were thus severed from the remaining French forces, cooped up in a corner with their bases gone, and faced with annihilation.

By 23 May, Boulogne was in German hands. A small British force, the Rifle Brigade, had been flung into Calais to hold that port and keep contact with the British Army. The Germans swept upon the town and hemmed in the garrison, and summoned it to surrender. It refused, and by its desperate resistance it held up the enemy advance for four vital days. In the end the riflemen were wiped out, but their sacrifice saved the British Army, which gained time to rally round Dunkirk, the only exit left to it from the narrowing ring of German steel.

It was incontrovertibly a lightning victory for Hitler. In seventeen days he had conquered Holland and Belgium, routed the French and British armies in northern France, and won those Channel ports toward which the Kaiser had vainly striven for four years during the 1914-18 conflict. The Nazi troops streaming across Flanders and Picardy had outflanked from the north the fabled Maginot Line on which French security policy had squandered a fortune during the past two decades. That vast nightmare of concrete and engineering lay derelict and purposeless on one side, while the enemy flood which it had been meant to dam poured down behind it into the heart of France.

WHAT WERE THE FRENCH DOING?

The swift advance of German forces across northern France seemed incredible to those in Britain who kept vivid memories of the long stagnation of stationary trench warfare in that very area during the struggle of twenty-five years before. Surely this flying column, thrusting so far ahead of the main force, would be cut off and annihilated! What were the French doing, that they did not sever this menacing but most vulnerable tentacle at its root?

Only by degrees did the truth become known, through reports of those who got back to Britain and through the march of events in France itself—the truth that the French and British armies were out-manoeuvred by armoured and motorized columns closely supported by air forces with unprecedented mobility and flexibility. Every device to increase the disruption of the Allied Command was practised in a fruitful atmosphere of dismay and near panic. Worse still, the French Army itself was riddled with Nazi sympathizers, who were quite ready to sell out to the enemy. Numbers of the officers belonged to that right wing of French politics which gave birth to the "Cagoulard" movement—a secret Fascist organization that plotted the overthrow of French democracy and a link-up with the Axis.

As hopes of security through the League crumbled during the appeasement years, French politicians fell into two schools: those who still based themselves on the conviction that Germany was the enemy, and that France's hope lay in solidarity with Britain; and others who felt that Germany was the coming power, that Britain was unready and unwilling to oppose her, and that the wise course was to take shelter under Hitler's wing, whatever the price he exacted. Hitler would at least make short work of their Socialist and

Communist opponents! With this divided mind setting her states-men one against another, France was paralysed. Her generals failed each other, and her war effort collapsed.

As Prime Minister, Churchill had access to all the information about this state of affairs which had been secretly furnished to the Government, but had been ignored by Chamberlain, who preferred on occasions to close his mind to unpleasant facts. Churchill, with his acute mind, was not slow to realize how desperate the outlook had grown, and how poor a chance there was of keeping up the struggle in France. He hinted at this in his very first broadcast to the nation as Premier, on 19 May.

The Germans had already broken through the French frontier and were driving into the old Somme battlefields. The picture was not yet as alarming as it would become in the next few days, and Winston expressed a hope that the breach in the Allied front might yet be repaired. But he did not conceal its danger. It would be foolish, he said, to disguise the gravity of the hour, though it would be still more foolish to lose heart or courage. Well-trained and well-equipped armies ought not to be overthrown by a raid of mechanized vehicles. Yet he was presently using words which hinted his fears of a disastrous turn of events on the continent in the near future.

> "After this battle in France abates its force there will come a battle for our island, for all that Britain is, and all that Britain means. That will be the struggle. In that supreme emergency we shall not hesitate to take every step, even the most drastic, to call forth from our people the last ounce and the last inch of effort of which they are capable. The interests of property and the hours of labour are nothing compared with the struggle for life and honour, for life and freedom, to which we vowed ourselves."

He ended this broadcast on a religious note which had of late been less frequently heard in the public utterances of political leaders.

> "Today is Trinity Sunday. Centuries ago, words were written to be a call and a spur to the faithful servants of truth and justice: 'Arm yourselves and be ye men of valour and be in readiness for the conflict, for it is better for us to perish in battle than to look upon the outrage of our nation and our altars. As the will of God is in Heaven, even so let Him do.' "

"There will come a battle for our island!" Winston was never disposed to deceive himself or the people by vain wishful thinking. He knew that the French and British armies were well able to stand up to any mere "raid of mechanized vehicles"; but he knew, too, that where treachery and mutual distrust have entered, the citadel may be betrayed from within.

The sudden capitulation of the Belgian King on 27 May, without any prior warning to his allies who had abandoned their defensive front to come to his aid in response to his appeal, was an unexpected and fatal disaster. At the time it was interpreted as another piece of treachery, the act of a royal Quisling, who had sold out to Hitler. Later, evidence was forthcoming that Leopold was no traitor. He had surrendered because he judged the fight lost, and wanted to spare his people needless massacre, He himself never made peace with Hitler, but treated himself as a prisoner of the invaders. His decision might be right or wrong. It was at least sincere and unselfish.

DIRE PLIGHT OF THE BRITISH FORCES

Yet, right or wrong, it destroyed any chance that the French and British forces trapped in the Pas-de-Calais could have of continuing the fight. When Churchill broke the news to the House on 28 May he had to admit that their situation was extremely grave. He later owned that at that time he doubted if twenty or thirty thousand of our army could be rescued. At the time his warning was:

> "Meanwhile the House should prepare itself for hard and heavy tidings. I have only to add that nothing which may happen in this battle can in any way relieve us of our duty to defend the world cause to which we have vowed ourselves, nor should it destroy our confidence in our power to make our way, as on former occasions in our history, through disaster and through grief to the ultimate defeat of our enemies."

At that moment it seemed certain that our entire army in northern France would be forced to capitulate. Dunkirk was the only port left to them, a little harbour which small vessels used at high water. It had already suffered by the German bombing of British lines of communication. Our troops were strung out as far as Arras, some of them being more or less cut off by interposing streams of German motorized forces. The enemy had local air superiority, and was using it to the full in an effort to annihilate them.

Then followed a week the story of which will live for ever in the annals of British history—a strange and wonderful week in which things unbelievable happened. Somehow, although the whole weight of the German Army—tanks, artillery, bombers—was flung savagely upon it, the narrow corridor of land leading to Dunkirk beaches was held by the retreating British and French troops, while their scattered detachments drew into and down it toward the coast. Held? It was more than held! British formations that found time on their hands, while waiting their chance of evacuation, turned round and waded joyously back into the fray, inflicting such ferocious punishment on the enemy's advancing front that he halted and stood off, dazed and incredulous, glowering at this cornered remnant that was so dangerous to touch.

THE LITTLE SHIPS AT DUNKIRK

Meanwhile word had travelled swiftly and quietly round all the coasts and creeks of south-eastern England, and a vast, fantastic flotilla of little ships—yachts and fishing smacks, Thames barges, pleasure steamers, old life-boats, dinghies—put out across the Channel to bring home the men of Britain. Drake would have been at home in that fleet, and Hawkins, Frobisher and Sir Richard Grenville: for the island people were on the old, familiar waters, in a daring venture such as their forefathers had loved.

A benediction was upon them. For that week storm and tempest were chained up, the winds were hushed and the restless Channel spread calm and waveless. Under clear skies, through the long sunlight of summer days, and brief nights lit by stars and the bright sickle of a waning moon, the little ships plied tirelessly to and fro, standing in to the Dunkirk beaches where weary men had waded far out into the shallow sea to clamber aboard the rescuing craft, and then swinging about to bear their living cargo back to the homeland.

All the available warships of the British Navy were there—two hundred and twenty of them—to share the task of transport and to protect that fleet of six hundred and fifty little ships against the U-boats and E-boats of the enemy. The R.A.F. threw into the battle the Spitfires of the Home Defence squadrons, and with the other fighters they met the massed formations of the Luftwaffe. Outnumbered, they dashed in with a glorious knight-errantry to turn the enemy again and again from the busy sea traffic. It was the first really serious check to the Luftwaffe.

Before the morning of 4 June the Dunkirk beaches were empty and the last of the little ships homeward bound. Instead of the twenty thousand or so which a week earlier had seemed to be the most we could hope to rescue, more than 85 per cent of the whole British Expeditionary Force had been brought safely home, as well as a large body of French troops. In all 337,131 French and British troops were snatched from death or captivity; and Hitler, who a week before had seen his claws closing around all the cream of the British Army, could now gaze only at the mocking ripple of the tide upon empty sands.

The nation had been profoundly alarmed by the spectacle of the new methods of German air attack used against the Dutch and Belgians. Those masses of paratroops dropped from the sky to seize and hold airfields and bridges, those spies and saboteurs floating down in civilian diguise to prepare the way for the enemy, were a menace against which the traditional shield of Britain, the Royal Navy, could offer no protection. A loud and insistent demand was made that every man should be empowered to join in the defence of the country against these foes, if they tried the same form of attack on Britain.

LOCAL DEFENCE VOLUNTEERS

Anthony Eden, the new War Minister, met this clamour by announcing on 14 May the setting up of a new, unpaid, home defence force—the "Local Defence Volunteers"—which would be enrolled in every town and village to defend its own area against any Germans attempting parachute landings. There were no weapons for them at first, or uniforms. They collected shotguns, bludgeons and knives, donned brassards, bearing the letters "L.D.V.," and assembled in schools, playgrounds, disused halls, to practise drill and hear lectures on street fighting, guerilla tactics and similar practical matters. L.D.V. guards and patrols set themselves to watch over cross-roads, bridges, gas- and water-works and other vulnerable points. Until weapons arrived for them from America—U.S.A. rifles, relics of the last war—they would have been at a hopeless disadvantage in tackling German paratroops armed with tommy-guns, but they had a limitless equipment of determination and fighting spirit. They were ready to fight to the death.

They were a symbol of Britain's mood, these volunteers who

INSPECTING THE HOME GUARD

The Local Defence Volunteers (afterwards the Home Guard) were formed in May, 1940, to repel a German invasion. "A force," said Churchill, "of more than a million and a half who are determined to fight for every inch of the ground in every village and every street."

streamed along to enrol while the Allied front in Flanders and northern France was crashing to ruins beneath the sledge-hammer strokes of Germany's blitzkrieg. The British were locking their jaws and gritting their teeth. The outlook was black; the hope of checking and defeating this Nazi machine seemed feeble. But there would be no surrender. Compromise was simply unthinkable.

That was magnificently expressed by Churchill in the speech he made to the House on 4 June, reporting the course of the war and the miracle of Dunkirk. There are some speeches which are more than words. They are deeds. The stroke of them shapes history. Such was the speech that Winston Churchill delivered in that critical and historical hour in the European crisis.

He began by surveying the march of events in Belgium and

northern France; the effect of the German sweep through to the Channel ports; the heroism of the four thousand riflemen at Calais whose self-sacrifice guarded the road to Dunkirk. He admitted that a week ago he had expected he would now have to report the loss of practically all the B.E.F. and the French First Army. Instead, he was able to tell the glorious story of their rescue, and did so in that rich and resounding language of which he is a master.

But he did not attempt to conceal the desperate nature of the resulting situation. The men had been saved, but all the masses of military stores and equipment—tanks, artillery, ammunition, supplies of every kind, practically the whole available output from our armaments industry—which had been poured into northern France for our expedition, had been totally lost. A drive had now been started in our factories to push on the production of munitions by night and day, weekdays and Sundays, to rearm our men for the struggle ahead.

> "I have myself full confidence that if all do their duty, and if nothing is neglected, and if the best arrangements are made, as they are being made, we shall prove ourselves once again able to defend our island home and ride out the storm of war and outlive the menace of tyranny, if necessary for years, if necessary ALONE!"

The grim foreboding of that word "alone" could not be overlooked by his hearers. He had hinted the same prospect in his broadcast a fortnight before. He knew, better than most of his audience, how fissured and unreliable was the Government and High Command of our only ally, France. But if they failed, he knew too that Britain was resolute to hold out to the uttermost, and he voiced her purpose in words that will go ringing down the corridors of history as the finest expression ever given to her unconquerable determination:

> "Even though large tracts of Europe and many old and famous States have fallen, or may fall into the grip of the Gestapo and all the odious apparatus of Nazi rule, we shall not flag nor fail. We shall go on to the end. We shall fight in France, we shall fight on the seas and oceans, we shall fight with growing confidence and growing strength in the air. We shall fight on the beaches, we shall fight on the landing-grounds, we shall fight in the fields and in the streets, we shall fight in the hills, we shall never surrender; and even if, which I

do not for a moment believe, this island or a large part of it were subjugated and starving, then our Empire beyond the seas, armed and guarded by the British Fleet, would carry on the struggle until in God's good time the New World, with all its power and might, steps forth to the rescue and the liberation of the Old!"

"We shall never surrender!" declared Winston; and the British said "Amen." But France had no Churchill to rally and lead her. Split into factions headed by corrupt and venal politicians, she was in no shape to make resolute war. Besides, our sea-girt isolation gave us a breathing-space in which to rally after defeat and prepare for a fresh struggle. France had no such respite. The blow which smashed the Allied armies in the north, driving our men home through Dunkirk, was delivered across the body of France; and if Hitler was baulked of his British prey, he swung round upon the opponent still exposed to his direct assault.

The Germans drove down across the Somme. To the east they passed the Oise and Aisne and penetrated Champagne, while to the west they swung down upon the lower Seine, approaching Rouen. Fresh British troops were shipped across, but so swift was the advance of the Germans that a number of them were trapped north of the Seine and six thousand were captured. From the sea to the Argonne a multiple assault was developed against the French, who had no coherent strategy with which to repel it. Lured by the prolonged lull of the "phoney war," they had failed to call up their reserves, and had no army of manoeuvre to reinforce their crumbling line. By 10 June a threat to Paris was apparent.

MUSSOLINI DECLARES WAR

Mussolini, who had hitherto remained neutral, decided that France was doomed, and chose this moment to declare war. He wanted to be in at the kill, and get his pickings of the carcass. Churchill addressed a last-minute appeal to him not to plunge Italy, whose traditional friendship with Britain was so strong, into this struggle, but he only got an insolent defiance in reply.

On 11 June the French Government abandoned Paris and travelled south to Tours, moving on shortly afterwards to Bordeaux. They declared that Paris would be fought street by street. But that heroic mood quickly evaporated, and on 13 June it was declared an open city. The Germans entered it next day.

315

WINSTON CHURCHILL AND GENERAL DE GAULLE

In June, 1940, France capitulated but large numbers of Frenchmen left the country and formed the Free French Army, later known as the Fighting French. The Commander of this force was General Charles de Gaulle, who arrived in Britain on 18 June. In this picture Mr. Churchill and General de Gaulle are at a troop inspection.

Churchill, with his passionate friendship for France, tried to stiffen the resolve of her quivering statesmen. On the day that Paris fell he renewed the pledge of the British people

> "to continue the struggle at all costs in France, in this island, upon the oceans, and in the air, wherever it may lead us, using all our resources to the utmost limits and sharing together the burden of repairing the ravages of war. We shall never turn from the conflict until France stands safe and erect in all her grandeur, until the wronged and enslaved states and peoples have been liberated, and until civilization is free from the nightmare of Nazidom."

The gesture was timely, for Winston knew that a strong group of French politicians were for surrender to Hitler. The enemy were pushing down the Loire, and France was a chaos of fleeing refugees and lost military units. Finally, on 16 June, he made the utmost offer of help that could be extended. He proposed to join Britain with France in a Federal Union, akin to that which united the States of the U.S.A. They should enjoy a common citizenship, joint organs of defence, foreign, financial and economic policies. A single Franco-British War Cabinet should direct the affairs of the Union. Thereby all the resources of the British Empire would be bound to France's service. Generosity could devise no bigger offer to a weak and collapsing ally.

MARSHAL PÉTAIN'S SURRENDER TO HITLER

"Ha! Britain wants to annex France!" sneered the Anglophobe members of the French governing cliques. All through the day cabinet meetings went on, and by evening Reynaud had been forced to resign and the defeatist Marshal Pétain took charge of the Government. He at once asked the Germans for an armistice. Rather than join with Britain, he and his confederates decided to be annexed by Hitler and the Nazis, the bitter enemies of France.

Whatever Pétain, Chautemps and Laval thought about their decision, the French people, who had not been consulted, were stunned and aghast. The bottom had dropped out of their world. They had seen Hitler's way with a conquered country, and they knew that whereas defeat by Germany in 1870 had meant humiliation and loss, in 1940 it would mean national annihilation.

It was at that black hour that another of the miracle words of the war was spoken. General de Gaulle had been made Under-Secretary for Foreign Affiairs by Reynaud on 6 June. When France was collapsing and the Reynaud Government falling, he managed to escape to England. On 18 June he broadcast from London to the French nation, calling on all French officers and men, engineers and skilled workmen, to rally to him. For France had lost a campaign, but she had not lost the war!

"Whatever happens, the flame of French resistance must not and shall not be extinguished. I speak with knowledge, and I tell you that France is not lost! The same methods which have brought about our defeat can quite well one day bring victory. . . ."

De Gaulle was hardly a second Churchill. But his stand and appeal in that moment of disaster was climacteric. It saved France's reason. Broken-hearted men listened, and raised their heads again. Yes, truly, France should live on. They would wait, and work, and hope for a new France to arise.

There was, unhappily, a second postscript to France's surrender, as painful and humiliating for her as de Gaulle's proclamation was honourable.

NAVAL ACTION AT ORAN

On 25 June Churchill told the Commons of the last messages that had flashed back and forth between him and Reynaud before the collapse. In them he made it clear that if France failed on her pledge to make no separate armistice, she must at least hand her fleet over to Britain. Reynaud accepted this, but Pétain ignored it and signed terms which involved placing the French Navy under the control of Germany and Italy.

Churchill was faced with a cruel dilemma. On one side of the scale was the near-certainty of Britain's destruction, on the other a harsh and ungracious blow at our friend and former ally. With a heavy heart he decided that Pétain's treachery compelled him to take the hard road. At whatever cost the French Fleet must be prevented from slipping into Nazi hands.

On 3 July he acted, swiftly and resolutely. Those units of the fleet in British harbours were seized, almost without incident. Those at Alexandria accepted internment. But a formidable part of the French Navy, including the two modern battle-cruisers, *Dunkerque* and *Strasbourg,* and other battleships, cruisers and subsidiary craft, lay at Oran, in Algeria. A strong British fleet appeared off Oran and invited the French Admiral either to join with the British, to let his vessels be interned in a British port, or to take them across the Atlantic and intern them at Martinique in the West Indies. If not, they must be sunk, to prevent them falling into enemy hands and becoming a deadly menace to Britain.

The Admiral, acting under German orders, refused all the alternatives. A ten minutes' bombardment followed, supplemented by bomber attacks. Despite the fire of the French naval vessels and their protecting shore batteries, the action was quite one-sided, for the British fleet suffered hardly at all, while the *Strasbourg* was damaged and beached, the other battleships and an aircraft carrier and two destroyers sunk or burned, while the *Dunkerque* escaped to Marseilles.

This deplorable but necessary deed had two good results. It made the French Navy useless for Hitler; and it convinced the world, more effectively than the most defiant speech, that Churchill really meant business. The man who ordered the Oran bombardment was not going to be cajoled into surrender!

ATTACK FROM THE AIR BEGINS ON BRITAIN

With France out of the war Hitler could give his undivided attention to Britain. But he had hardly expected to be dealing with her quite so soon, and there was much preparation to be completed.

The first part of the attack was committed to Goering and his "invincible" Luftwaffe, which had so decisively smashed in turn the Poles, the Dutch, the Belgians and the French. Air attack was to begin by destroying British shipping, ports and naval bases, and driving the Navy out of the narrow seas. It was then to blot out the airfields, overpower the R.A.F., and establish complete air mastery over the Channel and South-east England. After that it would paralyse the country by blows on London and the great cities and nerve-centres, while the Army, supported no doubt by swarms of paratroops, would put out from the French coast and sweep across the Straits into England.

Churchill was not sitting idle. During the weeks of waiting he strained every nerve to rush forward the expansion of the Royal Air Force, still woefully small for the task it would have to face. There

IN AN ANTI-AIRCRAFT GUN-PIT

On 17 October, 1941, Mr. Churchill paid a visit to anti-aircraft batteries. Girls of the A.T.S. are working the range-finders as practice aircraft approach, while the Prime Minister, with the help of an officer, is endeavouring to catch a glimpse of the incoming "raiders."

were a million and a quarter of troops in the country, and the Local Defence Volunteers—renamed by Churchill the "Home Guard"— grew swiftly till it exceeded a million. Coastal defences were strengthened, and pill-boxes erected beside roads, rivers and canals. Signposts and place-names were removed or obliterated, to deny help to invaders. The whole nation prepared itself, very grimly, to fight "on the beaches, in the fields and in the streets."

That Hitler had exceeded his own highest expectations in the speedy defeat of France is evident from the complete lack of any prepared plan to carry the fight to England. His first decision to prepare for invasion was made on 2 July when operation "Sea-lion" (the invasion of England) was authorized. The first prerequisite was clearly stated; complete air superiority over the Channel and South-east England.

The Luftwaffe began the fight in a desultory manner. The first target was the Channel shipping and south-coast ports, to drive the light naval forces farther afield. Throughout July, 1940, the weather was poor, but the Luftwaffe made a number of attacks. The coastal shipping took some losses as the defender's fighters were at a disadvantage with very short warning periods, but the losses inflicted on the German dive-bombers forced Goering to withdraw them from the battle. Dover was the only port seriously attacked, but the Navy was never forced to leave any southern port.

AIR DEFENCE BY THE R.A.F.

Meanwhile Goering prepared the great assault that would destroy the R.A.F. and make invasion possible. It was to be launched on 5 August ("Eagle Day") and last for four days, but "Eagle Day" was postponed day by day till 12 August. Then after a false start the blows fell. The full might of the Luftwaffe was thrown in against the R.A.F. bases and radar stations in South-east England. The R.A.F. fighter pilots covered themselves in glory. Outnumbered, they yet inflicted heavy losses on the enemy. On 20 August Churchill paid tribute in the House to the superb gallantry of our small band of fighter pilots. In phrases that are unforgettable he declared:

> "The gratitude of every home in our Island, in our Empire, and indeed throughout the world, except in the abodes of the guilty, goes out to the British airmen who, undaunted by odds, unwearied in their constant challenge and mortal danger, are turning the tide of war by their prowess and their devotion. Never in the field of human conflict was so much owed by so many to so few!"

It the last week of August, 1940, the Luftwaffe moved their attacks to the main sector airfields near London. For two weeks the attacks kept on. R.A.F. Fighter Command reserves of aircraft were perilously low, the pilot strength was even more strained, but they held on, inflicting heavy losses on the enemy.

Hitler's time-table could not wait. All preparations for "Sea-lion"

PRIME MINISTER AND "MEN IN THE STREET"

Not only did Mr. Churchill travel extensively abroad in the Second World War but he also frequently mixed among the ordinary people at home. He visited areas devastated by enemy action. He also inspected war factories and A.R.P. centres all over the country. In this picture, he is talking to workmen at a quayside in a dock area.

had been ordered for readiness by 15 September, including air superiority. The German Navy and Army declared they could be ready. Only the Luftwaffe could not guarantee its task completed. Britain's fighter pilots stood between them and their aim of air superiority. Hitler was to decide on 11 September whether to go on with the invasion. By now the German bombers were aiming at the heart of London. To paralyse the centre of administration and wreck the London docks was Goering's third step. Again the R.A.F. beat off his attackers. Hitler delayed his decision till 14 September, the R.A.F. replied with heavy air attacks on his barges at the Channel ports, the Royal Navy bombarded Calais, Boulogne, Ostend and Cherbourg. Hitler again demurred till 17 September; then "Sea-lion" was off. The threat was still to be mounted, the Luftwaffe was to keep up its attack on London, but Hitler, denied the essential condition for invasion of England—air superiority—began to look elsewhere.

On into October the Luftwaffe's effort continued. If it could not stand up to the R.A.F. in the daylight, it could still flit across under cover of the darkness to bomb London and other great cities and ports. Surely a few weeks of intensive bombing, of the kind that had crushed Warsaw and Rotterdam, would make those English squeal that they had had enough!

NIGHT BOMBING INTENSIFIED

Already a considerable amount of night bombing had taken place, as a part of the later stages of the Luftwaffe's programme. The first night raid was made on Central London on 26-27 August. This form of attack quickly grew in intensity. On the evening of 8 September Goering broadcast to Germany from his headquarters in northern France, saying: "A terrific attack is going on against London. Adolf Hitler has entrusted me with the task of attacking the heart of the British Empire!"

The *Hamburger Fremdenblatt* stated frankly on 11 September that the German objective was the complete devastation of London.

> "Another two weeks of attacks will make normal life and work in London impossible. In other words, the complete evacuation of London's eight million workers is the immediate danger the country has to face. When this happens, Germany will have attained its main objective, the clogging of all highways of other cities in England with homeless refugees, who must be transported, fed, housed."

German papers suggested that it might not be necessary to invade England, as she might collapse under the severe air-raid punishment inflicted on her.

(The figures of Luftwaffe losses in the Battle of Britain were circulated to Parliament on 14 May, 1947, by Mr. Noel-Baker, Secretary for Air. These figures were in correction of estimates issued during the course of the battle. German records revealed that between 10 July and 31 October, 1940, 2,376 German planes had been put out of action, of which 1,733 were destroyed and 643 damaged. The heaviest losses were inflicted on 15 and 18 August, when 147 planes were destroyed and 32 damaged.)

Britain's answer to that threat was given on the very same day by Churchill in Parliament. After sounding a warning about the possibility of a German attempt at invasion, he said:

THE PRIME MINISTER VISITS LONDON'S DOCKS

Though naturally overshadowed by her husband, Mrs. Churchill, too, engaged in a wide variety of public activities during the Second World War, the best known of them being her Red Cross "Aid to Russia" Fund. In this photograph Mr. and Mrs. Churchill are seen travelling by launch to visit some of the bombed areas in the London docks.

"These cruel, wanton, indiscriminate bombings of London are, of course, a part of Hitler's invasion plan. He hopes, by killing large numbers of civilians and women and children, that he will terrorize and cow the people of this mighty Imperial city and make them a burden and anxiety to the Government, and thus distract our attention unduly from the ferocious onslaught he is now preparing. Little does he know the spirit of the British nation or the tough fibre of the Londoners, whose forebears played a leading part in the establishment of parliamentary institutions, and who have been bred to value freedom far above their lives.

"This wicked man, the repository and embodiment of many forms of soul-destroying hatred, this monstrous product of former wrongs and shames, has now resolved to try to break our famous island spirit by a process of indiscriminate slaughter and destruction. What he has done is to kindle a fire in British hearts here and all over the world which will glow long after all traces of the conflagrations he has caused in London have been removed. He has lighted a fire which will burn with a steady and consuming flame until the last vestiges of Nazi tyranny have been burnt out of Europe and until the old world and the new can join hands to rebuild the temples of man's freedom and man's honour upon foundations which will not soon or easily be overthrown."

Germany's all-out air attacks in the Battle of Britain and in its continuation, the Battle of London, gave Churchill an opportunity, of which he made eager use, to thrust forward as the mouthpiece and symbol of the British spirit of defiant and confident resistance. Wherever the bombs had fallen thickest, there Winston would shortly be on the spot, and people grew familiar with Press photographs of his sturdy figure appearing among those scenes of desolation, or waving back indomitable encouragement to the pathetic crowds of homeless folk, who drew fresh courage and cheer from the sight of him and the sound of his heartening words. His voice was lifted in speech after speech, resolutely declaring that "we shall draw from the heart of suffering itself the means of inspiration and survival"; maintaining that the enemy attacks "steel the hearts of all to the stern and unrelenting prosecution of the war against so foul a foe"; that "neither by material damage nor by slaughter will the people of the British Empire be turned from their solemn, inexorable purpose"; giving as the British watchword for the 1940 winter the remark of an air-raid warden: "It's a grand life if we do not weaken!" and reassuring the nation that Hitler's failure to carry out an invasion "constitutes in itself one of the historic victories of the

British Isles and is a monumental milestone on our onward march."

The blitz went on all through the winter. Night by night the sirens sounded soon after dusk, and the crash of anti-aircraft artillery and the whistle and crump of falling bombs continued till dawn. Fires glared redly in the docks, the City and the West End. Whole streets of little homes in East London were levelled, and the total of casualties mounted grievously. But the "tough fibre of the Londoners" to which Winston had paid tribute never joined the casualty list. "We can take it!" became their motto. They took it, with a wry Cockney grin of defiance, till Hitler himself grew weary of his hopeless task, and searched his intuition for some new plan whereby to crush this unconquerable people.

The night bombings were not confined to London. They ranged far and wide over the rest of the country. Merseyside and Tyneside, Cardiff and Swansea, Bristol and Plymouth, Birmingham and the Midlands took their share of destruction. On 15 November a savage and concentrated attack was launched on Coventry—not on the great industrial plants on its outskirts, but on the little homes of its residential centre. Vast suffering and ruin were achieved. But the only tangible effect was to stimulate a marked speeding up of the rate of munition production in every factory all through the Midlands.

By the spring of 1941 the blitz was growing more intermittent. From time to time there would be a violent raid on London or some big provincial city, but the raid-free nights became more common. When, in June, Hitler turned round against Russia, the skies above Britain cleared and Londoners fell asleep with a sense of something strange, missing the thunderous uproar which had for so long been, from the beginning to the end of blackout, their nightly lullaby.

AERIAL BOMBING OF LONDON

Foiled in his effort to break the R.A.F., as a preparation for invasion Hitler turned his bombers on to London. On 26 August, 1940, raiders were over London all through the night. The attacks continued until the spring of 1941. Mr. Churchill is here inspecting the wreckage of the House of Commons after it was gutted in May, 1941.

DISEMBARKING FROM H.M.S. "PRINCE OF WALES"

*In this photograph, Mr. Churchill has just changed ship from H.M.S.
"Prince of Wales," and is being cheered enthusiastically by the crew
as he prepares to go ashore. It was aboard this ill-fated ship that he
sailed to the historic meeting with President Roosevelt at which the
Atlantic Charter was drawn up and signed on 9 August, 1941.*

CHAPTER XV

A WORLD IN FLAMES

WHEN, early in 1916, Colonel Winston Churchill was commanding the Royal Scots Fusiliers in France, a general who visited his battalion headquarters denounced their position as "positively dangerous!" Winston's retort was characteristic: "But, you know, this is a very dangerous war!"

Never blinkered by the illusion that a war can be won without taking risks, Winston knew that mere passive defence meant waiting for defeat. For two and a half years after he took charge Britain had to remain mostly on the defensive; but those years were packed with daring adventures.

At the very outset he took a tremendous risk. Italy's declaration of war closed the Mediterranean and turned it into a battlefield. With her considerable fleet and her numerous air bases Italy was in a position to dominate it, while from her African possessions she could thrust against Egypt and the Suez Canal, Britain's life-line to her Empire. Here in Britain we were expecting Hitler's invasion. We had barely rescued our army from Dunkirk, with the loss of all its equipment. Prudence might well urge that every tank, gun and military unit we possessed must be husbanded to meet the German attack. But Winston decided that we could never save our Empire by merely huddling behind the Channel. We must venture our scanty resources to hurl the enemy back.

He promptly dispatched a considerable force of tanks, guns and troops to Egypt. It was a three months' voyage for them, round the Cape of Good Hope. They might not arrive in time. He had to risk that, as he risked denuding our own defences. Today there is no doubt that his prompt action saved the Empire and was a vital step to our ultimate success.

Mussolini for his part lost no time in trying to realize his arrogant boast that the Mediterranean should become an Italian lake. Bombing attacks were made daily upon Malta. Military forces began to strike eastward at Egypt from Libya, and at the Sudan from

Abyssinia and Eritrea. From Abyssinia and Italian Somaliland, too, blows were struck at Kenya, and in August, 1940, his troops swept into the sandy wastes of British Somaliland. Little help could be given to its small defence force, and after a fortnight's gallant fighting, the British had to abandon the territory.

But the Duce's progress against Egypt was slow, for the British Mediterranean Fleet, based on Alexandria, could cover the narrow coast road. Greece, with her islands, looked like a useful base for him fronting Egypt across the sea. Mussolini decided to snatch it in the same way as Hitler had once seized Austria. On 28 October, 1940, he sent Greece an ultimatum demanding entrance for his troops, and the troops themselves followed hard on the heels of the message.

But Greece was not Austria. She accepted the challenge of the invasion, and fought back with a heroic abandon that recalled the glories of Marathon and Thermopylae. British aircraft were sent to her aid, and before long the Italians found themselves not the attackers, but the attacked, and were hustled back across southern Albania.

TROUBLES FOR THE ITALIANS

Meantime the tanks Churchill had dispatched arrived in Egypt, and so did troops from Australia and New Zealand. The Fleet Air Arm celebrated Armistice Day by raiding the Italian Navy at Taranto, crippling three battleships, two cruisers and two auxiliary craft. Four weeks later General Wavell started, with his numerically inferior forces, a dashing offensive against the Italians who had penetrated western Egypt. Sidi Barrani fell, and Italian prisoners were rounded up in tens of thousands. Taking advantage of his initial success, Wavell thrust forward into Libya. Sollum, Bardia, Tobruk, Benghazi were taken one after the other, and in a month from the start of the offensive all Cyrenaica was in British hands.

In the south, too, the British went over to the attack in Somaliland and Eritrea. On 24 January, 1941, the Emperor Haile Selassie re-entered Abyssinia to lead its patriot forces against the Italian invaders. There was, in fact, a complete change in the picture by the turn of the year. Our position in the Middle East was still compassed about with dangers, but we were no longer sustaining a forlorn hope there. Indeed, we were giving Mussolini much more than he had bargained for when he light-heartedly entered the war.

VISIT TO A FIGHTER SQUADRON

Inspecting an R.A.F. Establishment Mr. Churchill (in the uniform of an Air Commodore of the Royal Air Force) and Mrs. Churchill are talking to a senior officer during a visit to No. 615 Fighter Squadron. Mr. Churchill inspected the aerodrome and took tea in the Mess.

Any admiration that Winston may at one time have felt for Mussolini's achievement in tightening up Italian discipline, and developing her resources, had long been displaced by contempt for this pinchbeck Caesar who puffed himself up like a bullfrog with windy ambitions for Imperial pre-eminence, and whipped his unwarlike people into treacherous attacks on their inoffensive neighbours.

BRITISH CABINET IN THE SECOND WORLD WAR

In this photograph of the War Cabinet, taken in the grounds of Number 10 Downing Street on 16 October, 1941, are, standing from left to right:—Mr. Arthur Greenwood, Mr. Ernest Bevin, Lord Beaverbrook and Sir Kingsley Wood. Sitting:—Sir John Anderson, Mr. Winston Churchill, Mr. C. R. Attlee and Mr. Anthony Eden.

As the essential hollowness of the Duce's much-vaunted military and naval strength was gradually exposed under the test of real fighting, a note of contempt for him crept into Winston's references to the bumptious little Italian, and the public took great joy in the Premier's sharp and derisive shafts of ridicule.

Broadcasting to the French people on 21 October, Winston said that Hitler had by force and treachery managed to subjugate for a time most of the finest races in Europe, and "his little Italian accomplice is trotting along, hopefully and hungrily, but rather wearily and very timidly, at his side." He expressed the nation's disgust at the brutal and unwarranted invasion of Greece—"The Italian Dictator ... perhaps playing his part in some new predatory design, has in his customary cold-blooded way, fallen upon the small but famous and immortal Greek nation. We shall never cease to strike at the aggressor in ever-increasing strength from this time forth until the crimes and treacheries which hang around the neck of Mussolini and disgrace the Italian name have been brought to condign and exemplary justice."

Mussolini stuck out his chin. On 19 November he boasted that he had sought and obtained permission from Hitler for Italian aircraft to bomb London; and in fact, four days later, twenty Italian planes flew up the Thames estuary. But when the Spitfires met them they turned and fled, leaving seven of their number under the waters of the Straits of Dover. None of their bombs fell on London.

Churchill broadcast on 23 December a Christmastide message to the Italian people, reminding them of the ancient friendship of the two countries, and urging them to get out of the war before disaster overtook them. "Your aviators have tried to cast their bombs on London: our armies are tearing and will tear your African empire to shreds and tatters."

The situation, he declared, was the work of one man only, who in his lust for unbridled power had ranged the trustees and heritors of ancient Rome on the side of the ferocious pagan barbarians. "There lies the tragedy of Italian history, and there stands the criminal who has wrought the deed of folly and shame!"

He read the Note he had sent to Mussolini on 16 May, appealing to him not to attack France; and he read the Duce's surly answer to that appeal.

"Anyone can see who it was that wanted peace, and who it was that meant to have war. One man and one man only was resolved to plunge Italy after all these years of strain and effort into the whirlpool of war. And what is the position of Italy today? Where is it that the Duce has led his trusting people after eighteen years of dictatorial power? What hard choice is open to them now? It is to stand up to the battery of the whole British Empire on sea, in the air, and in Africa, and the vigorous counter-attack of the Greek nation; or, on the other hand, to call in Attila over the Brenner Pass with his hordes of ravenous soldiery and his gangs of Gestapo policemen to occupy, hold down and 'protect' the Italian people, for whom he and his Nazi followers cherish the most bitter and outspoken contempt that is on record between races. That is where one man, and one man only, has led you!"

As a pendant to that denunciation may be quoted Churchill's

ASSOCIATION FOOTBALL AT WEMBLEY—
ENGLAND v. SCOTLAND

On 4 October, 1941, an international football match was played at Wembley Stadium, England beating Scotland by two goals to nil. Mr. Churchill, always a keen sportsman, was the guest of the Football Association and is seen shaking hands with Denis Compton, the famous Arsenal footballer and England cricketer, just before the game.

comment, in his broadcast on 27 April following on Mussolini's trumpetings when the Germans turned his defeat in Greece into victory:

> "This whipped jackal Mussolini, who to save his own skin has made of Italy a vassal state of Hitler's empire, goes frisking up at the side of the German tiger, with relish, not only of appetite—that could be understood—but even of triumph."

If, as many dare to believe, the destinies of mankind are guided by a Higher Power, we may recognize the hand of Providence in the remarkable circumstance that, at this most critical hour for human civilization and for the survival of justice and moral standards, the leader of Britain was linked by ties of birth with that other great commonwealth of democratic and Christian traditions, the United

States. Little did Lord Randolph Churchill think, when he wooed and won his American bride, that their first-born would, by virtue of his dual heredity, be able to play a giant's part in drawing those two mighty countries into a common effort for the greatest and most vital cause the world has ever known.

Winston's familiarity with Americans made him at home with them, and they with him. In his daring, his restless originality, his mastery of words, and valiant deeds, they found him a man after their own hearts. No doubt America would in any case have found herself compelled to side with Britain as the war continued. But it might well have been a distrustful, uneasy partnership, hampered and frustrated by rivalry and divided purpose. The emergence of Winston as British Prime Minister wrought an instant change of attitude across the Atlantic, and vastly eased the task of the great-hearted President, Franklin Roosevelt, in directing the immense resources of the States to support the battle for world liberty.

In the early months of the war American sentiment was anti-Nazi rather than pro-British. But the change was apparent after May, 1940. On 10 June Roosevelt made his "Full Speed Ahead!" speech, calling for American help for the Allies:

> "We will extend to the opponents of force the material resources of this nation; and at the same time we will harness and speed up the use of those resources in order that we ourselves in the Americas may have equipment and training equal to the task of any emergency and every defence."

So popular had become the idea of helping Britain that Roosevelt was able to make it a star feature of his programme on which he fought and won his election for a third term of presidential office— an unprecedented achievement.

In September the Anglo-American Agreement was concluded, whereby Britain leased a number of naval and air bases to the U.S.A. in return for fifty destroyers. A promise was also given to America that in no circumstances would the British Fleet be surrendered or sunk, but if need be it would go overseas to maintain the fight from other parts of the Empire—though Churchill added that "these hypothetical contingencies seem more likely to concern the German Fleet, or what is left of it, than the British Fleet!"

In a broadcast on 29 December Roosevelt declared that America

335

must become "the great arsenal of democracy." They had furnished Britain with material support, and "we will furnish more in future. There will be no falling back in our determination to aid Great Britain."

He followed this on 6 January, 1941, by proposing to Congress his plan which has now become historic as the "Lease-Lend" scheme.

> "I do not recommend that we make them a loan of dollars with which to pay for these weapons—loans to be repaid in dollars. . . . Let us say to the Democracies: 'We Americans are vitally concerned in your defence of freedom. We are putting forth our energies, resources, and organizing powers to give you strength to regain and maintain a free world. We shall send you in ever-increasing numbers, ships, aeroplanes, tanks and guns. This is our purpose and our pledge."

It was in this speech that Roosevelt proclaimed his vision of the future days when mankind would possess the four essential Freedoms: "Freedom of speech and expression everywhere; the freedom, and the right, to worship God in their own way everywhere; freedom from want; and freedom from fear!"

On 9 February Churchill delivered another broadcast to the nation, at the end of which he quoted a verse from Longfellow's poem, "The Building of the Ship," which had been sent to him as a message by Roosevelt. He asked:

> "What is the answer that I shall give in your name to this great man, the thrice-chosen Head of a nation of 130 million? Here is the answer which I shall give to President Roosevelt: 'Put your confidence in us. Give us your faith and your blessing and under Providence all will be well. We shall not fail or falter. We shall not weaken or starve. Neither the sudden shock of battle nor the long-drawn trials of vigilance and exertion will wear us down. *Give us the tools and we will finish the job!'* "

That final phrase was hardly in the style of either Gibbon or Macaulay; but it was straight talk, such as Americans could appreciate. On 11 March, the Lease-Lend Bill was passed by Congress, and before the summer was over, a steady flow of arms and food was pouring across the Atlantic to sustain Britain in her front-line defence of world freedom.

Hitler, who in his New Year message to Germany had promised

TOUR OF INSPECTION IN AN ARMS FACTORY

During a tour of the North Country, Mr. Churchill is seen inspecting an engineering works in Bradford, Yorkshire. Accompanying him is Mrs. Churchill; they are talking to a nineteen-year-old girl who is carrying out an operation on a lathe. Behind is the then Mayor of Bradford. This was one of many similar visits paid by the Churchills.

that 1941 would bring them the completion of the greatest victory in their history, must have been rather disgusted at the poor showing of his henchman, Mussolini. The Italians had been given the job of seizing Greece and Egypt, to open the way for the Axis through the Middle East for the blockade of Russia from the south and for a thrust at India, that El Dorado of so many conquerors. They were failing miserably in Greece, and were rapidly losing all their African empire.

The Fuehrer decided to throw the might of Germany into the scale. He brought pressure to bear on Bulgaria and Yugoslavia to join the Axis, flung a considerable force of tanks and specially trained troops—his Afrika Korps—into Tripoli to reinforce the crumbling

Italian armies there, and infiltrated numbers of German agents into Syria, Iraq and Persia to swing those countries to his side.

Bulgaria joined the Axis on 1 March, and German troops promptly moved through the country to the Greek frontier. Three weeks later Prince Paul, the Regent of Yugoslavia, yielded to Hitler's demands, but his people were furious at this surrender, and a prompt *coup d'état* flung out his government and set up young King Peter at the head of a government of national defence.

Massed German aircraft and tank forces surged down on Yugoslavia and Greece, and there was small chance of saving them. But Churchill was already under promise to give all possible aid to Greece; and, when Yugoslavia formed her new government to resist Hitler, he gave her the same promise. In speeches on 27 March, 1941, he declared:

> "Early this morning the Yugoslav nation found its soul. . . . This patriotic movement arises from the wrath of a valiant and warlike race at their country being betrayed by the weakness of its rulers and the foul intrigues of the Axis Powers. We may therefore cherish the hope that a government will be formed worthy to defend the freedom and integrity of their country. Such a government will receive from the British Empire . . . all possible aid and succour. . . . Great Britain will recognize that government. Great Britain will give all the aid in her power to those who are defending their native lands, the heroic Greeks, the Turks if they are attacked."

So Wavell had to check his victorious campaign in Libya, to release troops for an expedition to the Balkans in fulfilment of these pledges. From the start our intervention was a forlorn hope, for the Germans had immense superiority both in the air and in armoured vehicles and artillery. We scored one gratifying victory, however. The Italian Fleet, ordered out by Hitler to interfere with our expedition, was caught by the British Navy off Cape Matapan, south of Greece, and soundly trounced. The battleship *Littorio* was severely damaged, and three cruisers and three destroyers sunk, while the British Fleet sustained neither damage nor casualties. But the land warfare yielded a story of darkening disaster.

On 6 April Hitler struck at Yugoslavia without warning, bombing the open city of Belgrade to ruins with a terrible massacre of its inhabitants. During the month his troops swept down through the country from Hungary and Bulgaria, thrust into Greece and hurled

ARCHBISHOP OF CANTERBURY AT DOWNING STREET

In this photograph taken on the terrace behind Number 10 Downing Street, Dr. William Temple, Archbishop of Canterbury from 1942 until 1944, and a former Archbishop of York, is posing for the camera with Mr. Churchill. Dr. Temple was the son of Frederick Temple, who was himself Archbishop of Canterbury from 1896 to 1902.

back the Greeks and British. The remnant of the British force was
evacuated, though for another month we stood our ground in Crete.
It was a gallant and heroic struggle against heavy odds, but one fore-
doomed to failure. We had kept faith with Greece. That was our
justification.

Meantime the weakening of our North African force, and the
formidable German reinforcement of the Italians, resulted in a series
of British reverses in Libya. Before the end of April our Army was
driven back inside the Egyptian frontier again, except for a garrison
left holding out in Tobruk, which the enemy utterly failed to dislodge
during the months that followed.

In Iraq, German intrigue brought about a *coup d'état* by which
the pro-German Rashid Ali seized power. He at once set to work to
stop British air communications through Iraq, and Imperial forces
had to be dispatched to restore our treaty rights. After some
desultory fighting Rashid Ali fled to Persia and a new government,
this time more friendly to Britain, was set up in Bagdad by the Arabs.

Hitler had hoped, with the connivance of the Vichy French
officials governing Syria, to get control of that country and of Iraq,
and to encircle Egypt from the north-east. German "tourists"
swarmed into Syria and German planes descended on its airfields,
where they were promptly bombed by the British; and on 8 June a
combined force of British and Free French marched into Syria to
combat the Axis danger. General Dentz, the Vichy commander,

RED ARMY PARADE

M. Molotov and Mr. Churchill watching the march past of the Red Guard at a Moscow airport during Mr. Churchill's visit to Russia in 1942. It was this regiment which took the oath "to stop Hitler or die" in the autumn of 1941. The world is familiar with the story of how that oath was kept. Hitler was stopped. M. Molotov stands on Mr. Churchill's right.

showed fight, but he was beaten and forced to accept the British terms on 13 July.

One last step remained, to bar the road to the Middle East against the Axis. In August the British and Russians sent simultaneous expeditions into Persia, to clean up the colonies of German agents and their confederates in that country and to establish a through route for British supplies from the Persian Gulf to Russia. After a brief show of resistance the Shah abdicated in favour of his son. The Germans were sent packing; and the Middle East was secured against the menace of German designs. No attack could now be launched against the strategically important Suez Canal from that quarter with any hope of success at all.

Although the Russians had been carefully observing their Treaty of Non-aggression with Germany, Hitler was not happy about them. Could they be trusted to remain passive if he became heavily involved in the West with the job of wiping out Britain, the last remaining anti-Nazi power in Europe? Stalin, he felt, was no fool, and Stalin knew quite well that, whatever Hitler's ambitions elsewhere might be, he unquestionably intended to conquer the Ukraine and the western provinces of Russia. The Russian would hardly be likely to sit still and watch his last potential co-belligerent being mopped up, knowing he would be left to face the German war machine alone.

It was a pity, thought Hitler, that the Reich was already at war with Britain, for it would be far better to deal with Russia before trying to settle with that tough and inaccessible island people in the West. Perhaps he could get them to stop their war with him while he defeated Stalin? Ribbentrop assured him that all the people who counted in England were loudly anti-Communist in sympathy.

Accordingly, on the night of 10 May his devoted henchman, Rudolf Hess, the Deputy Fuehrer, dropped from a plane into a Scottish field, looking for the Duke of Hamilton, through whom he imagined that he could contact those alleged pro-Fascist circles that might be persuaded to thrust Churchill aside and bring Britain into an alliance with Germany against Bolshevist Russia. The notion was hare-brained; the misjudgment, alike of the Duke of Hamilton, of the British people, and of the power or even of the existence of those pro-Fascist leaders was complete. The one result was that Winston got advance news of the threat to Russia, and warned Stalin of what was brewing. The news was not unexpected, and Stalin arranged for his summer manoeuvres to take place in western Russia.

The Hess stratagem had failed, but Hitler stuck to his plan. Russian resistance, he was sure, could be broken in about six weeks. He would not repeat Napoleon's mistakes. Was he not far cleverer than Napoleon, and with a far mightier army? On 22 June, announcing that his patience with Russia's insolent extortions was at an end, he sent his Panzer divisions across the frontier.

Bewilderment threatened world opinion at this falling-out of former confederates. If Hitler was dreaded, Bolshevism was highly unpopular with the British, and regarded with even sharper antagonism in America. What line should the West adopt to this Nazi-Bolshevik conflict?

Churchill had no doubts. His strong and oft-expressed dislike of Communism did not blind him to the fact that the first and foremost enemy to world peace was German militarism, fanned by the Nazi creed of race superiority. His prompt and emphatic declaration of support for Russia secured the consolidation of the anti-Nazi front.

On the day that Russia was attacked Churchill broadcast an announcement of policy which began by stigmatizing the treacherous Nazis in stinging phrases.

> "Hitler is a monster of wickedness, insatiable in his lust for blood and plunder.... This bloodthirsty guttersnipe must launch his mechanized armies upon new fields of slaughter, pillage and devas-

THE ATLANTIC CHARTER MEETING

The Atlantic Charter emphasized that the United Nations were fighting for no territorial aggrandizement but to protect the liberties of all countries while destroying Nazi Germany. It expressed a hope for the future "abandonment of the use of force." Above, President Roosevelt and Mr. Churchill with Staff chiefs at their historic meeting.

tation. ... Even the carnage that Hitler's victory—should he gain it—would bring, would itself only be a stepping-stone to an attempt to plunge the 400 or 500 millions who live in China and the 350 millions of India into that bottomless pit of human degradation over which the diabolic emblem of the Swastika flaunts itself."

He pictured the Russian peasantry, living peacefully on the soil their fathers had tilled from time immemorial, being overrun and crushed by "the dull, drilled, docile, brutish masses of the Hun soldiery, plodding on like a swarm of crawling locusts." He would unsay nothing he had formerly spoken against Communism, which he had never pretended to like.

"But I have now to declare the decision of His Majesty's Government, and I feel sure it is a decision in which the great Dominions will in due course concur. ... We have but one aim and one single, irrevocable, purpose. We are resolved to destroy Hitler and every

RETURN TO LONDON FROM AMERICA

On 27 June, 1942, Mr. Churchill returned by air from a visit to President Roosevelt in America. He was accompanied by Mr. Averell Harriman, President Roosevelt's personal representative. When he arrived in London, Mr. Churchill was met by Mr. C. R. Attlee, Mr. Anthony Eden and Sir Archibald Sinclair (reading from left to right).

vestige of the Nazi régime. From this nothing will turn us—nothing. We will never parley, we will never negotiate with Hitler or with any of his gang. We shall fight him by land, we shall fight him by sea, we shall fight him in the air, until, with God's help, we will rid the earth of all those who have shadowed it and liberate the peoples from his yoke. Any man or State who fights against Nazism will have our aid. . . . That is our policy and our declaration. It follows therefore that we shall give whatever help we can to Russia and to the Russian people. We shall appeal to all our friends and Allies in every part of the world to take the same course and pursue it, as we shall, faithfully and steadfastly to the end. We have offered to the Government of Soviet Russia any technical or economic assistance which is in our power, and which is likely to be of service to them."

The declaration was eagerly welcomed throughout Britain. Men's minds were cleared. The very fact that Churchill was so well known for his anti-Communist attitude now added strength to his pronouncement in favour of co-operating with the Soviets. If he, once the arch-enemy of Bolshevism, could join hands with Stalin to defeat Hitler, no one else need hesitate to follow his example.

A war is a many-sided event in history, and people looking for its causes and objects can trace all kinds of diverse grounds for it— personal ambitions, pressure of population, commercial rivalries, artificially incited fears and hatreds. All, no doubt, are present. But the dominating influence which plunged Britain and other lands into the war was moral and spiritual acceptance of the challenge which Nazism threw down to justice, good faith, humanity, religion, honourable dealing: in short, all the values on which Christian civilization rests. It was these non-material factors which roused and united the British to oppose Hitler's aggression. They also swung the strongly moral and idealistic popular sentiment of the United States of America to the same side.

THE ATLANTIC CHARTER

By now the war had involved many countries. Winston felt that, while any precise statement of the probable terms of a peace settlement was not yet possible, a definition of the principles on which the war was being fought, and on which a peace settlement should be based, was needed. Even if we ourselves did not require this, it would be necessary for our shattered allies and for the instruction of neutral opinion. Roosevelt thought the same, and so the two leaders of the English-speaking world arranged to meet to talk over this and other matters of mutual interest to their peoples.

They arranged a meeting at sea, off the American coast, where no Nazi spies could watch and report on their discussion. Churchill travelled in the new battleship, H.M.S. *Prince of Wales,* and Roosevelt was aboard the U.S. cruiser *Augusta.* Their military and diplomatic advisers accompanied them. The two statesmen took counsel together, and one outcome of their discussions was a declaration that became known as the Atlantic Charter. This constituted a statement of "certain common principles in the national policies of their respective countries on which they base their hopes for a better future for the world."

The Charter had eight short clauses. It recorded that Britain and

345

the U.S.A. sought no aggrandizement for themselves, and pronounced against territorial changes except by the will of the peoples concerned. It demanded the right of self-government for all nations, equal economic opportunities, progress and social security, freedom from fear and want, the disarmament of aggressor nations and the establishment of a permanent international system of security. Its terms were broad and general, but it showed quite plainly the kind of world its authors hoped for when the Axis had been crushed—a world of democratic freedom and fellowship, of active progress and greater human welfare.

After a visit to Iceland, where American troops were now sharing the task of garrisoning the island against any German invasion, Winston returned home and broadcast an account of his conference. He claimed that these discussions symbolized the deep, underlying unities which at decisive moments ruled the English-speaking peoples and the "marshalling of the good forces of the world against the evil forces." It was an historic taking-up by the English-speaking nations of the burden of world leadership in this critical hour.

He referred to the Russian campaign, where Hitler was advancing against very stubborn resistance, and to the terrible slaughter on both sides. Hitler, he said, was staggered by the opposition he had met, and was retaliating by the most frightful cruelties. "Since the Mongol invasions of Europe in the sixteenth century there has never been methodical, merciless butchery on such a scale. . . . We are in the presence of a crime without a name." After explaining some of the features of the Atlantic Charter, he said:

> "You will perhaps have noticed that the President of the United States and the British representative have jointly pledged their countries to the final destruction of the Nazi tyranny. . . . The question has been asked, how near is the United States to war? There is certainly one man who knows the answer to that question. If Hitler has not yet declared war upon the United States, it is surely not out of his love for American institutions. It is certainly not because he could not find a pretext. He has murdered half a dozen countries for far less. Fear of immediately redoubling the tremendous energies now being employed against him is no doubt a restraining influence. But the real reason is, I am sure, to be found in the method to which he has so faithfully adhered, and by which he has gained so much. What is that method? It is a very simple method. One by One!"

He pointed out how the failure of the democracies to stand

346

AT THE DUKE OF CONNAUGHT'S FUNERAL

Mr. and Mrs. Churchill were here photographed at the funeral of the late Duke of Connaught who died on 15 January, 1942, aged ninety-one. The Duke was the third son of Queen Victoria and had a distinguished military career, being on active service in Egypt and India. He was Governor-General of Canada from 1911 until 1916.

together had eased Hitler's path; and he emphasized that from now on the countries defending freedom must act jointly. A conference was to be held in Moscow between the U.S.A., British and Russian authorities to settle their plans of campaign.

CONFERENCE IN MOSCOW

Winston was never the man to satisfy his soul with a resolution, however fine-sounding. The Atlantic meeting had produced the Charter. But it also produced agreement on the practical lines of co-operation whereby the aims of the Charter were to be realized. On 24 August all the allied nations, including Russia, adhered to the Charter. On 29 August the Moscow Conference was opened. Two days later it ended in full agreement, and Britain and the U.S.A. undertook to give Russia practically all the help she asked in her struggle.

The German armies ground their way savagely forward in Russia, but not with the speed and success that Hitler had expected. He admitted in a speech on 3 October that he had no idea how gigantic had been Russia's preparations. However, he declared that the enemy now lay defeated and could not rise again! He had previously claimed the utter destruction of the Russian armies, and would repeatedly do so again. But November came and went, and his troops had still not reached Moscow. In South Russia they were beginning to be driven back. Winter had begun, and the spectre of Napoleon's *Grande Armée* wandered uncannily about the snowdrifts of the vast Russian plains.

In North Africa, too, Hitler was suffering reverses. On 18 November the British launched a surprise offensive along the Libyan frontier, and were soon advancing rapidly a second time into Cyrenaica. The U-boat war on British shipping was not going well, and sinkings were only a third of those that had been inflicted earlier in the war. American supplies were pouring into Britain. American shipbuilding was getting into its stride. Something fresh had to be done.

Hitler thought that it was time to call on the third member of the Axis, Japan, to fling in her weight. Japan had been waging war on China for five years past. Her avowed aims included the conquest of all the western Pacific area and eastern Asia—which would involve conflict with both America and the British Empire. Her

JOSEPH STALIN AND WINSTON CHURCHILL IN 1942

Before the days of the Second World War, Mr. Churchill was a stern enemy of Bolshevism, regarding it as a menace to European peace, but Germany's attack on Russia resulted in a strong Anglo-Russian alliance. Mr. Churchill twice visited Russia on diplomatic missions and he is here shown with Stalin in the U.S.S.R. news film.

secret aims were not less than Hitler's own—the Empire of the World.

The immediate business was, however, to embroil Japan with the U.S.A., and thus to divert American aid from Britain and Russia. Turning America into a belligerent was a further departure from Hitler's "one by one" strategy, but like the Kaiser a quarter of a century earlier, he underrated her ability to take an active part in a European war.

The Japs were nothing loth to attack the States. They had a limitless faith in their invincible strength, and were as unscrupulous as they were pitiless in their use of it. They sent a friendly mission to Washington to discuss with the U.S.A. various matters about which there was disagreement, particularly the Japanese penetration of

349

French Indo-China. Then on 7 December, 1941, while these discussions were being blandly pursued, Japanese carrier-borne aircraft and submarines made a massed attack on the American fleet anchored in Pearl Harbour, in Hawaii. The Americans, taken completely by surprise—they were not even observing regulation precautions—put up hardly any resistance, and the bulk of the fleet was sunk or disabled. Simultaneously, attacks were launched on the American bases at Guam, Wake and Midway Islands, and on the Philippines.

Four days later Hitler declared war on the U.S.A., and informed the bewildered Germans that it was Roosevelt who had plotted the World War and had incited the Poles to resist Germany. Italy followed suit next day.

JAPANESE ADVANCE IN THE FAR EAST

On that day, 11 December, Churchill gave one of his periodic reviews of the progress of the Libyan campaign, where Auchinleck had already reached and relieved the Tobruk garrison. The tale of Japanese attacks in the Far East, on the other hand, was gloomy. Their dive-bombers had sunk the *Prince of Wales* and the *Repulse*, when these powerful vessels, the pride of the Royal Navy, were trying to intercept the Jap transports pouring troops into Malaya. But he added that the total British and U.S.A. naval power was still largely superior to that of the three Axis states. There were hard times ahead, but behind Britain, America, Russia and China were ranged all the spirit and hopes of all the conquered countries. His remark a few days earlier that four-fifths of the human race were on our side might well be an under-statement. Gangs and cliques of wicked men and their military or party organizations had brought these hideous evils upon minkind. "It would bring shame to our generation if we did not teach them a lesson which will not be forgotten in the records of a thousand years!"

The traditional hostility to Britain which colours American ideas, as a legacy from their War of Independence, did not show itself where Winston Churchill was concerned. They remembered that his mother was American. He was given an enthusiastic reception when on 23 December, 1941, he arrived in the States to discuss with the President "all questions relevant to concerted war effort."

The world conflict had by now reached full stretch, and the Allies and the enemy were locked in combat on every battlefield. The fortunes of the day were various. In Russia, the Red Army had launched a counter-offensive against the Germans, who were ill-equipped for a Russian winter in which Hitler had not expected to be still fighting. In North Africa the British had driven Rommel out of Cyrenaica again for the time being. But in the Pacific the tale was bad and growing worse. Hong Kong surrendered to the Japanese on Christmas Day. The little yellow men were racing down through Malaya. They had invaded Borneo and Sarawak. They were capturing island after island in the Pacific. They had landed in force in the Philippines, where the Filipinos and Americans, led by General MacArthur, were putting up a gallant but losing fight against them. America, her Pacific Fleet crippled by the Pearl Harbour blow, was unable to come effectively to their aid, and had impotently to witness their defeat.

But Winston's confident and virile personality was a tonic of encouragement to the Americans, and Congress paid him the exceptional honour of inviting him to address, on 26 December, a joint meeting of both Houses. He spoke in a tone of bold and assured hope, though he dealt frankly with the outlook and did not promise the United Nations any easy victory.

FORECAST FOR 1943

Great Britain and the U.S.A., he warned his audience, had not been prepared for this conflict, and their resources, which were potentially immense, were not yet fully mobilized. But great progress had been made, and by the end of 1942—a year ahead—the Allies should be definitely in a better position, and the year 1943 would enable them to assume the initiative on an ample scale. It was a notably accurate forecast, like so many made by Winston Churchill at various times in his career.

Some people might be depressed, he said, when he spoke of a long, hard war; but he felt that their peoples should rather hear the truth, however sombre. In the defence of hearth and home, and of freedom in other lands, the question of whether deliverance came in 1942, 1943 or 1944 fell into its proper proportion in world history. So long as they had faith in their cause, and unconquerable will-power, salvation would not be denied.

He reviewed the progress of the war in the various battle zones, and told how the fact that the U.S.A. had "drawn the sword for free-

AT THE MICROPHONE IN THE U.S.A.

This photograph was taken in Washington in 1943, as Mr. Churchill lit his cigar just before broadcasting to the British people. He visited America for the purpose of conversations with President Roosevelt and the Allied military staffs. During the same tour, he reviewed the course of the world war in a masterly speech before Congress.

dom and cast away the scabbard" was quickening the hopes of all the oppressed peoples of Europe. As for the Japanese attack, it was difficult to reconcile their action with prudence and sanity. "What kind of a people do they think we are?" he asked. Did they not realize that the Allies would persevere until the Japs had received a lesson they and the world would never forget?

In conclusion, he stressed the necessity of common action by Britain and the U.S.A. to preserve world order and the essentials of civilization.

> "I avow my faith and hope that in the days to come the British and American peoples will, for their own safety and the good of all, walk together in majesty, in justice, and in peace."

Four days later Churchill addressed both Houses of the Canadian Legislature at Ottawa. There, too, he reviewed the war situation, and spoke of the successful conferences he had held with Roosevelt to ensure united action against the enemy. Speaking of the collapse of France, he deplored the refusal of the French Cabinet to go to Africa and to continue the war from there.

> "But their generals misled them. When I warned them that Britain would fight on alone, their generals told their Prime Minister and his divided Cabinet: 'In three weeks England will have her neck wrung like a chicken!'" He paused: "Some chicken—and some neck!"

He added some words in French to the French Canadians and to Frenchmen everywhere. He called on the people in occupied countries to maintain their passive resistance and to hold themselves in readiness to co-operate when the hour of deliverance should strike. In conclusion, he said:

> "Let us then address ourselves to our task, not underrating the difficulties of the task and its perils, but, in good heart and sober confidence, resolve that, whatever the cost, whatever the suffering, we shall stand by one another, true and faithful comrades, and do our duty, God helping us, to the end."

CHURCHILL WITH BRITISH TROOPS IN NORTH AFRICA

*In June, 1943, Mr. Churchill visited North Africa on his return
journey from the United States to Britain. It was his first chance to
congratulate the troops there upon their brilliant victories. He is
shown here in the amphitheatre of ancient Carthage.*

with automatic emptying ...
the two tubs separate for easy storage or
individual use. All this for only **49 gns.**

**The famous
Hoover Twosome** with heater
is now reduced to **55 gns.**
Powerful heater that boils.

Over 9,000 sho

THERE'S ALWAYS G

with sense of storm

THIS is the tribute by the Poet Laureate, John Masefield:

The divine fortune, watching
  life's affairs,
Justly endowed him with
  what fortune may,
With sense of storm and
  where the centre lay,
With tact of deed, in some
  wise witty way.

Fortune of parents came in
  equal shares,
With England's wisest
  mingling with the west,
A startling newness, making
  better best,
A newness putting old things
  to a test. . . .

So, when convulsion
  and direst need,
When, in a mess of r
  overthrown,
This England stood a
  and stood alone,
His figure, then comma
  stood as stone.

Or, speaking, uttered li
  very breed
of Francis Drake, d
  being near,
One solemn watchwor
  have done with fear.
Thence, without other
  beat, all took cheer,
Content with such a ca
  such a creed.

CHAPTER XVI

ON THE ROAD TO VICTORY

CHURCHILL had spoken truly when he forecast that 1942 would be a year of preparation for the final grapple with the enemy, rather than one in which we could hope for outstanding successes. He was wise enough to recognize that if the Allies would wait until they had mobilized their immense potential strength instead of frittering it away in premature and ineffectual offensives, they would eventually have a decisive superiority over the Axis which would make victory certain when the hour struck for their attack.

So, through the greater part of the year, the Allies hung on grimly, being attacked rather than attacking, and took heavy punishment on nearly every battlefield. It was a sombre time for the people, with bad news coming in day after day, first from Far East, then from Russia. What the news bulletins could not disclose was the scale of our preparations for future operations, the progress of our devices for destroying the enemy by sea, land and air, and the vast reserves of fighting men and war material that were being amassed.

For Winston it was a year of desperate activity. He was repeatedly flying backwards and forwards to hold the Allies together and to harmonize their war plans. The whole machinery of our co-operation with Soviet Russia had to be created. Our relations with Russia had to be improved and stabilized. The people at home, fretful and impatient at the absence of any sign of military initiative on our part, needed cheering and calming. Happily for the British cause Winston was a man of unquenchable activity. But in 1942 even he must have found twenty-four hours all too short an allowance of time for each day, in view of the amount of work to be packed into it. His hand was on every lever; his finger in every pie.

The opening months were dark with an unbroken series of calamities for the United Nations in the Far East. The British, Dutch and American colonial territories there were not held by forces designed or equipped to withstand assault by an enemy deploying the full weight of armaments on a European scale. Their functions had been on little more than a police scale—suppressing bandits and unruly tribesmen. The vigour of the colonial administrations had been sapped and softened by years of easy living in a tropical climate, so that they crumpled up when they were hit by the invading Japanese.

MALAYA OVERRUN BY JAPANESE

Malaya was overrun with startling rapidity. British and Indian troops fought well, but were outwitted by Japanese jungle tactics and infiltration. The Air Force was outnumbered, but, worse still, its aircraft were obsolete. No amount of courage could overcome the handicaps of inferior aircraft performance, lack of secure forward airfields and inadequate communication facilities. The Allied Forces fell back on Singapore, which base, unprepared for an assault from Malaya, was forced to capitulate.

Attack on the Dutch East Indies quickly followed, and by 7 March they, too, were in enemy hands. Rangoon fell next day, and the Japanese then drove northward through Burma. Their navy poured into the Indian Ocean and captured the Andaman Islands, sank freighters passing down the east coast of India, and bombarded the ports of Madras Province. On 6 May the last American resistance in the Philippines ended and Japan was left in unchallenged supremacy over many thousands of miles of land and sea from the Aleutians to the Timor Sea, and from the frontier of Assam to the Gilberts in the mid-Pacific. It seemed as if her dream of a vast Asiatic Empire was about to be realized.

Winston's first broadcast speech of the year was made on 15 February, in the midst of this developing tale of calamity. He pointed out that we could take comfort from the fact that Russia had not been crushed during the previous summer, and was in fact at that time fighting back successfully with the thrust of her winter campaign. For the first time they had broken the Hitler legend. The all-conquering Fuehrer had found in Russia

"so far, only disaster, failure, the shame of unspeakable crimes, the slaughter of vast numbers of German soldiers, and the icy wind that blows across the Russian snows."

The Japanese assault, he said, was something against which we could not in any case have made adequate counter-preparations, while we had "Nazi Germany at our throat and Fascist Italy at our belly." All he now had to offer was hard, adverse war for many months ahead. Many misfortunes, severe, torturing losses and remorseless and gnawing anxieties lay before us. But if we held firmly together we should win through this new ordeal.

"So far we have not failed, and we shall not fail now. Let us move forward steadfastly together into the storm and through the storm."

The Japanese advance in Asia made it specially urgent to seek to consolidate Indian opinion behind the British effort to defend that country against invasion. At the outset of the war the Indian Government had joined with the British against Germany, and all parties and classes had applauded the decision. But in the autumn of 1940, when Britain stood alone against the Nazi monster, Gandhi and the Congress leaders decided to start a campaign of civil disobedience in order to force Britain to hand over the reins of government to them. Persuasion and expostulation were fruitless, and in the end the authorities had to lay the sedition-mongers by the heels to protect the country from disaster.

POLITICAL SITUATION IN INDIA

It was an unhappy situation. Ever since the Round Table Conference of 1930 Britain had been trying to persuade the Indians to agree on the terms of an Indian constitution which would enable Dominion self-government to be set up in the Indian Empire. It had been a fruitless effort. Congress, the biggest single party in India, could not or would not come to terms with the large Moslem minority, nor with the Indian Princes, whose territories comprised about two-fifths of its area and a quarter of its total population. To hand over these and all the other Indian minorities without any safeguard to the tender mercies of the group of politicians running the Congress Party was of course unthinkable. But was no peaceable compromise possible? The sullen non-co-operation of Congress Hindus was particularly unhealthy with the enemy at the gate.

Winston was no enthusiast for Indian self-government, but he recognized and accepted it as the agreed national policy, and made a bold bid to achieve a reconciliation of the conflicting sections. On 11 March he announced that Sir Stafford Cripps was going to India to convey the Government's proposals for a settlement (to have effect

AT A BATTLEFIELD CEMETERY IN EGYPT

In August, 1942, Churchill went to talk with Stalin in Moscow. Travelling by way of the Middle East, he arranged in Cairo for Generals Alexander and Montgomery to command our North African armies. Above, he is seen near El Alamein, in the Western Desert.

immediately on the end of the war) that would give India full Dominion status and autonomy.

The choice of Cripps for this errand was a very happy inspiration. For Cripps was not only a brilliant advocate—he was an outstanding left-wing politician, warmly sympathetic to the demands of Indians, and also well known as a man of incorruptible honesty. He was one of those sharp-cornered, distinctive characters which England not infrequently throws up; high-minded, stubborn, self-willed. A left-wing Socialist, he was so little disposed to conform to the social verdict that he was for a time flung out of the Labour Party for recalcitrance. He was in fact a strong individualist in practice, accepting no decision, however big its majority, unless it was his own. But of his utter sincerity and benevolent purpose there was never any question. The Indians could trust him absolutely to bring no trap or bogus offer to them. Duplicity was impossible for him.

Another blotted page was added to the record of the Congress Party when, after at first welcoming the scheme that Cripps brought, they swung round on Gandhi's orders and turned it down. It came out later that Gandhi thought Britain to be incapable of defending India, and wished therefore to be free to enter into separate negotiations with Japan, which were out of the question while India remained inside the Empire. The miscalculation was tragic for India.

There was never any question of the British resigning India to the Japanese. Reinforcements were pushed out as soon as the menace grew serious. Thereby another problem was raised, for they had to travel round the Cape of Good Hope, and north past Madagascar, which was held by a Vichy collaborator with the Axis, Governor-General Annet. There was acute danger that he would allow the Japanese to take control, as Vichy officials had done in French Indo-China, and thus make Madagascar an enemy base, barring our route. To avert this an expedition was sent out which by skilful tactics managed to land and establish itself in the north of the island. After a long and tedious campaign the whole of Madagascar was wrested from Vichy and was placed under control of the Free French. Our high-road to India was then securely protected.

A GRIM SEASON FOR THE ALLIES

The summer of 1942 was a grim season for the Allies. Towards the end of May the Germans again took the offensive in Russia. They soon regained the ground they had lost during the winter, and thrust on farther, across the centre and south of that country. Sebastopol fell on 1 July, and a week later the Nazis were hammering at Voronezh, far to the south-east of Moscow, in an attempt to cut through behind the capital and its formidable frontal defence zone.

Hitler announced that Voronezh had fallen. But the claim was premature. It did not fall. So the enemy swept farther south to bear down on Stalingrad on the Volga, while other forces drove across the Kuban steppes to the Caucasus, seeking control of the rich oil-fields of Baku. All through the late summer and autumn the fight for Stalingrad went on. To the bitter disappointment of the Germans, the Russians chose to turn it into a battlefield rather than yield it to the enemy. Among the shattered debris of the once beautiful city which had been the proudest town-planning achievement of Soviet Russia, they fought with desperate defiance for every yard of ground and every stone of ruin. Hitler claimed its fall. But again he was unable to make good his word. Driven back to a thin line of wreckage on the

Volga bank, the defenders never relaxed their determined grip on the city's fragments, while the watching world marvelled at a spectacle of heroism never surpassed in human history.

In North Africa, too, Rommel launched a German offensive on the night of 26 May, and in five weeks had driven the British back, right across Cyrenaica and western Egypt, until he was halted at El Alamein, just out of reach of Alexandria. So confident were the Axis leaders of complete victory there that Mussolini had his white charger dispatched to North Africa, in readiness for the pageant of his entry into Alexandria. But the El Alamein lines held firm, and that triumphal march never happened. Later on we captured the horse.

ILL-INFORMED CLAMOUR FOR A SECOND FRONT

In Britain there was an incessant, though ill-informed clamour for the immediate opening of a "second Front" in western Europe against Hitler; a demand whose noisiest supporters were the Communists, who had discredited themselves with the British public by insisting, right up to the moment when Hitler attacked Russia, that the war against the Nazi horror was merely a "Capitalists' War," which no enlightened person should support! National impatience for a direct assault on the Continent was not, however, confined to them. It was widely felt. But Churchill had no intention of engaging in any premature venture of the kind. He remembered the Dardanelles, Andalsnes, Crete. He knew the immense difficulties of an amphibious expedition against a powerfully held enemy coast, and planned another and more promising operation of which the public were unaware. It would serve to try-out our invasion methods.

Raids by our Navy and Air Force were, however, kept up with increasing vigour, as the fruits of intensive production in factories and shipyards magnified our striking power. Small-scale Commando raids at selected points on the hostile coasts were being continually carried out, though few of them received publicity. A rather larger one was made on St. Nazaire on 27 March, to damage the docks and destroy a radio station, and on 19 August the Canadians were given a chance at Dieppe, where they fought a very gallant action.

The bombing of Germany and German-held territory grew steadily heavier, until on 30 May the first thousand-bomber raid was made on Cologne, followed by another, the next night, on Bremen.

A third was made on Bremen on 25 June, and a month later the first "block-busters" were showered on the Ruhr and Hamburg. Henceforward British air warfare became a major feature of the struggle, attacking the enemy's war industries and disorganizing his transport.

JAPANESE DEFEATS IN THE PACIFIC

In the Pacific the tide slowly began to turn. Japanese naval craft had raided down towards Australia early in May, but they ran into a strong American force in the Coral Sea, and were heavily defeated. Another big battle took place off Midway Island, where the enemy also suffered punishment. Some twenty of their ships were sunk by the Americans, including three aircraft carriers. An attempt to overpower the Australian garrison at Milne Bay, in the eastern corner of New Guinea, was smashed up. The Americans, having established themselves in the Solomons, began steadily to clean up the Japanese bases there and to prise the enemy out of one stronghold after another in difficult jungle warfare.

The Allied Nations were a coalition, with all the possibilities of weakness and dissension which that entails. In the First World War a French statesman was reported to have said that he was coming to feel that Napoleon's reputation as a general was overestimated; he had to fight only coalitions!

Winston was wide awake to this danger, and perhaps the greatest of his many services to the cause of victory were the untiring efforts he put forth to hold the Allies firmly together, to secure a combined strategy, to allay mutual distrust and disagreement. To this end he not only dispatched a number of missions east and west, and set up joint boards of various kinds such as the Combined Chiefs of Staff Committee, Combined Boards for Food, for Supplies, for Shipping and so on, but paid repeated personal visits to discuss matters at first hand with the leaders of the Allied Governments.

On 18 June, 1942, less than six months after his last visit to the United States, Churchill flew across the Atlantic to discuss with Roosevelt the secret plans for the next big move—the assault on North Africa. The moment was cheerless enough. On the second day of his visit, Roosevelt handed him the news of the fall of Tobruk—a military disaster in which twenty thousand men were captured with much material and food—and of the retreat of Auchinleck's forces in Libya. But the two statesmen went confidently on with their plans,

MR. CHURCHILL VISITS TEHERAN, PERSIA

On his way to Russia, the Prime Minister held some frank talks with the Shah of Persia in Teheran. He took the opportunity, also, of meeting officers and men of the Persia and Iraq Command. Above, Mr. Churchill is shown walking with Major-General A. Selby.

whose aim, they vaguely announced, was "the earliest maximum concentration of Allied war power upon the enemy." Where those plans would take effect remained a secret.

On his return Churchill found himself thrown on the defensive in the House of Commons, where public dissatisfaction with the defeat in North Africa and the British failure to strike effectively on the Continent found voice. He had to admit the deplorable and inexplicable character of the Libyan defeat, though there were brighter items elsewhere in the account—notably the amazing defence of Malta, which had been subjected to months of intense bombing attack, but still fought back in defiance of all war-time precedents and probabilities. The American shipping output was mounting rapidly. So was British tank production. Some two thousand tanks had already been sent to Russia and large supplies of them and other arms, as well as reinforcements, were going to Africa. India was now well armed. Russia was putting up a magnificent fight. And, anyhow, he was not going to share his supreme responsibility with anyone. In the division the House gave him a 17 to 1 majority. It might criticize, but it did not want to change him.

CHURCHILL TOURS ABROAD

Just over a month later, Churchill set off on a fresh tour, this time to the East, to talk with Stalin. On his way he visited Cairo, and arranged to place General Alexander in charge of the Middle East war zone, with Montgomery as the Commander of the Eighth Army. He also visited the troops at El Alamein. His love of battlefields was as strong as ever. Then, by way of Persia, he flew on to Moscow, and discussed the strategy of the war with Stalin, whose troops were standing up to the full weight of the German summer offensive.

He explained to the Soviet leader why Britain could not at present contemplate opening a "Second Front" in western Europe, but told him of the projected assault on North Africa and the Mediterranean "soft under-belly" of the Axis. Stalin was far from happy about this. The strain on Russia of the German thrusts at Stalingrad and the Caucasus was intense, and he was eager to gain the relief which a British landing in France would give to his front. Nevertheless he accepted the Anglo-American decision, and the two men established a good understanding. Back flew Winston to Persia, where he had a frank talk with the Shah; back to Cairo, for further discussions with all the chief figures in charge of Middle East affairs; and on 17 August he returned to London, where the British public were profoundly thankful to welcome him safely home again.

It had been a very crowded, but most fruitful tour. Allied strategy was now really concerted, and the plans had been agreed for the opening of the next phase: the advance to victory. On 8 September Churchill made his report to Parliament, and was able to assure his hearers that the Eighth Army was now reinforced, re-equipped and

ALLIED LEADERS CONFER IN CAIRO

In 1943 a big Allied conference met in Cairo. Above (sitting, left to right) are: Generalissimo Chiang Kai-shek, President Roosevelt, Mr. Churchill, Madame Chiang. Standing (left to right) are: Sir A. Cadogan, Mr. Eden, Mr. Winant, Dr. Chung-hui, Mr. R. G. Casey, Lord Killearn, Lord Leathers and Mr. Averell Harriman.

"stronger, actually and relatively, than it has ever been." He told of his visit to Stalin, with whom he had discussed matters for four days "with the utmost candour and thoroughness": though it had not been easy to make the Russians, who were "land animals," understand the problems of Britain and the U.S.A., who were "sea and ocean animals." He ended with a denunciation of the atrocious Nazi crimes against humanity, of which he had learned further details when in Russia, and reaffirmed the determination of the Government to bring the criminals responsible for them to justice.

The Germans continued to hammer at Stalingrad. A big convoy fought its way to Malta against a terrific concentration of attack by hostile aircraft and U-boats. On 1 September Rommel attempted an assault on the lines at El Alamein, but was thrown back. The R.A.F. dropped five hundred tons of bombs nightly on German targets. American shipyards poured forth vessels, and on 27 September Churchill sent them a message of congratulation. He knew to what high purpose some of those ships would shortly be devoted.

Then, on 23 October, Montgomery struck at Rommel; struck hard, inexorably, irresistibly. When he took over the Eighth Army, the General had told his officers: "I forbid the use of the word 'Counter-attack'; for a counter-attack implies that we have given ground and there must be no giving ground." There was none. The Germans counter-attacked vainly. Montgomery had organized complete co-operation between air and ground forces, and German tank formations were smashed up and their lines of communication and supply blasted. After ten days of titanic struggle Rommel's lines were hopelessly broken, and British troops were pouring forward through the gaps. Montgomery's Order of the Day on 4 November announced that the enemy was worn down and "is now in our power. We have the chance of putting the whole Panzer Army in the bag, and we shall do so!"

Three days later the total of prisoners had mounted to forty thousand, and an equal number of the enemy had been killed or wounded. The Germans left their Italian allies to their fate, stole their transport, and hurried off westward as fast as they could, with the British Army hotly pursuing them.

INVASION OF NORTH AFRICA

It was high time. On 8 November the greatest amphibious operation till then in history took place far away to the west. A vast fleet of American and British transports, secretly assembled in the Atlantic, suddenly swooped down on Algeria and Morocco, and the armies aboard them poured into French North Africa. In some places the Vichy garrisons were ordered by their Fascist-minded commanders to resist. But none could repel the invasion.

The American element was thrust well to the front of the picture in this invasion, to disarm any suspicion by the French that Britain had designs on their territory. The British Navy had the lion's share of the task of covering the operation and of dealing with shore batteries and U-boats, and the British First Army subsequently played the major part in breaking the back of German resistance in northern Tunisia. Supreme command of the operations was, however, entrusted to the American General Eisenhower.

This was no doubt a wise and tactful arrangement: but it had one serious drawback. The Americans were rather inexpert in European diplomatic matters, and were somewhat afraid of being led by British diplomats. Looking upon General de Gaulle as a close associate of the British, they would not "let him in on their stunt," and chose General Giraud, whom the British had secretly brought off from France in a submarine. But Admiral Darlan, the time-serving collaborator with the Nazis, somehow got wind of what was happening, and slipped across to Algiers in time to witness the American arrival. He decided to jump to the winning side. Shouldering past Giraud, he offered to secure the peaceful surrender of French North Africa, and the Americans, unaware how bitterly he was hated by every patriotic Frenchman, thought this an excellent idea. It may have momentarily eased their military task, but it was a disastrous blunder, which nearly brought to ruin all hope of collaboration between the Allies and the French patriots who were their real friends. Happily, Darlan was assassinated on 24 December, and French unity in the struggle with Germany again became possible.

HITLER FORCED ON THE DEFENSIVE

With the Anglo-American invasion of North Africa the whole picture of the war was changed. The initiative definitely passed from the Axis to the United Nations. Hitler and his satellites were henceforward on the defensive everywhere, and were being slowly but surely beaten back and ground down toward their inevitable doom.

The Fuehrer was acutely aware of the threat implicit in this new move, and took every possible counter-measure. He at once proceeded to occupy the rest of France—the centre and Mediterranean coast—which hitherto he had controlled cheaply by means of his Vichy lickspittles, Laval and Darlan and the doddering, Fascist-minded Pétain. The defence of his prize against Anglo-American attack needed tougher guardians than these venal or dull-witted turncoats.

He poured troops into Tunisia, which the Allied invasion had not yet reached, and he built up a formidable garrison there to hold the rear of the Axis forces in Libya, as they retreated westward before Montgomery's Eighth Army. But these moves were purely defensive. They could delay the Allied advance. They could not deflect it, still less reverse it.

When Churchill spoke on 10 November at the Mansion House

CHURCHILL VISITS BATTERED MALTA

On his way to the Cairo Conference, Mr. Churchill visited the island of Malta. He was much impressed by the evidence of the island's gallant defence under aerial bombardment. Above, he is walking among the ruins of houses in the shattered dockyard area.

in London he had new and obvious warrant for that cheerful confidence which he had never lost in the darkest hour. But he forbore to boast. "This is not the end," he warned his audience. "It is not even the beginning of the end. But it is, perhaps, the end of the beginning!" He could now say openly that the battle of Egypt had been timed to prepare for and match the Anglo-American descent in the West. He expressed his faith that France would rise again, and wished her "free and strong, with her Empire gathered round her and with Alsace-Lorraine restored."

As for the British Empire, we coveted no one else's territory, but we meant to hold our own. In a pointed aside to those critics on both sides of the Atlantic who found fault with its existence, he remarked: "I have not become the King's First Minister in order to preside over the liquidation of the British Empire. For that task,

ALLIED CONFERENCE AT CASABLANCA, FRENCH MOROCCO
In January, 1943, President Roosevelt met Mr. Churchill at Casablanca. "Unconditional surrender" was agreed upon for the Germans. Above, they are seen with Generals Giraud (left) and de Gaulle.

if ever it were prescribed, someone else would have to be found, and, under democracy, I suppose the nation would have to be consulted!"

Next day, in Parliament, Churchill could at last point to North Africa as the explanation of the seeming inertia for which he had, all summer long, been criticized. "I am certainly not one of those who need to be prodded," he said. "In fact, if anything, I am a prod!" This Algerian pot had secretly been brewing all the time. The unfulfilled talk of a "Second Front" had served its purpose in drawing considerable German forces to the West, away from Russia, but Stalin had known, if Hitler had not, what was our real intention. "I must say quite frankly that I hold it perfectly justifiable to deceive the enemy even if, at the same time, your own people are for a while misled. There is one thing, however, you must never do, and that is to mislead your ally."

The North African campaign rolled forward. In a month from the first blows of the El Alamein battle the Eighth Army had chased Rommel out of Egypt and right across Cyrenaica. Then the blitzkreig

368

slowed to a hard grind through Tripolitania and into Tunisia, where the First Army, the Americans and the French were also advancing. Fast or slow, it was the Allies who advanced, the Germans who gave ground.

In Russia the story was now the same. The heroic defence of Stalingrad was changed into a glorious victory. Stalin had seemed almost niggardly with his reinforcements for the gallant city. The explanation came when he suddenly struck, in mid-November, not from the Stalingrad front, but well to the north-west and to the south of the city, in a vast pincer attack. Hitler, having pledged his intuition for the capture of Stalingrad, refused to allow his troops there to withdraw, and presently the whole doomed army—more than three hundred thousand strong—was encircled and trapped. He brutally ordered it not to surrender, but to fight and die. Cornered on a shattered and shelterless landscape, in the snow and bitter frost of a Russian winter, the troops tried to obey him. The Red Army closed in for the kill. Finally, on 31 January, 1943, the German Commander, von Paulus, surrendered with fifteen other generals and the remnants of his fine army, now reduced to about twelve thousand men. It was the biggest single victory scored up to that time by either side in the whole war.

CONFERENCE AT CASABLANCA

On 13 January, 1943, there was staged at Casablanca, in French Morocco, an Allied conference of high moment and dramatic significance.

Churchill had repeatedly visited the United States to discuss with Roosevelt the grand strategy of the war. But this time the President, despite his physical disability, crossed the Atlantic to visit the region where his American troops had driven out the enemy, and to confer with Churchill and the heads of the Allied forces about their future plans for the defeat of the Axis Powers.

All the chief figures—naval, military, air, political—of both nations were gathered. It had been hoped that Stalin would come too, but he was extremely busy, organizing the rout of the German forces before Stalingrad and in the Caucasus, and could not leave his post. But de Gaulle and Giraud were brought into conference, and a beginning was made in healing over the gaping fissures that still divided the French patriots.

At the Conference the entire field of war was surveyed, theatre by theatre, and complete agreement was reached by both statesmen and staffs on their war plans to draw the utmost profit from the initiative they now held. These plans included the sending of all possible material aid to Russia and China. But perhaps the most momentous of all the decisions agreed at Casablanca was that with regard to the terms on which hostilities should be ended. Roosevelt told the Press representatives at the close of the Conference that the United Nations were determined that peace could only come to the world by the "unconditional surrender" of the Axis Powers, and the total elimination of their capacity for war. He suggested that the meeting should be known to history as the "Unconditional Surrender" meeting!

Churchill added that it was the most important and successful war conference he had ever attended. He also spoke of the triumphs of the Eighth Army against Rommel, saying that it had followed him one thousand five hundred miles from El Alamein, and "everywhere that Mary went the lamb was sure to go!" It may be doubted whether the Germans whom he had hunted across Africa thought the comparison of Montgomery with a lamb was really appropriate.

A NON-BELLIGERENT BUT FRIENDLY STATE

The Casablanca Conference was no sooner ended than Churchill was off farther afield, this time to Turkey, where on 30 and 31 January he discussed the situation fully with the Turkish President, while his supporting officials had interviews with Turkish political and military chiefs. A good understanding was reached with this non-belligerent but friendly State.

Back in England again, Churchill gave a full report of his tour and its results to Parliament on 11 February. He defined the dominating aim of the Allied leaders at Casablanca. It was to engage the enemy forces "by sea, land and air, on the largest possible scale and at the earliest possible moment, and to make the enemy burn and bleed in every way that is physically and reasonably possible, in the same way as he is being made to burn and bleed along the vast Russian front." The keynote of the Casablanca Conference was the unconditional surrender of the enemy; and while this did not mean any cruel treatment of whole populations, "justice must be done upon the wicked and the guilty, and, within her proper bounds, justice must be stern and implacable."

IMPERIAL CONFERENCE MEETS IN LONDON

In May, 1943, the Imperial Conference met in London to discuss Imperial co-operation in war and peace. Sitting (left to right) are: Mr. Attlee, Mr. Fraser (New Zealand), Mr. Mackenzie King (Canada), Mr. Churchill, Mr. Curtin (Australia), Field-Marshal Smuts (South Africa) and Mr. Eden. Standing (left to right) are: Lord Woolton, Mr. Oliver Lyttleton, Sir John Anderson, Mr. Bevin and Mr. Morrison.

There was reason for Churchill's warning of a coming retribution; for during the winter and spring appalling news began to leak through of the bestial savagery which Hitler's dehumanized hordes were practising upon the helpless peoples under their heel. The defeats which the Axis was suffering and the shadow of coming doom which darkened its prospects only seemed to intensify the sadistic cruelty with which it treated its victims.

Throughout Russia the Germans treated the inhabitants of the regions they had overrun as vermin, to be exterminated without pity. The able-bodied they carted off to slavery in the Reich. Girls were collected for soldiers' brothels. The rest were robbed of all food and left to starve; hanged by the score in towns and villages; bayoneted, shot, or driven into huts and churches and burned alive. As in the

BRITISH AND GREEK MINISTERS CONFER IN ATHENS

On Christmas Day, 1944, Mr. Churchill and Mr. Anthony Eden
conferred in Athens with representatives of the various conflicting
Greek political parties. Above, Mr. Churchill and Mr. Eden are on the
right of the Greek Regent, Archbishop Damaskinos.

course of 1943 the Russians advanced once again into their despoiled
territory, they found everywhere the traces of massacre and outrage,
the wanton destruction of all cultural buildings, monuments,
libraries, works of art, the almost total depopulation of the country.

But perhaps the worst horrors of Nazi savagery were practised in
Poland; for Hitler was impatient to use Poland for German coloniza-
tion, and accordingly took systematic steps to obliterate its population. The peasants were cleared from district after district, the healthy
men enslaved, the children deported to Germany, the rest carted off
to "an unknown destination." That destination, it presently trans-
pired, was one or other of the centres established by the Nazis for
mass murder. Special measures were taken to collect all Jews and
send them to these murder camps, where they were stripped of all
clothing, killed in gas chambers and buried in huge pits dug by
mechanical excavators. The Inter-Allied Information Committee in
London reported on 27 February, 1943, that up to the end of 1942
two and a half million Poles, including a million Jews, had been
executed or beaten to death in concentration camps. Jews were also

collected from Holland, Belgium and France and carried off to the Polish killing grounds.

The Allied advance into Germany later uncovered "horror" camps which shocked the world. Belsen became a new term for vile and bestial cruelty. Hitler's insensate hatred of the Jewish race had driven him on in a wild attempt to wipe it from the face of the earth. Also caught up in the Nazi schemes for mass destruction were all those who dared to oppose the party hierarchy. The subsequent trials of the leading personalities in the administration of these camps, and the stories of survivors helped to inform world opinion of the utter depravity of the Nazi mind. Winston's fierce denunciations and promise of stern justice were well merited.

The Germans were not alone in their cult of bestial and carefully studied cruelty. The Japanese, for whom everything is right if done for Japan, practised a similar savagery upon those who fell into their hands. On 21 April they announced the execution of some American airmen who, during a bombing attack on Tokyo a year previously, had been shot down and taken prisoner. The many thousands of European prisoners who fell into their hands during their victorious sweep through the Far East were herded into camps in conditions too bad for the Japs to permit neutral visitors to inspect them. On their release prisoners revealed that they had been starved and brutally maltreated, while thousands had been murdered or died of disease. The barbarities inflicted on some of them by their callous and cold-blooded captors were unspeakable.

Well might Winston denounce the Japanese massacres as "the most bestial, the most squalid, and the most senseless of all their offences," and declare that when Hitler was defeated Britain's whole strength would be turned on Japan, whose cities and other military centres should be laid in ashes, as they must be before peace returned to the world.

CEASELESSLY ON THE MOVE

In the months that followed, Winston was tirelessly on the move. On 11 May he arrived in Washington for fresh talks with Roosevelt. Conditions differed a good deal from those when last he had visited the States. Then he had been confronted with tidings of the fall of Tobruk and the rout of the British Army in North Africa. This time news came through, the day after his arrival, of the surrender of the

German Army in Tunisia and the complete deliverance of North Africa from Axis forces. During his former visit the Germans had been rolling forward across Russia in their greatest advance. Now the Russians were keeping up through the summer the momentum of their winter offensive, and relentlessly pressing the Nazis back in a series of crushing defeats.

Once again Winston addressed Congress. He had a heartening theme in the North African victories of the Anglo-American forces. The account, too, had just been published of the brilliantly successful bombing of the Möhne and Eder dams in the Ruhr. The Gettysburg of this war, he could assure Congress, was safely won. Now we had to finish off the job as quickly as possible.

On his way home, Churchill visited North Africa, where Eden met him and consultations were started between de Gaulle and Giraud to arrange a united Free French administration of the territories now free of Vichy and Axis control. When he got back to Britain, Churchill gave the Commons a cheerful account of the agreement reached between the French leaders.

While Churchill was at Washington, another gathering of great interest was taking place at Hot Springs, Virginia, where the representatives of forty-four nations unanimously agreed on a policy to mobilize, after the war, the world's food resources and to ensure that all mankind should get enough to eat. Discussions were also on foot for giving first-aid to the war-devastated countries when hostilities should end. On 11 June the "UNRRA" Agreement, setting up the United Nations Relief and Rehabilitation Administration, was published. After the war this organization did much to aid world recovery.

On 30 June Winston spoke at Guildhall, and renewed the promise that the British would proceed to crush Japan as soon as Hitler was disposed of:

> "Every man, every ship, and every aeroplane in the King's service that can be moved to the Pacific will be sent and will be there maintained in action by the peoples of the British Commonwealth in priority over all other interests for as many flaming years as are needed to make the Japanese in their turn submit or bite the dust!"

The war continued to march in favour of the Allies. Early in July, the Germans tried to embark upon a fresh offensive in Russia, but it quickly petered out, and the Soviet advance was renewed and extended. On 10 July, the next phase of the Mediterranean war was reached with an Allied invasion of Sicily, which was skilfully planned and boldly executed. In five weeks the island was completely in our hands and the remnants of the Axis troops there surrendered. The mounting disasters of Italy brought about Mussolini's downfall on 25 July, and the end of the Fascist regime.

On 10 August, Churchill arrived in Canada where a fortnight later Roosevelt joined him for further conferences. From Quebec Churchill broadcast on 31 August, stressing the importance of an early conference between himself, Roosevelt and Stalin. A week later, at Harvard, he pleaded for continued co-operation between Britain and the United States in the post-war period:

> "In my opinion, it would be a most foolish and improvident act on the part of our two Governments, or either of them, to break up this smooth-running and immensely powerful machinery the moment war is over. For our own safety, as well as for the security of the rest of the world, we are bound to keep it working and in running order after the war—probably for a good many years, not only until we have set up some world arrangement to keep the peace, but until we know that it is an arrangement which will really give us that protection we must have from danger and aggression."

In this speech he referred to the advantage of the possession by Britain and America of a common language, and advocated the teaching of basic English as a common speech throughout the globe.

On 3 September, Italy was invaded, and the new Italian Government under King Victor Emmanuel and Badoglio quickly signed an armistice, though the Germans holding down the country kept up the fight there in the natural fortress of the Appenines.

In the Balkans, Yugoslav patriot forces developed a harassing war on the Germans. The Portuguese lent the Azores to Britain as a naval base on 12 October, and the war on the U-boats took a still more favourable turn. Toward the end of October the Americans joined with the British at a Three-Power Conference in Moscow, where a clear understanding was reached about war measures and peace aims, and machinery was devised to secure future co-operation. On 6 November, the Ukranian city of Kiev was recovered by the Russians, and Hitler could mark the inexorable approach of ultimate doom.

Churchill's tireless journeying to and fro, to hold the front of the

United Nations together and ensure full agreement and joint action in their strategy, culminated during the closing weeks of 1943 in a grand orgy of conferences.

On 22 November, Churchill and Roosevelt met in Cairo for a conference to which all the military and diplomatic chiefs gathered. Plans were laid for future operations in all war theatres, including the Far East, where it was agreed that Japan must be stripped of all the ill-gotten gains she had acquired since 1895.

Then the two statesmen with their advisers travelled on to Teheran, in Persia, where Stalin joined them, and the long-hoped-for meeting of the world's three greatest figures took place. The joint statement issued at the close of their discussions recorded their full agreement as to military plans and future co-operation. It ended with the words:

> "No power on earth can prevent our destroying the German armies by land, their U-boats by sea, and their war planes from the air. Our attacks will be relentless and increasing. From these friendly conferences we look with confidence to the day when all the peoples of the world may live free lives, untouched by tyranny and according to their varying desires and their own consciences. We came here with hope and determination. We leave here friends in fact, in spirit and in purpose."

From Teheran, Churchill and Roosevelt went back to Cairo, where President Inönü of Turkey joined them for further discussions. These confirmed the good understanding reached between Turkey and the Great Powers as to plans and policy. Turkey had all along been Britain's non-belligerent ally.

But the unquenchable activity of Winston's spirit had outrun his bodily strength, and the climax of these three great conferences, following his incessant labours of the past years, brought about a collapse. Pneumonia set in, and an anxious world waited for the bulletins reporting his fight for life. Not many months before, he had been stricken with the same illness. Providentially, however, recent years had seen the discovery of the sulphonamide series of drugs, with their remarkable potency against the pneumococcus—particularly the drug known as M. and B. 693. "M. and B." had brought Winston safely through his former attack, and this time, too, it did not fail. Mrs. Churchill hurried out to him, to find him making good progress, and soon the bulletins could announce that he was out of

MR. CHURCHILL VISITS ALLIED SUPREME COMMANDER

Shortly after the Anglo-American armies had landed in France, Mr. Churchill crossed the Channel to visit the troops and watch the progress of their advance. In this picture Mr. Churchill is seen with Supreme Commander General Dwight Eisenhower, after a conference at the headquarters of the Allied military command in Normandy.

danger. He spent some weeks convalescing at Marrakesh, enjoying the warm winter sunshine of that Moorish capital, where eight years previously he had had an interesting holiday and had essayed to sketch the colourful streets and shady palm-groves.

On 18 January, 1944, Churchill arrived back in London, bronzed and fit. Already there had been announcements of the various staff appointments to the command of the Anglo-American forces which were being assembled to launch the "Second Front" attack on Hitler's "Fortress of Europe." The next weeks were spent in completing the preparations for the crucial operation, which were to deal the final blow to Nazi power and set free the enslaved peoples groaning under the brutalities of the Gestapo.

MOUNTING POWER OF ALLIED AIR RAIDS

The air assault on German industrial centres and on military installations and airfields in northern France and the Low Countries was now taking on a new intensity. Ever since the first "blockbusters" had been dropped on Hamburg in July, 1942, this war on the great munition and aircraft factories of the Reich had been developing in steady crescendo. In January, 1943, the Royal Air Force began dropping 8,000-lb. bombs on Berlin, while their attacks on the Ruhr turned Essen, like Hamburg, into a crumbled heap of ruins. Dusseldorf, Cologne, Frankfort, Mannheim, Ludwigshafen, Nuremberg, Karlsruhe, Bremen and more than a score of other mighty German cities were blasted and shattered. In the autumn of 1943 a series of big raids started in which over two thousand tons of bombs were dropped nightly and smashed up Berlin—till most of the German capital was smouldering wreckage.

The American Air Force, massing in huge strength in Britain for the final round of the struggle, took up the attack by day, until there was no hour of light or darkness when German war production was not being hammered and laid waste. While the heavy bombers were sweeping far into the heart of the Reich, medium and light bombers and fighters clouded the skies across the Channel and plastered camps and roads and railways, aerodromes and defence works, "softening up" the Continent in preparation for the entry of Allied troops.

Churchill realized far more fully than the noisy crowds that were shouting impatiently for a "Second Front" how immense were the

378

difficulties which this invasion would have to surmount. All North-
west France had been turned into a fortress. Its harbours were strongholds and its whole coastline bristled with elaborate defences, both
on land and below the waterline. Hitler had strained the genius of his
ablest military engineers in elaborating devices to baffle any invader,
and had used the slave labour of conquered Europe in the erection of
concrete works and emplacements at every vulnerable point. The
French Channel ports were garrisoned and protected with special care
because, after the Canadian raid on Dieppe, Hitler assumed that any
Allied invasion attempt would begin with an effort to capture a
harbour through which troops, tanks and supplies could be disembarked.

"MULBERRY" HARBOURS

While a fully equipped harbour would ultimately be necessary
for maintaining a successful invasion, the planners of Combined
Operations pointed out that the initial assault must be made on open
beaches; and even after a harbour had been captured it would take
weeks for the Allies to restore it. During that period the assaulting
forces would have to be maintained from the beaches. Why, it was
suggested, should not those beaches be given the protection of a
breakwater of blockships, and be equipped with floating piers;
turned, in fact, into makeshift harbours? It was a startlingly novel
idea, but Churchill had an instinctive fondness for novel ideas. So he
adopted the plan of establishing on the barren, shelving coast between
Cherbourg and Le Havre two prefabricated floating harbours,
through which two armies, one British, one American, could be
poured ashore in a matter of a few hours and temporarily maintained
with supplies and reinforcements, including even the most powerful
modern weapons. These harbours comprised a mole, made of
broken ships and concrete caissons, laid down a mile off shore.
From this, long arms enclosed a rectangle of a mile square. The
general construction was in a line of loosely jointed steel girder spans
anchored to the sunken piers.

Alike in their design and in their construction, these "Mulberry"
harbours were an astounding achievement. How closely Churchill
himself was associated with their planning is illustrated by the
Directive which, as far back as May, 1942, he sent to the Chief of
Combined Operations. It ran as follows:

C.C.O. or Deputy.

They *must* float up and down with the tide. The anchor problem must be mastered. . . . Let me have the best solution worked out. Don't argue the matter. The difficulties will argue for themselves.

W.S.C.

30.5.42

If the "Mulberries" themselves were a miracle of engineering skill, an even greater miracle was the fact that their parts were made, brought round to the south coast and accumulated there, and that thousands of workers must have known about them, but not a whisper leaked out to betray their secret to the enemy. A similar cloak of silence shrouded the assembly of the immense military equipment which was gathered with the armies in southern England, ready for the venture.

While Hitler could not be unaware that a stroke was impending, he knew neither its time, place nor method till it fell. The advance bombardment of the coastal defences in France was spread along their whole length. In the meantime, Montgomery had been appointed commander of the invading forces.

On the night of 5/6 June, a dark, wet, windy night, that seemed most unsuitable for such an attempt, a vast flotilla stole across the Channel, to swoop in on the Normandy shore. Shortly after midnight clouds of paratroopers and gliderborne troops showered down on the countryside beyond the points where the convoys were to make their landing. In the morning light and on a rising tide the Allied landing craft went aground; the liberating armies stormed ashore.

GERMANS TAKEN BY SURPRISE

The enemy were taken by surprise and a strong foothold was made in the first two days. The immediate German reserves were committed in a desperate attempt to dislodge the invaders, but fortunately the enemy were deceived by the Allied threat of another landing in the Pas-de-Calais and large forces were held there. The Allied build-up of forces in Normandy was drastically hampered by a violent storm on 20 June. The "Mulberry" in the American sector was destroyed, the one in the British sector badly damaged. But if the Allied reinforcements were delayed, so too were the Germans. The Allied air forces had effectively disrupted the rail complex of

MR. CHURCHILL VISITS THE WESTERN FRONT

The opening of the Second Front by British and American troops was the most important military event of 1944. Mr. Churchill, who visited the front several times, is seen with Field-Marshal Montgomery and Field-Marshal Sir Alan Brooke.

northern and eastern France, and the fighter bombers so menaced the approaches to the beachhead that movement was confined to the few hours of darkness.

The British forces striking at Caen came up against the main weight of the enemy armour. The Americans cleared the Cherbourg Peninsula, then ranged themselves on the right flank of the Allied bridgehead ready for the break into open warfare. This came in the last week of July. By mid-August the German armies south of the Seine were trapped in a pocket round Falaise. Unfortunately, large numbers of them got away, but they had lost all their equipment and were in headlong flight to the borders of the Reich. Paris fell to the Free French Forces, and was entered by General de Gaulle on 25 August. The American 3rd Army, under General Patton, which all through this campaign moved with extraordinary dash, swept along to the south of Paris and drove forward to Luxemburg and Alsace-Lorraine, while the British forced their way across the Seine and thrust at top speed through Picardy and Belgium in a headlong race for Brussels, Antwerp and the Dutch border. They by-passed for the moment the Channel ports, but stamped out the sites in northern France from which the Germans had been launching their V.1 flying-bombs—nicknamed "doodle-bugs" by the British—which had caused much damage in the London area.

FURTHER LANDINGS IN THE SOUTH

Needless to say, Churchill flew across to Normandy very soon after the Allied bridgeheads had been established there. Characteristically, he had wanted to take part in the assault aboard one of the British naval vessels, but was dissuaded by General Eisenhower. On 12 June he was touring the battlefront with General Montgomery. Then on 10 August he dashed over to Italy to have a look at the battlefield there and to discuss the Yugoslav situation with Marshal Tito. From Italy he sailed in a warship to watch the opening of "Operation Anvil," the invasion of France from the south on 15 August by a combined force of British, French and American troops. This was by comparison a far easier achievement than the Normandy landing, for there were no such formidable defences as the "Atlantic Wall" to be surmounted, and the German troops in southern France were much inferior in strength and equipment to those in the north. A number of landings were made between Toulon and Nice and rapid progress was made. By 20 August, American troops had reached Aix and French forces entered Toulon and captured Toulouse. Two days later, Marseilles was entered, while an American flying column reached Grenoble on 22 August. By this time all France was seething. Free, or as they now called themselves, Fighting French forces sprang up everywhere. The guerrilla warriors of the *Maquis*, who had for a long time past been getting arms, supplies and counsel from Britain, now thrust into the open, liberating Department after Department, overthrowing the Vichy French authorities and rounding up the German garrisons. Hitler's dominion over France melted away.

By 3 September, Lyons, Bordeaux and the whole of southern France from the Rhône to the Atlantic had been freed. In the north, the British, advancing two hundred miles in five days, liberated Brussels, while the Americans to the south captured Verdun and drove on to the Moselle. In three months from "D-Day," the code name for the date of the original landing in Normandy, the bulk of France and Belgium had been cleared of the enemy. Hitler's forces in western Europe had suffered upward of a million casualties, of which about half a million were prisoners of war.

These spectacular successes of the British, American, French and other Allied forces in the west were being paralleled by similar dramatic victories in the south and east of Europe.

ADVANCING IN ITALY AND IN RUSSIA

In Italy the British-American forces, reduced in strength because of the concentration of troops for the invasion of France, continued nevertheless to drive doggedly forward. Rome was entered on 4 June, two days before the Normandy "D-day," and in the next few weeks Leghorn and Florence fell. By the beginning of September the Allies were pressing against the "Gothic Line," Hitler's new defence system running through the heights of the Apennines and guarding the Po Valley.

Meanwhile the Russians never paused in their forward drive. All through the spring and early summer they had pressed on in the Ukraine, regaining Odessa, Sebastopol and the Crimea, and penetrating the frontier of Rumania. At the end of June they started a full-scale summer offensive along the Eastern Front to match the Anglo-American invasion in the West. From the Baltic to the Black Sea the Red armies swung forward, sweeping the Germans out of the Baltic States, hammering their way across eastern Poland toward the Vistula and Warsaw, thrusting at the frontiers of East Prussia.

By the beginning of August it seemed as if Warsaw was within their reach and the Polish "underground" army within the city rose to share in its liberation. But their effort had a tragic issue. The Russian armies were over-extended and the Germans rounded on their vanguard and beat it back. The prospect of an early capture of Warsaw faded. Whether for strategic or political reasons, the Russians delayed any further thrust forward on this part of the front for five months, and the valiant but doomed Polish forces in the city (who happened to be anti-Communist) were left to their fate. When at last the Soviet armies drove on again past the Polish capital it had become a depopulated ruin.

Early autumn saw the end of German domination in the Balkans. With Russian armies advancing across her territory, Rumania changed sides on 25 August, 1944, and declared war on Germany. The Russians entered Bucharest by the end of the month. During the last week of August Bulgaria tried to withdraw from the war. Russia refused to concede the Bulgarian claim to have become neutral. She declared war on her on 5 September and Bulgaria promptly imitated Rumania and in turn sided with the Allies. Early in October, Allied forces landed in Greece and, by the 13th, the British entered Athens. Next day the Russians, who had overrun Transylvania, were invited by Hungary to free her from Hitler. Russian troops reached Belgrade in Yugoslavia on 20 October, and the remaining Germans in the Balkans began to withdraw in a hurry, speeded by Marshal Tito's patriotic forces and the Allied "Land Forces, Adriatic," which were operating from Italy. Far to the north, Finland had signed an armistice with Russia on 10 September, and by 22 October the Russians reached the Norwegian border. All around, the walls were caving in upon Hitler's brief empire, which he had boasted would last a thousand years.

These crowded victories following one another in swift succession in less than five months from the "D-Day" launching of the "Second Front" were a dramatic realization of the plans laid at Teheran, and may be said to have vindicated Churchill's policy of making the most thorough preparation before delivering the great stroke.

FURTHER TRAVELS OF A STATESMAN

Amid the glow of these great events Churchill arrived in Canada on 10 September, where he was joined next day at Quebec by President Roosevelt for a conference on the future conduct of the war. Stalin had also been invited, but excused himself on the ground that the Russian armies were fighting on so broad a front that he could not leave the Soviet Union. However, Churchill visited him in Moscow a month later, on 9 October, to talk over not only the military but still more the political problems which the defeat of Hitler, now becoming an ever-closer reality, would set before the Allies.

384

"BIG THREE" CONFERENCE IN THE CRIMEA

In February, 1945, Churchill, Roosevelt and Stalin met at Yalta in the Crimea. This was the first time that Roosevelt and Stalin had met, and the three made final plans for the defeat of Germany. Above, Roosevelt and Stalin are admiring Churchill's headgear.

The autumn saw a bold bid by the British to rush the northern end of the German defence line in the west. On 17 September airborne troops were dropped at Nijmegen and Arnhem in Holland, to seize the bridges over the Maas and the Rhine, while the 2nd Army drove forward overland, cutting a corridor towards those key points. But bad weather hampered the stroke, which came short of success. Nijmegen was reached and passed, but not Arnhem. There the parachute troops held out very gallantly until 25 September, on which date the few remaining alive and uncaptured had to be withdrawn. During October and November the British and Canadians were occupied in clearing the entrance to the Scheldt and opening the port of Antwerp, while farther south the American and French forces cleared eastern France and Alsace-Lorraine.

December saw the ominous beginnings of that lamentable conflict in Greece between Communist and anti-Communist elements which was to develop into the drawn-out tragedy of the next five years. Both groups of partisans had been well armed by the Allies for war against the Germans. On the withdrawal of the enemy, they started to fight one another. The British troops who were in the country, and were appealed to by the newly-established Greek Government to restore order, tried to disarm and pacify the warring elements. The public at home heard with profound disquiet that our men were becoming involved in the conflict and having to shoot down Greek patriots. In an effort to retrieve the situation, Churchill flew out to Athens on Christmas Day, 1944, and started negotiations which led to an armistice.

The Allied advance in the West suffered a sharp setback in mid-December. A desperate counter-thrust by the Germans, made in atrocious weather which grounded the Allied air forces, temporarily penetrated the American front in the Ardennes. But the tough stand of the American infantry, the hammering of the German supply routes by the air forces as soon as the weather cleared, and the vigour of the Allied counter-attacks, turned the enemy's last major offensive into a vast failure, which cost him heavy and irreplaceable losses.

In the bitter weather of January and February, 1945, the Russian armies began their winter offensive. They rolled forward massively along their whole front, from East Prussia to the Carpathians. Before this onslaught the Nazi defences crumbled and collapsed. In a matter of days the Red Army swept across western Poland into Silesia and Pomerania. By February they were within fifty miles of Berlin.

CONFERENCE AT YALTA

On 4 February, when Belgium had been finally cleared of the last pockets of Germans, a conference opened at Yalta in the Crimea between Stalin, Churchill and Roosevelt, at which a plan was agreed, not only for co-ordinating the final military operations to complete Hitler's overthrow, but for the occupation and control of Germany after her surrender, for the elimination of all traces of Nazism, for the calling of a conference at San Francisco to frame the constitution of the United Nations, and for the re-establishment of order in

386

post-war Europe. Unhappily, however, Roosevelt was so eager at this conference to conciliate Stalin and engage his co-operation in post-war world affairs, that he insisted, against Churchill's strong opposition, on making concessions to him that later were to spell calamity in China and Korea, in Poland and the Balkans, in Germany, Austria and Czechoslovakia, and indefinitely to postpone European peace.

FINAL ALLIED OFFENSIVE

In the next month, an unusually mild and sunny March, the great Spring offensive was launched which would end only with the complete destruction of the German military might. The American forces had already begun their drive from Aachen toward the Rhine on 23 February. On 8 March Cologne fell. Meantime the American 1st and 3rd Armies had been making a headlong sweep down through the Rhineland and Palatinate, and on 7 March an advance guard of General Hodges' 1st Army won the bridge over the Rhine at Remagen before the Germans destroyed it. The British and Canadians pushed on with clearing the west bank of the lower Rhine, which, with an American Army on their right flank, they crossed on 24 March. With the Americans spreading out in the south and the British over-running North-west Germany the enemy faced a complete collapse in the West. German troops in the Ruhr were trapped, and between 1 and 19 April twenty-one divisions were rounded up there. The Russians were driving in from the East. Danzig had fallen on 30 March, Königsberg on 9 April, Vienna on the 13th. The Allied armies in Italy captured Bologna on 21 April and reached the River Po two days later. The eclipse of the Luftwaffe was so complete that black-out restrictions were lifted in Britain. On 24 April, Himmler offered to surrender the German Reich to the Governments of Great Britain and the U.S.A. He was the most loathsome figure among the Nazi leaders, and would cheerfully have betrayed his leader, Hitler, and all his comrades if thereby he could save his own skin. He saw that the game was hopelessly lost. Russians were penetrating the Berlin suburbs and encircling the town to the north and south. The British had reached Bremen and the Americans had crossed the Danube in South Germany and reached the Elbe in the middle of the country. The end was at hand.

During those two months of March and April, 1945, the speed of events rivalled, on a far vaster scale, the speed of Nazi successes

WHITEHALL CROWDS CHEE

*On 7th May, 1945, the German High Command signed the uncondition
surrender of all its fighting forces. The next day at 3 p.m., Mr. Church
announced the end of the war in Europe in a broadcast from the Cabin
Room at 10 Downing Street. He then proceeded to the House
Commons to make the official announcement of the surrender. F*

MR. CHURCHILL ON "V-E DAY"

...hanked the men of all parties for the way in which the liveliness of Parliamentary institutions had been maintained under the fire of the enemy. On his way to the House Mr. Churchill (seen on the left) received a tremendous ovation from large and enthusiastic crowds who made their way to Whitehall from all parts of the Metropolis.

in April and May, 1940; but this time it was the German armies that were falling one after another in swift collapse, while the countries they had once battered down now raised their heads anew in freedom. The last V.2 rocket bomb on England dropped at Orpington in Kent on 27 March; and when on 26 April Mr. Churchill was asked in the House of Commons whether he would make a statement about enemy rocket attacks, he gave the laconic answer: "Yes, sir; they have ceased!" By that date the German forces in the Reich were collapsing wherever the Allies penetrated. Verona and Milan had been liberated in Italy. Marshal Pétain, trying to flee from France, was arrested on the frontier. Two days later, on 28 April, Mussolini was captured by Italian partisans, who killed him and hung up his body in Milan. On 2 May the German armies in Italy surrendered unconditionally, while the British were thrusting across the Elbe into Mecklenburg, heading for the Baltic.

Hitler, trapped in his bomb-proof shelter in Berlin, toward which the Russians were battering their way, could not effect his escape, and committed suicide. The Germans announced his death on 1 May, and Admiral Doenitz took charge of the dying Reich. Next day Berlin surrendered to the Russians, and on 4 May, Montgomery received the unconditional surrender of all German forces in North-west Europe. Three days later the German High Command signed the unconditional surrender of all its fighting forces everywhere.

The war in Europe was over. The foulest tyranny that had ever set out by lies and treachery, by torture and mass murder, to enslave the bodies and souls of all mankind, lay dead at last amid the ruin to which it had brought its victims and its dupes.

Next day, when "V-E Day" was celebrated in the bomb-scarred streets of Britain's capital, cheering crowds of the nation, which had dared, even alone, to stand out against that monstrous power, now thronged to hail on a balcony in Whitehall a familiar figure who symbolized for them the finest fighting courage of their breed.

"Good old Winston!" they cried, as they listened to his simple yet noble confession of faith:

"Don't despair! Don't yield to violence and tyranny!
March straight forward and die, if need be, unconquered!"

CHAPTER XVII

LEADER OF THE OPPOSITION

WITH the passing of "V-E Day" a swift change came over the political sky. War was not yet ended. Japan had still to be defeated and, although the tide was now setting strongly against her, she was still holding most of her war-time gains. But, by contrast with Britain's past five years' experience, the Japanese war was remote and untroublesome. It did not scatter bombs or rockets on British towns or threaten the island with invasion. Indeed, the Japanese were being forced back on every front, and their ultimate collapse was not in doubt. Peace and the post-war world were just below the horizon, and men's minds turned to preparations for the coming dawn.

A general election was long overdue. The Parliament elected in 1935 had had its life prolonged to nearly twice the statutory span of five years, and Churchill had announced his intention of calling for a fresh election as soon as the ending of war conditions made it possible. The Labour Party had made it no less clear that they would not enter an election as members of a Coalition Government. Only in the prosecution of the war were they willing to co-operate with the Tories. For post-war reconstruction and peace-time domestic policy they had a programme with which Tories could not be expected to co-operate.

The prospect facing the Conservative party managers was bleak. In a free democracy it usually happened that the party which was in power when a war began was turned out by its rival after the war had ended. This happened in Britain to the Tories after the Boer War and to the Liberals after the First World War of 1914-1918. So it was in the U.S.A. with Woodrow Wilson's Democrat administration in 1920, and with Clemenceau in France.

Could not history suggest a way of escape? In 1900 the Tories, by holding the "Khaki Election" while the war was still on—though it seemed to be almost over—had scored a remarkable success. In 1918, at the "Coupon Election," they had been overwhelmingly victorious,

THANKSGIVING FOR VICTORY

After his broadcast announcing the end of the war in Europe, Mr. Churchill made a statement in the Commons on the German surrender. He expressed the opinion that the House had shown itself to be the strongest foundation for waging war that had ever been seen in Britain's long history. The House then adjourned and went in procession to St. Margaret's, where a service of Thanksgiving was held.

partly because there was little real opposition to the Coalition and partly because of the dazzling prestige of the Coalition Premier. Lloyd George, whom the nation rightly hailed as "The Man Who Won The War!" If an election were hurried on while the war with Japan was still undecided, if Churchill remained the Conservative leader, with a popular esteem for his war service as great and as justified as Lloyd George had enjoyed twenty-seven years before, and if, best of all, the Coalition could be maintained over the election, they might count on a renewed lease of power.

But these were difficult "ifs" to realize. A new electoral register was being drawn up which would not be ready till October, and the Labour Party were emphatic that the election, having been put off because of the war for five years, ought not now to be rushed on the old register when war was still in progress.

However, Churchill agreed to hold a General Election without waiting for either the end of the war or the coming into effect of the new register; and he agreed to remain leader of the Conservative Party for the election. He also wrote to Attlee asking him to consent to the Coalition being held together until the war with Japan was ended.

Attlee and his Labour colleagues refused to promise to maintain the Coalition for an indefinite period. The Japanese war might possibly drag on for a year or more, but need not prevent the nation from starting its reconstruction tasks. But they offered to maintain the Coalition until the end of the session in October. By that time the new register would be ready and an election could be held on party lines with a view to the future domestic policy of the country.

Churchill offered to hold a referendum to test popular opinion as to whether an election should be postponed till Japan was defeated, but the Labour Party rejected this proposal at its party conference at Blackpool, in May, 1945. There it formally adopted the programme of post-war policy set forth in the pamphlet "Let Us Face The Future," which it published on 21 April.

The Liberal Party also refused, after deliberating the question, to maintain the Coalition after the end of the session. A section of the Liberal Party led by Viscount Simon, however, pledged their continued support to the Conservative Party.

FIRST POST-WAR GENERAL ELECTION

Churchill then announced his decision to hold a General Election in July, and on 23 May he broke up the Coalition Government, and formed a fresh "Caretaker Government" to carry on over the election. Arrangements were made for Parliament to be dissolved on 15 June, and the election to take place on 5 July. Outstanding legislation was hurried through its final stages; the most notable of these last Acts brought in by the Coalition being the Family Allowances Act, which provided for Family Allowances to be paid by the State in respect of the second and subsequent children in a family. Legislation was also drafted to enact the schemes of Social Insurance and a National Health Service which had been proposed by the Beveridge Commission, but there was no time before the election to carry this through.

Political campaigning started actively in all parties. Labour already had its programme clearly set out in "Let Us Face The

Future," and was pledged to the nationalization of the Bank of England, the coal mines, railways and transport undertakings, electricity and gas supply and the steel industry. As for the Conservatives, Churchill had announced two years earlier, in his broadcast speech of 21 March, 1943, a Four Years' Plan of domestic reform, covering national insurance, agriculture, health, education, housing and town planning, financial reforms and extended State ownership of monopolies. But this had been a Coalition programme, common ground for all three parties and by no means exclusively or even characteristically Conservative. The progressive wing of the Party gladly adopted it as their election policy. But Lord Beaverbrook, who with Churchill and Brendan Bracken formed the operative directorate of the Party during the life of the "Caretaker Government," saw little prospect of winning the election by its means. Labour was ready to promise all this and much more.

A POLITICAL BLUNDER

Beaverbrook remembered, however, the devastating triumph which the Tories had won over Labour in 1924 by means of the Zinovieff "Red Letter" scare. There was no "Red Letter" available now, and it would hardly be appropriate to try to smear Labour with a charge of Bolshevik alliance, seeing that Churchill had associated with Stalin! But the end of the war had brought to light the appalling horrors that had been committed alike in Germany itself and in the countries overrun by the Nazis; and the Nazi Gestapo, the secret police, chief agent in these infamies, was a name to arouse loathing. It was thought that the Tories would succeed in the election by suggesting that British Socialism was akin to German National-Socialism and would set up a secret police organization if it got into power.

On 4 June Churchill made this suggestion in a broadcast election speech. The nation gasped in astonishment. For Churchill the War Premier they had an admiration that approached idolatry. But this utterance of stupid and unscrupulous party spite could arouse only sorrow and disgust, and remind them of the fact, formerly well known but half forgotten in their hero-worship, that Churchill, the great imperial and war-time statesman, was far from being equally distinguished as a domestic politician. His broadcast, they felt, was silly. Did he expect them to believe that Attlee, Bevin, Alexander

ROYAL FAMILY ACCLAIMED IN VICTORY CELEBRATIONS

On "V-E Day" vast crowds flocked to Buckingham Palace. The King and Queen and Princess Elizabeth and Princess Margaret came on to the balcony and received tumultuous cheers from the crowds below. The Royal Family again appeared later and when they were joined by Mr. Churchill the roar of welcome and celebration was prolonged.

and the other Labour leaders, who had been his trusted colleagues up to less than a fortnight ago, were merciless scoundrels of the breed of Himmler and Goering?

The speech was, in fact, a tragic blunder, bad in its immediate effect on public opinion, but no less in its election strategy. In the weeks immediately following "V-E Day," Churchill had been acclaimed in rapturous praise, not only at home but all over the world, as the chief architect and inspirer of victory for freedom and civilization. The *New York Times* commented on 13 May that the country appeared to be anti-Tory but pro-Churchill. If the Tories had any hope of averting a crashing defeat in the election, it could only have been through trying to damp down party conflicts as much as possible, persuading the voters that they, too, were as resolved as Labour to pursue a progressive policy, and appealing for popular support for the national hero, Churchill, as the best man to finish the war and lead the country into the post-war era of reconstruction.

But Churchill's broadcast shattered all hope of such an appeal, and convinced the people that Tory policy was still one of stubborn reaction.

The Churchill-Beaverbrook-Bracken triumvirate stuck doggedly to their chosen line. Churchill came again to the microphone to reiterate his thesis that a Socialist government would impose Gestapo rule on the country, and Brendan Bracken loyally backed him in a broadcast speech in which, like the fat boy in *Pickwick Papers,* he tried to make people's flesh creep. But it was of no avail. The artifice of the trumped-up charge was too evident. This was no election-winning "Red Letter." It was just a damp squib that fizzled and spluttered and finally blackened the hand that held it.

The General Election was held on 5 July. It was a formidable undertaking, for the troops serving abroad in Burma and India and other distant fields had also to be polled; and pending the arrival of their voting papers, the ballot boxes were sealed up and put away. Results were not to be announced until 26 July, three weeks after polling day.

Churchill took the opportunity, as soon as the election was over, to snatch a brief holiday. He had been carrying an immense load during the past war years. So he now slipped away to the south of France and spent a few days at the Château of Bordaberry on the Biscay coast, lent him by the Canadian Brigadier-General Brutinel. The easel came out and he renewed his old hobby of painting.

THE POTSDAM CONFERENCE

On 17 July he went with Attlee and Eden to Berlin, to join President Truman and Generalissimo Stalin in the Potsdam Conference. Nine meetings were held before the Conference was interrupted while the British Ministers returned on 25 July to learn the results of the General Election.

All the forecasts had suggested that there would be a very close result, that no party would get a clear majority of the total votes cast and that, in consequence, there might well be a delicate balance in the new Parliament. The votes proved to be very near, Labour polling about 49 per cent of the total; but despite the fact that slightly less than half the electorate voted for them, the Labour candidates swept the field everywhere and seats which had been regarded as absolutely safe Conservative strongholds returned Labour members.

396

CHURCHILL COMMENCES ELECTION CAMPAIGN

The Parliament elected in 1935, and prolonged by Coalition unity during the war, ended on 15 June, 1945, and a General Election was held on 5 July. Mr. Churchill made several extensive election tours throughout the country and received an enthusiastic reception from great crowds. Here he is seen in his constituency at Woodford, Essex.

By 26 July all but one of the results were known, and the Labour Party, with 393 Members, had a clear majority of nearly 150 over all other groups put together. The Conservative Party, with its Liberal allies, numbered 210. The Independent Liberals, who had put up only 300 candidates, were reduced to 11 members.

Churchill promptly tendered his resignation to the King, who invited Attlee to form a government. His Majesty offered Churchill the Order of the Garter, the highest and most ancient Order of Knighthood in the Kingdom, which is hardly ever conferred on a commoner, being usually reserved for royalty and holders of the more historic peerages. Winston took the unprecedented step of declining the honour. As leader of the Conservatives, he must stay in the House of Commons, and while he remained there he wanted to keep his familiar name, and he hesitated to see it changed into "Sir Winston!" Nor was it the time, he felt, for him to accept a peerage and to retire from party leadership into the House of Lords.

THREE-POWER CONFERENCE

*A historic meeting of the supreme war leaders of the "Big Three,"
Britain, the United States and Russia, opened on 17th July, 1945, at the
Cecilienhof Palace, Potsdam, and lasted until 2nd August. Winston
Churchill, President Truman, and Marshal Stalin headed the respective
delegations and among others who took part in the proceedings were
Clement Attlee, Anthony Eden, J. Byrnes, Admiral Leahy and*

OF WAR LEADERS AT POTSDAM

M. Molotov. *After the victory of the Labour Party in the General Election, declared on 26th July, Churchill's place was taken by Mr. Attlee, and Ernest Bevin, the new Foreign Secretary, succeeded Mr. Eden. Among the matters dealt with at the Potsdam Conference by the Three Powers were the treatment of Germany during the initial period of Allied Control, the demilitarization of Germany, and reparations.*

The war with Japan was still in progress, and he loved a fight. The Conservatives had just suffered a smashing defeat, and he could scarcely choose this moment to desert them.

His decision was perhaps inevitable. But it was in some respects unfortunate. Churchill had never been a notably orthodox Tory, and the "naughty boy" strain of erratic wilfulness which now and again appeared in his conduct made him sometimes an embarrassment to his colleagues. A minor drawback in a freelance, it is a grave handicap in a party spokesman. Besides, his magnificent war record had lifted him above parties and made him a great national and international figure; and this was the role in which he would be able to make his most valuable contributions in the years ahead to the progress of British and world affairs. The jangle of party brawls across the floor of the Commons was no worthy concern for him. Nor was he well equipped to guide the Opposition in considering the economic and domestic issues which would be Parliament's predominant concern in the difficult days of post-war reconstruction. He was no expert in economics, and to domestic problems his natural attitude was one of somewhat detached benevolence. His supreme interests lay in the fields of Imperial and international affairs.

NO PLACE IN THE COUNCILS OF THE ALLIES

The immediate result of the Conservative defeat was that Churchill lost his place in the councils of the Allies. The British delegation which returned to Berlin to complete the business of the Potsdam Conference consisted of Attlee and Bevin. Churchill and Eden were no longer in the party.

The Potsdam Conference set up a Council of Foreign Ministers to draft the terms of peace settlements with Italy, Rumania, Bulgaria, Hungary and Finland. It laid down the political and economic principles which were to govern the treatment of Germany during the initial control period; arranged for reparations to be exacted from her in the form of removal of German assets such as industrial equipment; agreed about the disposal of the German navy and mercantile marine; divided East Prussia between Poland and Russia; arranged for the trial of war criminals; and made a temporary settlement of Poland's western frontier. Unhappily for the world, the decisions taken at Potsdam, like those at Teheran and Yalta, were gravely influenced by the American obsession with the idea that

MR. CHURCHILL LEAVES NO. 10 DOWNING STREET

The General Election of July, 1945, swept the Labour Party into power with a large majority over its opponents, and Mr. Attlee went into occupation at the official residence of the Prime Minister. Here Mr. Churchill is seen with Mrs. Churchill leaving No. 10, in the background, Mary Churchill is saying goodbye to one of the staff.

Britain was an Imperialistic Power, whereas the Russians were without aggressive aims, and no adequate safeguards were supposed to be provided against Soviet bad faith.

While Europe was groping towards peace, the war in the Far East was approaching its final cataclysm. All through July, Japan was being subjected to terrible air bombardment and to shelling by the Allied navies. City after city disappeared in flames. On 26 July a joint announcement was made to Japan by Truman, Churchill and Chiang Kai-shek, warning her that unless she yielded, without further delay, her cities would be utterly destroyed.

The awful menace behind that warning revealed itself when, on 6 August, the first atom bomb fell on Hiroshima, and four square miles of that packed city were blasted away in a single instant, while many of the inhabitants who were not killed outright were so

401

damaged by the insidious gamma rays of the radio-active particles released in the explosion that death followed quickly or slowly. The first jubilation in the Allied countries at the news that our side now possessed so supremely potent a weapon of war steadily gave way to horror as accounts began to come through of the ghastly destruction it wrought and the deadly menace of its aftermath of radiation.

INTRODUCTION OF THE ATOMIC BOMB

Ever since Professor Rutherford had shown the possibility of changing atomic structure, scientists had foreseen the use of the atom as a storehouse of energy which could be released for human service. But the war had turned their minds to the possible use of the atom as an explosive and, in Britain, America and Germany, research with this object had been actively pursued. Eventually, the British and American scientists co-operated in American experimental stations where an atom bomb was ultimately made and exploded in a desert of New Mexico. News of this success was flashed to Potsdam, where the Conference was in its first stages, and Truman and Churchill made the momentous decision to use this bomb against the cities of Japan. After the first atom bomb had fallen on Hiroshima, another atom bomb was dropped, on 9 August, on the harbour of Nagasaki. Five days later the Japanese surrendered.

The Hiroshima bomb was estimated to have more than two thousand times the blast power of the biggest bombs hitherto used in the war. But the ruin it inflicted on the Japanese town was far from being the limit of its destructive work. It shattered the former world-fellowship of scientific research, with its free exchange of knowledge and discovery. Scientists became a secret service working behind heavily guarded doors to discover yet swifter methods whereby the human race may destroy itself. The search for knowledge had somehow taken a wrong turning and brought mankind to the gates, not of life, but of death.

Unaware as yet of the price to be paid for so swift a victory, the people celebrated 15 August as "V-J Day," marking the triumphant end of the Second World War. In the Far East there was still a good deal of tidying up to do, for Japanese forces were yet in possession of Malaya and Singapore, the Dutch East Indies and parts of Borneo, Burma, China and Korea. When they had been rounded up and removed it was found that the British, Dutch and French colonial

BRITAIN HONOURS EISENHOWER

On 12 June, 1945, General Eisenhower drove through cheering crowds to Guildhall where the Lord Mayor conferred on him the Freedom of the City of London. Mr. Churchill is seen here greeting the Supreme Allied Commander. Later in the day, Eisenhower was received at Buckingham Palace, where the Order of Merit was bestowed on him by the King.

territories they had overrun could not be restored to their former condition. Economically, they had been wrecked. Politically, they had been deeply changed in outlook, and would never resume their old status as mere dependencies of European Powers.

Amid the rejoicings of "V-J Day," the new Parliament met for the first time on 15 August, 1945, and the Labour Government, the first in British history to take office with a clear Parliamentary majority, put forward its programme of domestic legislation and foreign policy. At home the country was promised the fulfilment of the undertakings in "Let Us Face The Future." In international affairs, it was already becoming evident that Bevin was going to have difficulties with Russia and the countries which had come under her wing. In his speech to the House of Commons on foreign affairs,

Bevin warned his hearers on 20 August that the governments set up in Hungary, Rumania and Bulgaria had merely replaced one form of totalitarianism by another. In Poland the question of their secret police needed clearing up. There was danger in the establishment of the Polish frontier too far west and the transference of populations.

NO GREAT INTEREST IN DOMESTIC POLITICS

The re-assembly of Parliament in October brought Winston back to London, but he did not find the new House attractive. The Government was busily rushing forward an immense programme of nationalization. First came, on 10 October, a Bill to nationalize the Bank of England. Then, on 19 November, Morrison announced the intention to nationalize coal, gas, electricity, civil aviation, telecommunications, railways, canals, long-distance haulage, docks and harbours. Churchill had little sympathy with these ideas, but he did not during the early months of the new Government's existence lead any very heavy attacks upon them. He was influenced partly by a desire to give them a chance to prove themselves, and partly perhaps by a certain weariness of spirit after the strain of the war years, which made him loth to plunge forthwith into a new conflict. He had, moreover, no very intense interest in domestic politics. He had served his apprenticeship to them before the First World War, but then he was under the guidance and inspiration of his friend, Lloyd George, who was as much a predominantly domestic politician as Churchill was a predominantly imperial and international one. Ever since he had left the Exchequer in 1929, Churchill had concentrated his attention on international affairs, and he really had little taste for conducting a parliamentary war with the Labour Government about the nationalization plans. He did, however, make a speech on 28 November, in which he laid on the Labour Government the blame for the country's slow rate of recovery from the war, and spoke in praise of the Conservatives' four-year plan.

How far there was substance in his charge is a matter which future historians will debate. Most Conservatives were at heart far from sorry that the Labour Party had been landed with the thankless and complex task of coping with the country's post-war difficulties. It was a task which offered little hope of winning credit, and many opportunities of blundering, and a certainty of incurring blame and obloquy for the existence of conditions of hardship and shortage that were humanly unavoidable. It was also an advantage for the Party representing organized Labour to be in charge during the immediate post-war years, when there was certain to be much Labour unrest while industry was changing over from war work and men were being demobilized from the Services. After the First World War the change-over to peace had been marked by a series of grave strikes, and the end of the post-war commercial boom which resulted in a heavy slump and large-scale unemployment. This time, the fact that Labour's own leaders were in charge enabled measures to be taken which the workers would not have tolerated from a right-wing government. This was an important counter-weight to the Conservative claim that they possessed a greater number of statesmen experienced in the responsibilities of national administration.

BRITAIN'S ECONOMIC DIFFICULTIES

An intolerably difficult economic situation faced the country. For six years Britain had been devoting all her chief productive capacity to the works of war—guns and shells and war-planes and the like—whose net effect had been to destroy instead of increasing human wealth and happiness. Her cities had been devastated by bombs and her overseas investments were spent in purchasing supplies for her war effort. As a result, she had won deliverance for herself and the world, but had emerged insolvent. All Europe had been also stripped and impoverished and industrially wrecked by the Nazi conquest and the Allied fight to regain freedom. The Far East had similarly been devastated by the Japanese, and its former capacity to produce rice, oilseeds, tea, rubber, tin and other commodities had been temporarily destroyed. Outside the American continent, the world was desperately poor and, with its industries disrupted, its agricultural land neglected or derelict, its trade relations broken down, its governments unstable and changing, it was in very poor shape for starting on the long, steep climb back to order and prosperity. Britain, vitally dependent for her existence on world trade, by which alone she can buy the food for her forty-eight millions of population and the raw materials for the manufactures with which she pays the bill, was hard hit by post-war conditions. Countries from which she used to buy food and raw materials had none to sell; and she, with her industries disrupted, had not the means to buy.

Yet the British public, after doggedly enduring all the terrors and shortages of war, expected the peace to bring them a return of plenty. The Labour Party had been optimistic in its promises of the good times it would create if it got into power and the masses now expected the early arrival of more wages, less work and abundance of everything. The Government did, in fact, set about shortening hours; and wages rose. But since the need of the hour was for harder work, greater output and less spending while the production arrears of the war period were being made good, these concessions did not reduce the national insolvency.

THE END OF LEASE-LEND

During the war, American Lease-Lend had maintained the British economy at a subsistence level. This was only fair, because Britain was fighting America's battle as well as her own and by a mutual arrangement her whole industrial capacity was diverted to war production, while the United States kept her peace-time industry largely intact. But as soon as Japan was defeated, President Truman ended Lease-Lend, and the food and materials which Britain had been receiving without having to pay for them were stopped.

This meant that instead of peace bringing ease and plenty to Britain, it threatened her with starvation and collapse; for, as her overseas investments had been spent and her manufacturing capacity crippled, she was unable to purchase her essential supplies. It was not long before the American Government recognized this and, realizing that it would be disastrous to herself if she allowed Britain to fall into bankruptcy and ruin, she decided after considerable debate to offer a large loan of 3,750 million dollars, which could be drawn on between the end of 1945 and 31 December, 1951. The loan was to be used to help Britain to re-establish her industries, and to keep her going while she did so.

When the Agreement about the loan came before Parliament for approval on 13 December, 1945, Churchill announced his disapproval of the terms and conditions on which it was being offered and said that the Government had allowed itself to be browbeaten at the Bretton Woods Financial Conference, which aimed to revive and expand world trade. The Opposition would not oppose acceptance of the Agreement, but would not take any responsibility for the transactions which had culminated in the offer. He strongly advised

PLEA FOR ANGLO-AMERICAN PEACE-TIME TREATY

Early in 1946 Churchill visited the United States. At the University of Miami he received the honorary degree of LL.D. Later, accompanied by President Truman, he arrived at Fulton. There, in an address on 5 March, entitled "The Sinews of Peace," he urged close unity between the United States and the British Commonwealth and Empire. This would involve collaboration between military advisers, similarity of weapons and instruction manuals, interchange of officers and joint use of bases. Eventually there might come the principle of common citizenship. The speech aroused widespread interest and, in the House of Commons, Mr. Attlee stated that Mr. Churchill was speaking for himself only; the Government had no knowledge of the speech.

LORD WARDEN OF THE CINQUE PORTS

At Dover on 14 August, 1946, Churchill was installed with traditional ceremony as Lord Warden of the Cinque Ports. He is seen inspecting a Guard of Honour of Royal Marines.

his followers to abstain from voting either way but, in fact, 71 Tory Members went into the lobby against acceptance of the loan, along with 23 Labour, 3 National Liberal and 3 Independent Members. The loan was, however, agreed to by a sweeping majority.

At the end of the year, Churchill travelled to Belgium, where both Brussels and Antwerp presented him with the Freedom of their cities. He had previously been honoured in Paris in November, 1944, when he visited it just after its liberation and, in February, 1945, he received the Freedom of Athens. In the months that followed he was presented with the Freedom of a large number of cities, both in Britain and overseas.

In the New Year Honours List, published on 1 January, 1946, it was announced that the King had conferred on Churchill the Order of Merit, the highest honour in the gift of the Crown which does not confer any title upon its holder. The investiture took place on 8 January, and then Churchill left for a holiday in the United States, where he arrived on the 14th.

During his stay in the States, which lasted until 21 March, Churchill discussed the international situation with President Truman and received an honorary degree at Miami University. But the highlight of his visit was a speech which he delivered at Fulton, in Missouri, on 5 March, 1946. After surveying the international situation, and stressing the desire of the world for freedom from war and tyranny, and pleading for the United Nations to be equipped with an international force which might by degrees relieve States of the need to maintain national armies, he urged that the English-speaking peoples should give a lead to world unity by establishing among themselves a fraternal association. He wanted a special relationship between the British Commonwealth and Empire and the United States, involving collaboration between their military advisers, similarity of weapons and instruction manuals, interchange of officers and joint use of bases. Eventually there might come the principle of common citizenship.

AMERICAN REACTION TO THE SPEECH AT FULTON

He pointed out the threat to liberty and peace involved in Russia's establishment of the "Iron Curtain" which cut off Eastern Europe from the rest of the civilized world, and her efforts to build up Communist supporters in other countries. He did not think that Russia desired war, but she desired the fruits of war and the expansion of her power. The only hope of restraining her from pursuing this aim and establishing a genuine co-operation with her was for the Western nations to be strong and united. If the population of the English-speaking Commonwealth were added to that of the United States there would be "no quivering, precarious balance of power to offer its temptations to ambition or adventure. On the contrary, there will be an overwhelming assurance of security."

The speech created a great sensation, but by no means a uniformly favourable one. American opinion was far from being ready for any such marriage of the Eagle and the Lion as was being suggested by Churchill, and was unwilling to be stampeded into a betrothal. Certain sections of opinion, too, were averse from being thrust into a situation of avowed alliance with Britain against Russia. In a further speech at New York on 15 March, Churchill added touches to his Fulton proposals, emphasizing that he felt no antagonism to the Russian people, but pointing out that their 180 millions, and many more millions outside Russia, were in the grip of a handful of able men who held absolute power. Throughout the English-speaking world there was sympathy with the Russian people and readiness to co-operate with them. "If the Soviet Government do not take advantage of this sentiment—if, on the contrary, they discourage it, or chill it—the responsibility will be entirely theirs."

However wise in their conception and desirable in the interests of world civilization and peace, the Fulton proposals were thought to be somewhat untimely and premature. America and Britain may in fact be moving steadily towards some such close fellowship as Churchill was then advocating, but, at any rate, in the early stages of such a movement, the wider and deeper its roots strike before it makes much flourish on the surface, the better.

SOCIAL INSURANCE AND NATIONAL HEALTH SCHEMES

Churchill's American visit kept him out of the country during the early part of 1946, when the Government were bringing in several measures of major importance. Of these, the greatest was the new scheme of Social Insurance, introduced on 24 January, 1946. This measure was based upon the Report of Sir William (later Lord) Beveridge, planning the way in which the existing scheme of Social Insurance could be widened and improved so as to cover the whole nation. Adopting substantially the main recommendations of that Report, the new Bill set up a system under which everyone in the Kingdom, from duke to dustman, should be compulsorily insured for widows', orphans' and old age pensions, sickness and invalidity, and unemployment. It was substantially an agreed measure. Allied with this measure was the National Health Service Bill, introduced on 19 March, to provide free medical treatment for the whole population. Certain of the features of this Bill, particularly those dealing with the nationalization of hospitals, and the terms to be offered to doctors, gave rise to long and bitter disputes. The Bill was passed and its provisions operated from July, 1948.

After his return from the United States at the end of March, Churchill did not plunge actively into domestic party politics. It can be broadly said that from this time onward, although remaining titular leader of the Conservative Party, Churchill adopted in the main the role of an Elder Statesman, coming forward occasionally to utter a pronouncement on the questions of the hour, but by no

EL ALAMEIN REUNION AT ALBERT HALL

Veterans of El Alamein, the battle that turned the tide in the war, foregathered on 23 October, 1946, at the Albert Hall from all parts of the world to celebrate the fourth anniversary of the battle. Field-Marshal Montgomery and Mr. Churchill, seen giving his famous "V" sign, addressed the gathering and were given a rousing reception.

means devoting his constant efforts and whole time to the political struggle. Henceforward his chief positive contributions to public affairs were to be in regard to international relations.

In May, 1946, Churchill paid a visit to Holland as the guest of Queen Wilhelmina, and addressed both Houses of the States General at the Hague. He was given an honorary degree by Leyden University. On 4 May he intervened in the House of Commons to voice his disagreement with the Government's policy of total withdrawal from Egypt and the Suez Canal. In August he visited Luxembourg, and and on 14 August he was installed as Lord Warden of the Cinque Ports, an office which traditionally carries a residence at Walmer Castle, but no very onerous duties. Towards the end of September, he made a trip to Switzerland, and on the 19th made a speech at Zurich University in which he pleaded for the creation of a United

CALL FOR A UNITED STATES OF EUROPE

During a holiday in Switzerland in September, 1946, Churchill made an important speech at the University of Zürich. He made a strong plea for a United States of Europe and for Franco-German friendship. Later, he was a guest of honour in the Zürich Town Hall, above, and then proceeded to Berne, where he was cheered by 100,000 people.

States of Europe under and within the world concept of the United Nations Organization. He declared:

> "We must recreate the European family in a regional structure called—it may be—the United States of Europe, and the first practical step will be to form a Council of Europe. If, at first, all the States of Europe are not willing or able to join a union we must nevertheless proceed to assemble and combine those who will and those who can. . . . In all this urgent work France and Germany must take the lead together. Great Britain, the British Commonwealth of Nations, mighty America, and, I trust, Soviet Russia—for then, indeed, all would be well—must be the friends and sponsors of the new Europe and must champion its right to live."

This concept of a United States of Europe was not new. It had been advocated by M. Briand twenty years earlier, but at that time aroused little enthusiasm. The twenty years of mutual distrust, chaos and bloody disaster, which had intervened since Briand's idea had been declined by the European countries, were now powerful arguments in its support. Churchill's pronouncement, therefore, kindled a new hope in the hearts of many who had been gazing despairingly on the scene of post-war depression and disunion. It was welcomed with particular eagerness by thoughtful Germans, who saw in it the one prospect of a restoration of their country to fellowship with her neighbours; and for the other nations which also lay to the west of the "Iron Curtain" the idea held a promise of a powerful combination which would insure them against falling into the grip of totalitarianism dominated by the Kremlin.

For Churchill himself the notion of a United States of Europe, with which the British Commonwealth should be closely associated, became from this time forward a major interest. He saw in its furtherance a real contribution of statesmanship which he might make to the world order of the future. Six years before, in the bitterest crisis of the war, he had invited France to federate with the British Empire and Commonwealth. Now he began to press for a yet larger federation which would include all the free democracies of Western Europe.

BACK TO PARTY POLITICS

Churchill came back to England to attend the Conservative Party Conference, which was held at Blackpool from 3 to 5 October. The Party was still in low spirits and as yet showed no sign of recovering its former power. The Labour Government had not lost a single seat at any of the by-elections which had taken place since the General Election. Some of the more progressive spirits among the Conservatives put forward a proposal to change the party name to something which would secure an alliance with the Liberals; for, while the Liberals had sunk to a relatively small third party in the State, with no visible prospect of again winning a parliamentary majority, they still included a significant proportion of people prominent in the professions, commerce and industry. The three or four million votes which they could still command would also have been a valuable asset to the Conservatives. But the proposal was rejected.

Churchill wound up the Conference with a speech in which he described the main objects of Conservative policy as being the promotion of a free society, a property-owning democracy, with

CHURCHILL ATTACKS LABOUR GOVERNMENT POLICY

Speaking at a Conservative demonstration of 60,000 people in August, 1947, at Blenheim Palace, Woodstock, Mr. Churchill made a strong attack on the Government's economic and financial policy. He also advocated a closer association with the United States.

arrangements for profit-sharing and joint consultation in industry, and the status of partners for the wage-earners.

On 23 November, Churchill intervened in the debate in Parliament on foreign affairs to draw attention to the extent of Russian military strength in occupied Germany. He declared that today Russia's frontier was on the Elbe, and asked whether it was true that there were more than two hundred Russian divisions on a war footing in the Soviet-occupied countries of Europe. This suggestion was contradicted five days later by Stalin. But by now it had become all too sadly evident that the comradeship of Soviet Russia with the Western democracies during the war against Hitler was passing; that the Russian rulers were basing their international policy on the assumption that real friendship and collaboration between Communist and Capitalist systems was impossible, and that a "cold war" must be maintained against all the non-Communist governments— the Labour-Socialist administration of Britain as much as the Capitalist-Individualist administration of the U.S.A.

The weakness of the Western world in face of this scarcely veiled hostility of the Soviet system was that while behind the "Iron Curtain" one rule held sway over all the countries and peoples, from Berlin and Vienna to Vladivostok, the Western states were isolated from each other in their independent sovereignties. This made for military and diplomatic weakness, and for economic disorder. Churchill was convinced that the best hope for these nations was to build up as quickly as possible a close federation. At Fulton he had tried without much success to start a movement for Anglo-American federation. He now bent his energies to the task of constructing a United Europe. On 16 January, 1947, a Provisional Committee was set up under his chairmanship to promote this cause.

DEMANDS FOR SELF-GOVERNMENT

The British Government might well be excused for failing to devote much attention to this question. At home it was pressing forward eagerly with the legislation and the yet more difficult task of organization necessary to carry out its projects for nationalizing coal-mines, transport, electricity and aviation; it was struggling with the housing shortage and the economic perils associated with the country's adverse trade balance and dwindling reserves of foreign exchange, and it had its hands full of imperial and international problems. India was clamouring for the ending of the old regime, though her various sections, Hindu, Moslem and native Princes, could not agree as to the constitution of the Indian Government into whose hands the administration was to be given. Burma was demanding the same right of self-government as had been offered to India, with freedom to leave the Commonwealth if she chose. Malaya had been provided with a constitution which, on second thoughts, was found to be unsatisfactory, and the whole question had to be re-opened. Egypt, after being saved by British troops from conquest by the Germans and Italians, was insisting on the immediate withdrawal of Britain from both Egypt and the Canal Zone, and the premature termination of the existing treaty between the two countries. Palestine was in conflict, the Jews refusing to accept the policy, which had been laid down in a White Paper, of severe limitation of their right of entry and settlement, while the Palestinian Arabs, noisily supported by all the other Arab states, demanded a prompt ending of the whole policy of the Jewish National Home, set out in the Balfour Declaration of 1917 and in the Mandate from the League of Nations and from U.N.O. under which the country was being administered by Great Britain.

In Greece, the British were committed to supporting a rather unsatisfactory right-wing regime, as an alternative to letting Russia-supported elements in Greece and in its Soviet-controlled neighbours overrun the country and drag it behind the "Iron Curtain," thus giving the Soviet bases in the Mediterranean which would command the routes to the Middle East. In Persia, a Russian invasion of Azerbaijan had with some difficulty been induced to withdraw, but Russian pressure was being steadily exerted to secure concessions—and the Anglo-Persian oilfields were Britain's main source of mineral oils. On 8 August, 1946, Moscow sent a Note to Turkey, demanding Russian bases and facilities for Russian troops and equipment in the zone of the Dardanelles and Bosporus. France was in acute difficulties about her Constitution. During 1946 she held two general elections and two referendums, and had repeated changes of government. World food supplies were far short of the active demand for them. Western Germany, cut off from her former granaries in Pomerania and East and West Prussia, and crowded with refugees from those provinces and from Silesia, was with acute difficulty being kept at heavy expense just above starvation point by the British and Americans. France and Italy, too, were desperately short of food. The devastation of Burma, caused by the Japanese occupation and the war which had moved backwards and forwards over the country, meant that India and Malaya and other countries in the Far East dependent on Burmese rice had to be sent wheat for which Europe was clamouring. In Britain this situation made it necessary to introduce bread rationing on 21 July, 1946. Altogether, the year 1946 was a time of continual crisis, at home and abroad.

STRESS OF WEATHER

As if this were not enough, the 1946-7 winter was one of extreme severity. Blizzards swept the country and wrought havoc among the livestock. It was estimated that over two million sheep and lambs and many thousands of cattle were destroyed. The winter conditions went on far into the spring, and, when at last the thaw came, it brought disastrous floods that covered some of the most fertile agricultural land in the kingdom, delaying or altogether preventing the sowing of crops. By contrast, the summer that followed was so unusually hot

MEETING PLACE OF WARTIME HOUSE OF COMMONS

After the Chamber of the House of Commons was bombed in May, 1941, Members met in the Hoare Memorial Hall in Church House, Westminster. On 28 May, 1948, Mr. Churchill and Mr. Attlee jointly unveiled an oak panel commemorating the wartime use of the Hall. The Archbishop of Canterbury, Dr. Fisher, presided at the function.

and dry that the yield of such fields as had been sown or planted was much reduced and, in the autumn of 1947, potato rationing had to be introduced to enable the meagre crop to last out till the following summer. The year was, however, marked by one bright event, of great significance for Britain. In July the betrothal was announced of the King's heir, Princess Elizabeth, to Lieutenant Philip Mountbatten, formerly Prince Philip of Greece; and in November their wedding took place at Westminster Abbey, amid scenes of immense popular rejoicing. A year later, their first child, Prince Charles, was born, and in August, 1950, they had a daughter, Princess Anne.

Considerable progress was achieved during 1947 with the settlement of some at least of the external problems confronting the nation. On 18 February, 1947, the Foreign Secretary, Bevin, informed Parliament that as the Jews and Arabs of Palestine could not agree about the country's future, the issue would be referred to the United Nations. This was done, and a special Committee of the United Nations reported on 29 August in favour of ending the Mandate and partitioning the country. The British Government then announced that it would not impose any settlement by force of arms, but would return its Mandate to the United Nations and vacate Palestine at an early date.

EMERGENCE OF INDIA AND PAKISTAN

On 20 February the Prime Minister declared that the Indian problem could not be allowed to drag on indefinitely and that Britain would evacuate the country and transfer power to responsible Indian hands not later than June, 1948. This step forced the Hindu and Moslem factions in India to seek to compose their disputes, and under the tactful guidance of Lord Mountbatten, who replaced Lord Wavell as Viceroy, agreement was reached for dividing India into two Dominions, India and Pakistan. By 15 August these two new Dominions had been set up and the government of the country transferred to them. Unhappily, the transfer was followed by a tragic outbreak of communal rioting and massacres which lasted for several weeks. Burma, too, received her independence in the course of the year, by a Burma Independence Bill which received the Royal Assent on 10 December, and appointed 6 January, 1948, as the day on which Burma's connection with the British Commonwealth should cease.

Churchill was in the main only a spectator of all these develop-

CHANCELLOR SMUTS CONFERS DEGREE ON CHURCHILL

In June, 1948, Field-Marshal Smuts was installed as Chancellor of Cambridge University in succession to the late Earl Baldwin. Afterwards he conferred a degree on Winston Churchill, who is seen in the procession after the ceremony.

ments, which were beyond his control. On 1 March, 1947, he expressed disapproval of the Government's intention to give Burma full independence, for he had little sympathy with anything that savoured of "giving the Empire away." On 12 March he spoke in the debate on economic affairs, strongly criticizing the Government's handling of the situation, but the Opposition's amendment was defeated by 374 votes to 198. Against the Government's solid majority he was unable as Leader of the Opposition to take any effective action.

On 14 May, Churchill addressed a great gathering at the Albert Hall, and appealed for the immediate setting up of an organization to promote European unity. Less than a month later, on 11 June, he went on the sick list, and had an operation for hernia, but by 17 July he was back in his place in the House of Commons, where he received a warm welcome. In the following month he addressed a huge demonstration at Blenheim Palace. Speaking about the economic crisis which was facing the country, he declared that the Conservatives were ready to give their support to all sound proposals which were put forward by the Government to meet the situation; but he denounced what he described as the partisan legislation which was being brought in by the Labour Government, and he held it to be partly to blame for the country's troubles.

ECONOMIC CRISIS OF 1947

This economic crisis, which had been evident in 1946, became desperate in 1947. The country was nowhere near paying its way. Its total purchases from overseas—principally food, tobacco, raw materials and machinery essential for the restoration of its industries —greatly exceeded in value its total exports. The situation was especially difficult as regards dollars, for the United States was now the principal source of supply, not only for Britain but for all countries in the "sterling area"—countries whose currency values were dependent on the value of sterling—causing them to depend on Britain for dollars with which to buy goods from America. Britain's dollar deficit in 1947 exceeded four thousand millions. The American loan, which had been expected to last until 1951, and to see the country through to financial solvency, was practically exhausted before the year was out. On 20 August the free exchange of sterling and dollars had to be stopped, and all purchases of food from

America were cut short, badly though the food was needed. Other countries in western Europe, especially France and Italy, were in even worse straits, and there seemed an imminent danger that their finances might collapse.

The United States had been coming to the help of the worst hit countries with emergency loans, but finally, on 5 June, 1947, the American Secretary of State, George Marshall, made a momentous speech in which he called on the European nations to get together and see what had to be done to ensure their economic recovery, and how far they could attain this by co-operative efforts.

INTRODUCTION OF THE MARSHALL PLAN

Bevin promptly took up this challenge, and he and the French Foreign Minister, Bidault, arranged for a joint conference in Paris with Molotov to discuss the Marshall offer. This was held on 27 June, but Molotov strongly opposed combined action on the lines indicated by Marshall. Bevin and Bidault decided to go ahead, and on 12 July they summoned a conference which was attended by sixteen nations —all Europe (except Spain) outside the "Iron Curtain." This conference set up a continuing organization to prepare and carry out plans of co-operation for recovery, and to advise the United States about the financial aid that would be necessary to make the plans successful. On 6 July, 1948, the Agreement between Britain and the United States governing the terms on which Marshall Aid would reach Britain was signed in London by Mr. Bevin and Mr. Douglas, U.S. Ambassador, following a vote of approval in Parliament.

At the time it seemed very uncertain whether the American Congress would be prepared to vote large sums for the benefit of Europe. But in the following months the breach between the Western world and Russia widened deplorably, and this development, however unhappy in itself, made the Americans feel the importance of getting the free democracies of Europe on their feet, lest their collapse should play into the hands of the Communists. A European Recovery Aid Bill was eventually passed by the American Congress and was signed by President Truman on 4 April, 1948.

The Marshall Plan, and the economic co-operation which it forced upon the nations of western Europe, was a most potent factor to move them forward toward that European Federation which Churchill was advocating. Another move in the same direction was made in March, 1948, when a Five-Power Treaty was signed in Brussels between Britain, France, Belgium, Holland and Luxemburg, binding them to co-operate for their mutual defence. One of the terms of the Treaty was that by unanimous agreement between the original signatories, any other country could be admitted to the Five-Power Union. On 17 April, 1948, the five Powers held a meeting in Paris, at which they set up a Permanent Consultative Council.

Meantime, the Provisional Committee of which Churchill was Chairman had been pressing forward with arrangements for a gathering to be held at the Hague in May, 1948, for the purpose of starting a "Congress of Europe," a non-governmental assembly which should bring representatives of the free nations of Europe into systematic consultation with a view to the promotion of European federation. It was an idea which Churchill had cherished for a considerable time, and had proclaimed during the war. Now that he was without any ministerial responsibilities to pre-occupy him, it had become his main interest and purpose. In the circumstances, it was perhaps unfortunate that he held the post of Leader of the Conservative Party, because this made his activities for European unity suspect to a considerable section of the Labour Party, although they had publicly adopted the same policy; and Labour members, a number of whom were sympathizers, were officially discouraged from attending the Hague Congress.

The Congress was opened on 7 May by Churchill in a speech which many held to be the finest in his career as a world statesman. Defining the purpose for which the Congress of Europe was being set up, he said:

> "We seek nothing less than all Europe. We aim at the eventual participation of all peoples throughout the Continent whose society and way of life are not in disaccord with a charter of human rights and the sincere expression of free democracy. We welcome any country where the people own the Government and not the Government the people."

The Congress was not an alternative to a world organization. He envisaged the Council of Europe, "including Great Britain joined with her Empire and Commonwealth," as one group, which, along with the vast Soviet Union and the Western Hemisphere, would form the three pillars on which world organization would rest. He pleaded for co-operation to secure world peace:

UNITED EUROPE CONGRESS AT THE HAGUE

Mr. Churchill made one of the most notable speeches of his career when he delivered the opening address at the "Congress of Europe" held at The Hague in May, 1948. The Congress was attended by non-governmental representatives from twenty-three countries and its aim was the promotion of a federation of European democratic countries.

"How little it is that all the millions of homes in Europe represented here today are asking: a fair chance to make a home, to reap the fruits of their toil, to cherish their wives, to bring up their children in a decent manner, and to dwell in peace and safety. The freedom that matters most today is freedom from fear. Why should all these hard-working families be harassed, first, as in bygone times, by dynastic and religious quarrels; next by nationalistic ambitions, and finally by ideological fanaticism? Shall so many millions of humble homes in Europe, aye, and much of its enlightenment and culture, sit quaking in dread of the policeman's knock?

The Congress set up political and economic committees to examine various practical issues, and their reports were adopted on 10 May, when the Congress closed down. Churchill flew to Norway, where he spent from 11 to 15 May as guest of King Haakon. On 12 May the University of Oslo honoured him. In July and August he had exchanges of correspondence with Attlee about the scheme for a European Assembly which was being put forward by an International Committee of the movement for United Europe. The British Government poured cold water on this scheme, asserting that it would damage relations with the Commonwealth. But the movement received the blessing of the American State Department, and was urged by the Governments of Holland, France, Belgium and Italy. Eventually, in October, the Conference of Foreign Ministers agreed to set up a committee of the Brussels Treaty Powers to examine the proposal.

MOVEMENT FOR EUROPEAN UNITY

Churchill's Zurich speech of September, 1946, had in fact started an avalanche, and the movement for European Unity swept forward past the opposition of the British Government. The Brussels Treaty Commission proposed, on 5 February, 1949, the establishment of a Council of Europe consisting of a Committee of Ministers and a Consultative Assembly, and at the end of the month this Council held its inaugural meeting at Brussels. When opening the proceedings, M. Spaak, the Belgian Premier, paid a tribute to Churchill as "the most respected and illustrious of all" among those who had pressed the idea of European unity.

It was indeed no more than the truth that the lead Churchill had given to the movement could have been given by no other statesman; and the harassed, war-weary countries of the Continent rallied

CHURCHILL ATTACKS SOVIET POLICY

Mr. Churchill strongly criticized Soviet policy at the Conservative Party Conference at Llandudno on 10 October, 1948. "Nothing stands between Europe today and complete subjugation to Communist tyranny but the atomic bomb in American possession," he said. If the United States consented to destroy their accumulated stocks of atomic bombs, he declared, they would be guilty of murdering human freedom and committing suicide themselves.

eagerly at the call of the world-famous British leader to the concept of a fruitful and peaceful co-operation in place of their old rivalries. In August, 1950, some fifteen nations sent representatives to a great meeting at Strasburg of the Consultative Assembly, dreaming of the early establishment of a European Federation of which Britain would be a member. This, however, was a more advanced conception than Churchill was prepared to recommend, and certainly more than the British people would have agreed. Britain, closely linked with the overseas Dominions of her Commonwealth, has only one of her two feet in Europe, and cannot submerge her identity in a European federation. Churchill disappointed the Strasburg Assembly when he told them: "I have always thought that the process of building a European Parliament must be gradual, and that it should roll forward on a tide of facts, events and impulses, rather than by elaborate constitution-making." But the unwelcome advice was sound, and has been followed. By concerning itself with *ad hoc* practical issues, the Council of Europe has steadily gathered strength and momentum. Its discussion of economic problems played a part in the conception of the Schumann Plan, which produced the European Coal and Steel Community Treaty, an agreement whereby the coal, steel and iron ore resources and production of France, Holland, Belgium, Luxemburg, Italy and Western Germany are now pooled and free trade in them between these six countries has been established. The exclusion of defence matters from the deliberations of the Consultative Assembly broke down in practice when the Assembly was asked to support the action by the United Nations opposing Communist aggression in Korea. Thus the Council is becoming a growingly powerful agency for European fellowship.

THE NORTH ATLANTIC TREATY

If one of Churchill's main objectives in international affairs was to build up a United Europe, the other was to develop the closest friendship and alliance with the United States. This had been the theme of his Fulton speech in March, 1946, and he witnessed a big advance toward this goal when in the spring of 1949 the North Atlantic Treaty was drawn up and signed, binding the United Kingdom and the U.S.A., together with ten other countries, to joint organization of their defence resources against aggression. The North Atlantic Treaty Organization (commonly cited as NATO) is no mere paper pledge, but a practical system of defence co-ordination to keep the peace across the Western world from Turkey to America. A Three-Power Pact (known as ANZUS) to maintain peace in the area of the Pacific Ocean was later set up between the U.S.A., Australia and New Zealand. Thereby a new link was forged between America and the British Commonwealth.

In international affairs, the ideas of Churchill were thus progressively bearing fruit. It cannot be claimed for him that during his leadership of the Opposition he was equally constructive in his contributions to domestic policy. His notions about economic matters were based on the nineteenth-century theories prevalent in his youth, and he could not appreciate the necessity the country was under, in face of world-wide economic chaos resulting from two great wars, of adopting measures to control currency, finance, overseas trade and industrial activities. Though he had for a time, in the distant past, played, under Lloyd George's tuition, an active and useful part in social reform, his interest in it had diminished after 1911, when he became absorbed by external affairs. During the rule of the Labour Government, between 1945 and 1950, he paid intermittent visits to the Commons and poured forth rolling invective against the measures of nationalization they were swiftly pressing through Parliament. Fortunately for his Party, it included a group of progressive-minded younger members, headed by R. A. Butler, with up-to-date knowledge of economic and domestic problems and constructive ideas for their treatment. They produced two major statements of policy, "The Industrial Charter" in 1947 and "The Right Road For Britain" in 1949. Both statements received Churchill's benediction and were officially adopted at the party's annual conferences. But while Churchill sanctioned their preparation and accepted their proposals, he would hardly claim to have played much part in their composition.

Churchill devoted a large part of his time while out of office to writing his history of the Second World War. This was planned to fill half a dozen massive volumes. The first appeared in 1948, and the rest were published in the following five years. Packed as they are, not only with Churchill's own vivid personal narrative, but with a dense body of supporting documents—letters, cables, orders and directives—they form a collection of historical material of capital value brilliantly set out, and after-generations will be profoundly grateful to the author for making these records available to them.

Advancing years failed to diminish Churchill's energy. In addition to writing this monumental work, to preparing his speeches and articles, maintaining his parliamentary appearances and carrying out his task as leader of the Opposition and of the Tory Party, Churchill acquired during this period some five hundred acres of land near his Chartwell home, and engaged in farming. He also took up horse-racing, and his horse, Colonist II, competed in 1950 at Hurst Park in the Winston Churchill Stakes, where it came in second. He resumed his painting, and in 1948, three of his pictures were hung "on the line" at the Royal Academy. The artistic capacity of this distinguished amateur was so generally applauded that the Academy invented the special designation of "Honorary Academician Extraordinary" and conferred this title upon him.

In 1950 the five years for which the Labour Government had been returned would draw to their close, and Attlee decided to hold a fresh General Election in February. But when the results came out, it was found that the Labour majority had shrunk to six. The Government's days were clearly drawing to an end, for a majority of only six, subject to the hazards of sickness or unavoidable absence, was hardly adequate to support for any length of time a Government which had by its recent legislation excited very bitter party antagonism; and another election, when it came, was unlikely to restore the Socialist fortunes, for it is a fact of British politics that for well over a century no Government that has been continuously in office for six years or more has won a general election at the conclusion of that period. The situation appealed to Churchill's militant instincts, and he gaily led his party in for the kill, harrying the Socialists rather ruthlessly through the lobbies on every pretext. Attlee put up a gallant fight, keeping his party whipped together by day and night, and avoiding as far as he could any controversial activities. But it was a situation that could not last for long, and when, in April, 1951, Aneurin Bevan, his Minister of Labour, resigned and set to work to organize and lead a group of rebels within the party, who presently issued their manifesto attacking the Government's policy and the leaders of the T.U.C., it was clear that a breaking-point had been reached. Besides, the country was running into economic difficulties and sterner measures would have to be adopted than a weak Government could venture to undertake. On 5 October, 1951, Parliament was dissolved and 25 October was appointed for a fresh General Election.

CHAPTER XVIII

SIR WINSTON

WINSTON CHURCHILL and his supporters entered on the 1951 Election with good confidence. Their opponents, the Socialist Party, had now held office for just over six years. They were split by the Bevan faction and were believed to be losing ground with the floating voters. It was becoming known that the national finances were in a parlous state, and the Conservatives might be expected to inspire more confidence than the Labour Government in their ability to provide cautious and experienced handling of a financial crisis.

Tory hopes were realized, though only by a narrow margin. They and their allies gained a majority of seventeen over all other parties in the Commons, although their total poll was still slightly less than that secured by Labour candidates. On 26 October, Attlee resigned and the King invited Winston Churchill to form a Government.

Thus at long last, a month before his seventy-seventh birthday, Churchill reached his coveted goal. He was Prime Minister by election of the people. His war-time Premiership had not been so won. A national calamity had lifted him to that position despite years of neglect and ostracism by the leaders of his Party. In 1935 he had been returned merely as a private member, and when in 1945 he had with his magnificent record of war service gone to the country as the Tory leader, he and his Party had been cast out of office.

It was, however, no roseleaf bed to which he was called. If in 1940 he had taken control when Britain's war situation was desperate, her present plight in peace-time was hardly less critical. The huge American loan granted her in 1945, which was to last till 1951, had long since been dissipated, and the first instalment of its repayment was about to fall due. A Treasury Report showed that the country was increasing its external debt at the rate of £700 million a year, and that during the financial year its gold and dollar reserves would shrink by over £600 million. Coal stocks were down; those of household coal were only half what they had been a year earlier. National

429

bankruptcy was in sight, threatening a total inability to purchase the imports of food and raw materials without which the nation would starve and industry would run down.

Abroad, the prospect was hardly less sombre. In Korea, Britain was involved along with America and other members of the United Nations in a war to repel Communist aggression. In Malaya, she was maintaining without marked success a bitter struggle against insurgent Communist bandits who were trying to master the country. The Persian Government, in breach of treaties and contracts, had recently nationalized the oil industry of the Anglo-Iranian Oil Company, of which the British Government was the major owner; its British staffs had been flung out and the Abadan refineries abandoned and closed down. Egypt was conducting a violent agitation against the continuance of the British military station on the Suez Canal. Rioting was occurring in Cairo and attacks were being made on British troops. Worst of all, domestic finance and foreign policy alike were constantly bedevilled by the Soviet Union's "cold war" on the free nations, and the necessity of building up armaments and maintaining a solid front against this persistent threat.

CHURCHILL TAKES CONTROL

Churchill, however, was the last man in the country to be daunted by this array of perils and problems. He took control, as in 1940, with a resolute courage that was grim but gay, and warned the nation that for a time it would have to endure austerity and submit to strict economy in order to clamber back out of the pit of disaster into which it had been sliding. His programme, which he had sketched in a broadcast during the election campaign, was to provide a period of solid, stable administration, to restore the country's finances and reduce the controls which were hobbling enterprise and initiative. When the new Parliament opened on 6 November, 1951, the King's Speech promised security measures to strengthen the nation's defences, and an increase in the housing programme. But there was little offered in the field of legislation, apart from the repeal of steel nationalization and the restoration of private road haulage.

What somewhat surprised his critics, indeed, was the comparative tranquillity of Churchill's administration. They had anticipated violent upheavals of the existing system and sudden reversals of Government policy, in view of his vehement denunciations, while in

FAMILY GROUP

Taken in November, 1951, on the Pink Terrace outside Mrs. Churchill's sitting-room at Chartwell, this photograph shows, standing on the left, Mr. and Mrs. Duncan Sandys (Diana, Mr. and Mrs. Churchill's eldest daughter); their son Julian sits in front of them. On Mr. Churchill's knee is Emma Soames, daughter of Mr. and Mrs. Christopher Soames (Mary Churchill); Emma's brother Nicholas is seated on the cushion. On the right of the hammock stands Mr. Randolph Churchill; his son Winston sits between Mr. and Mrs. Churchill and his daughter Arabella is on Mrs. Churchill's left.

opposition, of Socialist economic planning and the continuing control of industrial supplies and of imports and overseas trade. But, if somewhat irresponsible in speech, Churchill, as his conduct of the war had demonstrated, was discreet and sure-footed in action, and he had about him, in his Cabinet, men who possessed a good understanding of the needs of the economic situation. So there was no sudden revolution of method. The Tory Party's much publicised aim to "set the people free" was pursued cautiously, not catastrophically. Only as the economic situation allowed were industries and commodities step by step freed from control and foods derationed.

Of Churchill's pugnacity there has never been any doubt. As he is always sure that he is in the right, it follows that all opponents are wrong and their causes are evil, so it is his duty and his delight to do battle with them. During the General Election, the most effective weapon in the Socialists' armoury was their warning that if Churchill returned to power he would land the country in another war. That suggestion may well have cost his party a number of seats. The *Daily Mirror*, indeed, went too far in an article charging him with war-mongering, and he brought a libel action against it, which was later settled in his favour out of court by the paper publishing full apologies and paying his costs and handing over a large sum to charity. But another aspect of Churchill's character is the swiftness with which he forgets a past quarrel and refuses to nurse old grievances. When he became Prime Minister during the war, he rejected all pressure to turn out of office those Tory leaders who for years had scoffed at him and exiled him from their counsels while they were letting the country drift to disaster. Instead, he worked in the frankest friendliness with them and with his former political opponents. In a speech at Oslo in May, 1948, he declared: "We must abandon all bitterness and all wish for revenge. ... We must not let such feelings go on into the future. Unless we remove the shackles from our feet we will drag behind us long trails of old grievances." When returned to power at the 1951 election his first word was to express the hope that "there will now be a lull in our party strife which will enable us to understand more what is good in our opponents, and not be so very clever in finding out all their short-comings." More recently, on 29 April, 1953, when the Commons were discussing the inclusion of General Speidel, a former colleague of General Rommel, in a visiting party of continental military observers, he remarked in the same vein: "Keeping alive of hatred is one of the worst injuries that can be done to the peace of the world!" If Churchill's capacity as a war minister was well established, such sentiments were warrants that he was no less capable of treading the paths of peace.

VISIT TO PRESIDENT TRUMAN

Always a believer in the value of personal contacts, Churchill paid a visit in January, 1952, to President Truman to talk over the international situation with him. While across the Atlantic, he also visited Canada and broadcast from Ottawa in support of the North

Atlantic Treaty, United Europe and a European Army that should include Germany. Back in Washington, he addressed a joint session of Congress, surveying the world situation and declaring in regard to Korea that if a truce there were reached only to be broken, the joint response of Britain and the U.S.A. would be "prompt, resolute and effective!" On his return to the United Kingdom, he was taken to task by the Opposition in Parliament for this pledge, which they held might commit the country to warlike operations against China; but he effectively quashed this charge by disclosing with puckish delight that the Labour Cabinet were on record in their minutes as having themselves agreed with the U.S.A. for action to be taken if necessary beyond the Korean frontiers.

DEATH OF KING GEORGE VI

On 6 February, the nation and Commonwealth were plunged into mourning by news of the death of King George VI. For some time he had been in poor health, and a serious operation on his lung in the previous September had indicated a condition likely before long to have fatal consequences. King George was greatly beloved by his people. From the time when, through his brother's abdication, the unexpected and undesired burden of monarchy had been thrust upon him, he had, despite physical handicaps, carried out its duties nobly and faithfully; courageous and indefatigable amid the perils of the Second World War; a model of constitutional propriety in his relations with changing ministers; a shining example in the stainless-ness and happiness of his domestic life. It fell to Churchill to broad-cast a tribute to him that evening, and the Prime Minister's eloquence was never more finely and sympathetically employed than when on this occasion he gave expression to the nation's regard and sorrow.

Princess Elizabeth, who now acceded as Queen Elizabeth II, was in Kenya with her husband, the Duke of Edinburgh, beginning a tour to Australia and New Zealand, when the King died. They flew back at once, and Churchill, accompanied by Attlee, Clement Davies and other Privy Councillors, met the young Queen at the airport and gave her his counsel and guidance in the heavy responsibilities that now fell on her. It can hardly have failed to be a great comfort to her in this difficult crisis that her First Minister was a man of such rich experience and long familiarity with State procedure and royal customs.

The funeral of the late King was conducted with the solemn dignity and faultless pageantry of which the British are masters, and then the nation began to prepare for the coronation of its young Sovereign. Hope and confidence ran high, for England has always been strong and prosperous with a Queen occupying the throne, and under the rule of their beautiful and accomplished young monarch, supported by so popular and highly qualified a Consort as the Duke of Edinburgh, the people might well anticipate a second Elizabethan Age, even more distinguished than the first.

During 1952 the domestic policy of Churchill's government was mainly directed to restoring the country's economic stability and to pressing on with a vigorous housing programme. On 11 March, the Chancellor of the Exchequer brought in the Administration's first Budget. It was, as the financial situation required and as Churchill had foretold, drastic and austere in some aspects. There was a further cut of £100 million in imports. The bank rate was raised from $2\frac{1}{2}$ to 4 per cent. Postal charges, car taxes and petrol duty were increased and an excess profits tax introduced, while food subsidies were cut down. But to avert hardship for poor folk, there were considerable concessions in the lower levels of income tax, that spelt total exemption for a further two million people, and there were increases in family allowances and pensions. Austerity and restriction alone, declared the Chancellor, were not enough. The weight of direct taxation on the lower and middle income groups must be lightened, so that people could feel that if they worked harder they would be allowed to enjoy a proper reward.

The effect of these measures, added to the drastic cuts and economies introduced by the Government on taking office, was soon evident. On 11 June, Churchill was able to tell the Press Association that the country had reached a position of equipoise.

EUROPEAN DEFENCE COMMUNITY PROPOSED

At the Strasburg meeting of the Council of Europe in 1949, Churchill had urged the creation of a unified European Army under proper democratic control, as a device for associating Germany with the other countries of Western Europe in their common defence. A number of plans had thereafter been advanced by various European statesmen for establishing such a force; for while it was generally recognized that Germany must somehow be enabled to take part

IN THE JERUSALEM CHAMBER AT WESTMINSTER ABBEY

In January, 1953, Mr. Churchill launched a nation-wide appeal to secure one million pounds for the restoration of Westminster Abbey. He is seen receiving from one of the choristers the gift of the Royal Family to the fund. The appeal achieved its objective in May, 1954, donations having been received from all over the Commonwealth.

in her own defence against any threat from Russia, no one was prepared—France least of all—to permit the re-creation of a German national army and General Staff. Eventually, in January, 1952, a measure of agreement was reached for the establishment of a European Defence Community (E.D.C.) including German divisions. A treaty incorporating the scheme was drafted on 9 May by the representatives of France, Belgium, Federal Germany, Italy, Luxemburg and the Netherlands, and was signed on 27 May.

The ratification of the E.D.C. Treaty by the signatory Governments was subsequently held up by hesitations on the part of both France and Western Germany, and by the rival problem of the conditions for securing unity of East and West Germany, which might be hampered by Western Germany's alliance with the Western Powers. But as the six signatories of the E.D.C. plan are those which constitute the European Coal and Steel Community (C.S.C.) under the Schumann Plan, they are already in close economic alliance under a supranational Authority of their own creation. The Council of Europe unanimously adopted on 30 May, 1952, a modification of its objects proposed by Eden, whereby both C.S.C. and E.D.C. were associated with the Council's activities and recognized as steps toward the realization of the United Europe advocated by Churchill.

TROUBLES IN MALAYA AND WITH MAU MAU

Conditions in Malaya, where Communist bandits had for years been carrying on a campaign of terrorism and assassination which the police were unable to check, engaged Churchill's prompt attention when he became Prime Minister. On 15 January, 1952, he announced the appointment of General Sir Gerald Templer as High Commissioner for Malaya, with full responsibility for all military and police operations, as well as for civil affairs. Templer arrived there three weeks later, announcing his object to be the restoration of law and order, and the carrying out of social and political reforms with the object of creating a completely self-governing Malaya. On 19 March he announced a full programme of reforms, including common citizenship, the creation of an effective police force and a Federation army (recruited from all communities in the country), medical, social and educational improvements, land settlement and economic measures to equip the country for its independence. The prompt steps he took to direct an effective warfare against the bandits soon brought about a dramatic change in the situation, and turned them from aggressors into fugitive bands, lurking hungry in the jungle. Presently large numbers of them came in and surrendered, and Templer took the bold step of recruiting some of them into his police forces to hunt out their former allies.

Malaya did not remain the only trouble centre in the overseas territories of the British Empire. In August, 1952, an outbreak of violent disorders in Kenya, which quickly developed into a campaign of murder and destruction, was found to be the work of a secret society, called "Mau Mau," which a group of unscrupulous agitators had set up among the Kikuyu tribes of British East Africa. Their aim was to kill or drive out all European settlers and other non-Africans, to stamp out Christianity and all civilized influences and to restore primitive paganism and the old savage tribal life. The simple-minded Kikuyu were being forced into the movement by the organizers, who compelled them to take a ritual oath of obedience and killed brutally those who refused. Indeed, although a number of European farmers and other residents were murdered by Mau Mau, the greater number by far of its victims were Kikuyu—loyal head-men, native Christians and others who refused to join the society. Considerable military forces had to be sent out to Kenya to assist the local police in dealing with this conspiracy and rounding up the terrorist bands that infested the colony.

UPHEAVAL IN EGYPT

Farther north in the African continent, an uprising of a far healthier character was taking place. The Egyptian Government had long been appallingly corrupt. The Court was a morass of profligacy and extravagance. Ministers of State were abusing their office and amassing huge private fortunes out of public funds. A group of army officers, headed by General Neguib, grew exasperated by this state of affairs, and on 23 July, 1952, they overthrew the Government by a *coup d'état,* and three days later compelled King Farouk to abdicate. Neguib took charge, and proceeded to clean up the political parties, to bring in a series of drastic reforms, and to break up the large estates and distribute their land to the oppressed fellahin.

British relations with Egypt had latterly fallen into a deplorable state, for Farouk had sought to divert attention from his own mis-government by blaming all the ills of the country on the presence of British forces in the Suez Canal Zone. Now that his replacement by the practical and efficient rule of Neguib caused some easing of the pressure to terminate British occupation of the Canal Zone—for Egyptian opinion had been so whipped up about this that full conciliation was impossible, at least for the time—a franker and more realistic handling of diplomatic issues with Egypt could be carried on, and in particular the difficulties which had obstructed agreement on a constitution for the Sudan were considerably reduced. Negotiations about this went rapidly ahead, and on 12 February, 1953, the Sudan Agreement was signed in Cairo. Since 1899, following on Kitchener's victory at Omdurman, whereby the Sudan had been liberated from its oppression under the Khalifa's dervishes, this country had been an Anglo-Egyptian Condominium, and while the Egyptians had done little or nothing for it, the British had equipped it with a college, with schools, courts of justice, a sound administration, a big irrigation scheme and a flourishing cotton-growing industry; they had also begun to train the Sudanese to conduct their own affairs. The grant to the Sudanese, in agreement with Egypt, of a constitution under which they would have independent self-government was the completion of this work.

A pleasant family episode occurred in August, 1952, when Anthony Eden, the Foreign Secretary, was married to Churchill's niece. The two men had long been close colleagues, and shared common sympathies about foreign affairs in those difficult days before the war, when Eden joined Churchill in exile from office rather than share in the miserable policy of appeasement of the Nazi-Fascist dictators. Eden was now Churchill's second in command of the Conservative Party, and was widely thought to be his probable successor; so this union of the two families was a happy circumstance.

THE FRUITS OF AUSTERITY

By the autumn, the policy of austerity which Churchill had imposed on the country was beginning to bear fruit, and in a speech he made at Woodford on 6 September, he was able to announce that during the second half of the financial year Britain would be in balance with the non-sterling world, though there could be no relaxing of efforts. He declared that he favoured the highest possible level of earnings in every industry, if warranted by increased output and

438

PRESIDENT TITO IN LONDON

Taken in Whitehall during the visit of President Tito of Yugoslavia to London in March, 1953, this photo shows on the left Dr. Vladimir Velebit the Yugoslav Ambassador, President Tito, Mr. Winston Churchill the Prime Minister, and Mr. Anthony Eden the Foreign Secretary. This was the first visit to Britain of any Communist ruler.

efficiency. The increasing association of employers and wage-earners with business and industry through joint consultation, profit-sharing and various forms of co-partnership, "certainly opens paths we should not hesitate to tread!"

Discussions with America were somewhat hampered during the latter part of 1952 by the fact that it was the presidential election year, and that a change of parties and personalities there might result. General Eisenhower had been induced to resign his post as Supreme Commander of the Allied Forces in Europe in order to stand as the Republican candidate; and at the election on 4 November he was returned with a record majority. This portended a complete change-round in the New Year of the men responsible for the conduct of American affairs, though it was less disturbing in its probable effect on America's foreign policy than it would have been if the isolationist Senator Taft had secured the Republican nomination and won the election instead of the General.

Between Eisenhower and Churchill a good comradeship had been developed during the past ten years, and the new President was closely familiar with European problems and anxious to promote their solution. Without waiting for Eisenhower's formal inaugura-

439

tion, which took place on 20 January, 1953, Churchill crossed to America at the beginning of the month to talk matters over with him. He spent from 5 to 9 January in New York and Washington, holding two interviews with the President-elect, and also meeting the outgoing President Truman and the retiring and incoming Secretaries of State, Acheson and Dulles. Among the topics discussed were the defence of Western Europe and the exchange of information about atomic weapons.

DEATH OF JOSEPH STALIN

Early in March, news came from Russia that Marshal Stalin was on his death-bed, and on 5 March he died. The world breathed a sigh of hesitant relief. Ever since Lenin died and Stalin seized power in Russia, brushing aside and subsequently liquidating Lenin's nominee, he had ruled the U.S.S.R. with a ruthless personal dictatorship, making himself the sole infallible source of Communist doctrine and policy, and obliterating all potential rivals on the pretext that they were deviationists from the true faith and would betray Russia to the capitalist foe. Under his direction, Russia, her satellites, and even her representatives abroad, had been sealed off from all contact with other nations, and it eventually was made a capital offence for a citizen to speak, unauthorized, with any foreigner. Now Stalin was dead. His henchman, Malenkov, stepped forward into his shoes, but it was not to be expected that he could fill them. He had neither the experience, the capacity nor the reputation with which to sustain Stalin's personal autocracy and compel blind, unquestioning obedience from all the leaders of the Soviet Union. People began to nurse a faint hope of some relaxation in the rigidity of Communist rule.

The earliest signs were hardly reassuring. Red planes shot down an American jet fighter cruising near the Czechoslovak frontier, and a British bomber travelling to Berlin along an authorized air corridor. But soon afterward the new Soviet administration showed a less aggressive attitude. Road traffic to Berlin was speeded up. The British were invited to a conference to discuss how future air incidents near the border could be averted. In the U.S.S.R. a general amnesty was proclaimed for all prisoners serving up to five-year sentences, and for certain other classes of prisoners. In Korea the Communists proposed an immediate exchange of sick and wounded

THE QUEEN WITH THE COMMONWEALTH PRIME MINISTERS

From left to right in this photograph, taken at a luncheon in June, 1953, at Buckingham Palace, are: Mr. Mohammed Ali (Pakistan), Sir Godfrey Huggins (Southern Rhodesia), Lord Brookeborough (Northern Ireland), Mr. Holland (New Zealand), Mr. Nehru (India), Mr. Bustamente (Jamaica), Sir Winston Churchill, Her Majesty the Queen, Mr. Menzies (Australia), Mr. St. Laurent (Canada), Mr. Senanayake (Ceylon), Dr. Malan (South Africa), and Dr. Borg Olivier (Malta).

prisoners of war, and asked for a resumption of the armistice negotiations that had been broken off some time before. It was also significant of the changes at the Kremlin that a group of Jewish doctors, victims of the anti-Semitic policy which Stalin had latterly introduced, who had been compelled to confess to plotting the death of leading Soviet Generals, had the charges withdrawn and their accusers denounced.

On 24 March, Queen Mary died. The widow of King George V, and grandmother of Queen Elizabeth II, she was in her eighty-sixth year, and had remained active and energetic to the last. Her long experience and sound judgment had been invaluable to the younger generations of the Royal House, and the nation held her in deep respect, mingled—especially in later years—with a growing affection. She was every inch a Queen, and over the radio and in Parliament, Churchill paid nobly phrased tributes to her unblemished record.

On Churchill's invitation, Marshal Tito, the remarkable ruler of Yugoslavia—the one Communist country outside the Iron Curtain —paid a short visit to London on 16 March. During the war, Churchill had established contact with him through his secret emissaries, Colonel Deakin and Brigadier Maclean, while Tito was carrying on a guerilla war of resistance against Hitler, and he now gave his guest a warm welcome in Britain. The Marshal told his own people on his return that Churchill had assured him that "We are your allies, and if Yugoslavia is attacked we shall fight and die together!"

The Chancellor's Budget statement in April brought the cheerful news that the severe economy measures Churchill had authorized had achieved the desired result, and that the country's finances were again on an even keel, though a more successful export drive was still needed to ensure the safety of sterling. A number of tax concessions were made, including reductions of the income and purchase taxes, larger allowances to industry and the aged, and relief of cricket and amateur sport from entertainment duty.

SIR WINSTON CHURCHILL

On 24 April, Queen Elizabeth expressed the high esteem in which Churchill was held throughout the nation and indeed all over the free world by conferring on him the Knighthood of the Garter. This most ancient and noble of the British Orders of Knighthood is rarely bestowed on any but Peers of high rank; but it was universally felt to be an appropriate honour for Winston Churchill, the most distinguished commoner in the realm, with a unique record of magnificent public service. The Garter had indeed been offered to him once before, when he ceased to be Prime Minister at the end of the Second World War, but he had then asked leave to decline it, fearing no doubt that acceptance might be taken to hint his intention of withdrawing from his activities as party leader in the Commons. But that status was now assured, and, until he should choose to retire, his leadership of his party would be undisputed; and the country

THE LORD MAYOR'S BANQUET AT GUILDHALL, 1953

*Reading from right to left there can be seen at the top table Lord
Simonds the Lord Chancellor, Lady Churchill, Lady Bowater the
Lady Mayoress, Sir Winston Churchill the Prime Minister, Sir Noel
Bowater the Lord Mayor of London, Sir Rupert de la Bere the retiring
Lord Mayor, M. Massigli the French Ambassador, and Lady de la Bere.*

was glad that he should be thus honoured by his Sovereign while
still actively engaged in the public service. Warm affection blended
with the slightly amused respect with which his fellow-politicians
began to address him as "Sir Winston."

It was a long and arduous road which Sir Winston Churchill had
travelled since as "a young man in a hurry," as Balfour described
him, he had first entered Parliament in 1900; a course beset by frus-
trations, set-backs and disappointments. Gifted though he was with
quite extraordinary ability and initiative, and with boundless
energy—Baldwin used to speak of his "hundred horse-power mind"

—and driven by unconcealed ambition, he was hampered by the distrust of his colleagues and of large sections of the public. Misfortunes had dogged the execution of some of his most brilliant and original ideas; and his indifference to the notions and prejudices of other men was a real handicap, causing him at times to blunder badly in his political tactics. It was forty years before chance thrust him that supreme charge of the nation's affairs toward which he had so long aspired, and fifty before the country deliberately chose him as its leader. His fitness for the post is now, at last, generally recognized; indeed, his speech on foreign affairs in Parliament on 11 May, 1953, was acknowledged by leaders of all parties to be a superb expression of the highest statesmanship, giving the world new hope that a peaceful settlement might be achieved between the rival policies of east and west. But whether in office or in opposition, Churchill has written his name large across the history of Britain and of the world, and has expended his brilliant gifts and quenchless energy in splendid achievements that have benefited his own generation and will endure for the good of generations yet to come. As the Rector of Oslo University said of him in 1948, Winston Churchill is "The man who wrote history, lived history, and made history!"

INDEX

Numbers in italics indicate illustrations

447

448